The Challenge of Change in Latin America and the Caribbean

edited by Jeffrey Stark

The mission of the North-South Center is to promote better relations and serve as a catalyst for change among the United States, Canada, and the nations of Latin America and the Caribbean by advancing knowledge and understanding of the major political, social, economic, and cultural issues affecting the nations and peoples of the Western Hemisphere.

The views expressed in these Agenda Papers are those of the authors, not the North-South Center, which is a nonpartisan, public policy and research institution.

To order or to return books, contact Lynne Rienner Publishers, Inc., 1800 30th Street, Suite 314, Boulder, CO 80301-1026, 303-444-6684, fax 303-444-0824.

Cataloging-in-Publication Data is on file at the Library of Congress

The challenge of change in Latin America and the Caribbean/ edited by Jeffrey Stark

p. cm.

Includes bibliographical references and index.

ISBN 1-57454-076-9 (alk. paper: paperback)

Printed in the United States of America

∞The paper used in this publication meets the requirements of the American National Standards for Information Sciences — Permanence of Paper for Printed Library Materials, ANSI Z39.48.1984.

06 05 04 03 02 01 6 5 4 3 2 1

Printed in the United States of America/TS

Contents

INTRODUCTION

The Challenge of Change in Latin America and the Caribbean: Development Amid Globalization in the 1990s

JEFFREY STARK

The decade of the 1990s was one of remarkable and rapid change in Latin America and the Caribbean. The nature of that change was manifold, involving not only fundamental and far-reaching neoliberal economic restructuring and state reforms, but also the strengthening of civil society and shifts in the understanding and expectations of citizens and political leaders in relation to national development. While aspirations for economic growth remained central, as the decade progressed, a richer and more complex set of questions involving social equity, democratic participation, unemployment, sustainable development, social service delivery, and race, ethnicity, and gender came more clearly into view.

These questions became increasingly acute, as they often arose between the Scylla and Charybdis of weak political representation within countries and the gathering force of globalization. It fell to elected leaders beset with multiple and competing domestic and international demands to choose among policy options and to craft political language that could explain or rationalize measures that dealt with these questions to diverse constituencies. While these challenges were common throughout the region, they played out in distinctive ways in the very different polities and societies of the hemisphere.

This reader of outstanding *North-South Agenda Papers*, in many places with new material and updating, offers analyses of country-specific experiences and key policy issues that provide empirically based insights into some of the dilemmas characteristic of the current phase of transition and transformation in the Americas. Part I closely examines three countries — Argentina, Brazil, and Trinidad and Tobago — in relation to the intricate and difficult puzzle of expanding initial political or economic progress into sustainable benefits widely shared by all social classes and sectors. In Argentina, the adoption of a fixed exchange rate extricated the country from a crisis of hyperinflation but then contributed to high rates of unemployment and growing social inequality. In Brazil, efforts to promote democracy and social justice were frustrated by the need to respond to global markets and the corrosive effects of political clientelism. In Trinidad and Tobago, privatization and rapid economic growth in the oil and gas sector could not paper over long-standing distributional conflicts and the tensions of racial politics. Together, the cases make apparent that the pervasive effects of globalization were, nevertheless, powerfully refracted through local historical experiences and political cultures, producing very different sets of policy concerns and outcomes in the different nations.

Part II is devoted to the examination of three key issue-areas: trade, health care reform, and sustainable development. First, the antecedents and stumbling blocks of what many consider to be the driving forces in contemporary inter-American relations — trade and economic integration — are discussed in an analysis of the progress toward the hemisphere-wide Free Trade Area of the Americas (FTAA), planned for completion by 2005. Second, a comparative case study of health care reform in Guatemala, Ecuador, and Chile examines the new model of social services delivery now evolving through collaboration and partnerships among governments, the private sector, and non-governmental organizations. Third, the real or perceived competing interests of environmental protection and economic development are explored in detail in relation to the politics of sustainable development and forest policy in Costa Rica. In each of these chapters, one sees evidence both of the strong disciplinary effects of economic globalization and the concomitant rise of social actors, pressing for the recognition of norms associated with a broader agenda related to basic quality-of-life issues and minimum standards of social welfare.

LATIN AMERICA AND THE CARIBBEAN IN THE LATE 1990S

In keeping with its overall pattern, the decade from 1991 to 2000 ended equivocally in Latin America and the Caribbean, with a general sense of disappointment about economic performance, leavened by a sense of relief that Brazil's January 1999 financial crisis had not been worse and with hopes that Mexico's 7-percent growth rate in 2000 could be duplicated elsewhere. However, a pattern of alternating cycles of hope and disappointment had become well entrenched. At the outset of the decade, there had been optimism that unprecedented economic and political reforms would produce considerably better results. This transitional moment in Latin American political economy was seen by many observers as the historic convergence of free markets and democracy in a part of the world that all too often had been sorely lacking in both.

Ideology aside, however, the new policies had been reached via a series of highly path-dependent and circuitous routes with important differences among the countries of the region. In the Southern Cone, transitions to democracy were achieved in the early to mid-1980s as the result of a combination of the military regimes' economic policy failures and the growing strength of civil societies that rejected the abuses and impunity of authoritarian rule.[1] In Central America, the end of the Cold War, the intractability of bloody military stalemates and the timely launching of regional diplomatic initiatives, led by Costa Rican president Oscar Arias, opened windows of opportunity for electoral transitions and reconciliation processes in such countries as Nicaragua, El Salvador, and Guatemala. In Mexico, in the early 1990s, the convergence of guerrilla rebellion, financial crisis, and political assassinations laid bare the bankruptcy of the one-party political system dominated by the Institutional Revolutionary Party (Partido Institucional Revolucionario — PRI) and opened the way to opposition control of the lower house of Congress and the eventual election of President Vicente Fox of the rival National Action Party (Partido Acción Nacional — PAN) in 2000.

The wave of economic reforms that swept through the region in the late 1980s and early 1990s similarly reflected not so much ideological conversion as the exhaustion of other means to redress prior policy failures. Import-substitution industrialization, which had produced periods of growth over several decades, began to flag in the late 1960s. With the stagnation of traditional agriculture, limited export sectors, a marked dependence on the importation of capital goods, and an activist role assigned to the state, Latin American nations were vulnerable to external conditions and had strong tendencies toward public-sector deficits. As a result, the impact of the 1973 oil crisis and subsequent petroleum price increases was severe. The fiscal gap was largely filled by tapping into a huge new international private financial market of Euro-currency and loans by multinational banks. The scale of borrowing was driven as much by willing creditors as by the solicitations of indebted Latin governments but, once in hand, these funds were often subject to mismanagement or wasted on white-elephant infrastructure projects. Growth slowed down significantly in the industrial countries, leading to a sharp recession in 1980-1982. This was accompanied by an alarming upward spike in interest rates, which compounded the indebtedness of the Latin American countries. The crisis became acute with Mexico's August 1982 declaration of a moratorium on payments of its public-sector debt. By 1982, the proportion of the region's current account deficit deriving from net payments of interest and profits surged past 100 percent (Griffith-Jones and Sunkel 1986).

Although the debt crisis brought the inadequacies of Latin America's protectionist/statist economic model to a head, there remained within the region a disposition to resist pressures to adopt doctrinaire programs of immediate and harsh market liberalization. An assortment of heterodox schemes to deal with inflation and stagnant growth failed in Argentina, Brazil, and Peru from 1982 to 1987. Inflation and hyperinflation remained rampant throughout the region — in 1991, inflation was 18 percent in Chile and Mexico; more than 25 percent in Colombia, Costa Rica, Venezuela, and Ecuador; 84 percent in Argentina; 139 percent in Peru; and 475 percent in Brazil (CEPAL 1998). The region's economies appeared to be stuck in a high-inflation/low-growth trap. At the same time, Latin American countries suffered from undisciplined fiscal policies, high levels of trade protection, and inefficient state-run enterprises that drained revenues, while providing low-quality goods and services.

It was in this context of frustration and failure that the package of neoliberal reforms, quickly labeled the Washington Consensus, emerged (Williamson 1990). The core of these reforms was trade liberalization, privatization, financial liberalization, and deregulation, accompanied by the elimination of subsidies, tax reform, market-driven interest rates and exchange rates, openness to foreign direct investment (FDI), and support for property rights. The sequencing and depth of the implementation of these reforms varied significantly from country to country, but they essentially blanketed the region by the early 1990s.

One significant advantage of the neoliberal reforms was that they provided a "road map" for policymakers (cf. Goldstein and Keohane 1993). By focusing on a fairly narrow set of economic indicators — inflation, money supply growth, interest rates, and budget and trade figures — a sort of thumbnail macroeconomic template could be employed with the endorsement of multilateral lenders, foreign governments, and export-oriented business sectors. However, domestic agriculture and industry faced intense external competition, labor unions were weakened, and the traditional circuits of political power were disarticulated. Privatizations were done in short order and often with little transparency. As governments sought to meet politically difficult International Monetary Fund (IMF) or World Bank targets for reduced fiscal deficits, a sense of urgency drove the process. In such a climate, there was increasing scope for abuses on the part of the executive, as exemplified in the presidencies of Fernando Collor in Brazil, Carlos Menem in Argentina, and Alberto Fujimori in Peru.

The reforms did produce several laudable achievements. As shown in Table 1, from a regionwide inflation rate of 199 percent in 1991, Latin America lowered inflation to an average of only 8.9 percent in 2000. Exports from Latin America more than doubled in the six years between 1991 and 1997, increasing in value from US$141 billion to a total of US$288 billion (Inter-American Development Bank 1998). As shown in Table 2, net foreign direct investment to the region increased sevenfold between 1991 and 1999, surpassing US$77 billion annually. A new study of privatizations in the telecommunications, electric power, and banking sectors concludes that they have been "predominantly positive," with "multiple firms competing in [each] sector, rather than just one state-owned monopolist," although "there is still plenty of room for more competition" (Grosse 2000, 12).

Table 1.
Variation in the Consumer Price Index
(inflation rate in percent)

	1991	1992	1993	1994	1995	1996	1997	1998	1999	2000
Latin America & the Caribbean	199.0	414.4	876.6	111.1	25.8	18.4	10.4	10.3	9.5	8.9
Argentina	84.0	17.6	7.4	3.9	1.6	0.1	0.3	0.7	-1.8	-0.7
Brazil	475.1	1149.1	2489.1	929.3	22.0	9.1	4.3	2.5	8.4	5.5
Colombia	26.8	25.1	22.6	22.6	19.5	21.6	17.7	16.7	9.2	8.8
Mexico	18.8	11.9	8.0	7.1	52.1	27.7	15.7	18.6	12.3	8.9
Peru	139.2	56.7	39.5	15.4	10.2	11.8	6.5	6.0	3.7	4.0

Source: CEPAL 2000, 88.

Table 2.
Net Foreign Direct Investment in Latin America and the Caribbean (in US$ millions)

	1991	1992	1993	1994	1995	1996	1997	1998	1999	2000
Latin America & the Caribbean	11066	12506	10363	23706	24799	39387	55580	61596	77047	54410
Argentina	2439	3218	2059	2480	3756	4937	4924	4175	21958	5000
Brazil	89	1924	801	2035	3475	11666	18608	29192	28612	30000
Colombia	433	679	719	1297	712	2795	4894	2432	1135	985
Mexico	4742	4393	4389	10973	9526	9186	12830	11311	11568	13500
Peru	-7	150	687	3108	2048	3242	1702	1860	1969	1185

Source: CEPAL 2000, 99.

These macroeconomic accomplishments, however, did not compensate for what was a disturbingly poor performance in relation to other economic indicators. Implicit in the neoliberal model was the assumption that once set free and disentangled from the distorting effects of the state, market forces would unleash a new surge of economic growth. Economic growth, after all, was the sine qua non of the neoliberal development ethos. As shown in Table 3, this did not occur as anticipated. For the decade as a whole, the gross domestic product (GDP) per capita grew in Latin America and the Caribbean at an average annual rate of only 1.5 percent. Some observers, who are relatively sanguine about these data, cite the 1980s as the "real world" baseline and note the tangible shift toward per capita growth in the 1990s, after a drop of about -1.0 percent in the prior decade. However, this perspective relies on using the infamous "lost decade" of Latin American development as the comparative baseline, a way of framing things that misses the larger historical context and obscures the pressing needs of the hemisphere's inhabitants. The average rate of growth in the region was 5.5 percent from the 1950s to the 1970s, and both the Inter-American Development Bank (IDB) and the Economic Commission on Latin America and the Caribbean (ECLAC) consider annual growth rates on the order of 5 to 7 percent necessary to reduce poverty significantly and begin to close the gap with the most highly developed countries (Ocampo 1998, 9). Moreover, national savings rates, often identified as the linchpin for jumpstarting growth, hovered at around 20 percent of GDP throughout the decade, far short of the target figure of 25 to 30 percent. In this context, the pace of economic growth in Latin America in the 1990s was disappointing.

Table 3 also reflects the devastating downturn produced by the 1994-1995 Mexican peso crisis (-7.8 percent growth in 1995) and the lesser effects of the 1999 Brazilian *real* crisis.[2] In both cases, Argentina suffered through harsh spinoff effects, with -4.1 percent growth in 1995 and -4.6 percent growth in 1999. These negative growth-rate statistics, however, are modest when compared to the impact on wages. For example, in Mexico in 1995, the minimum wage declined by 14.2 percent, and manufacturing wages declined by 15.3 percent (Godínez 2000).

Table 3.
Evolution of GDP Per Capita

	Variation Annual Rates in Percent										Average Annual Rate in Percent	
	1991	1992	1993	1994	1995	1996	1997	1998	1999	2000	1981 1990	1991 2000
Latin America & the Caribbean	2.0	1.3	2.2	3.4	-0.6	2.0	3.5	0.6	-1.3	2.4	-0.4	1.5
Argentina	9.1	8.1	4.3	4.5	-4.1	4.2	6.7	2.5	-4.6	-1.2	-2.1	2.9
Brazil	-0.6	-2.1	3.4	4.3	2.7	1.2	1.9	-1.1	-0.4	2.6	-0.4	1.2
Colombia	-0.1	1.6	2.6	4.0	3.2	0.1	1.5	-1.4	-6.0	1.2	1.6	0.6
Mexico	2.3	1.7	0.1	2.6	-7.8	3.4	5.0	3.2	2.0	5.5	-0.2	1.7
Peru	0.9	-2.2	3.0	10.9	6.7	0.7	4.9	-2.1	-0.3	2.3	-3.3	2.4

Source: CEPAL 2000, 86.

Further, as the Executive Secretary of ECLAC, José Antonio Ocampo, has pointed out:

> When crises involve a financial meltdown, costs are extremely high. Asset losses may wash out years of capital accumulation. [A] significant socialization of losses may be inevitable to avoid a systemic crisis, but this affects future fiscal (or quasi-fiscal) performance.... The financial sector itself becomes risk averse, affecting its ability to undertake its primordial economic functions (Ocampo 2000).

A closer examination of the data reveals a number of other important flaws in the performance of the neoliberal model. Income inequality — a category in which Latin America continues to lead the world — remained unchanged or worsened in countries across the region during the 1990s. A study by Miguel Székely and Marianne Hilgert (1999) of the IDB concluded that "there is no country in Latin America where we can confidently say that income inequality improved during the 1990s." Although ECLAC and the IDB reported slight gains in combating poverty in Latin America during the 1990s, approximately one out of three individuals lives on an income below US$2 per day. At current rates of growth, it is estimated that it could take 50 to 100 years (or longer in some countries) to eliminate such poverty (Lustig 1998).

The most serious immediate deficiency of the neoliberal model, however, has been its apparent inability to create jobs in sufficient numbers. While it may have been thought that opening the Latin American economies would create new opportunities for labor-intensive employment, this has not been the rule. As Table 4 shows, open urban unemployment steadily increased over the course of the decade. Meanwhile, according to the IDB, the rate of informal employment increased from 51.6 percent in 1990 to 57.4 percent in 1996, indicating that this large percentage of the working population is subject to reduced or nonexistent coverage of worker protection mechanisms and social security.

Table 4.
Open Urban Unemployment
(in percent)

	1991	1992	1993	1994	1995	1996	1997	1998	1999	2000
Latin America & the Caribbean	5.7	6.5	6.5	6.6	7.5	7.9	7.5	8.1	8.7	8.6

Source: CEPAL 2000, 89.

During the 1990s, wage differentials between skilled and unskilled workers increased substantially, especially in Peru, Colombia, and Mexico. Unemployment is consistently ranked in polls as the number-one concern of a plurality of respondents. Seven of 10 Latin Americans rate themselves concerned or very concerned about losing their jobs or being unemployed in the next 12 months (Lora and Márquez 1998).

The social panorama was further darkened by high levels of crime and violence. With approximately 20 homicides per 100,000 inhabitants, Latin America is the most violent region in the world (this rate is nearly double the U.S. rate). Surveys in Guatemala, Costa Rica, Mexico, and Ecuador found high percentages of women who reported physical abuse — 49 percent, 54 percent, 57 percent (urban women), and 60 percent, respectively (World Bank 1997). No direct cause and effect relationship can be specified between neoliberal reforms and increasing violence in Latin America; clearly, it is a phenomenon that is multicausal, with the illegal drug trade an important factor in a number of countries. However, most Latin American social scientists consider the economic model of the 1990s implicated in these social pathologies.

In general terms, health conditions have been steadily improving in Latin America and the Caribbean over the past quarter century. In Brazil, for example, life expectancy increased from 59 years in 1970 to 67 years in 1997, while the infant mortality rate decreased from 95 per 1,000 live births in 1970 to 37 per 1,000 live births in 1997. In Mexico, over the same period of time, life expectancy increased from 61 years to 72 years, while the infant mortality rate dropped from 79 to 29 (UNDP 1999, 168-169). In the 1990s, however, the region's governments were presented with "the juxtaposition of a backlog of accumulated problems and a series of emerging challenges" (Londoño and Frenk 2000). Health care systems struggled to deal more effectively with traditional concerns, such as common infections, malnutrition, and reproductive health, while at the same time facing a spate of re-emerging diseases, including malaria, dengue fever, cholera, and tuberculosis. The HIV/AIDs crisis significantly impacted many of the countries of the region, but it was felt most strongly in the Caribbean, which had the highest rates of infection outside of Africa. As democratic governments became more responsive to citizens' health care concerns, political pressures increased for better and more diversified services.

At the same time, as the urgency of the 1992 Rio Earth Summit began to fade, problems of environmental degradation mounted in the region, particularly in relation to forests, water issues, and the urban environment. For many countries, expanded agroexport industrialization was central to the new economic model, but the extension of the agricultural frontier was one of the main causes of deforestation, and it led as well to habitat conversion, threatening biodiversity. Although environmentalists had sounded the alarm when Latin America lost 6 percent of its forest cover from 1980 to 1990, the rate of deforestation continued unabated during the first half of the 1990s (UNEP 1999, 123). Even where conservation schemes were announced and ostensibly given legal status, implementation and enforcement often were absent. Water quality deterioration due to the discharge of domestic, industrial, and agrochemical wastes seriously compromised major rivers, and conflicts over marine and riberine resources in Central America, the Caribbean, and elsewhere raised new concerns about "environmental security" – the prospect for violence or social tensions short of war deriving from rising environmental pressures (McNeil 2000). In 1950, only 43 percent of the population of the region had lived in urban areas, but this had increased sharply to over 73 percent by 1995 (UNEP 1999, 132). As a consequence, governments faced enormous difficulties in providing even rudimentary levels of sanitation and urban waste disposal.

So where did all this leave Latin America and the Caribbean at decade's end? The mainstream reading of the performance of the politico-economic reforms of the 1990s held that, while they may have been necessary, they were hardly sufficient. The benefits of lower inflation and reduced fiscal deficits were evident, and increased trade and investment were encouraging; however, rising unemployment and under-employment, financial instability, stagnant or worsening inequality, weak political representation, serious public health concerns, and environmental degradation composed a daunting set of policy challenges. The neoliberal reforms could hardly be blamed for every woe, but the discussion about post-neoliberal development strategy in Latin America revolved around "second generation reforms," a very loose term that was construed alternatively by analysts to mean supplemental measures, refinements of past actions, course corrections, or more far-reaching changes in strategy and policies. The titles of books and papers published by the World Bank, IDB, and ECLAC — for example, "Development Beyond Economics," "Beyond Tradeoffs," "Beyond the Washington Consensus," and "Rethinking the Development Agenda" — all reflected the same sense that a significant shortcoming of the policy reforms of the 1990s was their inability to get at issues of poverty, equity, and social welfare. The spirit of the times increasingly had a "back to the drawing board" air to it.

Not, however, that there was any lack of ideas. Quite to the contrary, in fact. Whereas the development debate at the beginning of the 1990s became increasingly constrained, shoehorned into the parameters of the Washington Consensus, the discussions at the end of the 1990s actually fanned out in a number of different directions at once. New ideas continued to emerge from the international financial institutions and research institutes about how to strengthen institutions, increase productivity, enhance competitiveness, manage anti-cyclical macroeconomic policy, enforce contracts, promote workers' rights, create client-based social services, eliminate discrimination, decentralize education, stimulate microfinance, combine economic growth with environmental conservation, and, in a variety of ways, how to launch a much-needed social offensive (see, for example, Burki and Perry; 1997, Burki and Perry 1998; Birdsall, Graham, and Sabot, 1998; IDB 2000; Stallings and Peres 2000; Lloyd-Sherlock 2000; and UNEP 2000). Although there were in these studies broad areas of commonality, upon closer examination, they revealed divergent assessments of the performance and worth of Latin America's neoliberal reforms, and they offered policy frameworks and prescriptions that implied quite different understandings of the future structure and role of the state in the region.

As they reached the threshold of the twenty-first century, political leaders and government officials in Latin America and the Caribbean found themselves once again at a transitional moment. The neoliberal road map had become torn and tattered and no longer clearly marked the way forward, but no replacement map was readily at hand. Instead, advice was offered from different quarters, concerning any number of new, intermediate policy destinations (often in the spirit of post-ideological "third way" politics); unfortunately, these suggestions were without clear instructions as to how to "connect the dots" into a viable and coherent development strategy. Moreover, given the constraints of global markets and the preferences of investors, who generally favored the continued deepening of economic liberalization, these middle-range policy options often contained inconsistencies and trade-offs. Hence, the backdrop for the chapters that follow is a period of sustained change and rapid learning experiences, marked by periodic crises and a steady stream of new reforms, in which the pathways of policy were becoming more complex, and, in many ways, less certain.

THE CHAPTERS OF THE BOOK

In Chapter 1, Manuel Pastor, Jr. and Carol Wise provide a close examination of stabilization and economic reforms in Argentina, with a special emphasis on both the benefits and unintended consequences of the fixed exchange rate "Convertibility Plan" designed by Economy Minister Domingo Cavallo in the early 1990s — a topic of renewed relevance with the March 2001 return of Cavallo to the same government post (and some of the same dilemmas). The authors argue that this powerful policy measure was necessary in the context of high inflation (inflation was reduced from 84 percent in 1991 to less than 4 percent in 1994), but the rising value of the peso negatively impacted competitiveness and employment, a regressive value-added tax further aggravated inequality, and investment incentives favored non-tradable goods and capital-intensive manufacturing, providing few new opportunities for workers seeking to find their way in the rapidly changing economy. Meaningful adjustment assistance for small-and medium-sized enterprises (SMEs) was also lacking, even as larger firms prospered. External factors further exacerbated these problems, as the 1994-1995 Mexican peso crisis contributed to a sharp economic downturn in 1995, and the devaluation of the Brazilian *real* contributed to negative per capita GDP growth in 1999 and 2000. A fundamental shortcoming of the Argentine reforms, according to Pastor and Wise, was that they did not cohere into mutually reinforcing elements of a clear development strategy. Moreover, under President Carlos Menem, the reforms were enacted in an exclusionary fashion, with limited public dialogue and political consultation. The authors find that the Menem-era reforms need to be supplemented by sustained tariff liberalization, new policies to strengthen linkages between SMEs and larger firms, additional steps to advance labor market reforms, and increased levels of public investment in infrastructure for productive purposes.

In Chapter 2, William C. Smith and Nizar Messari trace the efforts of President Fernando Henrique Cardoso of Brazil to deepen democracy and reduce poverty, while also responding to the demands of investors and volatile international financial markets. Although many observers had high hopes for the progressive agenda of Cardoso, who was, after all, the author of such classic works as *Dependency and Development in Latin America* (Cardoso and Faletto 1979), the social democratic president was soon ensnared in a complex array of cross-cutting forces that nearly brought to a halt his plans for political, administrative, fiscal, and social security reforms. Smith and Messari describe how, in the face of clientelism embedded in a weak and fragmented party system as well as fiscal and political decentralization, Cardoso attempted to advance his agenda in piecemeal fashion, offering patronage along the way in hopes of gradually strengthening governability. However, the slow pace of the reforms meant that his focus soon shifted to his reelection campaign, which required the expenditure of both state largesse and political capital in order to pass a constitutional amendment allowing his reelection (as well as that of Brazil's governors and mayors). No sooner had Cardoso begun his second term than Brazil was hit by the full effects of a snowballing currency crisis and forced into a currency devaluation. Although the country's subsequent recovery was more rapid than anticipated, Smith's and Messari's analysis of the enduring political difficulties in pursuing a reform agenda in Brazil suggests that many, if not most, of Cardoso's social democratic goals will have to be left to his successors.

In Chapter 3, Anthony Maingot addresses the interplay between the forces of globalization and the realities of national political culture in Trinidad by placing globalization's powers of transformation in the context of the deep historical roots of Trinidadian political culture, which in many ways derives from racial competition between Afro-Trinidadians and Indo-Trinidadians. In Maingot's estimation, despite a shift in the economic thinking of government elites in the 1980s and 1990s, there still remains a gap between today's market-based ideology of neoliberalism and Trinidad's traditional, popular ideology of a central role for the state, especially as it pertains to addressing the economic needs of Afro-Trinidadians. Interviews with officials from the rapidly expanding oil and gas sector demonstrate that they are increasingly part of a cosmopolitan and internationally connected epistemic community with links to the political elite, but Maingot argues that it is still an open question whether the "thin," culturally detached, and abstract arguments for further economic liberalization will prevail over the "thick," culturally connected moral arguments for maintaining a degree of economic nationalism. Nevertheless, the author reminds us, sociological theory tells us that, over time, the incongruity between traditional ideology and the new economic model will have to be resolved at some yet-to-be-determined equilibrium point.

In Chapter 4, the focus shifts from country-specific analysis to the development of the best-known policy initiative in the region – the Free Trade Area of the Americas (FTAA), which is due for completion in 2005. Focusing first on the trade initiative's historical antecedents, Ambler H. Moss, Jr. points out that support for free trade has come from different parts of the hemisphere at different times. In 1990, President George H. W. Bush announced the Enterprise for the Americas Initiative, proposing the idea of hemispheric free trade largely as a counterweight to U.S. concerns that Europe and East Asia were developing their own trading blocs. Yet, in the fall of 1994, it was the strong desire on the part of Latin American governments for a free trade centerpiece at the Summit of the Americas in Miami that solidified U.S. support for the FTAA.[3] Once launched, the FTAA process benefited from a series of regularly scheduled trade ministerials, which slowly but steadily moved through the necessary steps of the process, compiling data; creating working groups; establishing a rotating, temporary administrative secretariat; and setting up preliminary (albeit flawed) mechanisms for gathering input from the private sector and civil society. Despite significant differences in the perspectives of the United States, which preferred moving more quickly, and Brazil, which preferred to move more slowly, first consolidating subregional integration through MERCOSUR and entering into separate free trade negotiations with the European Union, important progress was made in relation to business facilitation measures and the architecture of nine negotiating groups and three special committees. As Moss notes in his chapter, however, while he is optimistic that the FTAA will move forward as planned, much needs to be done to advance and invigorate the process. In the United States, President George W. Bush will need to find a way to gain Congressional approval of trade promotion authority (formerly fast-track authority), and a hard road lies ahead in dealing with the contentious issues of labor, the environment, the role of civil society and the private sector, and the handling of adjustment costs for smaller economies.

In Chapter 5, Alberto Cardelle analyzes new mechanisms for health care reform in Latin America, which in the context of diminished state resources and decentralization are marked by new forms of collaboration between governments and non-governmental organizations (NGOs), who increasingly serve as private sector contractors having the potential to improve the system's efficiency and effectiveness. However, government-NGO relations are problematic for a variety of reasons, including historical mistrust dating from authoritarian rule in the 1970s and 1980s as well as more immediate conflicts arising from the limited institutional capacity and weak financial foundations of "social change" NGOs that find it difficult to operate under the state's contractual regime, which emphasizes program management and administration. At the same time, NGOs often aspire to greater participation and voice in the planning and development of health care services, a prerogative that government officials often retain solely for themselves. Governments, for their part, are concerned about being able to verify the professional and technical capacities of NGOs, and they seek to hold them accountable. Cardelle's research in countries like Ecuador and Guatemala shows that, even where high-level officials maintain a strong commitment to the idea of government-NGO collaboration, the dissenting views of local officials and field managers can often undermine new modes of service delivery. Cardelle concludes that the new model of health care provision in Latin America can be improved by explicitly viewing this model as a public investment, rather than a mere contractual arrangement. Accordingly, he calls for such steps as the extension of funding cycles to NGOs, the establishment of contingency funds to cover temporary financial shortfalls, the development of NGO accountability measures to satisfy public sector regulations, and the creation of arenas of structured dialogue to discuss and clarify the goals and objectives of national public health policies.

In Chapter 6, Eduardo Silva details the difficulties of implementing forest policies in Costa Rica consistent with a multifaceted concept of sustainable development that balances economic growth, environmental protection, social equity, and citizen participation. In general, says Silva, three clusters of interests have vied for influence in Costa Rican forest policy: supporters of conservation as forest preservation; economic liberals concerned with market linkages and issues of importance to landowners; and those holding more communitarian perspectives, emphasizing the development of social capital among peasants and small-scale farmers. In the 1980s, on the basis of significant international funding, Costa Rica experimented with a number of innovative forestry projects, for the most part relying upon government regulation of the private sector and emphasizing the organizational development of smallholders. However, in accordance with the shifting ideological tides, the 1990s saw policies swing back toward administrative decentralization and market-oriented strategies. Although decentralization was intended in principle to bring improved client services and democratization, the author explains that it in fact weakened oversight and led to confusion over the interpretation of rules at the regional and subregional levels. Further, the liberalization of extraction undermined the goal of sustained-yield harvesting. At the same time, Silva points out, the turn toward market incentives hurt cooperatives and smallholder organizations unable to muster the necessary technical, managerial, and financial capacities to be competitive on a larger scale. The interests of these organizations were included within what Silva terms "the discourse of participation," but the prevailing "economic, institutional, and political asymmetries of power" emptied this discourse of real bargaining power. As a result, the author suggests that a more inclusive forest policy for Costa Rica could evolve out of renewed interest on the part of the international community and the conscious efforts of peasant and smallholder organizations to study more closely the core concepts of biodiversity conservation and sustainable development in order to be able to articulate more powerfully how the organizations' own interests fit and can be expressed within these concepts.

Taken as a whole, the chapters assembled in this volume represent a collection of rich empirical materials and detailed analyses chronicling the challenges of an era of transformation and reform in Latin America and the Caribbean across a broad spectrum of issue-areas: macroeconomic and microeconomic strategy, democracy and governance, poverty and inequality, trade and economic integration, health care and NGO-government relationships, and stakeholder participation and sustainable development. The authors provide abundant evidence that global influences are having an impact everywhere, but with very different local effects. They also indicate that, while the challenge of change in the region has been engaged with energy and determination, the achievements to date have been accompanied by a heavy load of unresolved issues and unfinished business. Clearly, the realization of enhanced levels of democracy, competitiveness, justice, prosperity, and equity in Latin America and the Caribbean remains very much a formidable work-in-progress.

Notes

1. In Argentina, the debacle of the Malvinas/Falklands war was decisive in restoring civilian rule.

2. A number of economists, such as Albert Fishlow (2000), believe that Brazil's ability to manage the devaluation of the *real* was related to lessons learned from the Mexican experience and improved monetary and fiscal policy. Financial crises are not likely to cease for Latin American countries, but there may be a basis for hoping that their negative effects can be better contained in the future.

3. According to Richard Feinberg, special assistant to President Clinton for inter-American Affairs at that time, opinion within the Clinton administration was divided as to whether to proceed with the FTAA. Some key officials felt that Uruguay Round legislation and fast-track renewal might be compromised by moving forward so soon after the bitter NAFTA debate. See Feinberg 1997, 71-78.

References

Burki, Shahid Javed, and Guillermo E. Perry. 1997. *The Long March: A Reform Agenda for Latin America and the Caribbean in the Next Decade*, Washington, D.C.: The World Bank.

Burki, Shahid Javed, and Guillermo E. Perry. 1998. *Beyond the Washington Consensus: Institutions Matters*, Washington, D.C.: The World Bank.

Birdsall, Nancy, Carol Graham, and Richard H. Sabot, eds. 1998. *Beyond Tradeoffs: Market Reform and Equitable Growth in Latin America.* Washington, D.C.: Inter-American Development Bank and The Brookings Institution Press.

Cardoso, Fernando Henrique, and Enzo Faletto. 1979. *Dependency and Development in Latin America.* Translated by Marjory Matingly Urquidi. Berkeley and Los Angeles: University of California Press.

CEPAL (Comisión Económica para América Latina y el Caribe). 1998. *Balance preliminar de las economías de América Latina y el Caribe.* Santiago de Chile: ECLAC.

CEPAL. 2000. *Balance preliminar de las economías de América Latina y el Caribe.* Santiago de Chile: ECLAC.

Feinberg, Richard E. 1997. *Summitry in the Americas: A Progress Report.* Washington, D.C.: IIE (Institute for International Economics).

Fishlow, Albert. 2000. "Brazil and Economic Realities." *Daedalus.* 129(2) Spring: 339-357.

Godínez, Víctor. 2000. "Economía política de las crisis recurrentes." In *Chile-México: Dos transiciones frente a frente*, eds. Carlos Elizondo y Luis Maira. Mexico D.F.: Editorial Grijalbo.

Goldstein, Judith, and Robert O. Keohane, eds. 1993. *Ideas and Foreign Policy: Beliefs, Institutions, and Political Change.* Ithaca, N.Y.: Cornell University Press.

Griffith-Jones Stephany, and Osvaldo Sunkel. 1986. *Debt and Development Crises in Latin America.* New York: Oxford University Press.

Grosse, Robert. 2000. *Moving Beyond Privatization in Latin America: The Government/ Business Relationship.* North-South Agenda Paper No. 40. (March 2000). Coral Gables, Fla.: The Dante B. Fascell North-South Center Press at the University of Miami.

IDB (Inter-American Development Bank). 1998. *Economic and Social Progress in Latin America.* Washington, D.C.: IDB.

Londoño, Juan Luis, and Julio Frenk. 2000. "Structured Pluralism: Towards an Innovative Model for Health System Reform in Latin America." In *Health Care Reform and Poverty in Latin America*, ed. Peter Lloyd-Sherlock. London: University of London, Institute of Latin American Studies.

Lora, Eduardo, and Gustavo Márquez. 1998. "The Employment Problem in Latin America: Perceptions and Stylized Facts." Paper prepared for the 1998 IDB/ICC Meeting, Cartagena, Colombia, March 1998.

Lloyd-Sherlock, Peter, ed. 2000. *Health Care Reform and Poverty in Latin America.* London: University of London, Institute of Latin American Studies.

Lustig, Nora. 1998. "Poverty and Inequality in Latin Amerian and the Caribbean: The Challenge Remains in Place." Paper prepared for the Sol Linowitz Forum, Inter-American Dialogue, Washington, D.C., March.

McNeil, Frank. 2000. *Making Sense of Environmental Security*. North-South Agenda Paper No. 39. (February 2000). Coral Gables, Fla.: The Dante B. Fascell North-South Center Press at the University of Miami.

Ocampo, José Antonio. 1998. "Beyond the Washington Congress: An ECLAC Perspective." *CEPAL Review*. 66 (December): 7-28.

Stallings, Barbara, and Wilson Peres. 2000. *Growth, Employment and Equity: The Impact of the Economic Reforms in Latin America and the Caribbean*. Washington, D.C.: Economic Commission on Latin America and the Caribbean (ECLAC) and The Brookings Institution Press.

Székely, Miguel, and Marianne Hilgert. 1999. *The 1990s in Latin America: Another Decade of Persistent Inequality*. Washington, D.C.: IDB.

UNDP (United Nations Development Programme). 1999. *Human Development Report 1999: Globalization With a Human Face*. London: United Nations Environment Programme/Oxford University Press.

UNEP (United Nations Environment Programme). 1999. *Global Environment Outlook 2000*. London: United Nations Environment Programme/Earthscan Publications Ltd.

Williamson, John, ed. 1990. *Latin American Adjustment: How Much Has Happened?* Washington, D.C.: Institute of International Economics.

World Bank. 1997. "Crime and Violence as Development Issues in Latin America and the Caribbean." Paper prepared for the Conference on Urban Crime and Violence, Rio de Janeiro, Brazil, March 2-4.

I.
Dilemmas of Economic and Political Reform

CHAPTER 1

Stabilization and Its Discontents: Argentina's Economic Restructuring in the 1990s

MANUEL PASTOR, JR., AND CAROL WISE

This chapter explores the political and economic conditions that prompted Argentine policymakers to adopt an economic management model in the 1990s that is generally considered to be less flexible than other approaches now prevailing in Latin America. Short-term outcomes as well as longer-term patterns of economic restructuring in Argentina are analyzed. The authors argue that Argentina became hemmed in by its own success: exchange rate targeting quelled inflation, but the resulting overvaluation limited export and employment growth; microeconomic reforms raised efficiency but threatened income distribution and hence political stability; exclusive styles of policymaking helped enact reform but led to corruption and policy insensitivity and contributed to rising social discontent. The chapter closes by suggesting how a "second generation" of reforms could tackle these issues and spread the proceeds of reform to a wider segment of the Argentine public.

INTRODUCTION

"Until not so long ago, Argentine economy minister Domingo Cavallo was fond of saying, 'Argentina is Mexico two years later.' When, in late December, the shockwaves of the Mexican devaluation caused a fall in the Buenos Aires stock market and an upsurge in demand for U.S. dollars, Cavallo changed his tune. 'Argentina,' he said, 'is not Mexico.'"

Latin American Weekly Report,
January 12, 1995

The authors thank The Dante B. Fascell North-South Center at the University of Miami, the United States Institute of Peace, the Social Science Research Council, and the Fulbright Commission in Buenos Aires for funding the research on which this article is based. María Barboza, Julie Jacobs, Rachel Rosner, and Walter Weaver provided excellent research assistance. Special thanks to Fernando Flint, whose help and support in Buenos Aires contributed greatly to this research; to Adolfo Canitrot for hosting this project at the Instituto di Tella in Buenos Aires; and to Ramón Borges-Méndez, Fernando Flint, Carol Graham, Robin King, Victoria Murillo, Bill Smith, and Néstor Stancanelli for their thoughtful comments.

On July 26, 1996, Argentina's flamboyant Economy Minister, Domingo Cavallo, was summarily removed from office by Argentina's equally flamboyant President, Carlos Saúl Menem. With the official announcement coming late on a Friday afternoon, markets had little time to react to the departure of an official who had been the architect and self-styled guarantor of the famed "Convertibility Plan," responsible for delivering Argentina from the throes of hyperinflation.

In fact, the peso held its value while stocks actually rose, suggesting the market's favorable assessment of Cavallo's replacement by Roque Fernández, a low-key former Central Bank president with a Ph.D. in economics from the University of Chicago. That same year, an opposition politician from the Radical Party captured the city's first open elections for mayor, a trend that continued into the 1997 congressional mid-term elections, which saw the highest levels of political competition in Argentina's entire history. In all, the country appeared to have made the transition from sole reliance on the credibility of just a handful of officials to a more fundamental faith in the macroeconomic laws now governing Argentina's economy, and the political rules characteristic of an established democratic regime.

Was this the moment for Argentina to be celebrating a sort of "end of history"— or at least its own history of erratic policy cycles, chronic macroeconomic instability, and prolonged bouts of social and political turmoil? While the Convertibility Plan purged the economy of inflation and fostered a return to growth, particularly as pent-up demand surged through the economy between 1991 and 1994, there were also some clear pitfalls to this strategy. Most obvious was a sharp appreciation of the exchange rate, which worked against the country's full realization of its export potential and made it difficult to trigger higher sustainable growth into the medium term. A major symptom of this dilemma was the precarious rate of unemployment, which in Buenos Aires had increased to around 13 percent by 1994 and then skyrocketed to 20 percent in the wake of Mexico's 1994 peso crisis. While the labor market later improved, much of the available work was temporary, and underemployment remained a serious problem. Not surprisingly, social tensions ran high in Argentina, with general strikes and violent protest the norm. Understandably, earlier public concern over hyperinflation gave way to the fear of "hyper-unemployment."

In this essay, we assess the Argentine experiment and speculate on its prospects. We suggest that the country's erratic economic performance and difficult employment and income trends were not just transitional costs related to market restructuring but, rather, predictable side effects of the chosen strategy. In particular, the government failed to coordinate its macroeconomic initiatives with the equally ambitious set of microeconomic reforms that were implemented since the late 1980s. Specifically, the negative effects of rigid management of fiscal and monetary policy under the Convertibility Plan, and the weight placed on workers and producers from an overvalued exchange rate, were not offset by programs designed to help economic agents adjust to the additional simultaneous challenges of trade liberalization and privatization. As a result, distribution worsened, and voters registered their dissatisfaction at the polls in increasing numbers. As Michel Camdessus, managing director of the International Monetary Fund (IMF), insisted, Argentina needs a "second generation" of reforms.[1] However, the current challenge involves more than the IMF's prescriptions for enhanced liberalization or a fine-tuning of the public sector; rather, the track record calls for a more cohesive set of market-supporting strategies and far more attention to repairing the distributional stresses and political strains that have been part and parcel of Argentina's contemporary political economy.

The remainder of this essay develops these arguments as follow: The second section analyzes and critiques the macroeconomic stabilization program that began with the implementation of Cavallo's Convertibility Plan in 1991. We agree that, in light of the prevailing hyperinflation, there was little alternative to the Convertibility Plan when it was adopted but argue that the resulting overvaluation dampened export and employment growth. The third section reviews the key microeconomic initiatives that were undertaken in conjunction with the Convertibility Plan. Here, we elaborate on the main sources of distributional stress engendered by the reforms, including underperforming labor markets, increasingly unequal household incomes, and growing disparities in the performance and asset base of small and large firms. We then review the politics of the reform process, noting that the Menem administration's autocratic and insulated style of decisionmaking did little to widen the "winners' circle" from reform, usually a necessary undertaking to ensure the consolidation of long-term political support. The last section sketches a "second generation" of strategies to deal with these shortcomings, with specific attention to the macro, micro, institutional, and political dimensions.

MACROECONOMIC STABILIZATION: CONTEXT, STRATEGIES, AND OUTCOMES

> "Argentina has always been a country with moderate growth — believing that spectacular growth and riches are right around the corner. And when a good year comes, the Argentines say, 'Ah-ha, here comes the life we've been waiting for and so deserve.'"
>
> Daniel Heyman, staff economist, UN Economic Commission for Latin America and the Caribbean, Buenos Aires[2]

Inflation, Convertibility, and Growth

The year 1989 marked a dramatic break with Argentina's past. In the midst of the worst economic crisis in the country's history, and for the first time ever, a democratically elected president from one political party was succeeded by a democratically elected president from another party (McGuire 1995, 200). Given the urgent task of completing the reform process left unfinished by the previous Raúl Alfonsín government (1983-1989), the incoming administration of President Menem attacked the country's formidable economic problems with renewed vigor. As the monthly inflation rate soared to 197 percent when Menem took office in July 1989 (see Figure 1), the president reached beyond the working class and populist roots of his own backers in the Peronist Party (Partido Justicialista — PJ) and sought the support of business interests and the middle classes to try to tame skyrocketing prices.[3]

Figure 1. Argentine Monthly Inflation, 1982-1996

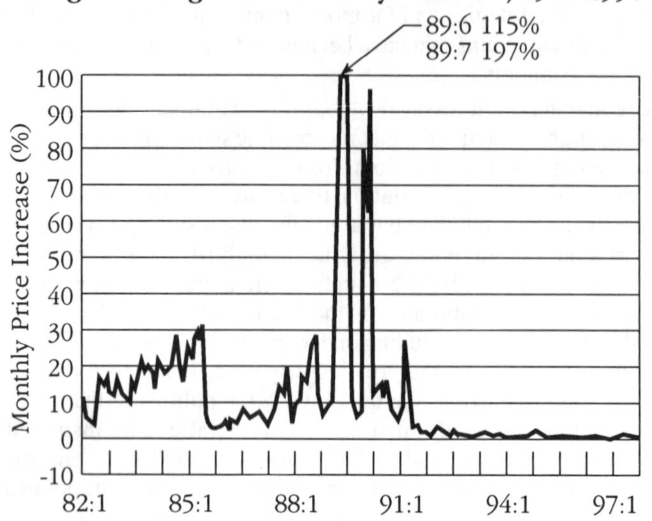

The Menem team moved gradually at first, launching a moderately heterodox stabilization program known as the "Bunge and Born Plan," named after the country's largest transnational firm, whose advisors had helped to design it. Relying on the same sort of price controls that had been implemented under Alfonsín's Austral Plan, the new program unraveled quickly when the government was forced to carry out a large step devaluation in December 1989. At this time, all price controls were eliminated, and the currency was allowed to float; not surprisingly, inflation exploded once again. This new round of price liberalization did at least slow the plunge in gross domestic product (GDP) that the Argentine economy had registered in the previous two years. Meanwhile, after the initial burst of prices in the first quarter of 1990, inflation slowed, albeit to a still worrisome rate of 11 percent per month.[4]

In January 1991, Domingo Cavallo was appointed economy minister and soon launched the now famous Convertibility Plan. Passed quickly by the Argentine Congress into formal legislation, the Plan obliged the Central Bank to 1) back up a fixed exchange rate by agreeing to convert national currency into foreign exchange at that rate and 2) calibrate the monetary base to the level of foreign currency assets. Much like the approach that evolved in Mexico between 1987-1994, the operative assumption was that a fixed exchange rate, when coupled with import liberalization, would provide an effective control against domestic price hikes. In general terms, the combination made for the sort of discipline that the gold standard historically had imposed. That is, if the economy became overheated, the resulting shortage of foreign exchange would force a contraction of the money supply and slow domestic economic activity.[5]

This new set of rules also enhanced the private sector's influence over the economy: if local investors were displeased with the course of economic policy, the exodus of their resources via capital flight could trigger a destabilizing recession. To bring the private sector more firmly on board in facilitating the process of disinflation, the government initially asked leading companies to "voluntarily" engage in price restraint. As the currency gradually stabilized, so did prices. By May 1991, monthly inflation had tapered down to around 3 percent and by 1992, the monthly average was less than 1.5 percent. By 1994, annual inflation was less than 4 percent, a trend more typical of a developed country.

On the fiscal side, the Menem administration had inherited a public sector deficit that averaged 9 percent of GDP through the 1980s.[6] Similar to other hyperinflationary crises that had erupted in the 1980s, for example in Brazil and Peru, the Argentine deficit reflected a disastrous combination of rampant public spending and a virtual collapse of the tax system. Clearly, tax reform was essential for maintaining the hard-fought victory of inflation reduction; moreover, because the Convertibility Plan excluded the possibility of domestic credit creation, the central government was under intense pressure to keep its fiscal house in order. As a result, the Menem administration moved aggressively to eliminate tax evasion and to improve tax administration and compliance. Legislative reform centered on increasing tax revenues on income, the implementation of an 18-percent value-added tax, and the construction of a regulatory framework for the privatization of state-owned companies and assets.

The impacts of these monetary and fiscal reforms on growth were initially positive. As can be seen in Figure 2, the first two years of the program prompted a buoyant recovery, with growth sustained at a slightly more moderate pace through 1993 and 1994. In regional terms, Argentina posted the second fastest growth rates for this period in Latin America, and the Argentine recipe was pronounced a success both at home and abroad. In light of the extreme policy swings and political

Figure 2. GDP Growth in Argentina, 1982-1996

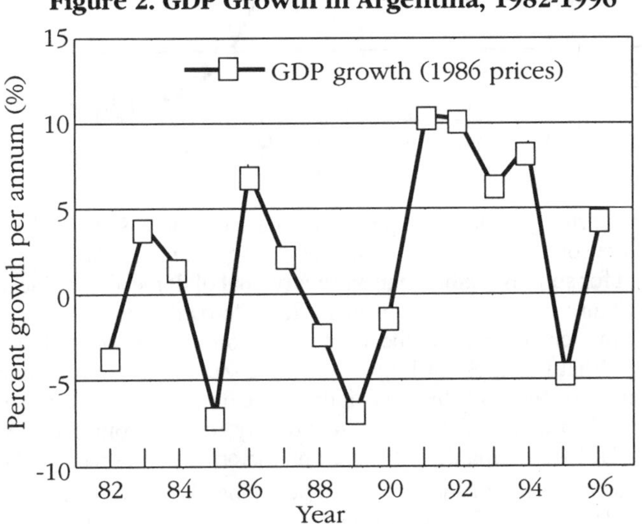

economic decline that had characterized the country throughout the post-war era, it appeared that Argentina had finally turned a necessary corner.

All That Glitters Is Not (the) Gold (Standard)

Or had Argentina turned the corner? By late 1994, some investors and financial analysts were again expressing concern about Argentina, particularly with regard to the rising value of the peso. In the aftermath of hyperinflation, it is typical for price movements to take time to stabilize completely. In this case, it took until 1994 before domestic inflation fell more or less in line with international inflation.[7] As a result, the real currency value steadily increased over the period, especially in the earlier, higher inflation years. This pattern is evident in Figure 3, which shows the average annual real exchange rate.[8] Discounting the upward surge in 1989 — hyperinflation episodes are often associated with a sharp decline in the value of the local currency — we can see that, by 1993, Argentina's real exchange rate had settled to about half the value it had held during most of the period following the 1982 debt crisis.[9]

Figure 3. Real Exchange Rate in Argentina, 1982-1996

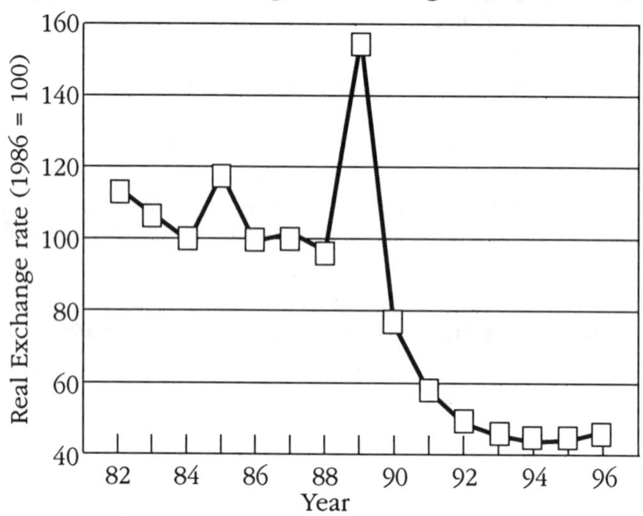

Both the rising value of the peso and the steady increase in GDP (and hence demand) were soon felt in the trade balance. In Argentina, export sales have often been a "vent for surplus" rather than a primary goal of domestic producers. As can be seen in Figure 4, exports were indeed briefly "crowded out" by the 1991-1992 resurgence in demand within the domestic economy, with moderate growth thereafter.[10] What was most striking in the trade sector was the dramatic surge in imports: between 1990 and 1994, the dollar value of imports swelled by more than 400 percent. The trade balance correspondingly moved from a US$8.6 billion surplus to a US$4.2 billion deficit, a shift on the order of 7 percent of GDP.

The sustainability of such a large deficit depends on two factors: the type of financing and the nature of growth in demand for both domestic output and imports.

With regard to financing, Figure 5 indicates the dramatic, though uneven, increase in portfolio investment; the huge inflow in 1993 partly reflects a spate of privatizations of state-held companies, including the state-owned oil company, Yacimientos Petrolíferos Fiscales (YPF) (de la Balze 1995, 93; Grosse and Yañes 1996). At the same time, non-privatization foreign direct investment (FDI) increased modestly, providing yet another cushion for reserves. There also seems to have been a substantial return of flight capital during this period.[11]

Figure 4. Exports, Imports, and Trade Balance

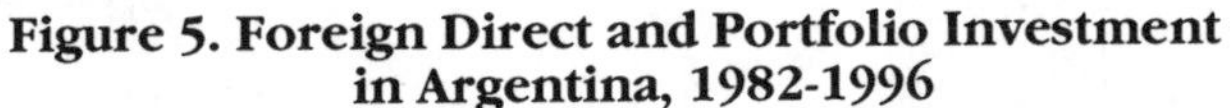

Figure 5. Foreign Direct and Portfolio Investment in Argentina, 1982-1996

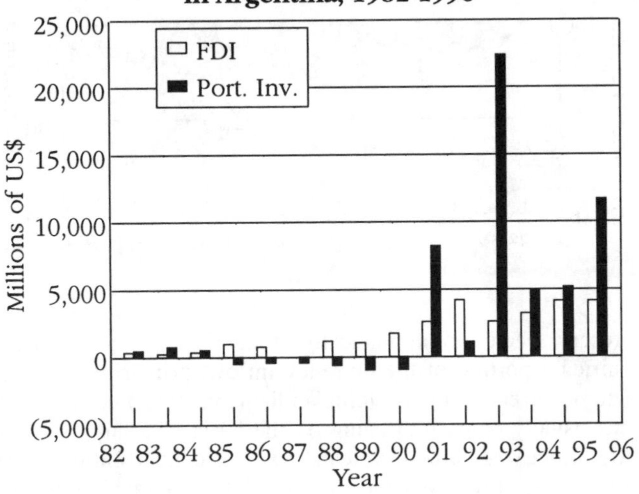

Figure 6. International Reserves in Argentina, 1982-1996

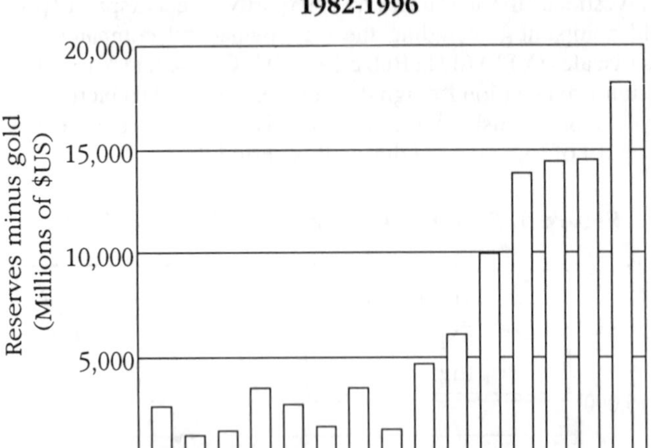

Figure 7. Consumption, Investment, and Imports as % of GDP in Argentina, 1982-1996

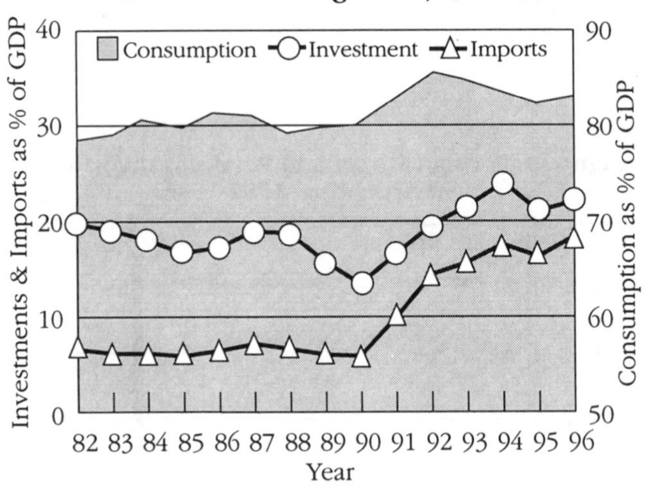

With reserves increasing dramatically through 1994, the government squirreled away a significant portion of the currency inflow, primarily to remonetize the recovering domestic economy. As John Williamson (1995) notes, currency board arrangements usually come into being on the basis of a large stock of foreign reserves; Argentina was an unusual candidate for convertibility in that it had a relatively small base of reserves at the outset of the program. At the beginning of the Convertibility Plan, however, the domestic money supply had also withered due to the inflation-induced flight of cash; as a result, a small base of foreign assets could provide the requisite backing.[12] As inflation subsided, the real demand for liquidity rose. To finance this typical post-stabilization need for remonetization, the government had to accumulate reserves.[13]

While the source and extent of financing is one aspect of understanding a country's ability to maintain a widening trade deficit, another key feature has to do with the nature of demand. If an expansion in imports and GDP is driven by investment, then the supply and export sides of the economy could benefit eventually; if the expansion is driven by consumption, then the deficit is less

Figure 8. Composition of Argentina's Imports, 1990 and 1994

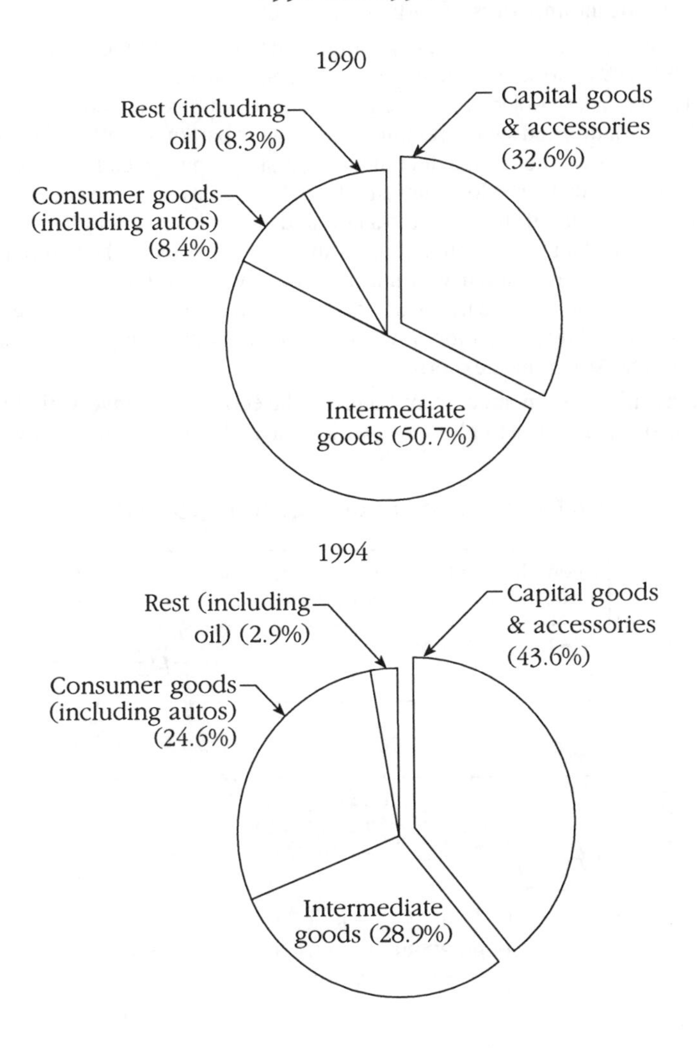

sustainable. To explore this issue, Figure 7 plots consumption, investment, and imports as a percentage of GDP. As can be seen, consumption was indeed on the upswing between 1990 and 1994, increasing by nearly 5 percentage points over this period. However, both the import and investment ratios rose even more dramatically, each increasing by about 10 percentage points from 1990 to 1994.

This suggests that investment did play a role in the import boom, an interpretation that is further verified by the composition of imports. Figure 8 compares Argentina's import composition in 1990 to that of 1994. As can be seen, imports of capital goods and accessories rose from around one third to nearly 44 percent of total imports. During this time, consumer goods rose dramatically as well, going from below 10 percent to nearly 25 percent of total imports. The relative loser in the import boom was intermediate goods; one reason may have been that final goods imports displaced old import-substitution industries, hurting firms that had been significant importers of parts for assembly.[14]

In any case, investment was a key component both of GDP and import growth over the 1990-1994 period. Enhancing business confidence and private investment had clearly been a key objective of the government's approach, and the commitments to low inflation and steady remonetization were part of this effort. However, it is difficult to know whether the documented burst in capital spending was due to pent-up demand — driven by low interest rates, a favorable exchange situation, and the need to rebuild capital stock — or to a new and higher level of long-term capital accumulation. The fact that the bulk of investment was devoted to the nontradeable sector implies that new capital was not directed toward building up the export sector's competitiveness.[15] As necessary as this would eventually be for overcoming the trend toward overvaluation, low value-added agricultural products continued to dominate Argentina's exports.[16]

Meanwhile, as is apparent from Figure 9, the economic recovery did little to alleviate the sharp rise in unemployment, which reached 13 percent in Buenos Aires

Figure 9. Unemployment in Argentina, 1982-1997

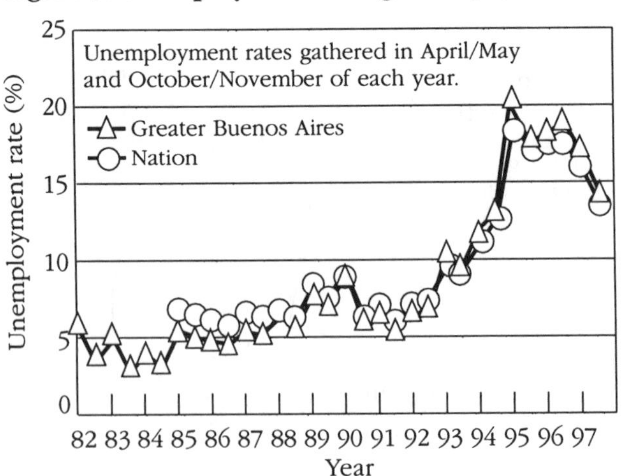

in late 1994.[17] To some extent, increasing labor market dislocation reflected a positive development, as companies streamlined their operations in response to new liberal economic incentives, and labor productivity increased dramatically.[18] However, in light of Argentina's historically low levels of unemployment and the context of economic boom that prevailed until 1995, the 1994 jump in the number of unemployed was especially alarming.[19]

By 1994, other troubling signs had also surfaced. The Menem administration's increasing reliance on a regressive value-added tax (VAT) only worsened distribution (discussed below), and the VAT's extension to food items and other basic necessities simply compounded its regressive character. While improved over the course of the program, Argentina's investment ratio was still running well below the 26.4-percent rate achieved in 1980, shortly before the debt crisis. With unemployment rising, an overvalued peso dampening exports, and investment distorted toward nontradeables, the Argentine strategy seemed to have hit an impasse. In December of 1994, one multilateral banker observed, "There actually is no 'model' beyond the adjustment plan which Cavallo introduced in 1991.... Argentina should start thinking hard about what it will do next."[20]

The 1995 "Crack" and Beyond

Before Argentine policymakers had a chance to address these mounting tensions, the Convertibility Plan itself had come under attack.[21] In the first few months that followed the December 1994 Mexican currency crisis, over US$8 billion exited from Argentina, an amount equal to about 18 percent of all deposits in the domestic banking system. As Economy Minister Cavallo observed in August 1995, "The fall in deposits between January and April was similar to that of the crack of 1929."[22] Publicly, the government reacted by holding a firm line on its quasi-gold standard; quietly, rules were bent to prevent a massive recession. The Convertibility Plan included a "loophole" that allowed the Central Bank to hold up to one-third of

Figure 10. Growth of Real GDP, Consumption, and Investment in Argentina, 1982-1996

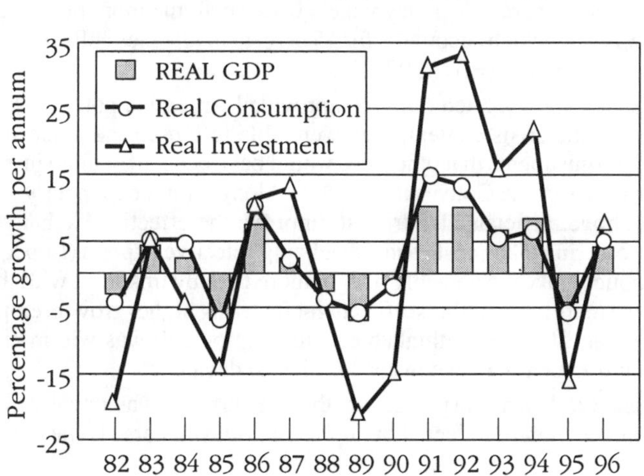

its assets as U.S. dollar-denominated government debt, while moving quickly to purchase the same debt in order to inject new dollars into the system. Previously steep reserve requirements in the private banking system were also cut by half, allowing for an expansion in liquidity.

The above measures helped to slow the decline in GDP, but investment continued to plummet through 1995 (see Figure 10). In May 1995, unemployment in Buenos Aires hit an alarming 20.2 percent and was compounded by a corresponding national rate of underemployment that was calculated at 11.3 percent for the same time period (Murillo 1997, 78). Although the country had more or less recovered its level of output by the end of 1996,[23] unemployment had dropped by just 2 to 3 percentage points. By October 1997, labor markets had improved somewhat, with unemployment in Buenos Aires dropping below 15 percent and national unemployment below 14 percent (see Figure 9). However, estimates show that half of the new jobs created were temporary. Moreover, projecting ahead from the 1996 GDP growth rate of 4.3 percent, it could take until 2010 before the unemployment rate settled back down to its 1992 level.[24] On this count, the composition of trade continued to constitute a bottleneck for future job creation; while the trade balance had shifted to a surplus and exports grew by 14 percent in 1996, the biggest increases were for primary products with little value-added, maintaining the pattern of earlier years. Meanwhile, portfolio investment staged a comeback, rising to about half of the level it had enjoyed in 1993. While this reassured some, it led others to wonder whether Argentina was again becoming vulnerable to the vagaries of international capital markets.[25]

While Argentina's 1995 economic slowdown has often been attributed to the so-called "tequila effect," following Mexico's peso crisis, there were ample reasons for economic growth to taper off that year anyway. Most noticeable was the continuing disarray of public finances, which some international observers said had returned to a deficit position in 1994 and 1995.[26] As the flow of one-shot revenues from privatization began to slow in 1994, the government's difficulties in strengthening tax compliance and cutting expenditures, especially spending by provincial governments, had become all too apparent. Because the Convertibility Plan made fiscal soundness imperative, policymakers became all the more dependent on the regressive VAT — which accounted for 45 percent of all taxes collected in 1996 — to help cover the deficit (EIU 1997, 13).

In a sense, the 1995 tequila shock provided Argentine policymakers with a "cover": given the crisis context, they were able to loosen the purse strings and finesse some adjustments that otherwise would have been difficult to justify within the strict confines of the Convertibility Plan. Along with the monetary maneuvers mentioned above, officials also tried to improve the effective exchange rate for exports by lowering labor costs and subsidizing selective exports (López 1997, 8). Although policymakers ostensibly bought more time by tinkering with the current strategy at the margins, was this sufficient for fostering higher growth, employment, and income gains? Or, as unthinkable as this option still was within elite policy circles, should Argentina have instead sought to devalue?

The answer depends in part on whether the currency was actually overvalued, a contention vehemently rejected by top-level policymakers. To tackle this issue, we followed the methodology developed by Ilan Goldfajn and Rodrigo O. Valdés (1996) in their study of currency appreciation episodes in 93 countries from 1960 to 1994. Gathering monthly data on the Argentine exchange rate for 37 years (from January 1960 to August 1997), we calculated an "equilibrium" (or purchasing power parity) real exchange rate, as well as deviations from this "equilibrium" value.[27] Our results suggest that the Argentine peso was modestly undervalued when Cavallo took office but crossed a 25 percent appreciation threshold (above the equilibrium rate) less than two years later.[28] Goldfajn and Valdés note that of the 71 cases they studied that crossed this threshold, less than 5 percent returned to within 5 percent of the equilibrium real exchange rate without a nominal devaluation; instead, most governments switched from a fixed to a floating rate, and in 90 percent of their cases, more than half of the movement back to equilibrium was done by currency depreciation, not by price shifts.[29]

There is no doubt that Cavallo had little choice but to fix the peso against the dollar at the outset of his tenure as economy minister. By 1991 the Argentine government had completely destroyed its credibility, and the Convertibility Plan offered a highly visible and essential signal of the government's commitment to fiscal and monetary discipline.[30] Over time, however, the Menem administration perhaps hung too much of its credibility on the exchange rate anchor, at the expense of cultivating a much broader range of confidence-enhancing signals within the country's economic and political institutions.

Argentine policymakers generally have well-rehearsed explanations for why the upward drift in the exchange rate does not constitute overvaluation. These arguments center on the facts that 1) the exchange rate has been validated by strong capital inflows, 2) the currency was initially undervalued, and 3) improved productivity by Argentine labor is a better route for achieving export competitiveness. These explanations would perhaps be more convincing if they did not resonate so closely with those recited by Mexican technocrats prior to that country's 1994 crash. The earlier strength of the Argentine program, based on the sanctity of the fixed exchange rate, has become its main weakness: rather than face the music now and adjust the strategy in a manner more conducive to sustainable growth, the government instead has opted for a slow and painful return to equilibrium — complete with excessive unemployment and high social costs.

THE MICROECONOMIC SCENARIO: THE POLITICAL ECONOMY OF ADJUSTMENT

> "It's not so much a question of having confidence in the market, as it is of creating markets."
>
> Bernardo Kosakoff, staff economist, UN Economic Commission for Latin America and the Caribbean, Buenos Aires[31]

> ". . .we support the model, but we don't want to be buried by it."
>
> Jorge Blanco Villegas, president of the Unión Industrial Argentina[32]

Microeconomic Initiatives

So far, we have focused on the macroeconomic stabilization strategy devised by the Menem administration. Yet, the government was also engaged in an ambitious program of microeconomic reforms, including trade liberalization, privatization, and deregulation. In this section, we review both the microeconomic initiatives and the distributional stresses that they, in conjunction with the prevailing macroeconomic strategy, triggered. We then turn to the politics of reform, suggesting how the Menem administration's style of closed, autocratic decisionmaking, much like exchange rate targeting, outlived its usefulness.

Trade Liberalization. Like many Latin American countries since the late 1980s, Argentina has simultaneously pursued its trade liberalization goals at the unilateral level, multilaterally through the Uruguay Round of the General Agreement on Tariffs and Trade (GATT) and World Trade Organization (WTO), and within a subregional context (Berlinski 1996; Tussie 1996; Wise 1998). Similar to Mexico's gradual, then rapidly accelerated commercial opening under the 1987 "Economic Solidarity Pact," Argentina first opened slowly in 1988, with considerable pressure and financial support from the multilaterals and as part of the bilateral integration thrust with Brazil that began in 1986. The reduction of tariff and non-tariff barriers was then escalated in 1990 and 1991, as Argentina followed in Mexico's footsteps, eventually linking trade liberalization with a fixed exchange rate as the centerpiece of its stabilization strategy under the Convertibility Plan. At the subregional level, Argentine officials committed to further liberalization and deregulation under the Southern Cone Common Market (Mercado Común del Sur — MERCOSUR) Customs Union (which includes Argentina, Brazil, Paraguay, Uruguay; and Chile and Bolivia as associate members) that was launched formally on January 1, 1995 (Guira 1997). Associate members were accepted later.

By April 1995, Argentina's average tariff was half of what it had been in October 1989, and some progress had been made in reducing the dispersion rate around the tariff (Artana and Navajas 1995, xiv).[33] Meanwhile, one standard measure of openness — exports and imports as a percentage of GDP — had risen from less than 17 percent in 1990 to over 30 percent by 1996.[34] As Figure 4 indicates, the growth in this trade ratio was lopsided: exports nearly doubled from 1990 to 1995, while imports jumped fourfold over this same time period.

There is certainly evidence to endorse Argentina's increased trade and outward orientation as the most direct route for expanding growth and incomes (Edwards 1995, chapter 5). It appears, however, that the extended lag in terms of the realization of employment gains can be partially explained by certain features of the trade regime itself. In the previous section, we noted that the long-term thrust of the country's commercial expansion has been dominated by low value-added exports of agricultural and energy products, as well as imports of final consumer durables and capital goods, a pattern that has not been conducive to rapid job creation.

The fact that this trend increased (low value-added natural resource exports jumped from about 25 percent of all exports in 1989 to 34 percent in 1994) reflected the limited progress made toward shifting to the kinds of higher value-added exports necessary for triggering future income and job growth (Edwards 1997; Toulan and Guillén 1997, 402). In regional terms, Argentina was certainly not alone in facing this need to generate higher value-added economic activities, essential for improving a given country's level of development. Policymakers responded to this challenge by granting a range of tax incentives to those producers who could credibly demonstrate an increase in their export capacities (de la Balze 1995, 117-122). The lackluster response of higher value-added exports to such policies appears to be a matter of other cross-cutting incentives that favored production for the domestic market, especially the adverse effect of an overvalued peso. In this sense, there was a lack of coordination between micro- and macroeconomic strategies.

Other structural factors worked against a trade-led reactivation of employment. The top conglomerates in the main tradeable sectors indeed increased efficiency and consolidated their assets and ties with foreign capital, though in a highly capital-intensive and concentrated manner. By 1994, the 30 largest exporting firms controlled 55 percent of all exports and in just four sectors: petroleum, foodstuffs, steel products, and motor vehicles (Toulan and Guillén 1997, 406-407). The country's 500 largest firms accounted for about 30 percent of GDP in 1994, but they employed only 20 percent of the workforce. Meanwhile, the primarily small- and medium-sized firms that form the core of the country's traditional industrial base had yet to make the transition to export-led production.[35] Operating mainly within the nontradeable sector, these smaller companies still lack the access to technology, skills, and market information that would enable them to participate more fully in the new market economy.[36] A special difficulty has been the lack of access to reasonably priced credit for financing modernization: in late 1996, large companies in Argentina's highly segmented credit markets reported paying from 8- to 10-percent interest on business loans, while smaller firms paid between 15- and 30- percent interest.[37]

In at least two respects, this adverse economic situation within the small- and medium-sized firms constituted a missing link in the market reform effort: On the demand side, although these firms traditionally accounted for the majority of jobs created, the squeeze on small manufacturing concerns in the 1990s contributed directly to the growing unemployment challenge. Between 1984 and 1994, for example, the total number of manufacturing establishments that employed 11 to 50 workers fell by 21 percent, as did the number of employees in these same sized companies (FIEL 1996, 140). On the supply side, the lack of integrated ties between small and large firms overlooked the essential role (for example, service inputs, innovation, flexibility) that the former played in launching successful export drives in other regions, such as East Asia.

Meanwhile, one of the most important factors in Argentine export growth did not involve liberalization per se but, rather, trade enhancement under the elaborate set of rules governing MERCOSUR. The share of Argentine exports going to Brazil rose from 11.5 percent in 1991 to nearly 28 percent by 1996; indeed, the increase in Argentine exports to Brazil accounted for nearly two-thirds of the entire increase in exports between 1991 and 1994, and the improvement in Argentina's trade balance with Brazil accounted for a full one-third of the trade adjustment over the difficult 1995-1996 period.[38] In one of the most dynamic growth sectors, the motor vehicles industry, higher levels of intra-industry trade resulted as much from competitive specialization and economies of scale as from MERCOSUR's balancing requirements (Bielschowsky and Stumpo 1995, 159; Mondino and Reca 1997, 189-192).

At face value, the rapid expansion of trade and investment ties reflects the extent to which these MERCOSUR partners succeeded in approximating their stated goals. But at the same time, there were some troubling trends that did not speak well for Argentina's increased competitiveness. Among them was the controversial question of MERCOSUR's diversion of trade from more competitive trade partners outside this subregional scheme (Yeats 1996). On the import side, despite some evidence of trade diversion for specific products, the overall trend within MERCOSUR was one of trade creation (Sepúlveda and Vera 1997, 9-10).[39] Even with some distortions, Robert Lawrence suggests that an arrangement like MERCOSUR's need not result in trade diversion if "changes in domestic regulations could give internal firms cost advantages over outsiders that resulted both in fewer imports from outside the region and in lower internal costs" (1996, 30-33). However, this scenario assumes that domestic firms across all economic sectors are achieving more efficiency and greater economies of scale as a result of their participation in a subregional scheme and that they are simultaneously reaching out to increase their share in other markets.

This assumption is doubtful for Argentina, given the price distortions related to exchange rate overvaluation, the dominance of MERCOSUR trade by just one sector (autos), and with one main trading partner, Brazil (Toulan and Guillén 1997, 404-406).[40] As long as Argentine exports to the more sophisticated Organization for Economic Cooperation and Development (OECD) markets continue to level off and local firms limit their outreach to the less competitive Brazilian market, it clearly will be difficult for Argentina to launch the dynamic export drive so necessary for sustaining productive growth.[41] This scenario was further clouded by ongoing instability and macroeconomic divergence between Argentina and Brazil throughout the 1990s (Nofal 1995). Although the two countries have implicitly harnessed their trade strategies to each other's macroeconomic stabilization program, the lack of policy coordination on this front resulted in erratic swings in the Argentine-Brazilian trade balance. The most recent situation was particularly precarious, as Brazil's 1999 devaluation quickly resulted in a burgeoning deficit for Argentina.

Privatization.[42] By the late 1980s, it was estimated that Argentina's approximately 400 state-owned companies accounted for 7 percent of domestic GDP and 21 percent of total gross investment. At the same time, the combined losses of the 13 largest public firms were US$4 billion in 1989, reflecting extremely low levels of productivity within the government enterprise sector. With inflation running at 5,000 percent that same year and public opinion rebelling against the horrendous quality of goods and services provided by state companies, the newly inaugurated Menem administration seized the opportunity to act against long-held preferences for state ownership in Argentina. Two laws were passed in 1989, the Economic Emergency Law and the State Reform Law, which together enabled the government to begin unloading state-held assets quickly.

This legislation initially authorized the president to place trustees in charge of state firms for up to one year, with the broad mandate to begin selling off as much as possible and by whatever means necessary. Assets were rapidly sold across all economic sectors, including airlines, oil companies, steel, petrochemicals, insurance, banks, telecommunications, and postal services. The positive impact on the fiscal balance, particularly in the crucial years of 1991 and 1992, can be seen in Figure 11 (the huge privatization yield from the 1993 sale of the state oil company was not applied to the fiscal accounts for that year, which would have shown a large divergence between government revenues with and without privatization).[43] Overall receipts were impressive: between 1990 and 1994, the federal government raised nearly US$10 billion in cash and absorbed an even larger amount of public bonds from the market. After this boom period, the pace of privatization slowed considerably. The receipts for 1995-1996 were approximately US$640 million, representing the sale of a handful of firms in the hydroelectric sector and one large petrochemical enterprise.[44]

Figure 11. Fiscal Performance in Argentina, 1990-1996

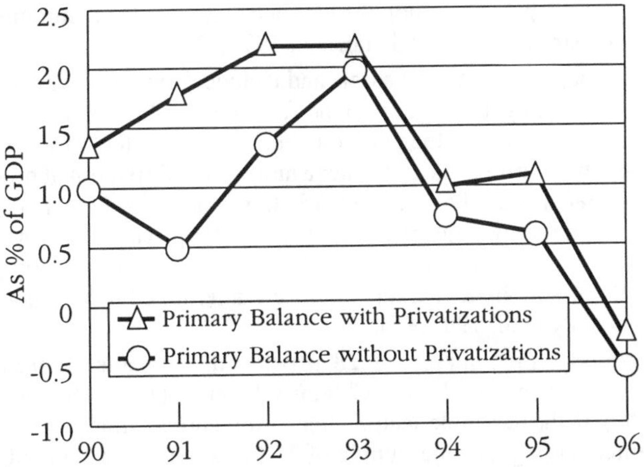

As % of GDP
2.5
2.0
1.5
1.0
0.5
0
-0.5
-1.0
90 91 92 93 94 95 96
Primary Balance with Privatizations
Primary Balance without Privatizations

Given the hyperinflationary context, the urgent need to reduce the fiscal deficit, and the dire slump in productivity, there is no doubt that the time had come for the Argentine state to rid itself of an increasingly parasitic government enterprise sector. In the aftermath of the ambitious sell-offs that were carried out through 1995, the privatization process simultaneously has been praised for placing Argentina in the vanguard of Latin America's market reformers and blamed as a main factor in the country's high rates of unemployment.[45] The data tell a slightly different story: because state firms traditionally accounted for just 3 percent to 4 percent of the country's total employment (de la Balze 1995, 88-89), it appears that the allegedly recessionary impact of privatization on the real economy may have had as much to do with the pace and manner in which assets were transferred from public to private hands as it did with retrenchment of the public workforce proper.

Research on the politics of privatization in Argentina supports this claim (Chudnovsky et al. 1995; Saba and Manzetti 1997). The key question was whether the shift to private ownership would trigger the efficiency and productivity gains that could attract further investment while laying the groundwork for employment expansion and sustainable growth over the long run. On this count, while the successes of the privatization drive were notable, so too were the failures. On the upside, the auction of assets ranging from ports to gas and petrochemical plants attracted world- class investors who, in conjunction with various local consortia, introduced those standards, know-how, and technologies most conducive to increased competitiveness. In particular, the widespread privatization of Argentina's public services holds strong potential for improving the quality of those nontradeable inputs essential for building a healthy, export-led development model.

On the downside, in its rush to balance the budget and produce some concrete results in the eyes of wary investors and inflation-weary voters, the government rode roughshod over some of the basic principles that have underpinned the privatization process elsewhere. For example, the record shows that not all state firms went to the highest or most sophisticated bidder and that the numerous sales in the early 1990s were made without a proper regulatory framework to prevent the emergence of costly private monopolies in such sectors as telecommunications and the airlines industry (Gelpern and Harrison 1992).[46]

Foreign majority control of assets and technical expertise were the rule, with domestic partners relegated mainly to the firm's lower-level administrative functions. But more to the point, the generous inducements offered to foreign bidders and their Argentine partners did not foster a more dynamic pattern of production and investment geared toward the external market. Instead, the general macroeconomic configuration and the specific incentive structure for privatization encouraged the pursuit of "very dynamic domestic market niches . . . which compete within predominantly oligopolistic market conditions determined by product differentiation" (Chudnovsky et al. 1995, 95).

Accordingly, in a survey of 28 privatized companies representing nine different individual sectors, Daniel Chudnovsky et al. (1995, 99) found that even those investing in the tradeable sector (such as food processing) did not embrace an export-oriented strategy; of the sample of 28 firms, only two adopted an outward export orientation (a meat-processing firm and a manufacturer of gear boxes), while the research and development activities of all but a handful of respondents were basically nil.

Deregulation. The mass of regulatory reforms that have been legislated since July 1989 represent nothing short of a revolution. Across sectors, fiscal and administrative barriers to competition have been removed, and the Argentine economy is now a considerably more stable and cost-effective environment for conducting everyday business transactions (de la Balze 1995, 99-104). A number of outdated state agencies have been abolished, most notably those that symbolized the incompetence and corruption that prevented the state from properly providing even the most basic public goods. And while foreigners have been granted the same rights and treatment as national investors since 1979, sectoral restrictions and prior authorization procedures were streamlined; indeed, Argentina's FDI laws are now so liberal that inscription into the national Registry of Foreign Investments is optional (Agosín 1995, 12).[47]

The one area where deregulation proceeded more erratically was within domestic labor markets. Admittedly, President Menem showed great political acumen in maintaining organized labor's backing while dismantling a statist model that many of his own labor constituents within the PJ still held dear. According to government sources, however, it was the remaining distortions in Argentina's labor markets — most of which originated during the heyday of Peronism in the 1940s — that were contributing both to high levels of unemployment and underemployment and to the flight of workers and producers into a quickly expanding informal economy.[48] For example, estimates showed that only 60 percent of the Argentine workforce was now formally registered (de la Balze 1995, 108).

The Menem government did make some headway in legislating new rules on health insurance and workers' compensation. However, a more difficult change, a reduction in payroll taxes and the replacement of severance payments for dismissed workers by an unemployment insurance scheme based on individual capitalization accounts with payroll deductions, remained. At the same time, the record showed that unions and employers increasingly met the challenge of market restructuring by proceeding with their own de facto "flexibilization" strategies. This included everything from the incorporation of productivity and work reorganization clauses into collective bargaining contracts; to the purchase by the unions of struggling firms in the represented sector; to union management of employee-owned stock of privatized state enterprises (Murillo 1997, 80-87). Given the extent of deregulation that had already occurred, it appeared that labor market rigidities were just one aspect of Argentina's persistent pattern of unemployment. The larger problem was the limitations on growth posed by 1) the country's exchange rate policy and 2) steep nonwage labor costs that constituted 50 percent of gross wages in Argentina (as compared with 30 percent for the OECD countries), which hampered the flow of workers from less productive employment to jobs in the more competitive sectors (Pessino 1997).

Another pressure point in the regulatory reform process was the government's mixed record in constructing effective oversight mechanisms for newly privatized firms providing such services as water/sewerage, telecommunications, natural gas, and electrical power. Again, the high presence of foreign investors in the privatization of public utilities (37 percent between 1992 and 1995) reflected the profitability conditions that were built into the transfer clauses and the captive nature of the domestic market (Chudnovsky et al. 1995, 40). The crucial role for public policy in overseeing the quality and price competitiveness of private service delivery under such circumstances was not lost on the Menem administration.

Yet, the regulatory bodies designed for this task varied greatly in their effectiveness (Urbiztondo 1997, 13-28). At one end of the continuum were the gas (ENARGAS) and electricity (ENRE) commissions that regulated numerous service providers, were funded autonomously, and fell under congressional jurisdiction. At the other end were the telecommunications (CNT) and water/sewerage (ETOSS) commissions, the targets of intense lobbying by one or two large firms that are funded by revenues that sometimes carried questionable political ties and were subject to frequent administrative interventions by the president and other local officials. Obviously, the latter pattern created lucrative opportunities for corruption;

in turn, this sheds light on the numerous scandals surrounding the Menem administration (Saba and Manzetti 1997).[49]

Distributional Outcomes in the Reform Process

Market reform usually promises to correct distributional inequities: in theory, liberal trade regimes are expected to generate new demand for labor, while a reduction in the realm of government is supposed to deter rent-seeking and favoritism toward elites. In practice, most of Latin America's market reformers have experienced distributional deterioration in the process of liberalization, marked by sizable transfers of wealth toward the top income deciles. Argentina is no exception.

Figure 12 illustrates the shift in income distribution over the course of the first five years of the Convertibility Plan, making use of a twice-a-year household survey collected for the Greater Buenos Aires area (which accounts for almost 40 percent of the population and more than 50 percent of national GDP). We plot two measures of income distribution: the percent of income received by the top 20 percent of households relative to the bottom 40 percent of households and the percent of income received by the top 10 percent relative to the bottom 10 percent. While there is some volatility, both measures show a pattern of worsening distribution over the course of the period.[50]

A detailed breakdown of the evolution of labor market trends after 1991 helps to explain some of this distributional worsening. By May 1993, the unemployment rate of blue-collar workers was four times that of university-trained professionals; although the jobless rate for the latter was half that of those with just a primary-level education, in 1994 the university-level unemployment rate began rising more quickly than any other education category. These trends follow a pattern typical of an economy that is downsizing, whereby those with the lowest levels of training

Figure 12. Income Distribution in Argentina 1990-1996

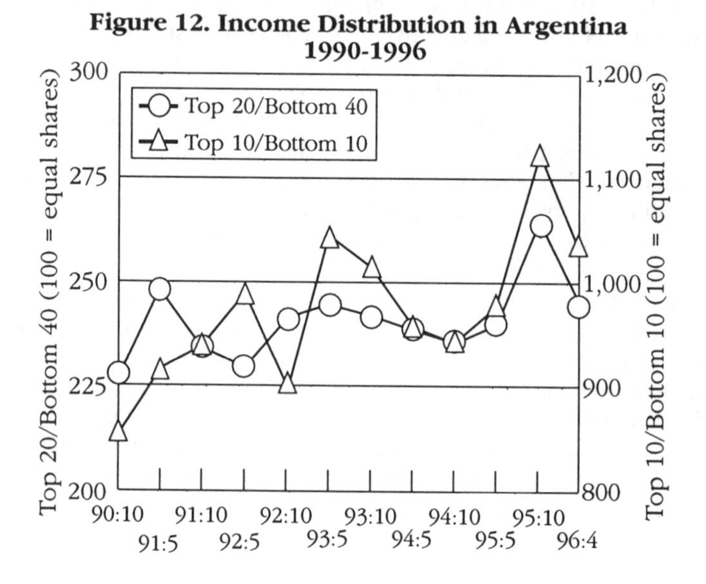

(primary and secondary education) are let go first, and then the more highly educated — whose skills become increasingly obsolete — are then laid off. By 1995, the skills required to obtain a new job were quite different from those needed in the past.

As a result, the segment of the population hit hardest by declining employment prospects was male heads of household with a secondary education. While the Menem administration blamed the country's rigid labor laws for the inability of this traditional core of the Argentine workforce to defend its economic interests, it is doubtful that a "flexibilization" of the labor code alone would prompt the levels of labor absorption necessary; moreover, the overvalued exchange rate worked against job creation in high value-added export ventures, while favoring nontradeable boom sectors such as financial services, which required fewer workers with much higher skills.

Adding to the distributional problem was a continuing concentration of assets on the business side. Even as the 1995 recession provoked higher unemployment and rising rates of bankruptcy throughout the economy, Argentina's top 200 companies increased their sales and profits that same year by 11 percent and 30 percent, respectively.[51] The restructuring of the financial system, particularly in the wake of the tequila shock, also resulted in asset concentration; while few banks went under in the midst of the 1995 crisis, many were absorbed by larger, more solvent banks, and by late 1996, the number of banks had fallen from over 200 to 148.[52]

Another distributional tension arose with regard to the relationship between the central government and the provinces. Until 1995, local governments had not been subjected to the same fiscal discipline as that imposed on the federal government. For one thing, the early growth boom generated a healthy increase in the local tax base.[53] For another, provincial officials often forced province-owned banks, not subject to convertibility regulations, to extend credit. Moreover, even in the midst of sharp cuts at the federal level, the central government actually increased its transfers to the provinces by nearly 2 percent of GDP between 1990 and 1992. Overall, from 1990-1995, federal resource transfers to the provinces more than doubled (Gibson and Calvo 1997, 8). In the face of such largesse, local level state reform was postponed, a pattern that tended to ameliorate political difficulties.

However, when the 1995 recession hit and the federal surplus declined, provincial budgets quickly fell into a state of fiscal crisis. As the provincial deficit rose to US$3 billion in 1995 (slightly over 1 percent of GDP), the provinces finally quickened what had been an exceedingly slow pace in the realm of privatization; since provincial banks were a prime target for such privatization, the option to borrow locally was now foreclosed to provincial officials.[54] With finances tightening, local officials postponed payments to suppliers, state employees, and pensioners (World Bank 1996). Social tension percolated, then exploded; in May 1997 alone, there were more than 40 incidents of local protest, including roadblocks and clashes with the police.

In many other countries with similar distributional stresses, including Bolivia, Chile, and Mexico, governments devised short-term, "safety net" strategies to soften the pains of adjustment and win political support for reform (Graham 1994). Because of the buoyant growth rates from 1991-1994, the fiscal stringency imposed by the Convertibility Plan, and the "hands-off," ideological fervor of the Cavallo team, the Menem government rejected this sort of approach. With the recession of 1995 and the full impact of economic restructuring sinking in at the level of the real economy, the president put aside earlier fiscal concerns and launched a social plan. Since this was also an election year, Menem began selectively targeting compensation toward valued constituents (Weyland 1997, 21-22). But the transparency of the ploy and its timing were lost on few citizens.

The Politics (and Anti-Politics) of Reform

Until 1995, the Menem administration appeared to have accomplished the nearly impossible task of winning over one of the region's most feisty electorates, while launching the most far-reaching set of economic reforms in the country's history. Despite the lack of a safety net strategy to garner political support for market adjustment, the alarming jump in unemployment in 1994, and the steep recession that followed from the Mexican crisis, President Menem easily won re-election to a second term in 1995. Yet, by early 1997, support for Menem in national public opinion polls had plummeted to just 10 percent. The country experienced a string of militant general strikes, beginning in mid-1996 (in contrast to one general strike during Menem's first term); street crime was on the rise; and even pensioners on fixed incomes were protesting.

Understanding Argentina's political dynamics requires that we analyze, first, why Menem enjoyed such an extended period of support and, second, why it evaporated. One crucial factor was the willingness of the public, in the wake of hyperinflation, to tolerate austerity in exchange for price stability and the promise of future economic gains (Starr 1997). There were, however, several key political tactics that also helped sustain some degree of support for reform.

The first tactic was the masterful overhaul of Menem's PJ, expanding and diversifying the party's mass base while diminishing greatly the traditional Peronist trade unions' influence.[55] By exploiting the party's weak rules for leadership turnover and its historically strong ties to the country's working classes, Menem seized the leadership role, replaced the PJ's typically populist agenda with his own program of market reform, and was thereby able to draw a larger business and middle-class segment into the party. He also managed to maintain organized labor's loyalty in spite of its outright marginalization within the party, due most likely to labor's lack of other political alternatives.

The second tactic involved playing off constituents in Argentina's urban centers against their compatriots in the country's less developed provinces. As noted above, the provinces had largely been spared the pain of fiscal adjustment until 1995, at which point the tequila shock forced the federal government's hand. As Edward Gibson and Ernesto Calvo (1997, 7) explain, "Peronism's seeming invincibility at the polls . . . was due not to organized labor in the metropolis, but to its ties to clientelistic and traditional networks of power and mobilization in the periphery." Hence, a winning electoral coalition was maintained nationally by the phasing-in of harsh adjustment measures to the regions at a much later point.

Thus, as noted earlier, central government transfers to the provinces actually increased while the urban centers were subjected to a tight fiscal shock; moreover, during the 1989-1994 period, although the federal government workforce was cut by 77 percent, public sector employment in the provinces held steady. The force with which fiscal retrenchment was hitting the regions, where public employment traditionally had been a mainstay, shed light on why social protest erupted later and with such vehemence in the periphery.

Menem, similar to many other heads of state in Latin America of the 1990s, relied heavily on executive decrees in order to overcome lingering anti-market sentiments within Congress and the wider political arena (Teichman 1997). Executive decrees were utilized, for example, in raising taxes and revising tax laws, in modifying public and private contracts, and in setting various rules that were vital to the trade regime — decisions that typically require broader input and consensus (López 1997).[56] The previous Alfonsín administration issued just eight decrees of "necessity and urgency" during its entire tenure; in contrast, between July 1989 and December 1993, more than 12,000 executive decrees and 308 decrees of "necessity and urgency" were passed, the latter composing the core of the reform program (López 1997, 15).

Given the measured success of these tactics, what explains the sharp drop in political support? In a compelling study, Susan Stokes (1996, 508) argues that an "intertemporal" response ("no pain, no gain") to the sacrifices invoked by market adjustment can eventually shift to a "distributional" response ("my pain is your gain") on the part of voters, even those who have been traumatized by hyperinflation: ". . .support for reforms began high among all classes and remained relatively high among the rich but declined notably among the poor. . . . No one was willing to suffer catastrophic losses, such as unemployment, on the promise of future prosperity or with the excuse of ghosts of the past" (Stokes 1996, 516-517).

The "distributional moment" arrived in Argentina. The Radical Party victory in the June 1996 mayoral election in Buenos Aires — where Menem's party garnered only 18 percent of the vote — reflected the distinctly distributional mood that had settled in amongst urban voters worried over whether they would actually see some light at the end of the economic tunnel. The provinces followed suit in the October 1997 mid-term elections, when the Peronists lost control of their majority standing in the lower house of the Chamber of Deputies ("La gobernabilidad está asegurada," *Clarín*, 1997). While this loss, in and of itself, did not impair seriously Menem's ability to govern (Perry 1997), it was compounded by the fact that all previous political tactics for garnering support had run into difficulties.

The reworking of the Peronist party wore thin, as the party's traditional base constituency within organized labor was all but consumed with its own immediate economic survival. The postponement of market reform in the provinces provoked a political backlash among those who thought they had escaped the inevitable pain of adjustment. The president's strong reliance on legislative decrees undermined executive legitimacy, as many of these decisions became enshrouded in charges of corruption. Both the business and labor sectors came to oppose an almost purely autocratic decision-making style, with points of conflict centering on Menem's repeated circumvention of Congress, frequently in defiance of the Constitution, and his ready resort to other underhanded tactics, such as the stacking of the Supreme Court with members guaranteed to support executive-level policy directives.[57]

To its credit, the Menem team took command of a shipwrecked economy, imposed an economic rationale on a society that had long been accustomed to "storming the state," and, in the process, secured the longest political honeymoon since the Peronist era. As effective as this style may have been for initiating and implementing market reforms, the successful consolidation of the reform process required the development of technocratic expertise and political skills beyond just the Economics Ministry and the office of the executive. It became imperative that two challenges be met for the next phase of market reform in Argentina: distributional improvement and increased public accountability.

THE NEXT PHASE FOR ARGENTINA

> "There is no relation between unemployment and economic policy."
>
> Domingo Cavallo,
> *Latin American Weekly Report*, August 3, 1995

> "What is this dollar to peso, one-to-one? The rest of Latin America is laughing at us. . . . This has been an act of inhumanity over the last six years. They have destroyed the technical schools, destroyed education, destroyed the base of the future. They will be judged."
>
> anonymous businessman,
> Buenos Aires, July 1995

This analysis has pointed to the disjuncture between Argentina's higher growth rates and lower inflation and its historically high unemployment and distributional upheaval. We argue that this gap between macroeconomic "success" and microeconomic "stress" is directly related to the policies that were adopted in Argentina under the aegis of market reform. At the macroeconomic level, a fixed exchange rate and the offering of government investment incentives that favor services, nontradeables, and capital-intensive manufacturing (cars), made it difficult for skilled and unskilled workers to find their new place in the emergent market economy. Such a transition was further slowed by microeconomic approaches (or the lack thereof), which did not materialize fully in the areas of labor market reform and adjustment support for small and medium-sized firms. In the end, however, perhaps the greatest challenge to successful sustainability of market reforms in Argentina was the political backdrop that has framed the policy-making process.

To elaborate further on these points, we turn to an analytical model devised by Dani Rodrik (1991), which provides a useful framework for assessing the medium-term sustainability of a market reform effort such as Argentina's. According to Rodrik, 1) the reforms must be technically sound enough to produce the desired economic result and, hence, the basis for a new coalition; 2) technocrats must be sufficiently insulated so that short-term lobbying pressures can be withstood until the reforms take full effect; and 3) the "winners" from the reform effort — who may not have been an obvious interest group at the beginning of the process

— must be persuaded or induced to develop a collective voice to maintain the new policy regime.

In our view, Argentina's track record gives cause for concern on all three counts. With time, the technical coherence of the reform program that Rodrik insists upon fell into question: while the convertibility experiment had positive effects on dampening inflation, this strategy discouraged investment in the production of manufactured exports; while privatization boosted the fiscal coffers from 1990-1994, later deficits reflected the extent to which these revenue flows had slowed and hence the continuing need for serious fiscal reform; while liberalization produced a welcome increase in productivity, unemployment lingered at high levels, and liberalization's effects on overall competitiveness were quite mixed. Meanwhile, policymakers shied away from initiatives that could readily shape the economy in a higher value-added direction; instead, they allowed market forces to breathe new life into some sectors, such as services, that offer little in the way of value-added elements.

As for Rodrik's notion of insulating technocrats to filter out societal pressures during the initiation of market reforms, it appears that the Menem administration went overboard in two respects. First, by issuing more emergency presidential decrees than the total number issued by all constitutional presidents in the past 130 years (Teichman 1997, 27), Menem secured his program but also effectively silenced the kinds of debate and input that would now be useful as the reform program moves into the medium term. Second, hindsight has gradually shown that the Menem team was perhaps too friendly with or not insulated enough from Argentina's powerful private sector conglomerates (for example, Techint, Compañía del Plata, and the Pérez Companc Group) — all of whom have benefited disproportionately in the 1990s (Teichman 1997, 31).

This excessive identification with wealthy interests, a seeming lack of concern about the employment and distributional consequences of reform, and an early determination to forego social policy also did little to expand the "winners' circle" in Argentina. The Menem team rightly prided itself on having purged the country of its self-destructive, populist past. Indeed, perhaps the most telling aspect of the October 1997 mid-term elections was the emphasis that the winning opposition candidates placed, not on populist-style expansion, but on the need for a second round of social and institutional reforms (especially anti-corruption initiatives) to correct for past shortcomings and to facilitate the country's adjustment to a market economy more effectively.[58]

As a first cut at defining more clearly what a "second phase" reform effort would consist of, the approach taken by Chilean policymakers in the mid-1980s offers some helpful lessons (Graham 1994; Edwards 1995; Velasco 1994). This shift in Chile, which occurred simultaneously at the level of the macroeconomy, the microeconomy, state institutions, and social policy, included the following changes: a more flexible and pragmatic macroeconomic policy, including the use of the exchange rate as a competitive tool; selective industrial interventions, particularly with regard to export promotion, financial incentives, and strategic support to foster an outward orientation within the small- and medium-sized firms; a badly needed overhaul of those state institutions most relevant to the policy-making process; and the development of social programs to help compensate the losers in the market, with special emphasis on the very poorest households.[59]

How would measures in all four areas translate into a second reform phase in the Argentine case? At the macroeconomic level, the two most powerful tools for improving growth and incomes are fiscal policy and exchange rate management. With regard to the former, the Menem administration made some important headway in increasing tax compliance, simplifying the tax structure, and modernizing the country's budgetary process (Artana and Navajas 1995). At the same time, however, Argentine fiscal policy in the 1990s followed a procyclical pattern, expanding during the good times and abruptly contracting when bad times set in, just the reverse of what was needed, for example, during the 1995 economic downturn. Also, fiscal policy in the 1990s was clearly manipulated for political purposes, most obviously in the provinces. A second-phase fiscal reform required that policymakers shift to a counter-cyclical strategy, tightening the administration and collection of direct taxes on income, and resisting the excesses of political spending that marked earlier national elections.

As for exchange rate policy, since the implementation of the Convertibility Plan in 1991, Argentina has defied conventional wisdom within the economic community, which favors a more flexible approach to currency management (Corden 1994, 304; Edwards 1995). Despite the rigid policy options intrinsic to the currency board, growth and export rates have been respectable, and the recovery from the tequila shock more rapid than expected. (Note: the domestic money supply must adjust automatically to changes in the country's foreign exchange reserves, and the board is not permitted to create credit.) Yet, the track record to date pales when Argentina's comparatively rich factor endowments are taken into account, and we are left to wonder whether the country could better maximize its economic potential through the adoption of a more flexible exchange rate strategy. In terms of a second-phase exchange rate policy, at least two additional points recommend a more flexible approach.

First, while the strict tightening of fiscal and monetary policy enabled Argentine officials to survive the tequila crisis with the Convertibility Plan intact, this adjustment was facilitated by bending the rules on reserve requirements and by the simultaneous expansion of Brazilian demand for Argentine products. With the Brazilian devaluation of early 1999 and the slowdown in its economy, forecasters negatively adjusted their projections concerning Argentina's growth prospects.

This leads into the second point: Convertibility's two remaining stabilization tools, high interest rates and wage and employment compression, also seem less favorable as options in the current economic environment. Given today's high levels of international volatility and the clear domestic exhaustion with recessive stabilization measures, Convertibility's time-honored reliance on austerity-driven adjustments may well face a credibility challenge. Hence, it is at least worth contemplating a more flexible second-phase exchange rate strategy.

On the microeconomic front, one puzzling aspect of the Argentine restructuring during the Menem administration was the absence of an explicitly stated development strategy. As Chile found out the hard way in the early 1980s, market reform in and of itself is not a development strategy. Rather, it is a set of policies meant to promote an outward orientation and a stronger foothold in international markets. Take Mexico as another example: although the country has had its own share of problems in implementing an outward-oriented development model based on higher value-added manufactured exports, there has never been any doubt as to the government's intention to pursue such a strategy (Pastor and Wise 1997, 429-440). In Argentina, despite the impressive strides that have been made in liberalization, privatization, and deregulation, the question of how these policies add up to a development strategy proper was not made clear.

A second-phase strategy at the microeconomic level demands a more explicit linking of market reforms with the outward-oriented model that is ostensibly being pursued and a more vigorous effort to remove distortions that impede market performance. Microeconomic reform is clearly the most complex and challenging component of market restructuring. To help simplify the discussion, we touch briefly on four interrelated issue areas:

1. *Tariffs on trade,* which have risen in terms of MERCOSUR's common external tariff, are still too upwardly flexible with regard to Argentine trade with non-MERCOSUR partners. A more confidence-enhancing, second-phase trade strategy is to continue to pursue the commitment to trade openness.

2. *Support for the small- and medium-sized enterprise sector* has been articulated in domestic legislation (FIEL 1996) but weakly implemented. Preliminary survey research suggests that smaller industrial firms have made some headway in shifting to an export-oriented mode of production, but greater gains could be achieved with the help of a more assertive public policy framework to guide this economic restructuring (Robbio 1997; Kosacoff and Ramos 1997). Into the second reform phase, support for this sector means an explicit, neutral, transparent set of public policies to strengthen horizontal and vertical links to larger firms; publicity and marketing; technical know-how; and more direct ties between education, job training, and employment expansion in these firms.

3. *Labor market reform,* interestingly, was not raised as a major point of debate by business or labor in the October 1997 mid-term elections. Why were political candidates allowed to skirt this important issue? At least partially because the legislative record since 1991 confirmed that a series of piecemeal deregulatory laws had increasingly introduced flexibility, productivity, and other cost-cutting clauses into labor contracts. And, these measures forced major adjustments in Argentine labor markets in the 1990s (Murillo 1997, 77-82). The remaining gaps in labor market reform and the failure of politicians to push a comprehensive legislative package through Congress perpetuated a credibility problem, particularly from the standpoint of foreign investors. A second-phase labor market reform bill was at last approved by the Senate in April 2000 in slightly watered-down form, after clashes between unionists and police. Although investors were somewhat assuaged, it was still unclear whether the measure would significantly address unemployment.

4. *Public investment in infrastructure for productive purposes* (railways, irrigation, and industrial facilities) dropped to historically low levels. The high concentration of public expenditure on current allocations in the 1990s was especially detrimental to the country's interior provinces and worked against the

broader expansion and diversification of production in industrial activities. In line with the second-phase fiscal reforms mentioned above, this deficit in productive investment must also be addressed.

The success of these macroeconomic and microeconomic second-phase reforms will hinge on the extent to which a badly needed overhaul of the most relevant public sector institutions is carried out (Naim 1995). While notable progress has been made in modernizing the state's main economic institutions, other public entities such as the judiciary, the regulatory commissions, the social ministries, and provincial governments are still too easily permeated by corruption and outside interests. Thus, and with good cause, the Argentine public has continued to view state institutions with suspicion. One benchmark of the importance of institutional reform to the long-term success of market policies was the IMF's remarkable 1997 offer to open a new line of credit for Argentina based on "good governance."[60] More to the point, during this second and more challenging phase of market reform, public institutions are crucial conduits for guaranteeing greater equality of economic opportunity and wider participation in the benefits of growth.

There is also the issue of social policy. As Argentina boasts the region's highest per capita income (US$9,387),[61] the most highly educated population, and relatively wide welfare coverage, the Menem administration was able to launch a first phase of market reform without resorting to the safety-net compensation schemes that were adopted in poorer countries like Bolivia and Peru (Graham 1994). However, since 1991, the combined effects of the convertibility stabilization program and government incentives that favor low value-added investments and higher levels of market concentration — including ownership, production, and exports (CEP 1997) — led to an increase in poverty (Burki and Edwards 1996, 8) and a worsening of distributional trends (see Figure 12). We argue that this social downturn is directly related to government policy and could be corrected in the second reform phase through 1) better targeting of social expenditures toward high-risk groups and 2) a more concerted effort at encouraging the kinds of high value-added investments and concomitant educational training that would offer employment opportunities for a much broader segment of the Argentine population.

Finally, opening the policy process up to more citizen involvement may generate a reform agenda that is less ambitious, but a coalition that is capable of sustaining market reform into the longer term (Graham 1998); this could also provide some badly needed accountability checks that will induce policymakers and political leaders to harness market policies more closely to the productive and distributive tasks for which they were originally designed.

Notes

1. See "Camdessus Calls for 'Second Generation' of Reforms in Argentina," 1997, *IMF Survey* 26:11 (June 9), 175-176.

2. Statement made during an interview conducted by the authors on August 1, 1996, in Buenos Aires.

3. Data sources for all figures are listed in the Appendix at the end of the paper.

4. Stabilization was made possible in part by the earlier "Plan BONEX," in which state debt was converted into 10-year, dollar-denominated bonds; this allowed the government to extend the maturity of public debt from less than one month to 10 years and to eliminate the quasi-fiscal deficit (a savings estimated to equal approximately 5 percent of GDP). Both outcomes made fiscal constraint easier to manage within the confines of the Convertibility Plan. See Rodríguez (1995) and Tanner and Sanguinetti (1996).

5. For a detailed look at the specific rules of the Convertibility Plan and currency board in Argentina, see Ades (1995); for a general view of the role of capital mobility in Latin American development and stabilization, see Mahon (1996). As we also note below, Argentina's program differed from a more orthodox currency board in that the Convertibility Law permitted part of the monetary base to be covered by dollar-denominated Argentine Treasury bonds. This gave the government a bit of breathing room when the 1995 crisis hit.

6. On Argentine fiscal reform, see Acuña (1994), Canitrot (1994), de la Balze (1995, 70-72), Artana and Navajas (1995), and Berensztein (1996).

7. For a brief review of a model that explains the tendency toward currency overvaluation during a disinflation process, see Dornbusch (1995).

8. As per the usual practice, declines in the real exchange rate imply increases in the domestic currency.

9. The effect of the exchange rate overvaluation was tempered somewhat by the tax system. In 1992, the government decided to offer a "general reimbursement" on exports with the same value-added scale structure as had been established for imports. Thus, wheat was exported with a subsidy of 2.5 percent and imported at a duty of 2.5 percent (Cristini 1996, 2.9). These mirrored tariffs and rebates ranging from 2.5 percent to 20 percent; the effect was a fiscal devaluation.

10. Likewise, Cristini (1996, 2.4) notes that the higher levels of exports from 1988-1990 were due to both a decline in domestic activity and incentives to earn dollars. Models of macroeconomies with such export dynamics are offered in Arida and Bacha (1984) and Pastor (1987, chapter 5).

11. Argentine investors were estimated to have stashed nearly US$45 billion abroad by 1987, an amount equivalent to over 75 percent of the country's external debt (Pastor 1990).

Since hyperinflation in the late 1980s induced the exodus of even more monies, there was ample flight capital to return home.

12. Starr (1997) also stresses hyperinflation's impact on the initial monetary base. As it turns out, the Central Bank initially had full coverage in terms of gross but not in terms of net reserves; the latter did not occur until 1992 (Williamson 1995, 9). Thus, part of the reserve accumulation in this early period was related simply to building up the appropriate monetary backing.

13. A failure to remonetize would have raised interest rates and choked investment, a problematic prospect given that the revival of the private sector was a key policy objective of the government.

14. By 1996, intermediate goods had staged a modest comeback, as firms imported intermediates to be able to export; capital goods had fallen to 41 percent of imports and consumption goods to 20 percent.

15. Chisari, Fanelli, and Frenkel (1996, 233) suggest that the very nature of relative prices channeled investment into the nontradeable sector; see also Gerchunoff and Machinea (1995). Chudnovsky (1996) argues that there was some investment expansion into tradeables in 1993 and 1994, but the strongest investment was in MERCOSUR-related sectors (automobiles, for example), reflecting the growing relationship with Brazil and the relative appreciation of the latter's currency. Bielschowsky and Stumpo (1995, 159) note that FDI was also drawn primarily into nontradeables, with the largest flows going toward services and toward petroleum, the latter being mostly a domestically oriented industry in Argentina.

16. The main export products were also capital-intensive, implying that this growth was not conducive to the creation of new jobs. For a review of export performance and composition from the 1970s to 1990, see Bisang and Kosacoff (1996); for a review of the contemporary period which suggests that there was no export boom in manufactures, see Cristini (1996).

17. While we present unemployment figures for Buenos Aires and the provinces, we believe the former to be more reliable than the latter. However, the Economy Ministry has stressed an improvement in the national unemployment rate, which has been lower than the rate for Buenos Aires in the last several years. This shift coincides with a methodological improvement in the government's labor market survey, which recorded the number of active job searchers in Buenos Aires but did not do so for the provinces. See Ernesto Kritz, 1997, "Tribuna abierta: ¿Qué hacer con las mediciones de empleo?" *Clarín,* April 7.

18. Labor productivity reportedly rose by 4.1 percent per annum in the 1990-95 period; see "Insufficient Growth Limits Job Creation," 1997, *CEPAL News* 27: 6 (June), 1. On the other hand, Argentine real wages grew by just 0.2 percent annually from 1990-1995 (compared to 5.1 percent for Brazil and 4.4 percent for Chile), with the rising wage-productivity gap indicating one reason for the worsening distribution of income.

19. According to Pessino (1997), the unexpected severity of labor market adjustment was directly related to the higher relative price of labor with respect to capital in the aggregate, a simultaneous increase in the labor force and a shrinking of job opportunities, and virtually no change in long outdated labor market regulations.

20. Quoted in "The Markets Are Getting Nervous," *Latin American Weekly Report,* December 15, 1994.

21. There was an earlier scare in November 1992, but the government stuck by the convertibility rules and, as Williamson notes (1995, 9), "the crisis passed rapidly." Also see Starr (1997).

22. See "IMF Allows a Deficit This Year," 1995, *Latin American Weekly Report,* September 14. This section on government policy responses to the 1995 financial crisis draws, in part, on authors' interviews with frontline managers at the Argentine Central Bank in Buenos Aires during July 1996. See García (1997).

23. See Figure 2, as well as Charles Newberry, 1996, "Argentine Growth Pickup and Lower Rates Seen," *Bloomberg Business News,* December 26. The financial system also had been shored up: in November 1996, bank deposits rose to US$53 billion, up sharply from the US$38 billion low of April 1995.

24. Another worrisome feature is the deteriorating quality of employment. According to a recent Labor Ministry study, permanent jobs actually fell by nearly 6 percent over the course of 1996; the improvement in employment, which helped keep the unemployment rate basically steady through that year, came from a dramatic expansion in temporary positions (EIU 1997, 19).

25. Oil, for example, rose 41 percent in value, while raw materials increased by 21 percent. See "Growth of 6% Forecast," from *Latin American Economy and Business* (LAEB-97-03). Meanwhile, exports of industrial manufactures actually fell by 1 percent (Economist Intelligence Unit 1997, 29).

26. ECLAC, 1996, *Preliminary Overview of the Economy of Latin America and the Caribbean, 1996* (Santiago: United Nations, ECLAC), 42. The official government data, presented in Figure 11, do not show the non-financial sector going into a deficit until 1996.

27. The actual procedure involves regressing the log of the real exchange rate on time (entered linearly and as a square) and using the result to obtain predicted values of the equilibrium rate (see Goldfajn and Valdés 1996, 7). We did not use a multilateral, trade-weighted exchange figure for our calculations. To the degree that the dollar fell in international value, we may be overstating the extent of the peso's appreciation. It is interesting to note that the equilibrium value of the peso has been rising over time, implying that Argentine officials may be partially right when they point to the peso's appreciation as a long-term, sustainable trend. However, this real adjustment is a very slow process, and the movement of the actual rate has gone well beyond the long-term value.

28. We should note that, since 1970, every time Argentina crossed this threshold for more than two months, the deviation from the real exchange rate continued to the point of a financial explosion. In the recent episode, the threshold was crossed in a sustained fashion, which subsequently was followed by a modest downward trend; thus, the effect was one of a financial "simmer," rather than a full-blown crisis.

29. Argentina managed to generate some real depreciation without nominal devaluation. In 1996, inflation was only barely above zero, which, given ongoing international inflation, produced a slight depreciation in real terms, and the real exchange rate finally dipped below the 25 percent "risk" threshold in April 1997.

30. For more on credibility, highly visible signals, and the Convertibility Plan, see Canavan and Tommasi (1996). On the politics of the Convertibility Plan, see Corrales (1997) and Starr (1997).

31. Statement made during an interview conducted by the authors on August 1, 1996, in Buenos Aires.

32. Quoted in "Cavallo Provokes Crisis, Keeps Job," 1995, *Latin American Weekly Report,* September 7.

33. The policy has been slightly more activist than the image. In 1993, for example, the government introduced restrictions and antidumping measures on the imports of some goods, hoping to shrink the growth in the trade deficit. See Tussie (1996) for further detail.

34. Measured as exports, imports, and GDP in constant 1986 pesos, these figures derive from the data compiled by the Argentine Economy Ministry. While other measures (such as in current pesos) will show different specific numbers, all reveal a general growth in trade as a percentage of GDP.

35. As of 1994, 99 percent of these companies employed fewer than 50 workers, and it is this group that accounts for 70 percent of all employment and 22 percent of GDP (FIEL 1996, 14).

36. Authors' interviews with Bernardo Kosacoff at ECLAC and Omar Chisari, Director, Instituto de Economía, Universidad Argentina de la Empresa, August 1, 1996, in Buenos Aires.

37. Authors' interviews with eight members of the Confederación General de la Industria, a business chamber that represents all small- and medium-sized firms in Argentina, on July 26, 1996, in Buenos Aires. See also FIEL (1996).

38. Data taken from Table 8.1.2, exports, imports and balance, by economic region and principal countries, *Statistical Yearbook of the Republic of Argentina, 1995* (CD-ROM); and *Síntesis de la Economía Real,* No. 9, November 1997, from the Centro de Estudios para la Producción (CEP), Buenos Aires.

39. The November 1997 decision to raise MERCOSUR's Common External Tariff to 25 percent, as a defensive response to the shocks emanating from Asia's multiple currency crises, was admittedly not an encouraging sign in terms of further trade creation.

40. While auto producers within MERCOSUR have advanced quickly in modernizing their operations and increasing their export ratio, the "price" for this sophisticated system of protection has been the continued inability to compete effectively outside the subregional market, not to mention higher auto costs for consumers within the MERCOSUR bloc (Agosín, 1995; Chudnovsky et al., 1995).

41. While intra-MERCOSUR exports quadrupled in the 1990-1996 period, the expansion of MERCOSUR exports to the rest of the world grew by an average rate of just 8 percent in the same period (Sepúlveda and Vera 1997, 1). As for Argentina, exports to the European Union, for example, expanded by 2 percent in 1996, while exports to Brazil grew by nearly 20 percent. In other words, Brazil captured 27.8 percent of Argentine exports in 1996, compared to 5.9 percent in 1985 (CEP 1997, 54).

42. This section draws on Gelpern and Harrison (1992); Chudnovsky et al. (1995); de la Balze (1995, 88-99); Artana and Navajas (1995); and Saba and Manzetti (1997).

43. While Figure 11 suggests that 1996 saw a modest primary deficit, other reports indicate that there was a much larger, 5.9 billion peso deficit for the consolidated public sector. This (non-primary) measure takes into account the higher interest rates paid by the state in the wake of the 1995 crisis (EIU 1997, 8).

44. These figures are reported in the *Statistical Yearbook of the Argentine Republic, 1997,* 13, INDEC, 480-483.

45. See, for example, Anthony Faiola, 1997, "Argentine Private Enterprise Draws Public Opposition." *The Washington Post,* June 22, A20.

46. A study by Daniel Azpiazu found that 66 of Argentina's 200 largest companies emerged out of the privatization program, with the 50 most profitable firms receiving 60 percent of all profits generated by the larger group of businesses; see "Big Profits for Privatized Services," 1997, *Latin American Regional Reports-Southern Cone,* March 4, 3. An earlier study by Fundación Capital, a private think tank, found that just three privatized firms accounted for 40 percent of the total turnover of the 70 companies quoted on the Buenos Aires Stock Exchange (see "Argentina's Drift Toward Concentration," 1995, *Latin American Weekly Report,* October 5).

47. Authors' interview with Jaime Campos, Director of INVERTIR, August 7, 1996, in Buenos Aires. Campos notes that these rules also make it more difficult to track new FDI flows into Argentina.

48. Information provided by Felipe Frydman, Economics Attaché at the Embassy of Argentina, Washington, D.C., in a lecture on "Argentina Under the Convertibility Plan," Johns Hopkins University, School of Advanced International Studies, November 13, 1996, Washington, D.C.

49. According to Saba and Manzetti (1997, 363), "In less than four years the [Menem] administration suffered some 19 scandals resulting in 29 ministers and senior advisers being dismissed —with privatization scandals extremely prominent."

50. At the same time, poverty rates fell steadily between the start of the program in 1991 and its 1994 peak (Petrecolla 1995). Such improvements are common in the wake of hyperinflation and can, in fact, be consistent with a relative worsening of income distribution. This pattern is usually politically acceptable, unless the absolute improvement is suddenly arrested, as it was in Argentina in 1995. In that year, the poverty rate rose (see Beccaria 1996) as income distribution continued to deteriorate.

51. Information on sales and profits in 1995, from "Big Profits for Privatized Services," 1997, *Latin American Regional Reports-Southern Cone,* March 4, 3. An earlier report also suggested that the biggest firms had seen their turnover increase even as the economy plummeted in the first half of 1995 (see "Argentina's Drift Toward Concentration," 1995, *Latin American Weekly Report,* October 5). As for bankruptcies, there was a 26 percent increase in the number of firms filing for bankruptcy between the first half of 1994 and the first half of 1995; see "Going Bust," 1995, *Latin American Weekly Report,* August 3.

52. See EIU (1997, 15); information also garnered from authors' interview with Roberto Bouzas, FLACSO, July 30, 1996, in Buenos Aires.

53. As Artana and Navajas (1995, vi) note, a turnover tax accounts for 50 percent of provincial own-source revenues; half of the remainder stems from property taxes. Both revenue sources were boosted by the 1991-1992 recovery.

54. According to the World Bank (1996), "Over a dozen provincial banks were privatized . . . social security systems were transferred to the streamlined national system, salaries were cut, and a number of redundant public employees were let go." For more on the privatization of the provincial banks, see Banco Central de la República Argentina, 1996, *Bulletin of Monetary and Financial Affairs,* January-March. 13-14.

55. This point, as well as our elaboration on it, borrows from Levitsky (1997).

56. Corrales (1997, 65-66) describes a more inclusive executive decision-making process, with stronger congressional oversight — an argument we find unconvincing when the legislative track record is closely scrutinized.

57. See "Menem's Decrees 'Unconstitutional,'" 1997, *Latin American Weekly Report,* January 7, 16; and "Back to Square One on Labour Reform," 1997, *Latin American Weekly Report,* May 20, 232.

58. Comments made by Senator Graciela Fernández Meijide (FREPASO/Radical Alliance) at an event entitled "Discussion on Results and Significance of the October 26 Elections in Argentina," The Brookings Institution, Washington, D.C., November 17, 1997. Also see Calvin Sims, 1997, "New Broom Is Sweeping in Argentina," *The New York Times,* November 10, A11.

59. Obviously, such policy shifts need to occur without recourse to the heavy-handed tools of political repression available to the Chilean regime during this period.

60. This included, for example, higher spending on health and education, an overhaul of the tax system, improved court practices and judicial independence, stronger guarantees on private property rights, and more transparency in government accounting. See Paul Lewis, 1997, "IMF Seeks Argentine Deal Linking Credit to Governing," *The New York Times,* July 15, D1.

61. J.P. Morgan, 1998, *Emerging Markets: Economic Indicators* (New York: Morgan Guaranty Trust Company), January 9, 22. The somewhat distant runner-up is Chile, with an estimated annual per capita GDP of US$5,591.

References

Acuña, Carlos H. 1994. "Politics and Economics in the Argentina of the Nineties (Or, Why the Future No Longer Is What It Used to Be)." In *Democracy, Markets, and Structural Reform in Latin America*, eds. William C. Smith, Carlos H. Acuña, and Eduardo A. Gamarra. Coral Gables, Fla: North-South Center Press, the University of Miami.

Ades, Alberto F. 1995. "Currency Boards and Its Implications for Argentina." *Economic Research Paper* (February). New York: Goldman Sachs.

Agosín, Manuel. 1995. "Foreign Direct Investment in Latin America." In *Foreign Direct Investment in Latin America,* ed. Manuel Agosín. Washington, D.C.: Inter-American Development Bank.

"Argentina's Drift Toward Concentration." 1995. *Latin American Weekly Report,* October 5.

Arida, Pérsio, and Edmar Bacha. 1984. "Balanço de pagamentos: Uma análise de desequilíbrio para economias semi-industrializadas." *Pesquisa e Planejamento Econômico* 14 (1): 1-58.

Artana, Daniel, and Fernando Navajas. 1995. "Stabilization, Growth and Institutional Build-Up: An Overview of the Macroeconomics of Argentina 1991-1995." Special Report. (October) Buenos Aires: Fundación de Investigaciones Económicas Latinoamericanas (FIEL).

"Back to Square One on Labour Reform." 1997. *Latin American Weekly Report*, May 20.

Banco Central de la República Argentina. 1996. *Bulletin of Monetary and Financial Affairs,* January-March.

Beccaria, Luis. 1996. "Reconversión, mercado de trabajo y distribución del ingreso." Buenos Aires: University of Buenos Aires, Department of Economics. Unpublished manuscript.

Berensztein, Sergio. 1996. "Rebuilding State Capacity in Contemporary Latin America." In *Latin America in the World Economy,* eds. Roberto Korzeniewicz and William Smith. New York: Praeger Books.

Berlinski, Julio. 1996. "Institutional Issues of Trade Liberalization for Manufacturers: Argentina, 1988-93." In *Trade and Industrialization Policies in Argentina,* ed. Montague J. Lord. Working Paper Series 206. Washington, D.C.: Inter-American Development Bank.

"Big Profits for Privatized Services." 1997. *Latin American Regional Reports-Southern Cone,* March 4.

Bielschowsky, Ricardo A., and Giovanni Stumpo. 1995. "Transnational Corporations and Structural Changes in Industry in Argentina, Brazil, Chile and Mexico." CEPAL Review, No. 55: 143-169.

Bisang, Roberto, and Bernardo Kosacoff. 1996. "Manufacturing Exports in an Economy in Transition: Surprises in Argentina." In *Trade and Industrialization Policies in Argentina,* ed. Montague J. Lord. Series 206. Washington, D.C.: Inter-American Development Bank.

Bouzas, Roberto. 1996. Interviewed by authors in Buenos Aires, July 30.

Burki, Shahid, and Sebastian Edwards. 1996. *Dismantling the Populist State*. Washington, D.C.: The World Bank, Latin American and Caribbean Department, Viewpoints Series.

"Camdessus Calls for 'Second Generation' of Reform in Argentina." 1997. *IMF-Survey* 26:11 (June 9).

Campos, Jaime. 1996. Interviewed by authors in Buenos Aires, August 7.

Canavan, Chris, and Mariano Tommasi. 1996. "Visibility and Credibility: On Nominal Anchors and Other Ways to Send Clear Signals." Boston: Boston College, Department of Economics, and Buenos Aires: Universidad de San Andrés. Unpublished manuscript.

Canitrot, Adolfo. 1994. "Crisis and Transformation of the Argentine State." In *Democracy, Markets, and Structural Reform in Latin America,* eds. William C. Smith, Carlos H. Acuña, and Eduardo A. Gamarra. Coral Gables, Fla: North-South Center Press at the University of Miami .

"Cavallo Provokes Crisis, Keeps Job." 1995. *Latin American Weekly Report,* September 7.

CEP (Centro de Estudios para la Producción). 1997. "Exportaciones y concentración de mercados." *Notas de la Economía Real,* No. 5 (December): 47-55.

Chisari, Omar. 1996. Interviewed by authors in Buenos Aires, August 1.

Chisari, Omar O., José María Fanelli, and Roberto Frenkel. 1996. "Argentina: Growth Resumption, Sustainability, and Environment." *World Development* 24 (2): 227-240.

Chudnovsky, Daniel, et al. 1995. "New Foreign Direct Investment in Argentina: Privatization, the Domestic Market, and Regional Integration." In *Foreign Direct Investment in Latin America,* ed. Manuel Agosín. Washington, D.C.: Inter-American Development Bank.

Chudnovsky, Daniel, et al. 1996. *Los límites de la apertura: Liberalización, reestructuración productiva y medio ambiente.* Buenos Aires: Alianza Editorial.

Confederación General de la Industria. 1996. Members interviewed by authors in Buenos Aires, July 26.

Corden, Max. 1994. *Economic Policy, Exchange Rates, and the International System.* Chicago: University of Chicago Press.

Corrales, Javier. 1997. "Why Argentines Followed Cavallo: A Technopol Between Democracy and Economic Reform." In *Technopols: Freeing Politics and Markets in Latin America in the 1990's,* ed. Jorge I. Domínguez. University Park, Pa.: The Pennsylvania State University Press.

Cristini, Marcela. 1996. "Convertibility and Argentine Industrial Exports: A Sustainable Change?" In *Trade and Industrialization Policies in Argentina,* ed. Montague J. Lord. Working Paper Series 206. Washington, D.C.: Inter-American Development Bank.

de la Balze, Felipe A.M. 1995. *Remaking the Argentine Economy.* New York: Council on Foreign Relations Press.

Dornbusch, Rudiger. 1995. "Progress Report on Argentina." In *Reform, Recovery, and Growth: Latin America and the Middle East,* eds. Rudiger Dornbusch and Sebastian Edwards. Chicago: University of Chicago Press.

ECLAC (Economic Commission for Latin America and the Caribbean). 1996. *Preliminary Overview of the Economy of Latin America and the Caribbean,* 1996. Santiago: United Nations, ECLAC.

"Economía elevaría a 3.5% la tasa estadística." 1997. *Clarín,* May 2.

Edwards, Sebastian. 1995. *Crisis and Reform in Latin America: From Despair to Hope.* New York: Oxford University Press.

Edwards, Sebastian. 1997. *The Disturbing Underperformance of the Latin American Economies.* Washington, D.C.: Inter-American Dialogue.

EIU (Economist Intelligence Unit). 1997. *Argentina, Country Report,* 1st quarter.

Epstein, Edward C. 1995. "Anti-Poverty Policy and Market Economics in the New Chilean and Argentine Democracies." Presented at the XIX International Congress of the Latin American Studies Association, Washington, D.C., September 28-30.

Faiola, Anthony. 1997. "Argentine Private Enterprise Draws Public Opposition." *The Washington Post,* June 22.

Fernández Meijide, Graciela. 1997. "Discussion on Results and Significance of the October 26 Elections in Argentina." Washington, D.C.: The Brookings Institution, November 17.

FIEL (Fundación de Investigaciones Económicas Latinoamericanas). 1996. *Las pequeñas y medianas empresas en la Argentina.* Buenos Aires: FIEL.

Frydman, Felipe. 1996. Lecture on "Argentina Under the Convertibility Plan," Johns Hopkins University, Washington, D.C., November 13.

García, Valeriano F. 1997. *Black December: Banking Instability, the Mexican Crisis and Its Effect on Argentina.* Washington, D.C.: The World Bank, Latin American and Caribbean Department, Viewpoints Series.

Gelpern, Anna, and Malcolm Harrison. 1992. "Ideology, Practice, and Performance in Privatization: A Case Study of Argentina." *Harvard International Law Journal* 33 (1): 240-254.

Gerchunoff, Pablo, and José Luis Machinea. 1995. "Un ensayo sobre la política económica después de la estabilización." In *Más allá de la estabilidad: Argentina en la época de la globalización y la regionalización,* ed. Pablo Bustos. Buenos Aires: Fundación Friedrich Ebert.

Gibson, Edward L., and Ernesto Calvo. 1997. "Electoral Coalitions and Market Reforms: Evidence From Argentina." Paper presented at the XX International Congress of the Latin American Studies Association, Guadalajara, Mexico, April 17-19.

"La gobernabilidad está asegurada." 1997. *Clarín,* October 28.

"Going Bust." 1995. *Latin American Weekly Report,* August 3.

Goldfajn, Ilan, and Rodrigo O. Valdés. 1996. "The Aftermath of Appreciations." Boston: Brandeis University, Economics Department, and Santiago: Banco Central de Chile. Unpublished manuscript.

Graham, Carol. 1994. *Safety Nets, Politics, and the Poor: Transitions to Market Economies.* Washington, D.C.: The Brookings Institution.

Graham, Carol. 1998. *Private Markets for Public Goods: Raising the Stakes in Economic Reform.* Washington, D.C.: The Brookings Institution.

Grosse, Robert, and Juan Yañes. 1996. "The Privatization of YPF: Lessons for Management and Government." Discussion Paper 96-1. Coral Gables, Fla.: International Business Center, University of Miami.

"Growth of 6% Forecast." 1997. *Latin American Economy and Business.* LAEB-97-03.

Guira, Jorge M. 1997. "MERCOSUR as an Instrument for Development." *NAFTA: Law and Business Review of the Americas* 3:3 (Summer): 53-102.

"IMF Allows a Deficit This Year." 1995. *Latin American Weekly Report,* September 14.

INDEC (Instituto Nacional de Estadística y Censos). 1995. *Statistical Yearbook of the Argentine Republic* (CD-ROM).

INDEC. 1997. *Statistical Yearbook of the Argentine Republic* 13. Buenos Aires: INDEC.

"Insufficient Growth Limits Job Creation." 1997. *Clarín,* October 28.

Kosacoff, Bernardo. 1996. Interviewed by authors in Buenos Aires, August 1.

Kosacoff, Bernardo, and Adrián Ramos. 1997. "Consideraciones económicas sobre política industrial." Centro de Estudios para la Producción. *Notas de la Economía Real,* No. 5 (December): 15-21.

Kritz, Ernesto. 1997. "Tribuna abierta:-Qué hacer con las mediciones de empleo." *Clarín,* April 7.

Lawrence, Robert Z. 1996. *Regionalism, Multilateralism, and Deeper Integration.* Washington, D.C.: The Brookings Institution.

Lewis, Paul. 1997. "IMF-Seeks Argentine Deal Linking Credit to Governing." *The New York Times,* July 15.

Levitsky, Steven. 1997. "Crisis, Party Adaptation, and Regime Stability in Argentina: The Case of Peronism, 1989-1995." Paper presented at the XX International Congress of the Latin American Studies Association, Guadalajara, Mexico, April 17-19.

López, Juan J. 1997. "Private Investment Response to Neoliberal Reforms: Implications of the Argentine Case, 1989-1996." Paper presented at the XX International Congress of the Latin American Studies Association, Guadalajara, Mexico, April 17-19.

Mahon, James. 1996. *Mobile Capital and Latin American Development.* University Park, Pa.: The Pennsylvania State University Press.

"The Markets Are Getting Nervous." 1994. *Latin American Weekly Report,* December 15.

McGuire, James. 1995. "Political Parties and Democracy in Argentina." *Building Democratic Institutions,* eds. Scott Mainwaring and Timothy R. Scully. Stanford, Calif.: Stanford University Press.

"Menem's Decrees 'Unconstitutional.'" 1997. *Latin-American Weekly Report,* January 7.

Mondino, Guillermo, and Alejandro Roca. 1997. "Toward a Hemispheric Free Trade Area: The Case of Argentina." In *Integrating the Hemisphere,* eds. Ana Julia Jatar and Sidney Weintraub. Washington, D.C.: Inter-American Dialogue (March).

Morgan, J.P. 1998. *Emerging Markets:-Economic Indicators.* New York: Morgan Guaranty Trust Company.

Murillo, Victoria. 1997. "Union Politics, Market-Oriented Reforms, and the Reshaping of Argentine Corporatism." In *The New Politics of Inequality in Latin America,* ed. Douglas Chalmers et al. New York: Oxford University Press.

Naim, Moisés. 1995. "Latin America's Journey to the Market." Occasional Papers No. 62. San Francisco: International Center for Economic Growth.

Newberry, Charles. 1996. "Argentine Growth Pickup and Lower Rates Seen." *Bloomberg Business News,* December 26.

Nofal, María Beatriz. 1995. "Mercosur: Evolution, Opportunity, Challenges." *MERCOSUR Journal* 1:1 (December): 2-44.

Pastor, Manuel Jr. 1987. *The International Monetary Fund and Latin America: Economic Stabilization and Class Conflict.* Boulder, Colo: Westview Press.

Pastor, Manuel Jr. 1990. "Capital Flight from Latin America." *World Development* 18 (1): 1-18.

Pastor, Manuel Jr., and Carol Wise. 1997. "State Policy, Distribution and Neoliberal Reform in Mexico." *Journal of Latin American Studies* 29 (2): 419-456.

Perry, William. 1997. *The 1997 Argentine Legislative Elections: Pre-election Report.* Study Series, No. 6. Washington, D.C.: Center for Strategic and International Studies, Western Hemisphere Election, October 15.

Persson, Torsten, and Guido Tabellini. 1994. "Is Inequality Harmful for Growth?" *American Economic Review* 84 (3): 600-621.

Pessino, Carola. 1997. "The Labor Market During the Transition in Argentina." In *Labor Market Reform in Latin America: Combining Social Protection and Market Flexibility,* eds. Sebastian Edwards and Nora Lustig. Washington, D.C.: The Brookings Institution.

Petrecolla, Diego. 1995. *Pobreza y distribución de ingresos en el Gran Buenos Aires: 1989-94.* Working Paper No. 10. Buenos Aires: Universidad Torcuato di Tella.

Robbio, Jorge. 1997. "Primeros resultados de una Encuesta sobre Pequeños Exportadores Industriales." Centro de Estudios para la Producción (CEP). *Notas de la economía real,* No. 5 (December): 61-64.

Rodríguez, Carlos Alfredo. 1995. "Ensayo sobre el Plan de Convertibilidad." Working Paper No. 105. Buenos Aires: Centro de Estudios Macroeconómicos de Argentina (CEMA).

Rodrik, Dani. 1991. "Policy Uncertainty and Private Investment in Developing Countries." *Journal of Development Economics* 36 (1): 229-242

Saba, Pedro Pablo, and Luigi Manzetti. 1997. "Privatization in Argentina: The Implications for Corruption." *Crime, Law & Social Change* 25 (4): 353-369.

Serra, Jaime, et al. 1997. *Reflections on Regionalism.* Washington, D.C.: Carnegie Endowment for International Peace.

Sepúlveda, Carlos, and Arturo Vera Aguirre. 1997. *MERCOSUR: Achievements and Challenges.* Working Paper Series No. 222. Washington, D.C.: Inter-American Development Bank, Integration and Regional Programs Department (August).

Sims, Calvin. 1997. "New Broom Is Sweeping in Argentina." *The New York Times,* November 10.

Starr, Pamela K. 1997. "Government Coalitions and the Viability of Currency Boards: Argentina Under the Cavallo Plan." *Journal of Interamerican Studies and World Affairs* 39 (2): 83-133.

Stokes, Susan. 1996. "Public Opinion and Market Reforms: The Limits of Economic Voting." *Comparative Political Studies* 29 (5): 499-519.

Tanner, Evan, and Pablo Sanguinetti. 1996. *Structural Reform and Disinflation: Lessons from Argentina's Convertibility Plan.* Discussion Paper 96-3. Coral Gables, Fla.: International Business Center, University of Miami.

Teichman, Judith. 1997. "Democracy and Technocratic Decision Making: Mexico, Argentina, and Chile." Paper presented at the XX International Congress of the Latin American Studies Association, Guadalajara, Mexico, April 17-19.

Toulan, Omar N., and Mauro F. Guillén. 1997. "Beneath the Surface: The Impact of Radical Economic Reforms on the Outward Orientation of Argentine and Mendozan Firms." *Journal of Latin American Studies* 29 (2): 395-418.

Tussie, Diana. 1996. *Argentina in the Global Economy: Facing the Dilemmas.* Documentos e Informes de Investigación No. 202. Buenos Aires: Facultad Latinoamericana de Ciencias Sociales (FLACSO).

Urbiztondo, Santiago. 1997. "Direct Foreign Investment in Argentina: Evolution, New Challenges and Perspectives." Paper presented at the XX International Congress of the Latin American Studies Association, Guadalajara, Mexico, April 17-19.

Velasco, Andrés. 1994. "The State and Economic Policy: Chile 1952-92." In *The Chilean Economy: Policy Lessons and Challenges,* eds. Barry P. Bosworth, Rudiger Dornbush, and Raúl Labán. Washington, D.C.: The Brookings Institution.

Weyland, Kurt. 1997. "Swallowing the Bitter Pill: Sources of Popular Support for Neoliberal Reform in Latin America." Nashville, Tenn.: Vanderbilt University, Department of Political Science. Unpublished manuscript.

Williamson, John. 1995. *What Role for Currency Boards?* Washington, D.C.: Institute for International Economics.

Wise, Carol. 1998. "The Trade Scenario for Other Latin Reformers in the NAFTA Era." In *The Post-NAFTA Political Economy: Mexico and the Western Hemisphere,* ed. Carol Wise. University Park, Pa.: The Pennsylvania State University Press.

World Bank. 1996. "Argentina." From: *Trends in Developing Economies,* 1996. http://www.worldbank.org/html/extdr/offrep/lac/argentin.htm.

Yeats, Alexander J. 1996. *Does Mercosur's Trade Performance Justify Concerns About the Effects of Regional Trade Arrangements?* Washington, D.C.: The World Bank, International Trade Division.

APPENDIX:-DATA SOURCES

Argentine monthly inflation, the real exchange rate (calculated as the nominal rate multiplied by the U.S. wholesale price index, and then divided by the Argentine CPI), exports, imports, trade balance, capital flows, and international reserves are from the International Monetary Fund's *International Financial Statistics.*

Growth of real GDP, investment, and consumption; shares in GDP of investment, consumption, and imports; and unemployment rates are taken from the Ministerio de Economía of Argentina (see <http://www.mecon.ar>, specifically <http://www.mecon.ar/ctas-nac/c1-1.htm> for the GDP figures and <http://www.mecon.ar/ftpdata/indec/communica/cp70001.txt> for the unemployment rates). Fiscal performance data gathered from various issues of *Informe Económico,* as posted at <http://www.mecon.ar>; 1995 and 1996 figures as a percent of GDP involve some estimation by the authors.

The unemployment figures are collected by the Instituto Nacional de Estadística y Censos (INDEC); INDEC is also the source for the distributional data in the text that was provided by special arrangement to the authors. Composition of imports and exports taken from INDEC, *Statistical Yearbook of the Argentine Republic, 1995* (CD-ROM version); *Statistical Yearbook of the Argentine Republic, 1997, 13, INDEC, 480-483;* and *Síntesis de la Economía Real,* No. 9, November 1997, from the Centro de Estudios para la Producción, Buenos Aires.

CHAPTER 2

Democracy and Reform in Cardoso's Brazil: Caught Between Clientelism and Global Markets?

WILLIAM C. SMITH AND NIZAR MESSARI

This chapter explores President Fernando Henrique Cardoso's record during his first term in office (1995-1999) and his successful reelection in October 1998 over the challenge of Luiz Inácio Lula da Silva, candidate of the Workers' Party (Partido dos Trabalhadores — PT) and the left. These events are examined in the context of a central, inescapable dilemma of contemporary Brazilian politics: how to reconcile the exigencies of the market and globalization with the equally compelling needs to promote democracy while combating poverty, violence, and social exclusion. The chapter concludes with analyses of the first year of Cardoso's second term and of various alternative politico-economic scenarios for Brazil during the period before the next presidential elections in 2002.

INTRODUCTION

Brazil is a mosaic of contrasts and contradictions. It is the third most populous democracy after India and the United States. It ranks fifth in the world in the size of its national territory, fifth in population (nearly 170 million), and eighth in gross national product, surpassing China. Brazil is wealthy, but it is also a country of tremendous poverty and inequality saddled with the legacy of an authoritarian past. Confronting these contradictions, President Fernando Henrique Cardoso (FHC) has attempted simultaneously to democratize Brazilian politics and society and make Brazilian capitalism more competitive in a volatile world economy. Many Brazilian and international observers praise Cardoso for abandoning an earlier flirtation with anachronistic, if not dangerous, leftist ideas. Meanwhile, erstwhile Cardoso admirers interpret his policies as Brazil's leader as the capitulation of a former radical to the blandishments of the global market and Washington orthodoxy. Despite containing elements of truth, the Manichean polarities of such facile ideological formulas fail to capture adequately the complex realities of Brazil at the beginning of the twenty-first century.

In the 1970s, FHC attained international acclaim as a sociologist for his seminal work on dependency theory (Cardoso and Faletto 1979) and his role as one of the most influential critics of the post-1964 military dictatorship and its model of "associated-dependent" development (Cardoso 1973, 1975, 1979). Important elements of the basic worldview he forged during this period remain intact. Cardoso's protestation that he continues to be a "man of the left" and has "never been a neoliberal" rings true (Cardoso 1996c; *Esquerda* 1996; *Folha de São Paulo* 1996).[1] In the early 1990s, shortly before he assumed the post of finance minister in Itamar Franco's government (1992-1994), FHC spelled out his vision of Latin American social democracy. He wrote that, in contrast to "populism, national-statism and renovated liberalism," social democracy must assume "responsible positions concerning the necessity of accumulation and economic growth, added to the qualities of a moral and concrete political force in favor of income redistribution and social welfare policies." Cardoso then added that

> the real goal for contemporary social democracy concerns knowing how to increase economic competitiveness — leading to increases in productivity and the rationalization of the economy — and how to make the vital decisions concerning investments and consumption increasingly public ones, that is, how to make them transparent and controllable in society by consumers, producers, managers, workers and public opinion in general, not only by impersonal bureaucracies of the state and the private sector (Cardoso 1993: 286, 287).

Once in the presidency, however, FHC has seen this social democratic goal of combining capital accumulation with a thorough democratization of Brazil's state, political regime, and civil society thwarted by the rigors of economic restructuring made worse by governability problems and the institutional constraints of the Brazilian political system, for example, an unrepresentative electoral system, weak parties, and a dysfunctional federal system. In fact, the difficulty of securing passage of reform legislation he considered crucial led FHC to believe that his own reelection to the presidency was the best guarantor of the continuity of market reform.

This conviction led him to downplay the need for social change in favor of strengthening ties with both the local and transnational business communities and his political allies from the center-right and right. FHC's rationale rested on the optimistic premise that a second four-year term would be the most practical route to the delayed but still very important social and political transformations he has always advocated. It made sense, then, that he resorted to the old-fashioned politics of clientelism, patronage, and elite conciliation, although these practices ran counter to his earlier insistence that the democratic reform of Brazil's archaic political institutions was required if capitalist development were to serve the interests of the country's poor majority. Thus, FHC's intellectual and political commitment to deepening democracy had to accommodate the enduring realities of elite privilege and domination. This accommodation resulted in a limited program of modest social reforms conditioned by the realities of globalization and subordinated to the twin imperatives of economic stabilization and Cardoso's own reelection.

Would this scenario, in which democratic social reform took a back seat to the economy, be reversed following FHC's successful October 1998 reelection to a second four-year term? Having defeated his leftist rival, Luiz Inácio Lula da Silva, the candidate of the Workers' Party (Partido dos Trabalhadores — PT), could FHC refurbish his somewhat tarnished social democratic credentials? To address these questions and to speculate on possible future developments, this chapter examines a central, inescapable dilemma of contemporary Brazilian politics: how to reconcile the exigencies of the market and globalization with the equally compelling need to promote democracy while combating poverty, violence, and social exclusion? Probing these issues, we find that Cardoso the sociologist is often the best critic (and adviser) of Cardoso the president.

THE PLANO REAL AND THE SOCIAL AGENDA IN AN "UNJUST SOCIETY"

Stabilization and Economic Growth

Fernando Henrique Cardoso won the presidency in 1994 with 54 percent of the vote, defeating Lula, the PT candidate.[2] Cardoso's victory was largely due to the optimism generated by the Plano Real, designed under his tutelage as finance minister during the government of Itamar Franco.[3] During the 12 months before the Plano Real's advent in July 1994, inflation had skyrocketed to a stunning 5,200 percent, yet, the Plano Real very rapidly brought mega-inflation under control, with prices rising during the rest of the decade at the slowest pace since the early 1950s. As Figure 1 shows, the Plano Real's success contrasted favorably with previous stabilization plans.

Figure 1. Plano Real Versus Previous Stabilization Efforts (Monthly Inflation Rate in %)

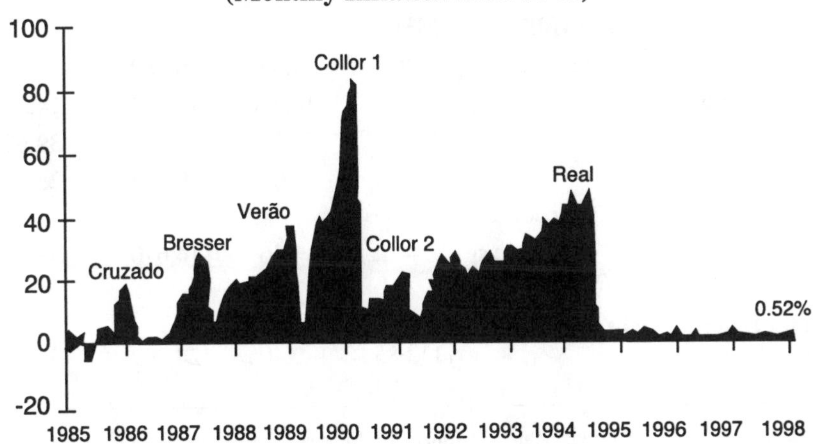

Source: Consumer price index (CPI) compiled by the Fundação Instituto de Pesquisas Econômicas (FIPE) from January 1985 to May 1998. See SECOM 1998a.

Table 1.
Selected Economic Indicators for Brazil

	1990	1991	1992	1993
Real Gross Domestic Product (GDP)[a] (Average Annual Growth Rate)				
Total GDP	-4.2	0.3	-0.8	4.2
Manufacturing	-9.5	-2.4	-4.1	7.9
Agriculture	-3.7	2.8	5.4	-1.2
Construction	-9.7	-3.5	-6.6	4.9
Gross Domestic Investment	-10.9	-1.8	-8.6	7.2
Non-Financial Public Sector (As Percent of GDP)				
Operational Balance (-Deficit)[b]	1.3	1.4	2.2	0.3
Prices, Salaries, and Unemployment (Average Annual Growth Rates)				
Consumer Price Index	2,937.7	440.9	1,008.7	2,148.5
Real Wage[c]	-42.7	14.9	5.3	-1.4
Unemployment Rate	4.3	4.8	5.8	5.4
Real Effective Exchange[d]	100.0	125.3	139.3	123.6
Balance of Payments (Millions of US$)				
Current Account Balance	-3,823	-1,450	6,089	20
Trade Balance	10,747	10,578	15,239	14,329
Exports	31,408	31,619	35,793	39,630
Imports	20,661	21,041	20,554	25,301
Capital Account Balance	35	42	54	81
Change in Reserves (-Increase)	-474	369	-14,670	-8,709
Total External Debt (Millions of US$)				
Total Debt	111,085	110,405	124,449	136,610

— = Not available. p= provisional e= estimate f = forecast

Notes: a) GDP at market prices. Sector of Origin at factor cost; b) Excludes monetary and exchange correction; c) Minimum wage; d) *Reais*/US$; End of Period; Index 1990=100.

Table 1.—*continued*
Selected Economic Indicators for Brazil

1994	1995	1996	1997	1998[p]	1999[e]	2000[f]
Real Gross Domestic Product (GDP)[a] (Average Annual Growth Rate)						
6.0	4.2	3.0	3.0	0.1	0.8	3.8
8.0	1.6	0.8	—	—	—	—
7.5	5.9	3.1	—	—	—	—
5.8	0.1	5.5	—	—	—	—
12.6	13.4	1.8	8.5	3.0	—	—
Non-Financial Public Sector (As Percent of GDP)						
1.4	-4.9	3.5	-2.4	—	—	—
Prices, Salaries, and Unemployment (Average Annual Growth Rates)						
2,668.6	84.4	18.2	7.5	3.0	8.6	6.5
-16.0	8.5	7.0	2.5	6.3	—	—
5.1	4.6	5.4	5.7	7.6	7.7	7.3
105.4	90.4	89.3	85.2	85.5	—	—
Balance of Payments (Millions of US$)						
-1,153	-18,136	-23,602	-33,840	-34,945	-24,380	-23,000
10,861	-3,157	-5,554	-8,364	-6,438	-1,203	2,500
44,102	46,506	47,747	52,990	51,120	48,009	55,000
33,241	49,663	53,301	61,354	57,558	49,212	52,500
173	352	462	407	31	—	—
-7,215	-12,920	-8,667	7,907	8,491	—	—
Total External Debt (Millions of US$)						
149,857	158,230	178,037	191,084	235	240	240

Sources: 1989-1998 data from Inter-American Development Bank, Statistics and Quantitative Analysis Unit. Basic Socio-Economic Data, April 2000; 1999 estimates and 2000 forecasts from *Latin American Monitor: Brazil,* March 2000.

A more stable economy reversed the stagnation of the early 1990s. The four years preceding the Plano Real had witnessed an average negative growth rate of 0.2 percent. Between 1994 and 1997, the gross domestic product (GDP) grew 17 percent at an average rate of 4 percent a year. Including 1998, Brazil achieved six consecutive years of economic expansion, something not seen since the late 1970s. Moreover, GDP per capita increased at an average annual rate of 2.6 percent, rising above $5,000 (all data is expressed in US dollars unless otherwise noted) in 1997 (SECOM 1998a).

The macroeconomic stability facilitated by the Plano Real also encouraged domestic investment, which, though still significantly lower than in Argentina or Chile, stood at approximately 18 percent of GDP in 1998, after floating around 15 percent since the beginning of the decade. Net foreign investment has been particularly dynamic, rising to $17 billion in 1997 and $26 billion in 1998, a more than tenfold increase since 1993 (SECOM 1998a).[4] Spurred by liberalization policies enacted by Fernando Collor de Mello (1990-1992), Brazil's international trade has grown by 140 percent since 1990, from $50 billion to a peak of about $110 billion in 1997. A substantial increase in imported capital goods (currently about 27 percent of total imports) is a sign of a vigorous industrial modernization process, which is reflected in data on productivity gains and the competitiveness of manufacturing exports (SECOM 1998a; *LARR: Brazil* 1997a, 1998d). Table 1 presents the relevant macroeconomic indicators for the 1990s.

However, what about social reform? During the 1994 presidential campaign, Cardoso spoke eloquently about Brazil's "social debt" and the urgent need to attack the gaping inequalities between the wealthy elite and the privileged upper-middle classes and the urban and rural poor. Have stabilization and structural adjustment policies diffused prosperity broadly? Alternatively, have market-oriented reforms resulted in greater social exclusion? Here it is necessary to distinguish between poverty, which tends to decline with economic growth, and redistribution of income and wealth, which requires more fundamental transformations in the political economy and the class structure.

Poverty and Equity

The major achievement of the first Cardoso government on behalf of social justice was the Plano Real's effective repeal of the "inflation tax" (see Figure 2), a repeal that allowed millions of Brazilians to increase their consumption. In mid-1994, the minimum wage could purchase only 60 percent of the basket of basic goods required for a family of four; by 1995, the same minimum wage purchased 90 percent of this basket; and, by 1998, a family might even have a little extra left over after meeting its basic food needs. According to the Brazilian Institute for Geography and Statistics (Instituto Brasileiro de Geografia e Estatística — IBGE), food consumption has increased across the board. Since 1994, chicken consumption jumped 40 percent, beef consumption 27 percent, and soft drinks 71 percent. Consumption of durable consumer goods also increased, with refrigerator sales up 55 percent, washing machines 69 percent, and color televisions 57 percent; in addition, sales of "popular" cars (less than 1,000 cubic centimeters) doubled. According to Cardoso's economic team, millions of Brazilians, for the first time, gained access to piped water, electricity, garbage collection, and telephone service. Reflecting these trends, official statistics show that extreme poverty (an income of less than about $50 per month) declined from approximately 35 percent of the population in 1994 to 25 percent in 1997 (SECOM 1998a).[5]

Figure 2. Inflation Versus Poverty

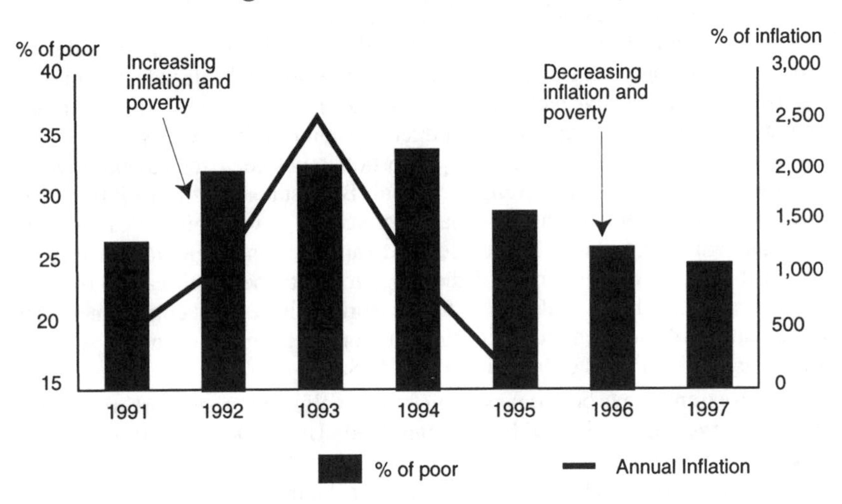

Sources: Instituto de Pesquisas Econômicas Aplicadas (IPEA) and Fundação Instituto de Pesquisas Econômicas (FIPE). See SECOM 1998a.

President Cardoso trumpeted these gains on July 1, 1998, the fourth anniversary of the Plano Real, when he announced that, according to the most recent data compiled by the United Nations Development Program (UNDP), Brazil ranked for the first time among the top 50 countries as measured by the "human development index" (*Jornal do Brasil* 1998d; *O Globo* 1998). Brazilians' prosperity is a welcome achievement, but due to other factors highly impervious to short-term amelioration — concentration of land ownership, an elitist educational system, racial and gender discrimination, and a huge informal economy — the reduction of extreme poverty does not necessarily translate into redressed inequalities. In fact, available data indicates that the post-1994 economy recovery left the deeply rooted structural inequities unchanged.

Household surveys confirm that the Gini coefficient, which measures inequality, has improved only slightly (0.614 in 1995, 0.58 in 1996, and 0.575 in 1998) in recent years, thus explaining the basic stability of income distribution. In fact, Brazil is one of the most unequal societies in the world: the richest 10 percent continue to appropriate around 46 percent of the nation's wealth, the poorest half of the population makes do with only 14 percent, and the most impoverished 20 percent receive only about 2 percent of national wealth (Londoño and Székely 1997; Lustig and Deutsch 1998; Barros, Mendonça, and Rocha 1995; *Brazil Focus:*

Weekly Report 1999d). Thus, measured against the magnitude of the problem, the progress achieved so far has been of the *ma non troppo* variety. As FHC observed in his 1994 campaign, "Brazil is no longer an undeveloped country, it is an unjust country" (*New York Times* 1998b).

Industrial Restructuring, Unemployment, and Urban Violence

Disturbingly, examination of the impact of the Cardoso government's economic modernization policies reveals new manifestations of social exclusion. Reflecting, in part, strong import competition due to trade liberalization, industrial output increased only 6.3 percent in the first seven years of the decade. Despite this sluggish growth, intensive technological innovation and vigorous industrial reconversion significantly boosted labor productivity but did little to raise real wages. Moreover, considerable job loss and a proportionately steep rise in unemployment have also been reported. According to official IBGE statistics, from 1990 to 1997, the number of manufacturing jobs has declined by a whopping 38.1 percent.[6] Consonant with trends throughout the region (Tardanico and Menjívar Larín 1997), this led to a rapid destructuring of the labor market: the combination of rising unemployment in the formal sector, fewer workers in regular employment, and multiplication of those employed in the burgeoning informal economy, who are without legal protections or benefits (*Veja* 1998a).

These trends have been devastating for the welfare of urban workers and their families. Survey data collected by the Inter Trade Union Department of Statistics and Socio-Economic Studies (Departamento Intersindical de Estatística e Estudos Socio-Econômicos — DIEESE), a well-known labor-affiliated research center, revealed that unemployment in greater São Paulo, Brazil's largest, most developed, and wealthiest metropolitan area, rose from 10.2 percent in 1990 to an unprecedented 18.9 percent in April 1998. Using a different methodology, the IBGE reported an average unemployment rate above 8 percent throughout 1998, up from 4.6 percent in 1995 (SECOM 1998a). Similar increases in joblessness are seen in the other major metropolitan areas of Rio de Janeiro, Belo Horizonte, Porto Alegre, and Salvador.

Urban violence and criminality have also risen sharply in recent years. Brazil ranks third among Latin American countries in homicides, with a rate of 19.7 per 100,000 inhabitants, roughly twice the U.S. rate and eight times the rate for Western European countries. Homicides are the number one cause (58 percent) of early death in Brazil, far surpassing auto accidents. Moreover, other forms of violence and criminality — drug trafficking, gunrunning, bank robbery, and kidnappings — have increased dramatically. Civil and military police are frequently perpetrators of the violence, particularly against shantytown dwellers, Afro-Brazilians, and street children (Pinheiro 1997; U.S. Department of State 1998). Although it would be a mistake to attribute violence and criminality solely or directly to market restructuring, there is little doubt that some of the consequences of economic reform, particularly high and rising unemployment, are linked to these problems. As recent studies (Ayres 1998; Morrison, Buvinic, and Shifter 1999) suggest, failing judicial systems, urban poverty, restricted employment opportunities, and inadequate housing, education, and social infrastructure are among the main causes of the rise in violence and the general erosion of citizen security in Latin America.

Agrarian Reform and the Sem-Terra Movement

These transformations and their consequences in the urban areas of Brazil have noteworthy parallels in the countryside. The expansion of modern, export-oriented agro-industry has generated pockets of impressive prosperity, but living conditions for many of the rural poor continue to deteriorate. This deterioration has given rise to an unexpected "ruralization" of national politics, whose most salient expression is the revival of agrarian reform as a hotly contested issue.

Land tenure in Brazil is becoming progressively more concentrated in fewer large units. According to recent studies, some 44,000 large landholdings (about 1.6 percent of the total) encompass about 155 million hectares, or 50 percent of all Brazil's farmland, an area roughly the size of Venezuela and Colombia combined. A middle group, consisting of about 394,000 farms (12 percent of the total), controls 32.1 percent of the arable land. In contrast, approximately 2.75 million small farmers (85 percent) eke out a living on only 18.9 percent of the nation's arable land. Another 4.5 million rural families (comprising as many as 30 million persons) are squatters (*posseiros*), renters, sharecroppers, and rural salaried workers who enjoy little legal access to land ownership (Fernández Franco 1997; SECOM 1998a, 1998c).

These highly skewed patterns of land tenure help explain the political influence of militant social movements seeking the democratization of access to land and the improvement of wages and rural working conditions (Pereira 1997a, 1997b). The Landless Workers' Movement (Movimento dos Trabalhadores Rurais Sem-Terra — MST), which claims 5,200 full-time "professional militants" and 300,000 active participants, is the most politically visible of these groups and one of the most powerful grassroots social movements in Latin America. The MST has carried out hundreds of illegal occupations and, according to the newsmagazine *Veja*, has taken over 7.2 million hectares of land, settling 130,000 people and creating 55 small rural cooperatives (FBIS 1998). Other important organizations include the National Confederation of Agricultural Workers (Confederação Nacional dos Trabalhadores na Agricultura — CONTAG), Brazil's oldest and largest rural labor movement; the Struggle for Land Movement (Movimento de Luta pela Terra — MLT); and the Pastoral Land Commission (Comissão Pastoral da Terra — CPT), a group with ties to the National Bishops Conference of the Catholic Church (Fernández Franco 1997; *El Mercurio* 1998a, 1998b; FBIS 1998).

Although land invasions have taken place in virtually every corner of Brazil, the focal points, in what sometimes resemble battlefields in a low-intensity civil war, are in the Pontal do Paranapanema region in the far west of the state of São Paulo and in the northern state of Pará. Land invasions in these regions often are violently repressed by police and, with increasing frequency, by private armed militias of modern-day *jagunços*, thugs hired by landowner organizations such as the Democratic Rural Union (União Democrática Ruralista — UDR) and the National Association of Rural Producers (Associação Nacional dos Produtores Rurais — ANPRU). More than 1,100 labor leaders and peasant activists involved in rural mobilizations have been assassinated since 1985 as a result of these confrontations. The partial collapse of state authority evidenced in the failure of law enforcement and the judicial system (Pinheiro 1997; U.S. Department of State 1998; Holston and Caldeira 1998; Pereira 2000) to punish human rights violations in the countryside means that perpetrators of these crimes, whether police or hired guns, normally enjoy total impunity.

The conflict, moreover, has taken on a radical political tone. The MST's principal leader, João Pedro Stédile, announced in 1997 that the movement's ultimate aim is to "finish off the neoliberal model" advocated by the government; he also warned that Cardoso's reelection would mean the "Colombianization" of Brazil, suggesting that uncontrolled violence and perhaps even armed conflict could engulf the countryside (*LARR: Brazil* 1997c; MST 1996). For his part, the then agrarian reform minister, Raúl Jungmann, who claimed that the "*latifúndio* is politically dead at the national level, though it still retains some power at the local level,"[7] charged that MST leaders "have three motives: politics, politics, and elections" (*LARR: Brazil* 1998a). Rhetoric aside, the government's response has been to make pragmatic concessions in an attempt to isolate the more radical MST leadership from its followers. Many land occupations have been legalized as the pace of agrarian reform has accelerated. However, although surveys by the National Colonization and Land Reform Institute (Instituto Nacional de Colonialização e Reforma Agrária — INCRA) reveal many unproductive estates of up to 1.2 million hectares in size, only a handful of these large *fazendas* have been expropriated (*Folha de São Paulo* 1998a). The Cardoso government claims that in its first three years it has settled 190,000 families, exceeding the agrarian reform efforts of all previous governments combined (INCRA 1998).[8] Land purchases are expensive, as is the provision of credit assistance to the families granted parcels. The government allocated $4 billion to reach the official goal of settling 100,000 families in 1998, with plans announced to spend more than $16 billion for this purpose by 2002 (SECOM 1998a; INCRA 1998).

Nevertheless, the Cardoso government's efforts to placate the landless have backfired politically. As the government itself has recognized, state attempts to address the crisis in the rural sector have set off a spiral of rising expectations fueling new demands as the growing supply of land made available stimulates competitive mobilization by the MST and other rival organizations such as CONTAG, which the government had cultivated in the past as a counterweight to MST (*LARR: Brazil* 1998c). Although they do not condone the use of violent methods and would lose nothing by the expropriation of large *fazendas*, a majority of middle-class Brazilians in urban areas support the goal of agrarian reform and tell pollsters they view the Sem-Terra movement sympathetically. It remains to be seen how this diffused support will play out, but it is clear that rural social movements supporting agrarian reform are likely to play a key role in efforts to overcome poverty and construct a more participatory civil society (Cadji 2000; Navarro 2000).

FISCAL HYPERACTIVITY VERSUS GLOBAL FINANCIAL MARKETS

The success of the Plano Real hinged on a delicate balance among fiscal restraint, tight monetary policy, and access to adequate inflows of foreign capital. The goal of this strategy was to control inflation and prepare Brazil for a more competitive integration with the world economy. The consequence was that Brazil's external vulnerability to global market forces, particularly its vulnerability to the vagaries of short-term flows of "hot money" in volatile financial markets, significantly increased.[9] The "tequila effect" of 1995 that followed the Mexican meltdown in late 1994 presented the first challenge to the strategy of embracing globalization. The effects of the Asian financial crisis in October 1997 posed a second major test. A third challenge came in August 1998, when the economic meltdown and political crisis in Russia foreshadowed the need for modifications in the Plano Real to reduce Brazil's exposure to the contagion effects of international financial instability.

The response of Cardoso's economic team on these three occasions was to cling tenaciously to its "dirty" float policy within broad exchange rate "bands," which allowed the *real* to gradually devalue in relation to the U.S. dollar. Reacting to the Asian crisis, for example, the Central Bank quickly boosted interest rates to 43.4 percent and reaffirmed the no-devaluation policy by spending $10 billion from its abundant international reserves to shore up the currency. These actions were followed, in November 1997, by an emergency austerity package of higher taxes and spending cuts equivalent to 2.3 percent of GDP (*Jornal do Brasil* 1997a; *Latin American Monitor: Brazil* 1997b; *LARR: Brazil* 1997e). Although many of these measures were never effectively implemented, the response worked, at least in the short-term: markets stabilized, and investors trusted Brazil again, thus allowing the Central Bank to gradually lower interest rates to their pre-crisis level and to rebuild international reserves, which soon rebounded too an all-time high of $74.9 billion in July 1998. However, the Central Bank's intervention in currency markets in response to the Russian crisis, a plunge of 40 percent in local stock markets, and the downturn on Wall Street provoked a net loss of more than $10 billion in reserves during August 1998.

Although the Plano Real's basic premises emerged intact, these episodes nevertheless highlighted the risks of the government's strategy in a world of globalized markets (*Folha de São Paulo* 1997b, 1998d). Since Thailand's devaluation of the *baht*, Brazil has been buffeted by successive bouts of skittishness of foreign investors, international bankers, and pension fund managers fearful of a new "contagion." In this environment, the Achilles heel of the Plano Real's hard-won macroeconomic stability is the "fiscal hyperactivity" of the Brazilian state, whose public sector, at 31.2 percent of GDP, is one of the largest of Latin America.[10]

The net public sector debt doubled during Cardoso's first government, surpassing $300 billion (or about 36 percent of GDP) in early 1998 (*Folha de São Paulo* 1998f, 1998h; *Estado de São Paulo* 1998c). Not only was the debt huge, but, under the impact of the Asian crisis, its average maturity declined from nearly 11 months to less than eight months (*Jornal do Brasil* 1998l). The cancellation of several debt auctions, when the government authorities refused to pay the interest rates demanded by investors, underscored the seriousness of this problem. The Central Bank was forced to roll over expiring debt by issuing bonds indexed to the overnight interest rate, a practice not widely used since the late 1980s, an era of economic uncertainty and rampant inflation. Naturally, the Central Bank's accumulation of dollars — necessary to bolster reserves, maintain the exchange rate, and ward off speculative attacks against the currency — increased the money supply. This move left the economic team two unpalatable options: either accept higher inflation (threatening stability) or issue government bonds to soak up the extra liquidity, thus boosting interest rates and choking off growth (*Folha de São Paulo* 1998d, 1998g; *Economist Intelligence Unit* 1998; *New York Times* 1998a).

The vicious circle set in motion by the state's fiscal hyperactivity also aggravated the public sector's deficit. Although government revenues were at an all-time high in 1997, government spending rose even faster. By the end of 1998, Central Bank data revealed that the nominal fiscal deficit of the consolidated public sector (federal government, plus the states, municipalities, and state enterprises) had reached 8 percent of GDP. A primary cause of the deficit, of course, was the need to make high, at times astronomical, interest payments on the public debt. The postponement of reforms of the social security system and the public administration (together responsible for 11 percent of GDP) also exacerbated the fiscal deficit. A related problem was that the revenue the state governments received from the privatization of public enterprises, which was to have been used to reduce their debt, has been spent (some say squandered) on high-profile public works projects, payrolls, and other current expenditures (*Folha de São Paulo* 1998g, 1998j; *Estado de São Paulo* 1998b; *Jornal do Brasil* 1998a).

The perverse feedback loop between the state's fiscal hyperactivity and volatile global financial markets had serious negative implications for economic growth as well. According to Central Bank data, because of growing deficits, the public sector's share of the country's financial savings jumped from 62 percent of the total in December 1995 to 85 percent in April 1998. Conversely, the private sector's share declined from 38 percent to only 15 percent in the same period (*Folha de São Paulo* 1998g). In theory, the public sector's voracious appetite for capital could be due to massive investments in education or infrastructure, which would result in both better equity and more rapid economic growth. However, in practice, financial resources have been used for interest payments, salaries, and to shore up the social security system. The private sector has been partially crowded out, obliging firms to resort to foreign loans, which increases Brazil's international reserves but potentially creates other problems. The reality is that the basic economic model has changed: rather than the state, the model now looks to the private sector to engender economic growth. But the government's inability to rein in a lax fiscal policy means that monetary policy has to be tighter, thus putting companies in a bind and making it hard for them to invest. This combination, of course, fuels problems, such as an overvalued currency and imbalances in the trade and current accounts, not to mention sluggish economic growth.

Against this background, the government's partial shift to relying on floating-rate bonds and dollar-linked debt was an intelligent response to the challenge of rolling over debt in a reluctant market. However, this tactic raised concerns of repeating the Mexican *tesobonos* debacle, when the buildup in foreign currency debt provoked a liquidity crisis after the Mexican government devalued. The risks of floating-rate bonds have always been severe, but, in the 1990s, these risks worsened due to the greater volatility of exchange markets and the dramatic global upswing in speculative attacks against currencies in emerging markets.

Many economists, such as MIT's Rudiger Dornbusch, insisted that, by the outbreak of the Asian crisis, the *real* was overvalued by at least 15 percent vis-à-vis the dollar (*Miami Herald* 1997), explaining, in part, why the growth in imports outstripped that of exports. After 1995, the trade deficit rose by more than 140 percent, and the current account deficit ($33.6 billion in 1998) jumped by more than 150 percent, surpassing the International Monetary Fund's (IMF) benchmark threshold of 4 percent of GDP. Concomitantly, economic growth slowed gradually. After a healthy rate of 6 percent in 1994, GDP growth was 4.2 percent in 1995, 3 percent in 1996, and 3 percent in 1997 (see Table 1 above). The loss of dynamism was even more pronounced in 1998, when the economy stagnated badly and per capita income dropped sharply.[11]

The continued volatility of international financial markets served as a reminder that, although Brazil successfully defended its currency during the worst of the Asian crisis, the high fiscal deficit still left the economy extremely vulnerable to external shocks. In this context, the 1998 electoral campaign introduced new elements of uncertainty, thereby underscoring that the interaction among several key factors — global financial market volatility, rising fiscal deficit, the current account deficit, and political contingencies — could once again force Cardoso's economic team to sacrifice growth — and progress on equity issues — in favor of defending the currency and protecting monetary stability. All this highlighted the urgency of major fiscal reform, which would allow both a looser monetary policy and a less rigid exchange-rate regime without triggering fears of a return to inflation. In fact, eventually, just such a fiscal adjustment was probably inevitable. The danger was that the more time passed, the riskier the Cardoso government's postponement of reforms became.

CONSTITUTIONAL REFORMS AND THE COSTS OF THEIR DELAY

For President Cardoso and his economic team, these risks to macroeconomic stability and long-term growth were of paramount concern as the 1998 elections neared. To address the need for improvements in democratic governability and to provide a permanent solution to the fiscal crisis, four main sets of constitutional reforms were proposed: social security reform, administrative reform, fiscal/tax reform, and political and institutional reforms. The following section presents a very schematic and simplified summary of an extremely complex set of reform proposals with highly Byzantine legislative histories.[12]

- *Social Security Reform.* The social security system (*previdência social*) operates with chronic deficits, forcing the government into the unsustainable use of tax revenues to pay for the benefits of retired public employees. Reform is needed to impose a reduction in benefits, to introduce tax deductible private pension plans, and to substitute time of contribution for time in service, with the introduction of a minimum age of retirement (55 for women and 60 for men). The two latter modifications were part of the government reform project but were rejected by Congress. However, a cap was instituted on monthly retirement paychecks for public employees (about $1,050). Some special retirement regimes were suppressed, although some officials, such as politicians and judges, continue to receive special perks. Reforms enacted prior to the October 1998 elections were considered a good start but fell far short of the government's initial proposals.

- *Administrative Reform.* Although the bloated federal and state administrative apparatus has shrunk somewhat since 1995, the government's efforts to modify constitutional protections in order to reduce the number of employees, curtail waste and corruption, and improve the quality of public services met stiff resistance from politicians, many of whom accumulate various public salaries and retirement pensions, as well as from the unions, especially those affiliated with the National Labor Central (Central Única dos Trabalhadores — CUT). The 1995 Camata Law mandates that public payrolls not exceed 60 percent of revenues, but it was never enforced (22 states were out of compliance by early 1998). Watered-down legislation approved in January 1998 ended guarantees of lifetime employment, imposed a cap of about $10,400 on monthly payments by the state (accumulation of salary and pension), prohibited receipt of more than two governmental paychecks, and eliminated some special privileges enjoyed by public officials.
- *Fiscal/Tax Reform.* The roots of Brazil's intractable fiscal problems lie in its system of "incomplete federalism." The 1988 Constitution mandates revenue sharing with the state and municipal governments but not a commensurate shift in responsibilities for major programs. Unable to pass constitutional amendments or to make fundamental changes in the tax system, FHC resorted to partial fixes, chief among them the creation of the Fiscal Stabilization Fund (Fundo de Estabilização Fiscal — FEF), which allows the federal government to retain transfers to states and municipalities in an attempt to rein in ballooning deficits. Other ad hoc measures to bolster tax receipts included the special tax (Imposto Provisório sobre Movimentação Financiera — IPMF) on checks and other financial transactions approved in 1994 when Cardoso was finance minister and the Temporary Tax on Financial Transactions (Contribuição Provisória sobre a Movimentação Financiera — CPMF) approved in 1996, with revenues earmarked exclusively for the Health Ministry.
- *Political Reforms.* Academics and legal experts have long called for wholesale changes in Brazil's political system, including strengthening of party fidelity to enhance party discipline; one-person, one-vote measures to redress unequal regional representation; changing from an open to a closed-list proportional representation system; adopting a "mixed" electoral system, similar to the German model; establishing threshold barriers

of 3 to 5 percent to reduce the number of parties in Congress; beefing up controls on contributions to electoral campaigns; tightening criteria for the creation of new municipalities; and enacting judicial reforms to reduce case loads, eliminate nepotism, and increase public confidence. With the exception of a few minor reforms approved in 1995 that dealt with party fidelity and campaign finances, virtually none of these proposals has been enacted. The only significant political reform was enacted in June 1997, when the government pulled out all the stops to secure passage of a constitutional amendment permitting Cardoso's own reelection, along with that of governors and some mayors.

The government and business interests claimed that passage of these reforms promised substantial rewards. For example, the government calculated that administrative and social security reforms would together trim nearly $34 billion from the fiscal deficit within three years. Government economists also warned that failure to act would leave the government with no options but either to print money (thereby risking higher inflation) or raise taxes. However, if the reforms were approved, government economists estimated the economy could grow 6 to 7 percent per year. For its part, the powerful Federation of Industries of the State of São Paulo (Federação das Indústrias do Estado de São Paulo — FIESP) argued that a delay in approving the government's tax, administrative, and social security reforms would reduce potential annual GDP growth by 3.7 percentage points. FIESP economists insisted that passing these reforms was the only way to boost the investment rate up to 25 percent of GDP and to achieve annual growth of 6 percent, increases that are needed to keep pace with the growth of the economically active population (*Latin American Monitor: Brazil* 1997a; *LARR: Brazil* 1998b).

POLITICO-INSTITUTIONAL DEADLOCK

Given the stakes, why did the Cardoso government make such scant progress in winning approval for these fundamental reforms? Although the reforms involved complex and controversial economic issues, the problem did not stem from a lack of technical expertise in the Cardoso government. Nor does an alleged lack of political will in the administration or Congress explain the situation very much. FHC the sociologist would agree that the obstacles to reform are systemic and that they raise fundamental questions regarding institutional design and the rules of the game in Brazil's postauthoritarian political system.

When FHC came into office, he enjoyed considerable enthusiasm in the general population and had broad support among the members of the political class. As Figure 3 demonstrates, Cardoso's original congressional coalition, made up of his own center-left Brazilian Social Democratic Party (Partido da Social Democracia Brasileira — PSDB); the conservative Liberal Front Party (Partido da Frente Liberal — PFL); and the center-right Brazilian Labor Party (Partido Trabalhista Brasileiro — PTB) could only marshal a maximum of 182 votes out of 513 in the Chamber of Deputies. Soon, however, the attractions of power brought new allies to the Cardoso camp: the catch-all Party of the Brazilian Democratic Movement (Partido do Movimento Democrático Brasileiro — PMDB) and the rightist Brazil-

Figure 3.
Parties and Coalitions in the Chamber of Deputies

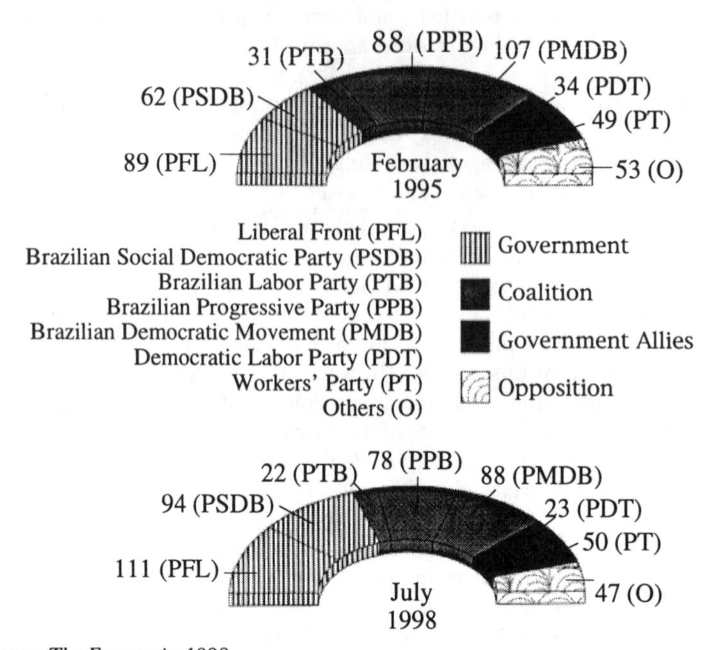

Source: *The Economist* 1998.

ian Progressive Party (Partido Progressista Brasileiro — PPB) led by ex-São Paulo Mayor Paulo Maluf.

On paper, this broad coalition gave the government an ample majority of more than 75 percent of the votes in Congress and should have guaranteed easy sailing for the proposed constitutional amendments. Instead, Cardoso's reform agenda stalled badly. Major responsibility for this failure must be laid at the doorstep of the federal system, electoral legislation, and the lawmaking procedures consecrated in the Constitution of 1988 (Rosenn 1990; Zaverucha 1997; Reich 1998).

Brazil is one of the most politically and fiscally decentralized of all developing countries. Modifications introduced in 1988 oblige Brasília to transfer a large share of tax revenues to the 26 governments, the Federal District in Brasília, and more than 5,500 municipalities, without a commensurate transfer of programs, thus leaving the national government with the same or expanded responsibilities but with fewer resources (Selcher 1998; Montero 2000). Paradoxically, this devolution of power and resources simultaneously holds out the promise of grassroots democratization while also strengthening local oligarchies and the forces of parochialism, clientelism, and patrimonialism.[13] In fact, in a modern-day variant of Brazil's "politics of the governors," state and local political machines and their constituencies operate as veto players in constant struggles over scarce resources with national authorities. While tempering possible abuses of centralized power, this system of "state ultrapresidentialism" (Abrúcio 1994; Selcher 1998), in which governors wield extraordinary power, erodes democratic governability by undermining the national government's management of the macroeconomy (Bonfim and Shah 1994).

Governability is further challenged by constitutional rules that seriously distort congressional representation. The Chamber of Deputies has 513 members, with a minimum of eight seats and a maximum of 70 per state. Because of the tremendous regional variations in demographics, six of the least populous states (with less than 6.5 percent of the national electorate) send 72 deputies to Brasília, while the state of São Paulo, Brazil's economic powerhouse with 22 percent of the electorate, sends only 70 deputies. Thus, a vote for federal deputy in the sparsely populated Amazonian state of Amapá is "worth" 14.5 times the vote of a citizen of São Paulo. Similarly, each state sends three representatives to the Senate, which permits the smaller, more rural, and more traditional states to overpower the larger, wealthier states. The distortion is so massive that only 40 percent of Brazil's population elects a majority of the Chamber of Deputies, and half the Senate is elected by less than 10 percent of all Brazilians (Sola 1994; Dos Santos and Schmitt 1995; Selcher 1998; Souza 1997).

The national electoral system of open-list proportional representation with statewide electoral districts introduces additional complications. Voters cast their ballots for a specific party or an electoral coalition or for a particular candidate affiliated with a party. Large districts make it easier for small parties to elect deputies, thus encouraging a multiplicity of parties and making it all but impossible for voters to hold their representatives accountable (Ames 1995a, 1995b, 2000). Regarding their offices as personal prizes rather than public trusts, deputies enjoy maximum freedom to switch allegiance from one party to another; this facilitates the formation of interparty alliances while undermining party coherence and discipline.

The combination of geographical distortions and electoral rules systematically favors politicians from less populated rural areas belonging to amorphous, catch-all centrist and rightist parties. Conversely, politicians belonging to the more modern or ideological parties of the center-left and the left, with urban constituencies, are strongly disadvantaged (Mainwaring 1992-1993, 1995a, 1995b, 1999; Power 2000a, 2000b). This gives rise to regional voting blocs organized along a north-south (poor-rich) cleavage in which alliances of conservative deputies and senators from the north, center-west, and northeast with rent-seeking, special-interest agendas have the upper hand over rivals from the more industrialized states of the south and southeast (Selcher 1998).

In addition, hard-to-meet requirements for the passage of constitutional amendments constitute a final institutional arrangement with far-reaching consequences. The main problem is that the 1988 Constitution is replete with provisions usually handled in most countries by ordinary legislation. Therefore, virtually all the reforms needed to assure democratic governability of the macroeconomy require constitutional amendments. Such amendments must be approved in two separate sessions by three-fifths super majorities of the full membership of both the Senate and the Chamber of Deputies. Moreover, because the mechanism of a U.S.-

style conference committee to resolve differences does not exist, even minor changes in constitutional amendments made by one chamber require the other's agreement before final passage.

A weak and fragmented party system makes congressional initiatives on broad social or economic questions virtually impossible; such initiatives can originate only with the executive branch (Abranches 1993; Mainwaring 1995a, 1995b, 1997, 1999; Weyland 1996a, 1996b). Nevertheless, their ability to delay and obstruct executive initiatives permits politicians to reap tremendous benefits in the game of "physiological politics" (*política fisiológica*). In the Brazilian version of pork and patronage, politicians use their bargaining leverage with the executive by exchanging their vote for jobs for family members, friends, and supporters and for special federal projects benefiting narrow interests in their states, municipalities, or specific constituencies (Diniz 1982, Hagopian 1996, Weyland 1996a, 1996b; Power 2000a). This perverse practice forces presidents to grant concessions to state, regional, and local elites, and it forces governments to forge cumbersome, constantly shifting ad hoc congressional coalitions in order to pursue agendas on key national issues (Weyland 1998; Power 2000a, 2000b).

The institutional arrangements emerging from these rules, reinforced by political patronage, resemble a huge collective action dilemma in a complex game involving numerous players: governors, clientelistic politicians, entrepreneurs, and other influential interest groups. Maneuvering in this game, Cardoso eschewed frontal assault in favor of advancing his reforms in sequential fashion. Cardoso's strategy has been to exploit the players' conflicting interests, supporting those whose demands overlap with his own agenda, and compensating the losses of those whose demands conflict with his project. Playing off clientelistic politicians' short-term interests against their long-term goals, FHC and his political operatives want to win maximum immediate patronage while guaranteeing their access to future patronage. Because of the highly uncertain nature of their careers in electoral politics, politicians discount future benefits and focus almost exclusively on obtaining short-term rewards. Cardoso's gamble has been to offer patronage up front in exchange for votes for constitutional changes he hopes to use to strengthen state capacity and reinforce governability, while also advancing a project of democratization and institutional modernization that will sharply limit patronage in the future (Weyland 1998).

How has this game played out to date? Cardoso's strategy achieved some initial victories during his first year in office, when Congress was persuaded to pass several "economic order" amendments to the Constitution, including beginning the privatization of state enterprises in telecommunications, coastal shipping, gas distribution, and a limited "flexibilization" of the Petrobrás petroleum monopoly. Foreign firms were also put on an equal legal footing with national companies (Fleischer 1998). However, the initial success of the Plano Real in rapidly bringing mega-inflation under control dissipated the impetus for further reform.

Since early 1996, the main proposals for constitutional change — social security reform, administrative reform, fiscal/tax reform, and political reform — have fallen victim to legislative gridlock as escalating demands for costly concessions produce paralysis and repeated congressional postponement of final approval.

For all his intellectual and leadership skills, many of Cardoso's reform ambitions have been effectively gutted by the veto players, who have successfully minimized most costs to themselves and their constituencies while extracting an exorbitant price in patronage in exchange. In Brazil, although legislative proposals of presidents usually prevail, at least in formal terms (Figueiredo and Limongi 1997a), this may mean that the executive branch simply decides not to insist on a vote or is obliged to accept substantially watered-down legislation. In the case at hand, more permanent solutions to the state's fiscal crisis were stymied, forcing the government to forego constitutional reforms and to continually resort to executive decree powers (*medidas provisórias* — MPs) to pass "important and urgent" stop-gap legislation (Figueiredo and Limongi 1997b; Power 1998).[14] Ad hoc partial remedies (such as the Fiscal Stabilization Fund and taxes on financial transactions) managed to stave off collapse but at high economic and political cost. Therefore, even Cardoso's great victory, his passage of the reelection amendment in May 1997, was marred by allegations of widespread payoffs to special interests and rent-seeking politicians.[15]

The reaction of Brazilian society to the political experiment represented by Cardoso's reelection bid was illuminating. Abuses were emphasized not only by those facing incumbent candidates but also by the press and the courts. These abuses were generally worse in the smaller states. The costs to Brazilian democracy of allowing the reelection of the president, governors, and mayors must be weighted against the eventual advantages of longer terms without reelection. More important, the 1998 election certainly gave new ammunition to those who, like Cardoso before he became president, have always defended parliamentarism.[16]

THE 1998 ELECTORAL CAMPAIGN

On October 4, 1998 Brazil's huge electorate of 106 million eligible voters would not only decide on Cardoso's reelection but would choose a new Congress (all 513 seats in the Chamber of Deputies and a third of the 81 Senate seats) as well as 27 governorships and 1,059 state legislators. Was Cardoso unbeatable and his reelection inevitable? Did the government's concessions to clientelistic politicians alienate the electorate and undermine FHC's capacity to govern? If reelected, would the president have any coattails that would strengthen his hand in passing reform legislation?

In the run-up to the October elections, Brazilians still credited FHC with taming inflation and also liked and admired the president for his personal characteristics; according to polling data, although Cardoso was seen as distant from the "real" people, he was considered to be honest, courageous, elegant, cultured, and intelligent, as well as a good family man. In one area, however, polls reported in *Veja* (1998b) detected vulnerability: specifically, voter dissatisfaction with high unemployment, low wages, and poor public health care. The public considered the Cardoso government's social policies to be "center-right" measures that hurt the interests of public employees, workers, the landless, and the poor in general, while favoring the rich, bankers, industrialists, and politicians. In short, although public opinion of FHC was positive for his record on stabilizing the economy and his personal qualities but negative for his performance on distributive questions and social issues, which meant that, in theory, the president was not unbeatable at the polls. Moreover, focus groups and simulation exercises revealed that if a credible opposition candidate could convince voters that he could maintain economic stability and, besides that, improve the lot of the majority, he might compete effectively against Cardoso (*Veja* 1998c; *Istoé* 1998c). Although this was precisely the strategy attempted by his opponents, the odds still heavily favored a Cardoso victory.

Electoral demographics and geography worked strongly to Cardoso's advantage. The recently published *Atlas Eleitoral do Brasil* reveals that Collor's victory in 1989 came from the hefty margin he racked up in smaller municipalities where low education levels and high social inequality prevail; politics in such regions generally remain dominated by local oligarchs and clientelistic party machines (*Jornal do Brasil* 1997c). Cardoso's 1994 victory was similar, except that, in addition to winning large majorities in smaller municipalities, he also won by smaller margins in the more competitive urban areas. In contrast, the highest returns for Lula were in large metropolitan areas and more industrialized municipalities where voters tend to be better educated. These regions are precisely where the PT; unions (especially those grouping public employees) affiliated with the more militant labor confederation (Central Única dos Trabalhadores — CUT); and grassroots social movements are best organized. Exceptions to Lula's generally poor showing in the countryside came only in regions (for example, in Rio Grande do Sul, Santa Catarina, and Paraná) where the MST first emerged and is most consolidated.

In short, while voters in "archaic" Brazil favor candidates like Collor and Cardoso who present themselves as symbols of "modernity," citizens in the most developed, industrialized, and sophisticated regions of Brazil are disproportionately more inclined to vote for Lula, who is often denigrated by his critics as "the candidate of backwardness." The main difference between archaic and modern Brazil is that the former has always been reliably pro-government, whereas the developed urban centers are more likely to be oppositionist. Paradoxes aside, 1998 was the first time a sitting president had ever sought reelection, and the odds were that the votes of those states, politicians, and voters most dependent on the federal government's largesse would favor the incumbent.

Large disparities in political, organizational, and financial resources had a similar effect on the probable outcome of elections. Taking full advantage of his incumbency, FHC cobbled together a broad coalition comprising his own PSDB and the conservative PFL, along with other centrist to rightist parties, including Maluf's PPB, the PTB, and the small Social Democratic Party (Partido Social Democrático — PSD) [See Figure 3]. Although not a formal member of the coalition, the large PMDB did not field its own candidate, and the majority of its leaders supported the president. Finally, the Cardoso campaign was fueled by a planned budget of more than $60 million, most of its contributions coming from corporations and wealthy individuals (*Jornal do Brasil* 1998f).

In contrast, Lula's coalition, the "Popular Unity/Change Brazil" (União do Povo-Muda Brasil), consisted of his own PT plus the Democratic Labor Party

(Partido Democrático Trabalhista — PDT) headed by his vice-presidential running mate, populist war-horse Leonel Brizola, along with the small but growing Brazilian Socialist Party (Partido Socialista Brasileiro — PSB) led by Pernambuco Governor Miguel Arraes, and the remnants of the two minuscule Marxist parties, the Brazilian Communist Party (Partido Comunista Brasileiro — PCB) and the Communist Party of Brazil (Partido Comunista do Brasil — PC do B). The PT was rent by internal conflicts pitting dogmatic intransigents versus "renovators" of a more social democratic cast (Nylen 1997, 2000). In addition, the PT's electoral strategy conflicted on many points with the union strategy of the CUT as well as with the militant tactics of the MST and some other grassroots social movements (Martin 1997; Hochstetler forthcoming). Moreover, Lula's coalition did not have the huge cadres of elected or appointed officials of its opponent coalition. Nor could Lula's electoral front's organizational weakness be compensated for with expensive tactics because of the paltry funds raised by the Lula campaign (*Jornal do Brasil* 1998f; *El País* 1998a). Ciro Gomes, the third-place candidate in public opinion surveys and ex-governor of Ceará who briefly served as Itamar Franco's last finance minister, was backed by a weak coalition of small parties, including the Popular Socialist Party (Partido Popular Socialista — PPS) led by ex-communist Roberto Freire and the small Liberal Party (Partido Liberal — PL). However, the Gomes campaign was relatively well financed and spent considerably more than Lula's coalition (*Jornal do Brasil* 1998f).[17]

Cardoso's final advantage during the campaign was the access to free radio and TV time. Brazilian legislation allocates free air time to candidates according to the size of their party or coalition's congressional representation, thus introducing a huge bias favoring a large multiparty coalition such as the one supporting Cardoso. Therefore, Cardoso's campaign had about one-half of all the free time divided among the 14 candidates (*Estado de São Paulo* 1998d).

Nevertheless, despite multiple handicaps, in May-June 1998, the Lula campaign managed to jolt the president's camp by scoring an *empate técnico*, or technical tie, with FHC in several opinion surveys. In various polls, the difference between the two candidates approached the margin of statistical error. One of the main causes of the narrowing gap was a sharp drop in support for Cardoso in the cities.[18] Polls showed public irritation with several unfortunate extemporaneous remarks by FHC (for example, he called people who retire before age 50 "lazy bums"). Moreover, the public was increasingly critical of rising unemployment and the government's failure to respond effectively to the huge fires raging in the northern state of Rondônia and the drought affecting millions in the Northeast (*Jornal do Brasil* 1998b; *Istoé* 1998a).

The Cardoso campaign demonstrated quick reflexes, however, and mounted an effective, two-pronged counterattack. First, Lula's opposition to the Plano Real and hints that a sizable currency devaluation might be necessary, together with his strong opposition to the privatization of state enterprises (particularly the 1997 sale of the Vale do Rio Doce mining giant and the July 1998 breakup and sale of the Telebrás telecommunications conglomerate), were used to paint him as a dangerous, irresponsible radical — the "candidate of chaos" who would scare away investors and bring back hyperinflation (*Jornal do Brasil* 1998c). Lula's platform calling for massive job creation, speeding up of agrarian reform, and a "pact of production" to assure 5 to 7 percent annual growth, while safeguarding stability, did not win large numbers of new recruits from among entrepreneurs or the middle classes (*Jornal do Brasil* 1998e). Many analysts argued that Lula's electoral support was nearing its maximum ceiling of approximately 30 percent of the electorate.

The second tactic of the Cardoso campaign's anti-Lula offensive was more positive: to project a confident, optimistic image of a take-charge president promising a better future for all Brazilians. Resembling U.S. president Bill Clinton's "bridge to the twenty-first century" and British prime minister Tony Blair's "New Labour" and the "Third Way," Cardoso's strategy was innovative for Brazil. FHC did not deny the problems facing his government in areas such as poverty, unemployment, or the crisis in public health. Rather, he talked about these issues and sought to politicize them to his advantage. The rationale was to "educate" people about the underlying causes of unemployment, for example, technology, industrial modernization, and globalization, in order to deflect blame away from the president, who represented himself as offering positive solutions for intractable problems (*Jornal do Brasil* 1998l, 1998j; *Estado de São Paulo* 1998a).[19]

Cardoso's economic team assisted the public relations strategy by announcing a series of major spending initiatives, including offering subsidies for reduced interest rates for middle-class mortgages, selling government stocks of rice and beans to force prices down, and expanding the National Program for Family Agriculture (Programa Nacional de Fortalecimento da Agricultura — PRONAF) to provide assistance for 500,000 family farmers. The centerpiece of this effort was the highly publicized "Brazil in Action" program, which was launched in 1997. This program projected spending more than $70 billion for 42 infrastructure projects in transportation, electricity, water, housing, and food production. The emphasis was on job creation, "social action," and future-oriented plans to "redesign the country" (SECOM 1998b).

Cardoso's campaign skillfully frustrated Lula's efforts to capitalize on the government's perceived weaknesses on potent social issues, including jobs, agrarian reform, and inadequate education, among others, by appropriating the left's reform agenda as his own. In the final months before the elections, Cardoso renounced some of his earlier austerity measures as "unnecessary evils." Instead of laying off public sector workers or pursuing cost-cutting measures such as cracking down on fraudulent pensions, for example, the president skillfully turned a court order forcing the government to give civilian employees the same pay increase earlier received by the military to raise civil service wages; this popular measure cost more than $400 million in 1998, plus an estimated $2 billion in future years. He also inaugurated spending projects of more than $5 billion for low-cost housing, promised billions of dollars for rural credits, and announced a minimum income scheme for poor families with children in school (*New York Times* 1998c; *El País*, 1998b).

Through such initiatives, Cardoso's main success in his first government, the Plano Real and economic stability, was skillfully linked to an optimistic vision of the marvelous things Cardoso could do if given a second, four-year mandate. All this was accompanied by a massive advertising campaign extolling the victories of the

Plano Real and promising much more. In fact, at the rhetorical level, a subtle inversion of priorities seemed to have taken place in Cardoso's platform: democracy first, followed by the "social question," with the economy in third place. In the 1994 elections, macroeconomic stabilization had been the absolute priority.

This offensive rapidly permitted Cardoso to recoup his popularity with voters and fueled his hopes for a first-round victory. By late September 1998, a *Datafolha* poll showed that he had reestablished his earlier lead: 40 percent supported FHC versus 25 percent who favored Lula; 9 percent backed Ciro Gomes; 3 percent favored Enéas Carneiro, the eccentric leader of the extreme right nationalist party (Partido de Reedificação da Ordem Nacional — PRONA); 6 percent said they would cast a blank or null vote; and the remaining 9 percent were undecided (Fleischer 1999, Table 1). Troubling for the president, however, was Lula's margin in the large states of Rio de Janeiro and Rio Grande do Sul and the way he had cut into the president's lead in the crucial state of São Paulo. The FHC camp found comfort in the fact that early polls systematically underestimate center-right votes that usually go to the incumbent (less educated persons define their vote late and are more susceptible to last-minute government patronage).

With a first-round victory within striking distance, Cardoso's ultimate win and his second term were not at serious risk. The real stakes on October 4, 1998 was whether FHC could win a majority or be forced to confront Lula in a second-round runoff. More in doubt than his victory was whether the president's showing at the polls would garner him the strong mandate he would need in 1999 and beyond to push his controversial package of constitutional changes through a reluctant Congress.

AFTER THE ELECTIONS: POLITICO-ECONOMIC SCENARIOS

Let us pause here quite literally to revisit our own perceptions on the eve of the 1998 elections. As the elections approached, our analysis placed strong emphasis on the nature of the interaction between domestic politics and economics and the global economy — particularly the upturns and downturns in global financial markets — and the peculiarities of Brazil's politico-institutional arrangements. Assuming Cardoso's successful reelection,[20] we envisaged three broad scenarios: 1) a worst-case outcome characterized by an adverse international environment, erratic economic performance, and rising domestic conflicts; 2) a "muddling through" path similar to Cardoso's first term but crucially lacking the earlier confidence that conditions would improve shortly; and 3) an optimistic trajectory in which major constitutional reforms, together with favorable international circumstances, might permit Cardoso to initiate a phase of renewed economic growth and deepening democracy. Let us recapitulate each of these possibilities in turn.

Not Apocalypse Now, Maybe Tomorrow?

A Cardoso victory over Lula would not mean easy sailing for the next Brazilian government. Even with an FHC victory, a worst-case scenario could possibly erupt at any moment, triggered by, for example, a total collapse of markets in Asia and Russia, which could touch off a speculative run against the *real*. Brazil's national accounts might not be able to withstand this type of contagion effect, especially as the current accounts balance had shown cumulative deficits since 1995, with the gap in 1997 and 1998 exceeding $30 billion.[21] The primary fiscal deficit was about twice the 3-percent level considered acceptable by the IMF. In addition, the exchange rate remained significantly overvalued. Though high interest rates and other measures taken in late August 1998 to prevent capital flight demonstrated the government's readiness to defend the *real* at any cost, they also exacerbated the already onerous domestic debt burden. The need to maintain high international reserves to ward off speculators inflated the money supply and, in a vicious circle, required large emissions of treasury bonds, further adding to the debt and leaving the economy vulnerable to new international financial shocks.[22]

To counter the effects of an "Indonesian" or "Russian" scenario, the new government might be forced to announce a surprise economic package right after the elections. Such a package might be accompanied by urgent appeals to the IMF and the Clinton administration for an emergency bailout. The desire to avoid this ominous scenario was one of the reasons Cardoso hoped to win reelection outright in the first round of voting: uncertainty and the risk of a misstep would be high during the interregnum before the runoff. This, then, would strengthen old-line politicians, as Cardoso would need their support and the help of their electoral machines at almost any price. This, then, would certainly frighten investors and Brazilian holders of liquid assets. Consequently, the longer that necessary corrective measures were postponed, the tougher any surprise *pacotaço* (big package) of austerity measures would have to be to shore up Brazil's credibility in global markets.

In this worst-case scenario, given Brazil's lethargic growth rates, tough austerity measures could well provoke a recession, and unemployment rates — already high — could climb. Depending on the depth of the crisis, social unrest and political instability could increase, given the absence of the social safety nets that cushion downturns in the United States and Europe. The repercussions of the crisis in the countryside might strengthen the MST and could stimulate a wave of new land invasions and rural violence. In this negative chain of events, FHC's hopes for advancing a democratic reform agenda would quickly vanish.

More of the Same, or Back to the Future?

After the elections, a second scenario was that of the Cardoso government muddling through, with conditions continuing more or less as they were or perhaps even improving to some extent. A speculative attack on the *real* might not occur. Even though the social security and administrative reforms approved in Cardoso's first term were greatly diluted, they did improve national accounts somewhat and sent the encouraging message to global financial markets and domestic investors that Brazil was serious about reforms. The subtext of this message was that investors should be patient, given that there were limits to what Cardoso could accomplish within the constraints of Brazil's cumbersome institutional arrangements.

Several developments prior to the elections reinforced the likelihood of this second post-electoral scenario. Accelerated privatization of state enterprises was projected to bring in revenues of about $50 billion in the 1998-2001 period.[23] Moreover, assuming that U.S. interest rates remained low, the Asian financial crisis was not rekindled, and the August 1998 meltdown of the Russian economy did not provoke a total collapse of Latin American markets, the Central Bank might eventually be able to reduce interest rates further. Lower borrowing costs would enable the economy to grow faster, thus bringing in more tax revenues and trimming the fiscal deficit. The risks of a speculative attack on the currency could thus diminish appreciably. These circumstances could conceivably permit Cardoso both to eschew unpopular emergency measures and to advance his reform agenda. This agenda would likely consist of more fiscal reform, the second stage of social security reform, tighter administrative controls, party and electoral reforms, and judicial reform. The announcement in late August 1998 of several moves to redouble efforts to reduce the fiscal deficit (for example, reduction of tax rates while broadening the scope of those subject to income taxes; greater discipline over spending by state and municipal governments; and combating corruption, improving efficiency, and firing excess civil servants) foreshadowed such an agenda (*Jornal do Brasil* 1998m; *Estado de São Paulo* 1998f).

As seen on the eve of the elections, what were the prospects for the success of Cardoso's reform agenda during his second term? According to our analysis, it faced major obstacles. The president's allies in the PFL, PMDB, and PPB were likely to compete aggressively with the PSDB for control over the Chamber of Deputies and the Senate and to insist on naming their luminaries to key cabinet posts. In response, Cardoso would have to employ, once again, the same tried-and-true methods of elite conciliation and patronage politics. Moreover, FHC's strategy of neutrality and failure to support fully some longtime, loyal allies in their contests against the candidates of other parties in his reelection coalition threatened to distance Cardoso from the leaders and rank and file of his own party. Indeed, in several important states, Cardoso was reluctant to appear on local platforms with candidates from his own party so as not to alienate allies from other parties, as national and state alliances often did not coincide. Consequently, even if elected, these PSDB candidates might remain resentful of the lack of support from the president during the electoral campaign.

The risks of Cardoso's reelection strategy were that the PSDB might emerge significantly weakened and that the president might not be able to count on the support of many governors from his own party. The governors of several of the larger states might turn out to be only nominally allied with Cardoso, as they would be busy positioning themselves as possible presidential candidates for the year 2002. These governors probably would actively manipulate their parties and their followers in Congress in ways certain to make life difficult for Cardoso. For example, if Maluf were to win the São Paulo state house, the PPB's support for FHC might last only as long as Maluf found it profitable. Similarly, in the PMDB, the ambitions of Itamar Franco and José Sarney to return to the Planalto presidential palace were well known. The aggressive César Maia, the PFL contender in the governor's race in Rio de Janeiro, had similar designs. There was then a real risk of anticipation of the 2002 presidential campaign. This might make Cardoso hostage to the careers of rival politicians and immobilize whatever reform agenda he had for the country. Instead of debating policies, Brazil would debate politics and the names of Cardoso's possible successors.

In short, even if the economy were to turn in a reasonable performance, Cardoso might face a more obstreperous Congress. As in his first term, Cardoso might only be able to win approval of a much weakened version of his reform agenda and then only when aspirants to his office agreed to help him. Needless to say, in this second possible scenario, the cost for Cardoso (and for Brazilian democracy) would be an excruciatingly slow process of change, fraught with potential for scandal and future instability.

Growth and New Style Social Democracy — Finally?

The third scenario one could envision following the elections was an optimistic one. In the short run, the economic situation probably would resemble the modest performance sketched for the muddling-through trajectory. The factor differentiating the two scenarios would be essentially political, but the potential medium- and long-term consequences for economic growth and efforts to combat poverty and inequality could be highly significant. Still, a major downturn in the world economy would severely undermine any realistic chance for this third, more optimistic scenario.

In the second "muddling through" scenario, the stress was on the possible erosion of FHC's political coalition and strengthening of powerful veto players. Events might unfold differently, however. The elections could bring Cardoso good tidings. For one thing, the PSDB had grown into a *partido ônibus*, that is, a broad, amorphous, catch-all party. Together with its support for liberal economics, this characterization certainly clashes with the PSDB's center-left social democratic image,[24] but this type of evolution would not be all bad: with greater numbers of deputies and senators, the president's party could assume control of one of the legislative chambers and key committees in both parliamentary bodies. Greater control over the legislative agenda by Cardoso's party might thwart clientelistic appetites and help smooth the way for the passage of necessary constitutional reforms. Similarly, although the president's PSDB allies faced up-hill battles in crucial states such as São Paulo and Minas Gerais against their PPB and PMDB rivals, they might succeed in retaining their current governorships. Additionally, Cardoso's much criticized alliance with powerful Bahia politician Antônio Carlos Magalhães might strengthen Cardoso's hand with the conservative PFL and help in approving reform legislation.

Further, if Cardoso were to emerge from the elections politically stronger, he might be emboldened to attempt to refurbish his credentials as a new-style social democrat. His campaign strategy — emphasizing more growth, employment generation, and investment in infrastructure, education, and other social areas — could conceivably signal a shift in the orientation of his economic project. In fact, there were some indications that efforts in this direction might already be underway. A presidential advisory group, the Grupo de Análise e Pesquisa da Presidência da República (GAP), was reported to be working closely with the National Bank of Economic and Social Development (Banco Nacional de Desenvolvimento Econômico e Social — BNDES) and the Institute for Applied Economic Research

(Instituto de Pesquisa Econômica Aplicada — IPEA) in the elaboration of an ambitious economic agenda for Cardoso's second term (*Folha de São Paulo* 1998e; *Jornal do Brasil* 1998g).

While reaffirming a commitment to a market-driven model, the idea advocated by the presidential advisory group was to move beyond the sterile debate over stability versus growth to position Brazil to confront the challenges of globalization, particularly the strengthening of the Southern Cone Common Market (MERCOSUL) and the creation of the Free Trade Area of the Americas (FTAA). This two-fold project entailed a concerted effort to rebuild the state's capacity to provide strategic guidance of the economy. The rationale underlying this inchoate plan was to forge strategic partnerships with essential local and transnational economic groups and to encourage technological innovation and increase Brazil's competitiveness in world markets.

Cardoso himself publicly recognized (*Folha de São Paulo* 1998m) the need for a new "Southern Consensus," reaching beyond Washington orthodoxy in order to tackle second generation reforms that would focus on social issues, microeconomic reforms, and stronger state capacity. Consonant with this view, some members of Cardoso's team argued that the next phase of Brazilian growth should be propelled initially by three official banks: the BNDES, the Banco do Brasil (BB), and the Caixa Econômica Federal (CEF). These institutions, which would be given greater autonomy from the finance ministry and the Central Bank, were to assume a more activist role in financing dynamic sectors that generate employment and have strong multiplier effects, such as paper and cellulose, steel, telecommunications, energy, transportation, low-income housing, and others (*Jornal do Brasil* 1998e).[25] In short, the state would be called upon to play a strategic role in the economy that would differ from that of the previous authoritarian period and from current neoliberal orthodoxy.

In the months before the October 1998 elections, Cardoso began to impose stronger, more direct, and more personal control over key ministries, with an eye toward removing them from the fray of clientelistic bargaining and competition over spoils among the members of his political coalition. In the event of Cardoso's reelection, analysts anticipated the possibility of a major ministerial reorganization (creating a Ministry for Production and a Foreign Trade Ministry, for example) and appointments in the BNDES and in the finance, planning, education, and health ministries that could indicate how determined Cardoso might be to reorient his economic project.

HYBRID PATHWAYS IN CARDOSO'S SECOND TERM

What course did events actually take following the 1998 elections? Did one or another of the three scenarios we envisioned prevail over the other possibilities? Many factors, some of which are beyond Brazil's control, shape the future course of events. Nevertheless, the evolution of the international order and strong elements of path dependence and continuity deeply rooted in Brazil's political economy, caution against realization of the optimistic scenario. If the possibility of apocalypse — now or tomorrow — can be pretty much discarded, it certainly is equally true that, regardless of Cardoso's preferences, Brazil is not on the threshold of a bold social democratic project. The scenario that is unfolding looks rather like a hybrid amalgam of a "back to the future" pathway with excruciatingly slow incremental reforms that leave the country's accumulated social inequities largely untouched. To explain this somber prospect, we must begin with a brief discussion of the electoral results themselves and then turn to the first year of Cardoso's second term.

Electoral Outcomes

Turnout in the first round of voting on October 4, 1998 was an impressive 57.6 percent of the electorate of 106 eligible million voters.[26] These voters were confronted not only with 12 candidates for the presidency but also with 14,406 persons contesting elections for 26 state governors, the governor of the Brasília federal district, 27 federal senators, 513 federal deputies, and 1,059 state deputies. FHC garnered 53.1 percent of the valid votes, only marginally less than in 1994 (54.3 percent) but significantly less than the president and his allies had expected. Lula finished with 31.7 percent (compared with 27 percent in 1994), while Ciro Gomes scored a strong third-place showing with 11 percent (see Table 2). As the polling data and analysis of the 1989 and 1994 contests predicted, Cardoso fared poorly in the larger cities, losing in Brasília and in 10 of 26 state capitals. He lost to Lula by a significant margin in the state of Rio Grande do Sul (49 percent versus 40 percent) and was defeated in Rio de Janeiro state (42.32 percent versus 42.28 percent) in a narrow cliffhanger, while also losing to Ciro Gomes in the latter's home state of Ceará (34 percent versus 30 percent).

In the simultaneous legislative elections, the president's broad parliamentary coalition remained almost unchanged. In the Chamber of Deputies, the governmental bloc shrank somewhat (down from 396 to 381) but this was compensated for by the defeat of 65 "dissident" members of FHC's legislative alliance who had frequently voted against priority government policies. The PFL became the largest party in the lower house, while Cardoso's PSDB became the second party, and the reverses suffered by the PMDB relegated its bloc of deputies to third place. On the right, Paulo Maluf's PPB was the big loser, while the principal leftist parties — Lula's PT and Ciro Gomes's PPS — gained seats. Of course, the resulting alignment was only provisional. Weak party discipline and the ideological incoherence of the party system guaranteed the perpetuation of the traditional "musical chairs" in which deputies migrate from party to party in hopes of extracting personal benefits and improving their chances of reelection.[27] Although some analysts argued that these changes might give the government a more cohesive support base, numerous defections from the PSDB during 1999 left Cardoso's party deeply split, and the president's coalition actually found itself more fractured than ever. Nor were things much different in the Senate. With 27 seats at stake in the upper chamber, the pro-FHC coalition retained a very substantial majority, although the leftist opposition parties (PT, PSB, PC do B, PDT, and PPS) succeeded in electing four new senators, and left-leaning candidates ran second in 13 states.

Recalling that the same constitutional reform that permitted FHC to seek immediate reelection also gave state governors the same right, it is ironic that the

Table 2.
Results of the First Round Presidential Elections: October 4, 1998

Candidate	Party	Number of Votes	% of Electorate	% of Votes	% of Valid Votes
Cardoso	PSDB	35,936,918	33.87	43.14	53.06
Lula	PT	21,475,348	20.24	25.78	31.71
C. Gomes	PPS	7,426,235	7.00	8.91	10.97
Enéas	PRONA	1,447,076	1.36	1.74	2.14
Others		1,437,470	1.36	1.73	2.12
Total Valid Votes		**67,723,047**	—	—	**100.00**
Blank		6,688,612	6.31	8.03	—
Null		8,884,426	8.37	10.67	—
Total Votes Cast		**83,296,085**	—	**100.00**	—
Abstention		22,798,904*	21.49	—	—
Electorate		**106,094,989***	**100.00**	—	—

Note: Cardoso's coalition: PSDB, PFL, PTB, PPB, and PSD.

Lula's coalition: PT, PDT, PSB, PCdoB, and PCB.

C. Gomes' coalition: PPS, PL, and PAN.

Other Candidates: Thereza Ruiz (PTN); Sérgio Bueno (PSC); José Maria de Almeida (PSTU); José Maria Emayel (PSDC); João de Deus Barbosa de Jesus (PTdoB); Vasco de Azevedo Neto (PSN); Alfredo Sirkis (PV); and Brig. Ivan Moacir de Frota (PMN).

* Includes 6.4 million suspected *fantasmas*. Thus, abstention could be reduced to 16.4%.

Source: Fleischer (1999) based on data from the Tribuno Superior Eleitoral (TSE).

most uncomfortable results for the president came in the 26 races for state governorships. Of the 22 incumbents who chose to seek immediate reelection, 15 were winners. While FHC's allies were elected in 21 states, a few key states, formerly governed by members of his party or by governors belonging to his coalition partners, went to opposition parties or to unreliable allies.[28] For example, while *tucano* (or PSDB) ally Mário Covas won in the runoff in the powerhouse state of São Paulo, the important states of Rio de Janeiro (won by Anthony Garotinho of the PDT) and Rio Grande do Sul (won by Olívio Dutra of the PT) went to the opposition. In addition, the governorship of the pivotal state of Minas Gerais was captured by ex-president Itamar Franco of the PMDB, an erstwhile FHC friend and ally but now a strong critic yearning to play the role of spoiler during the president's second term. These results produced resentment and mutual recriminations in the Cardoso coalition, with defeated PMDB and PPB candidates bitterly criticizing the president's television commercials on behalf of his fellow PSDB associates and complaining about the role played by Cardoso's cabinet ministers.

Currency Devaluation and Financial Crisis

Cardoso took the oath of office for the second time on January 1, 1999 with these partisan passions still running at fever pitch. One question was on everyone's mind: Would the $41.5 billion rescue package announced in November 1998 with the IMF (as well as with the strong support of the Clinton administration) prove sufficient to stave off a Russia-style financial collapse in which speculative attacks might rapidly exhaust Brazil's dwindling hard currency reserves? The answer was not long in coming. During the new administration's first week, newly elected Governor Itamar Franco of Minas Gerais declared a unilateral moratorium on all of his state's debts to the federal government, foreign creditors, and most suppliers of goods and services. Dramatically demonstrating both the vitality as well as the hazards of Brazil's federal system, in which forceful governors frequently act on the national stage as major veto players, Itamar's bold step was aimed at forcing the federal government to restructure state debts, which had already been renegotiated on very favorable terms in 1997-1998 (*Istoé* 1999a). Although somewhat reassured by Brasília's strongly voiced disapproval in response to the challenge from Minas, foreign and domestic investors viewed this rebellion as a major warning signal of Cardoso's weakness vis-à-vis key state governors and well-organized political and economic interests.

Less than a week later, on January 12, 1999, these fears reached critical mass when capital outflows hit $1.2 billion, causing panic on the São Paulo and Rio de Janeiro stock exchanges. The next day, the most ardent defender of the crawling peg foreign exchange regime, Central Bank president Gustavo Franco, resigned, and his successor, Francisco Lopes, announced a moderate widening of the acceptable "bands" for currency fluctuation. With the government's credibility shattered, capital outflows jumped to $1.8 billion on January 14, forcing the Central Bank to abandon the main cornerstone of the Plano Real by letting the currency float freely against the dollar.[29] This took the exchange rate to record lows, reaching 2.2 *reais* to the dollar in February, before stabilizing and ending 1999 at the renegotiated target of 1.95 *reais* to the dollar.[30]

Despite the trauma it caused, the consensus view among market players was that this devaluation was both necessary and inevitable, although there were questions about its timing. Indeed, a few weeks after the new exchange rate policy was unveiled, the economic team headed by Finance Minister Pedro Malan agreed that payment of the future tranches stipulated in the IMF rescue package would be contingent upon the Cardoso government's ability to meet newly revised macroeconomic targets requiring even tougher austerity measures that included greater cuts in spending and heftier tax increases. As the previous analysis of Brazil's fiscal hyperactivity underscored, the problem was that although the devaluation and currency float met the immediate threat, they worsened the burgeoning public debt, since the outstanding stock of domestic debt (most of which is based on bonds that pay variable rates of interest) immediately skyrocketed. Consequently, by virtue of the devaluation, the cost of servicing Brazil's debt rose dramatically, driving the nominal fiscal deficit (including interest payments on the debt) up from about 8 percent of GDP in late 1998 to around 10 percent of GDP in late 1999.[31]

Economic Recovery?

Ironically, the financial crisis provided a short-term boost for Cardoso. The government managed to rally its troops to overwhelmingly approve most of the fiscal measures in the IMF package, including the increase in civil service pension contributions for active and retired public employees, a measure that Congress had previously rejected on four occasions. However, any assumption that his large congressional majority meant that FHC would have a free hand in advancing his reform agenda soon proved misleading. Cardoso made several attempts to strengthen the cohesion of his parliamentary bloc by distributing cabinet posts and other top jobs in his second administration to reward loyalty and to punish recalcitrant alliance partners, but his weakened leadership undermined this tactic's credibility. Similarly, efforts to pass a "party fidelity" law that would have forced members to vote their party's line failed, as did the attempt to turn Congress into a "limited" Constituent Assembly (thus setting aside requirements for super-majorities and two rounds of voting in each house) in order to make it possible to approve constitutional reforms by a majority vote (Fleischer 1999).

These setbacks highlighted FHC's political vulnerabilities and made it clear that the institutional problems discussed previously guaranteed that in FHC's second term the government's congressional majority would continue the practice of *política fisiológica.* Once the immediate shock of the devaluation crisis was over, therefore, few politicians had much stomach for firing public employees, enacting pension reforms, reducing or eliminating fiscal incentives, or raising tax rates on key electoral constituencies. Moreover, as 1999 advanced, it became apparent that all the major parties and political figures were focusing obsessively on the municipal elections to be held in 2000 and that Cardoso would have to labor mightily to avoid becoming a lame duck well in advance of the 2002 presidential and congressional elections.

Challenges from the judiciary also exemplified another aspect of Cardoso's political and institutional weakness. The Supremo Tribunal Federal declared unconstitutional the plan (approved by the lame-duck Congress during the January 1999 devaluation crisis) to increase the social security tax from 11 percent to 25 percent for active federal workers and, for the first time, to impose a social security tax on the benefits and pensions of retired employees. Unless reversed by new legislation, this decision blew a major hole in the government's strategy of fiscal austerity and dealt yet another blow to its ill-fated plans for "reform of the state" (*Istoé* 1999m and 1999n; *Brazil Focus: Weekly Report* 1999c).

If party politicking, clientelism, and judicial setbacks gave him little respite on the domestic front, the discipline demanded by international capital flows did not afford FHC much maneuvering room before the exigencies of globalized market forces. This was made clear when congressional investigations into alleged irregularities surrounding the January currency float forced the resignation of Central Bank president Francisco Lopes.[32] In a move charged with symbolism, Cardoso reached beyond his circle of technocratic and academic supporters to replace Lopes with Armínio Fraga, a top employee of U.S. billionaire speculator, investor, and philanthropist George Soros. Despite nationalist protests and unsubstantiated charges that Fraga might have passed insider information to his previous boss, this appointment bolstered the prestige of the orthodox wing of Cardoso's economic team. More concretely, Fraga's evident financial savvy and privileged entrée at the IMF, the World Bank, and the top echelons of Wall Street and European banks soon helped to calm foreign investors and to restore Brazil's credibility in Washington and in international financial markets.

The orthodox fiscal and monetary policies counseled by the IMF, moreover, succeeded in avoiding a Russian- or Indonesian-style catastrophe. In the wake of the devaluation crisis, most pundits, as well as the IMF and the government itself, predicted a deep recession in which Brazil's economy would shrink by a calamitous 4.5 percent; moreover, many analysts expressed concern that consumer prices might rise substantially to 15 percent or more. But the Brazilian economy proved much more resilient than expected, and fears of an impending collapse were seen to be greatly exaggerated. At around 9 percent, inflation in 1999 was lower than expected and came in at the upper range set by official targets. On the negative side, the weakness of the real meant that even though Brazil met the 1999 target of a fiscal surplus (before interest payments) of 3.1 percent of GDP, the public debt stood at 49.95 percent of GDP, which meant that the cost of financing the deficit risked "sucking the blood out of the economy," in the graphic phrase used by the *Financial Times*. Nevertheless, in contrast to its Spanish-speaking neighbors, many of which confronted the sharpest economic contraction since the early 1980s, Brazil actually experienced a very modest recovery and, instead of shrinking the economy, actually managed a 0.8 percent minuscule expansion (see Table 1) in 1999. (*Economist* 1999; *Latin American Monitor: Brazil* 1999; *Brazil Focus: Weekly Report* 1999e; *Latin American Monitor: Brazil* 2000b).

The problem was that a decline of 7.3 percent in manufacturing jobs and a second straight year of sharply negative per capita growth (-5.5 percent) was hardly what FHC promised Brazilians during the 1998 campaign. Moreover, stability and "getting the prices right" were clearly inadequate to resolve the country's chronic problems of unemployment, poverty, and inequality. On this score, IMF recipes offered little cause for optimism. The devaluation of the *real* did not produce the hoped-for reversal of Brazil's trade imbalance as envisioned in the original IMF target of an $11 billion trade surplus. In fact, this target proved quite ludicrous — although improved from $6.6 billion the previous year, Brazil labored mightily to achieve a deficit of around $1.6 billion in 1999. The current account deficit for 1999 was approximately $24 billion (about 4.4 percent of GDP), and international reserves stood at approximately $36 billion, far below the $75 billion registered in mid-1998. In contrast, at close to $30 billion, direct foreign investment exceeded expectations (*Latin American Monitor: Brazil* 1999; *Brazil Focus: Weekly Report* 1999e, 1999f).

Why did the expected surge in export-led growth fail to materialize? A number of reasons can be highlighted: Brazil's imports fell much less than expected because, among other factors, the price of imported petroleum rebounded sharply; the prices of Brazil's principal commodity exports dropped in world markets; and, finally, exports to Argentina, a key MERCOSUL partner, declined by more than 20 percent due to that country's deep recession (caused, in part, by the devaluation of the *real*).[33]

However, this is just part of the story. Unfortunately, even if Brazil's exports demonstrate greater dynamism and competitiveness, the macroeconomic and welfare consequences for most Brazilians will be quite modest. The reason is that merchandise exports represent only 6.6 percent of GDP, while consumer spending accounts for about 80 percent of GDP. Aggregate demand by both firms and households is likely to remain weak because of a combination of a lack of substantial domestic private investment (hurt by very high real interest rates, which remain at nearly 20 percent after initially soaring to 45 percent) and a tight fiscal policy that has sharply curtailed public-sector investments. Finally, although direct foreign investment and capital inflows continued at very high levels in 1999, this would be difficult to sustain in the future because of a combination of lingering fears of turbulence in emerging markets and the fact that the number of high-profile privatizations is dwindling (*Gazeta Mercantil Latinoamericana/El Nuevo Herald* 1999).

The Logic of Opposition

Given this panorama, it is hardly surprising that maintaining macroeconomic equilibrium and satisfying most IMF targets failed to earn many kudos from most Brazilians. Instead, Cardoso and his economic team were criticized for the explosive rise in real interest rates on consumer credit and the precipitous rise in unemployment, which, according to credible surveys conducted by union-affiliated DIEESE researchers, hovered near the 20 percent mark.[34] From their own personal experience, most Brazilians also knew a second year in a row of economic stagnation meant falling standards of living for their families. In fact, with per capita income now lower than in 1995 when FHC first assumed office, the Plano Real's much ballyhooed improvements in social welfare clearly ground to a halt, with little expectation of significant improvements on the horizon.

In this context, declarations by leading politicians and high profile technocrats touting Brazil's more-rapid-than-expected economic recovery contributed to a misleading perception that *o pior já passou* — "the worst is over."[35] This unfounded optimism had particularly perverse consequences for Cardoso and his market reform policies by providing an opening for many politicians — especially those considering mayoral races in 2000 or eyeing the 2002 presidential contest — to criticize the government's economic strategy and to charge the president with a "lack of sensitivity" regarding the social costs of the priority placed on macroeconomic stability. Fair or not, these criticisms undercut the president's and the economic team's calls for continued sacrifice and austerity. Obviously the next step for many politicians of the left, right, and even the center was to call for more rapid growth and to promise redistributive measures designed to appeal to their electoral constituencies.[36]

Ciro Gomes of the PPS, the third-place finisher in 1998, showed considerable skill in playing this game. His proposals for attacking the burgeoning fiscal deficit by renegotiating the domestic debt as part of a broader plan to promote long-term growth favoring the poor attracted considerable attention from various sectors (including PSDB politicians dissatisfied with the government's preference for stability over growth) and propelled him into early presidential contender status (*Estado de São Paulo* 1999b; *New York Times* 1999). But no one, neither Ciro Gomes nor even Minas Governor Itamar Franco, who, in February 2000, lost face when he was obliged to cancel his debt moratorium (*Financial Times* 2000), surpassed Antônio Carlos Magalhães, the 71-year-old veteran politician from Bahia, as a grand master in playing this game.

As president of the Senate, ACM (as Magalhães is commonly known) was one of Cardoso's main allies in keeping the fractious governmental coalition in line, but this did not prevent him distancing himself from the president in order to win a position on the national stage as a potential candidate for the 2002 presidential elections. Despite his notorious ties to the post-1964 military regime and his status as one of the leading figures of the Brazilian right, Magalhães abandoned his previous support for Finance Minister Malan and seized upon Cardoso's sagging popularity to criticize the government's conservative economic policies as anti-growth and anti-poor. In fact, he aggressively sought to co-opt the left's platform by calling for an expensive anti-poverty program to be financed with 6-8 billion *reais* in new taxes on business and the wealthy (*Istoé* 1999d and 1999g).

The attacks of ambitious politicians like Itamar Franco, ACM, and Ciro Gomes not only sullied Cardoso's image but also contributed to worsening tensions between the so-called monetarists and developmentalists in the economic team and among the president's closest advisors. Dramatic evidence of these conflicts became public in early September 1999 when Development Minister Clóvis Carvalho, a long-time personal friend of the president, made an ill-tempered televised attack on Finance Minister Malan's orthodox policies. He called upon the government to be more "daring" and to "take more chances," proclaiming that "an excess of caution, at this point, is but another name for cowardice."[37] Although Malan and Central Bank president Armínio Fraga won this particular showdown by forcing Carvalho's firing and marginalizing the few remaining developmentalists to posts of secondary importance (*Istoé* 1999k), thereby successfully reasserting orthodox hegemony of economic policy, this episode clearly foreshadowed future fissures and conflicts within the Cardoso coalition.

Avança Brasil?

From Cardoso's perspective, these challenges to his authority could not have come at a less propitious moment. A "March of 100,000" took place in Brasília in late August 1999 with the participation of public servants and thousands of local residents under the leadership of the PT, other leftist opposition parties, and union groups such as the CUT. The militantly oppositionist posture of this large demonstration (the organizers claimed to have mobilized 130,000 participants while the *Folha de São Paulo* calculated the crowd at 75,000) set the tone for subsequent, smaller marches and demonstrations by public school teachers and the MST (*Istoé* 1999i). Moreover, in September and October, other groups such as agricultural producers, with far less radical political and economic agendas, also conducted their own high-profile marches and demonstrations in Brasília.

In the midst of this surge in popular protests, Cardoso announced his budget proposals for the 2000-2003 period. With considerable hoopla that deliberately recalled his 1998 campaign slogan of *Avança Brasil* ("Advance, Brazil"), the president's objective was to regain political momentum by highlighting a distinction between the themes of his first term — stabilization, privatization, deregulation, and the market — and the forward-looking goals — primarily decisive action on behalf of growth and development — he hoped the population would see in his second mandate. The heart of this strategy was an optimistic prediction of 4 percent growth (versus the World Bank's prediction of 2.5 percent) in 2000 and 5 percent in 2001 and the pledge to create 8.5 million new jobs in four years with a $580 billion spending plan on social development and infrastructure (*Istoé* 1999l; *Brazil Focus: Weekly Report* 1999a; *El Clarín* 2000). Regardless of its merits, however, politically, this attempt by the government to re-launch itself risked falling on deaf ears.[38]

Cardoso's support among the population seemed to be in free fall. According to public opinion surveys, by September 1999, the president's approval rating had sagged to 8 percent while his rejection rate (the sum of "bad" and "terrible" evaluations) had risen to an unprecedented 65 percent, the lowest rating for any president since the return to civilian rule in 1985.[39] Of direct policy relevance, over 40 percent of the population believed that the government's stabilization efforts were not working as well as expected, and fully 44 percent said the government should abandon the IMF targets.[40] The same polls asked respondents to evaluate the proposals of potential opposition candidates for 2002: 40 percent approved the ideas of Ciro Gomes, while 42 percent agreed with those of Lula. Although Lula, the veteran three-time candidate of the PT, remained quite popular, Ciro Gomes's meteoric rise in the polls was interpreted by analysts to mean that the political vacuum caused by FHC's fall in popularity had been filled by Gomes, the newcomer to presidential politics.

Although FHC's popularity subsequently recovered somewhat (for example, in February 2000, only 49 percent rated his performance as "bad" or "terrible"; see *Brazil Focus* 2000), his reduced public support, combined with an increase in popular mobilization in the streets, created a Catch-22 situation: after the Congress had sat on its hands for most of the year, the government urgently needed approval of politically controversial reforms to stimulate growth. But, by the same token, Cardoso simultaneously needed to show that his program could generate growth in order to encourage the Congress to approve the reforms. Without growth, many of his allies were increasingly nervous that continued support for Cardoso's strategy might inexorably lead to electoral defeat in the 2000 municipal elections and, beyond that, to dismal prospects for the governing coalition in 2002.[41]

CONCLUSION

In discussing FHC's first term in the present study, it was observed that Brazilian politics resembles a huge, multi-level collective action dilemma with numerous actors, each with contradictory interests and agendas. In this context, the success of Cardoso's governing strategy hinged on a big gamble: by offering patronage up front in exchange for support for constitutional reforms, the president hoped to strengthen state capacity, while advancing a project of economic modernization and political democratization that could limit patronage in the future. This gamble clearly paid off for FHC when constitutional changes were approved, permitting his own reelection. However, most of Cardoso's ambitious reform proposals were greatly diluted, if not completely gutted, by the actions of veto players, particularly the state governors, most of whom succeeded in avoiding any costs to themselves or their constituencies while taking advantage of fiscal federalism to make a mess of subnational finances. If anything, the record of the first year of Cardoso's second government only reinforces this pessimistic view.

Why are Brazil's problems so intractable, even for a gifted president like Cardoso? The crux of the problem, this argument suggests, lies at the intersection of deeply entrenched structural inequalities of truly egregious proportions and a complex ensemble of politico-institutional arrangements: geographic distortions in representation, open-list proportional electoral rules, a weak and fragmented party system, and incomplete federalism with willful governors acting as veto players. Although the causation is obviously circular, if the focus is limited to the span of one or two presidential terms, then politico-institutional arrangements clearly constitute the primary obstacles to meaningful reform. These obstacles are, of course, compounded by the impact of global financial volatility, which tempts many politicians to hang back and watch the government implode while they prepare to step into the vacuum.

These institutional arrangements, reinforced by the *aggiornamento,* or modernization, of traditional forms of clientelism and patronage, strengthen the tendency of most politicians and well-organized collective actors to *apostar no fracasso* — in Brazilian political parlance, to "bet on failure." A sophisticated, if intuitive, political calculus impels the most powerful players to eschew "cooperation" in favor of "defection" as their dominant strategy. Given prevailing rules and arrangements, this strategy is eminently "rational" for self-interested actors (operating within notably crude and constrained parameters) because there are few if any institutional disincentives or sanctions for defection. Consequently, politicians, whose short-term interests revolve around the acquisition and dispensation of patronage, usually can ignore party ideology and discipline and change parties with near total impunity, and they may even abandon a sinking presidential ship, all without paying virtually any cost.

Since the 1985 return of civilian rule, all governments have suffered from this syndrome, with the partial exception of that of Itamar Franco, who came to office in a unique moment of unity caused by his predecessor's impeachment and who left office on an upswing caused by the early successes of the Plano Real. Conversely, from the perspective of these perverse rules-of-the game, those politicians who cooperate, for instance, by supporting measures to reduce patronage, increase transparency and accountability, or who favor the general welfare over narrow personal or sectoral interests, are, in effect, acting "irrationally" and are generally rewarded with the "sucker's payoff" and marginalized from the centers of power.

A further complication stems from the frequently perverse interaction between the institutional rules and arrangements and the performance of the economy. While elected leaders and major collective actors in other democracies frequently cohere during crises and downturns, Brazil has few institutional mechanisms to encourage such behavior. In good times, this problem is less apparent. When the economy is growing, patronage resources are abundant, and electoral coattails are available, extreme political bandwagoning tends to be the rule, as occurred under José Sarney in 1986, when the Cruzado Plan temporarily vanquished inflation, or when the euphoria of the Plano Real caused politicians to ally themselves with Cardoso. In periods of relative bonanza, therefore, winning electoral coalitions can be forged relatively easily, and governing coalitions in parliament are more likely to be sustained, despite the fragmenting pull of weak parties, representational bias, and incomplete federalism.

But in economic hard times, politicians' time horizons shorten and distributive conflicts sharpen and spill over into the political arena. Consequently, in downturns, particularly of the more recent sort associated with international financial volatility, the problematic institutional arrangements discussed here are particularly crucial because weak institutions allow transgressors and political speculators to go unpunished, thus proving that defection is almost always a winning strategy. Of course, opportunistic bandwagoning and speculative behavior by pragmatic politicians are normal in all democratic polities, but, in Brazil, they assume particularly exaggerated forms and have especially perverse consequences. This exaggeration helps explain the fragility of Cardoso's governing coalition and why, despite his overwhelming majorities in Congress, his reform proposals have stalled so badly, particularly when the Plano Real began to go sour and growth ground to a halt. The exaggeration also provides a useful perspective on the reasons why Cardoso's PSDB-PFL-PMDB alliance risked implosion in the president's second term.[42]

As this chapter's subtitle suggests, Cardoso is "caught between clientelism and global markets." But Cardoso's travails are not unique and prompt us to revisit a question raised at the outset of this chapter: Is FHC a neoliberal or a new-style "third way" social democratic reformer? A clear pattern stands out in post-1985 Brazil: center-left parties cannot govern and remain cohesive at the same time.[43] Under Sarney, new adherents from the right, many of whom had supported the previous military dictatorship, first swelled the ranks of the PMDB. Subsequently, the PMDB lost its left wing when the PSDB, led by Cardoso, was founded as a new progressive party. The PSDB came to power with Cardoso's election and the pattern repeated itself: opportunistic politicians with centrist and center-right credentials flocked to the party and, following the 1998 elections, the progressive wing of the PSDB, its reformist ambitions blocked, began to exit in droves.

In short, there seems to be a clear tradeoff between maintaining identity or governing, which requires pragmatic compromises with powerful conservative forces. FHC has chosen the ugly task of governing Brazil, but, increasingly, the "authentic" *tucanos* of the PSDB are tempted to choose the former. This logic highlights an important aspect of the emergence of Ciro Gomes and his PPS as significant political actors, but it also points to the risks that make the PPS a future candidate for, and victim of, the same phenomenon. Only the PT runs alone and would govern alone, although accepting the support of other forces. However, after three consecutive defeats, the PT will have great difficulty winning at the national level.[44] Apparently, Brazilian "social democrats" can neither win nor govern alone. Governing in coalition with the right, first under Sarney and now FHC, has proved demoralizing and disintegrating to the historic center-left.

In light of this pattern, was Cardoso correct to gamble the promise of real social, economic, and political reform for the chance for four more years in the presidency?[45] FHC the sociologist no doubt is fully aware of the ironies implicit in this question. If it is true that the past frequently serves as a prologue to the future, then the verities of Brazilian politics point to the costs both to democracy and the economy of FHC's gamble and of his reliance on clientelistic modes of governance. But if a social democratic Cardoso legacy is now almost unthinkable, the president can at least strive to leave Brazil better prepared — meaning, with fundamental political, institutional, and fiscal reforms approved — to meet future challenges. If he fails in this task, he will only be remembered as the "man of the Plano Real," as yet another failed reformer. Ultimately, the decisive test of Cardoso's leadership during his remaining time in the presidency will be his ability to cajole Brazil's fractious political class toward credible modernization and democratization of the country's institutions. Failing this, the denial of full citizenship to millions of Brazilians will continue, as will their exclusion from participating in the benefits of the market and globalization in a more just society.

Notes

1. For analyses of Cardoso from two critics to his left, see Cammack (1997) and Dos Santos (1998). Also see Goertzel (1999) for a recent intellectual biography of Cardoso by a U.S. sociologist.

2. See Amaral (1995) for a useful collection of essays on the political, social, and economic circumstances surrounding the 1994 elections.

3. For an early analysis of the Plano Real by one of its leading advocates and the subsequent president of the Central Bank, see Franco (1995). See Kugelmas and Sola (1997) for an analysis of the "Machiavellian moment" facilitating the launching of the Plano Real.

4. U.S. investment in Brazil doubled from 1994 to 1997, rising from $17.9 to $35.7 billion, with most recent investments (64 percent) concentrated in the manufacturing sector. Germany, which currently ranks second in foreign investment (at $13.5 billion), has been challenged recently by Spanish investors (at approximately $12 billion), who have made major commitments in the telecommunications and banking sectors. See *O Estado de São Paulo* (1998f).

5. The reduction in poverty reflected in official statistics appears somewhat optimistic. For example, Londoño and Székely (1997) found that "extreme poverty" had declined from 26.2 percent of the population in 1990 to 18 percent in 1994 and that "moderate poverty" had declined from 53.3 percent to 45.1 percent in the same period. Despite the data, however, press coverage may have led many Brazilians to believe that poverty has increased, not declined. See, for example, the convoluted explanation of IBGE data in *Folha de São Paulo* (1997a).

6. According to IBGE data, manufacturing jobs declined by 11.2 percent in 1996 and by an additional 5.7 percent in 1997 (*Folha de São Paulo* 1998i).

7. A *latifúndio* is a large-landed estate.

8. Vice President Marco Maciel made the even more optimistic claim that 280,000 families were settled between 1995 and 1998 (*El País* 1999). According to Fernández Franco (1997, 72n), the José Sarney government (1985-1989) promised to settle 1.4 million families but gave land to only 140,000; the Collor de Mello government (1990-1992) announced plans to settle 500,000 families but did not settle any; and the Itamar Franco government (1992-1994) promised to give land to 100,00 families but managed to settle only 20,000.

9. For a sophisticated analysis of how international capital flows shape domestic political and macroeconomic policies, see Mahon (1996).

10. For discussions of the fiscal hyperactivity of the Brazilian state, see Sola (1994, 1995) and Kugelmas and Sallum Júnior (1993). For a related but broader analysis of the "hyperactivity syndrome," see Lamounier (1996). For comparative data on the size of the public sector, see IADB (1997).

11. Because the economically active population grows by 1 to 1.5 million persons each year, growth rates below about 6 percent imply rising unemployment. See *Jornal do Brasil* (1998k).

12. Tedious references to journalistic sources are dispensed with here. The *Latin American Monitor: Brazil* is a good English-language source for following the path of these reforms through Congress. For a broad defense of the importance of state reform, see Bresser Pereira (1997); see Diniz (1997) for a more critical historical perspective on state reform in Brazil.

13. See Hagopian (1996) for an insightful analysis of the survival of regional oligarchies into the postauthoritarian period. Power (2000b) provides an in-depth discussion of the right wing sectors of Brazil's political class and their ability to use traditional methods to adapt to the exigencies of competitive politics.

14. In 1991, FHC strongly criticized Fernando Collor's use of *medidas provisórias*; faced with governing, however, FHC has signed 108 new MPs, an average of 2.84 per month, slightly higher than Collor's average of 2.75. In his first 38 months in office, FHC also reissued the same MPs 1,839 times, 24 times Collor's rate. See *Folha de São Paulo* (1998k).

15. The scandal centered on the recently deceased Sérgio Motta. Allegations charged that Motta, then the minister of communications and one of FHC's closest friends and advisers, had orchestrated the securing of the votes of several obscure PFL deputies in exchange for money ($187,000 each). The threat united the government alliance, and the opposition's efforts to hold congressional hearings were unsuccessful. Of course, this display of solidarity within the government coalition was costly, both in material and political terms. A succinct summary of this episode may be found in *Latin American Monitor: Brazil* (1998b). Literally dozens of press reports during the first half of 1997 detailed constant exchanges between the executive branch and congressmen of funds and favors for votes for the constitutional change permitting FHC's reelection. See, for example, *Folha de São Paulo* (1998b, 1998c) for typical accounts of this wheeling and dealing.

16. Thanks to Tim Power for his insight on the issues discussed in this paragraph.

17. See Samuels 2000 for a useful discussion of Brazil's campaign finance legislation and the role of money in Brazil's democracy.

18. In fact, in mid-1998, more than half of better-educated voters said they would not vote for Cardoso (*Jornal do Brasil* 1997b, 1997c).

19. Strictly speaking, the president's penchant for publicly analyzing Brazil's many social problems was nothing new. As president, FHC continued to speak frequently as the sociologist about social, economic, and political consequences of Brazil's encounter with the forces of globalization. See, for example, Cardoso (1996b, 1996c).

20. We omit the fourth scenario — a possible, but unlikely, victory by Lula and his left coalition — which was included in the original, *North-South Center Agenda Paper* version of this chapter. The following discussion of these scenarios is mostly unchanged from the original text, except for minor editing.

21. However, as Finance Minister Pedro Malan and other members of the economic team insisted, Brazil was in a stronger position than in October 1997 to face a major crash in international markets. In late 1997, Brazil's hard currency reserves were 1.8 times the current account deficit; in August 1998, in contrast, this ratio was 2.25 times, with international reserves of approximately $73 billion and a $32 billion current account deficit (*Jornal do Brasil* 1998m).

22. According to forecasting models developed by Standard and Poor's DRI group, an "Asian Armageddon" scenario would "clobber" the Brazilian economy, sharply increasing inflation and cutting exports. See *Washington Post* (1998).

23. However, save Petrobrás, whose sale was unlikely for reasons of nationalist symbolism, after the $19 billion sale of Telebrás in late July 1998, there were no more large, highly visible privatizations available for the government to demonstrate its commitment to continued market reform and to buttress foreign investors' confidence.

24. See Power (1997) and Power, Fleischer, and Marques (2000) for pertinent reflections on the identity crisis afflicting the *tucanos,* or party affiliates, of the PSDB.

25. Such a project may have serious short- and medium-term difficulties. For a sobering critique of some of the implications of the pattern of investments, see the analysis of well-known economist Antônio Barros de Castro in the *Folha de São Paulo* (1998l).

26. For detailed analyses of the October 1998 elections, see Albuquerque (1998) and Fleischer (1999).

27. By the end of September 1999, 81 deputies had changed their party label, thus threatening the record set in 1995, when 83 switches occurred. See Melo (1999).

28. Indeed, to a great extent, FHC received legislative support for the reelection amendment precisely because he offered the governors the same right to run again. However, this created incentives for opposition governors to remain in office. The success of the incumbents in achieving reelection in 1998 suggested that the turnover in the ranks of state governments that might have helped FHC solicit new supporters for his agenda might be low. That could mean that the opposition governors that get in, stay in, producing more sustained subnational opposition to reform.

29. On these events, see *Istoé* 1999b. Also see *Istoé* (1999c) for an interview with Cardoso in which he admits that errors were made in the handling of the devaluation and denies that the IMF was imposing policies on Brazil.

30. In September 1999, the *real* already reached the $2 mark before recovering somewhat. However, the October 1999 elections in Argentina, the looming constitutional crisis in Venezuela, Ecuador's default on its foreign debt, the ongoing Colombian civil war, plus the U.S. Federal Reserve's tighter money policy all made it difficult to prevent the currency's erosion.

31. See the monthly data published in *Latin American Monitor: Brazil* (1999, various issues). Here again, it must be stressed that it is domestic, not foreign, debt that is the problem. In the last two years, domestic debt has almost doubled and currently stands at nearly R$200 billion, or about $205 billion dollars. By contrast, the foreign debt has only increased 13 percent in the same period. See *The New York Times* (1999) and the detailed analysis in Sáinz and Calcagno (1999).

32. The Lopes resignation followed several earlier scandals associated with the privatization of the Telebrás communications conglomerate that forced the ouster of several top Cardoso associates, including, most prominently, André Lara Resende, president of the BNDES, and Communications Minister Luiz Carlos Mendonça de Barros. See Simonens da Silva (1999) for a detailed critical study sponsored by the Catholic Church's Peace and Justice Commission, of scandals in the financial sector.

33. Rising tensions with Argentina over the future of MERCOSUL not only threaten Brazil's policy of integration with regional trading partners but also undermine its bargaining

position on the future Free Trade Area of the Americas with the United States. Thirty percent of Argentina's exports go to Brazil, and, in recent years, a considerable part of Argentina's trade surplus has come from its trade with Brazil. Consequently, the devaluation of the *real* not only struck a blow against Argentine exports but also fed an (exaggerated) impression that its markets were being "invaded" by cheap Brazilian products. The Brazilian devaluation also put pressure on Argentina's currency board, which locks the peso tightly to the U.S. dollar. President Cardoso's support of fiscal incentives to encourage the location of a major installation by automaker Ford in the northeastern state of Bahia provoked Argentine protests against its neighbor's "unfair practices." The ensuing tit-for-tat imposition of sanctions and restrictions on each other's exports plunged MERCOSUL into deep crisis. Although tensions subsequently subsided, bilateral trade between both countries was down some 20 percent, and prospects for a deepening of regional integration were in doubt. Of particular concern were the two countries' contrasting exchange-rate regimes, which make macroeconomic coordination and micro-level planning by firms problematic.

34. For detailed survey data, see the data bank (http://www.dieese.org.br) maintained by the Inter Trade Union Department of Statistics and Socio-Economic Studies (Departamento Intersindical de Estatística e Estudos Sócio-Econômicos — DIEESE). It should be stressed that DIEESE surveys are limited to the 10 largest urban centers, so they disproportionately reflect trends in the industrial sectors, particularly the older, import-substituting sectors. According to data released by the Federation of Industries of the State of São Paulo (FIESP), the level of industrial activity for the first 8 months of 1999 was 7.6 percent below that of the same period the previous year (*Brazil Focus: Weekly Report* 1999c).

35. See *Istoé* (1999e) for examples of claims that the "worst is over." For a scathing critique in which FHC is belittled as the "Queen of England," see the interview by outspoken economist Maria da Conceição Tavares in *Istoé* (1999h).

36. Similarly, well-organized lobbies and their parliamentary appendages (such as the infamous *bancada rural*, comprised of politicians of all parties tied to agricultural interests) championed expensive projects in Congress, thereby forcing the government to brandish its veto powers and to expend its dwindling political capital to defend its commitment to the IMF austerity package. See Acuña and Smith (1994) for a more formal explanation of why rational actors — both principals and agents — will step up their demands for redistributive policies well *before* a sustainable economic recovery is actually at hand.

37. Interestingly, this showdown occurred at a special meeting of the PSDB called to debate the topic "Development with Stability" and to hammer out a coherent political and economic strategy in order to overcome party divisions. For details see *Brazil Focus: Weekly Report* (1999b).

38. The government preferred not to highlight other figures in its 2000 budget proposals. For example, the budget bill projected that 43.7 percent of federal expenditures would go to servicing the public debt (up from 18.1 percent in 1997, 31.2 percent in 1998, and 34 percent in 1999). In contrast, health expenditures (11 percent in 1997, 8.1 percent in 1998, and 7.7 percent in 1999) were slated to decline to 6 percent in 2000, with education's share (5.5 percent in 1997, 4.5 percent in 1998, and 4.2 percent in 1999) of public spending to shrink to 3.8 percent in 2000 (Schmidt 1999).

39. According to polls conducted by Vox Populi and commissioned by the National Confederation of Industry, the previous record was the 60-percent rejection for Sarney in March 1990 as he left office with inflation raging at a monthly rate of 80 percent; even Fernando Collor, on the eve of his impeachment in mid-1992, had a 57-percent rejection rate (*Estado de São Paulo* 1999a; *Brazil Focus: Weekly Report* 1999c and 1999d).

40. Brazilians were not rejecting the need for austerity per se. In February 1999, following the devaluation, when asked if they "were willing to make further sacrifices" to avoid the return of inflation, 51 percent answered "No" and only 37 percent responded "Yes"; eight months later, those objecting to further sacrifice declined to 35 percent while those who answered "Yes" had risen to 57 percent. For details and analysis of polling trends, see *O Estado de São Paulo* 1999a; *Brazil Focus: Weekly Report* 1999c and 1999d.

41. These problematic prospects were foreshadowed by difficulties in approving the budget in timely fashion, thereby forcing FHC to call for a special legislative session for January and February 2000. Focused on the October 2000 municipal elections, many members of Cardoso's coalition frequently treated his priorities as a mere "wish list," while simultaneously exhibiting a more independent demeanor by strengthening Congress's oversight power by threatening to limit the presidential powers to use *medidas provisórias* to implement urgent measures. See *New York Times* (2000) and *Latin American Monitor: Brazil* (2000a) for an idea of the concern this provoked among foreign observers.

42. Strong parties and coherent state institutions matter, as the comparison with Chile suggests. In Chile, the Concertación government confronted its third consecutive election intact, even as the economy experiences what is (by Chilean standards) a mild recession. For an interesting analysis of the strength and "encompassing" nature of institutions in Chile, see Weyland (1997).

43. The following analysis owes much to conversations of the senior author with Tim Power, who wonders whether Brazilian social democracy has fallen victim to an "impossible game" described by O'Donnell (1978) for Argentina between 1955 and 1996. See Korzeniewicz and Smith (2000) for a more general discussion of the possibilities of "third way" alternatives in Latin America.

44. It should be noted that the PT has been willing to forge alliances behind candidates of other parties at the local and state levels, as its support for the PDT in Rio de Janeiro indicates. Although PT support for another party's presidential candidate (for example, in support of Ciro Gomes and the PPS) remains highly unlikely, a contest pitting a divided centrist alliance against a divided center-right alliance might conceivably lead to a PT victory. In this scenario, in which the center-left supported Ciro Gomes, then the PT perhaps could defeat a PFL-led coalition in first round balloting. Unless runoff elections are eliminated, however, it would be extremely difficult for the PT to win in a second round.

45. For an uncommonly blunt "no" response along these lines, see the interview with Thomas Skidmore, a prestigious U.S. *brasilianista*, in *Istoé* (1999j).

References

Abranches, Sérgio Henriques. 1993. "Strangers in a Common Land: Executive/Legislative Relations in Brazil." In *Political Constraints on Brazil's Economic Development*, ed. Sigfried Marks. Coral Gables, Fla.: North-South Center Press at the University of Miami. 105-129.

Abrúcio, Fernando L. 1994. "Os Barões da Federação." *Lua Nova* 33: 165-183.

Acuña, Carlos H., and William C. Smith. 1994. "The Political Economy of Structural Adjustment: The Logic of Support and Opposition to Neoliberal Reform." In *Latin American Political Economy in the Age of Neoliberal Reform: Theoretical and Comparative Perspectives,* eds. William C. Smith, Carlos H. Acuña, and Eduardo A. Gamarra, 17-66. Coral Gables, Fla.: North-South Center Press at the University of Miami.

Albuquerque, José Augusto Guilhon. 1998. "As Eleições de 1998 no Plano Nacional: Avaliação dos Resultados Parciais." Paper presented at the Konrad Adenauer Stiftung seminar on the 1998 elections, São Paulo, October 8.

Amaral, Roberto, ed. 1995. *FHC: Os Paulistas no Poder*. Niterói, Brazil: Casa Jorge Editorial.

Ames, Barry. 1995a. "Electoral Rules, Constituency Pressures, and Pork Barrel: Bases of Voting in the Brazilian Congress." *The Journal of Politics* 57 (May): 324-343.

Ames, Barry. 1995b. "Electoral Strategy under Open-List Proportional Representation." *American Journal of Political Science* 39 (May): 406-433.

Ames, Barry. 2000. *The Deadlock of Democracy in Brazil.* Ann Arbor, Mich.: University of Michigan Press.

Ayres, Robert L. 1998. "Crime and Violence as Development Issues in Latin America and the Caribbean." *World Bank Latin American and Caribbean Studies*: Viewpoints. Washington, D.C.: World Bank.

Barros, Ricardo, Rosane Mendonça, and Sônia Rocha. 1995. "Brazil: Welfare, Inequality, Poverty, Social Indicators, and Social Programs in the 1980s." In *Coping with Austerity: Poverty and Inequality in Latin America*, ed. Nora Lustig, 237-274. Washington, D.C.: The Brookings Institution.

Bonfim, Antúlio, and Anwar Shah. 1994. "Macroeconomic Management and the Division of Powers in Brazil: Perspectives for the 1990s." *World Development* 22: 535-542.

Brazil Focus: Weekly Report. 1999a. "Special Report — FHC Obliged to Sack Clóvis Carvalho." September 5.

Brazil Focus: Weekly Report. 1999b. "FHC Drops in Polls [Again]." September 11-17.

Brazil Focus: Weekly Report. 1999c. "FHC Rejection Rate Stabilizes — IBOPE." October 2-8.

Brazil Focus: Weekly Report. 1999d. "PNAD." November 27-December 3.

Brazil Focus: Weekly Report. 1999e. "Economics." December 25-January 3, 2000.

Brazil Focus: Weekly Report. 2000. " Cardoso's Rejection Rate Increases." Feb. 19-25.

Bresser Pereira, Luiz Carlos. 1997. "State Reform in the 1990s: Logic and Control Mechanisms." *Cadernos Mare*. Brasília, D.F.: Ministério da Administração Federal e Reforma do Estado.

Cadji, Anne-Laure. 2000. "Brazil's Landless Find Their Voice." *NACLA Report on The Americas* 33 (5) March/April.

Cammack, Paul. 1997. "Cardoso's Political Project in Brazil: The Limits of Social Democracy." In *Socialist Register 1997: Ruthless Criticism of All That Exists*, ed. Leo Panitch, 223-243. London: Merlin Press.

Cardoso, Fernando Henrique. 1973. "Associated-Dependent Development: Theoretical and Practical Implications." In *Authoritarian Brazil: Origins, Policies, Future*, ed. Alfred Stepan, 142-178. New Haven, Conn.: Yale University Press.

Cardoso, Fernando Henrique. 1975. *Autoritarismo e Democratização*. São Paulo: Paz e Terra.

Cardoso, Fernando Henrique. 1979. "On the Characterization of Authoritarian Regimes in Latin America." In *The New Authoritarianism in Latin America*, ed. David Collier, 33-60. Princeton, N.J.: Princeton University Press.

Cardoso, Fernando Henrique. 1993. "The Challenges of Social Democracy in Latin America." In *Social Democracy in Latin America: Prospects for Change*, ed. Manuel Vellinger, 273-296. Boulder, Colo.: Westview Press.

Cardoso, Fernando Henrique. 1996a. "Consequências Sociais da Globalização." Presentation at the Indian International Centre, New Delhi, India, January 27.

Cardoso, Fernando Henrique. 1996b. "O Impacto da Globalização nos Países em Desenvolvimento: Riscos e Oportunidades." Presentation at the Colegio de México, Mexico City, Mexico. February 20.

Cardoso, Fernando Henrique. 1996c. "In Praise of the Art of Politics." *Journal of Democracy* 7(3): 7-19.

Cardoso, Fernando Henrique, and Enzo Faletto. 1979. *Dependency and Development in Latin America*. Berkeley, Calif.: University of California Press.

Diniz, Eli. 1982. *Voto e Máquina: Patronagem e Clientelismo no Rio de Janeiro*. Rio de Janeiro: Paz e Terra.

Diniz, Eli. 1997. *Crise, Reforma do Estado e Governabilidade*. Rio de Janeiro: Editora Fundação Getúlio Vargas.

Dos Santos, Theotônio. 1998. "The Theoretical Foundations of the Cardoso Government." *Latin American Perspectives* 25 (1): 53-90.

Dos Santos, Wanderley Guilherme, and Rogério Augusto Schmitt. 1995. "Representação, Proporcionalidade e Democracia." *Monitor Público* 2 (March-May): 49-57.

Economist, The. 1999. "Brazil's Unsteady Recovery." August 28.

Economist Intelligence Unit. 1998. "Brazil: Fiscal Ambitions." March 6.

El Clarín. 2000. "En el 2000 vamos a crecer un 4 por ciento." Interview with Central Bank President Armínio Fraga. January 9.

El Mercurio. 1998a. "Los 'Sin Tierra' no dan tregua." March 28.

El Mercurio. 1998b. "Los sin tierra lanzan nuevo plan de invasión." April 5.

El País. 1998a. "La falta de dinero hace naufragar la campaña electoral de Lula en Brasil." August 5.

El País. 1998b. "Cardoso se apropia de la agenda social de su mayor oponente electoral en Brasil." August 14.

El País. 1999. "Los 'Sin Tierra' son un instrumento de la oposición brasileña." November 30.

Esquerda. 1996. "Entrevista: Presidente Fernando Henrique Cardoso." 21 (January-February).

Estado de São Paulo, O. 1998a. "FH Promete Tudo em Dobro." July 23.

Estado de São Paulo, 1998b. "Governo Têm de Dar Sinais de Controle do Déficit." August 5.

Estado de São Paulo, 1998c. "A Angústia dos Tucanos." August 8.

Estado de São Paulo, O. 1998d. "FHC Domina Espaço no Horário Nobre da TV." August 9.

Estado de São Paulo, O. 1998e. "FHC Mantém Chances de Vitória no Primeiro Turno." August 14.

Estado de São Paulo, O. 1998f. "Investimentos de Americanos no Brasil Duplicaram" and "Portugal e Espanha Investem US$ 16 Bi no Brasil." August 16.

Estado de São Paulo, O. 1999a. "FHC Bate Recorde de Rejeição e Supera Collor." September 14.

Estado de São Paulo, O. 1999b. "O Fenômeno Mobiliza Oposição e Precipita Calendário Político. October 3.

FBIS (Foreign Broadcast Information Service). 1998. "Brazil: Spread of Agrarian Reform Violence Viewed." FBIS-LAT-98-103, April 13.

Fernández Franco, Lorenzo. 1997. "El movimiento de los trabajadores rurales sin tierra y la reforma agraria en Brasil." *América Latina Hoy* 17 (November): 63-76.

Figueiredo, Argelina C., and Fernando Limongi. 1997a. "Presidential Power and Party Behavior in the Legislature." Paper presented at the XX International Congress of the Latin American Studies Association, Guadalajara, Mexico. April 17-19.

Figueiredo, Argelina C., and Fernando Limongi. 1997b. "O Congresso e as Medidas Provisórias: Abdicação ou Delegação?" *Novos Estudos CEBRAP* 47: 127-154.

Financial Times. 1998a. "Brazil: Fiscal Position Worsened in April." July 9.

Financial Times. 1998b. "Brazil: Fiscal Deficit Worsens." August 4.

Financial Times. 1999a. "Brazil: Doing the Sums for the Budget." September 10.

Financial Times. 1999b. Special supplement on Brazil. November 2.

Financial Times. 2000. "Brazil: State Calls Off Block on Debt Repayments." February 7.

Fleischer, David. 1997. "Democracy in Brazil: An Assessment, 1997/1998." Paper presented at the Study Group on the "Sustainability of Latin American Democracy." The Americas Society, New York, November.

Fleischer, David. 1998. "The Cardoso Government's Reform Agenda: A View from the National Congress, 1995-1997." *Journal of Interamerican Studies and World Affairs* 40 (4) Winter.

Fleischer, David. 1999. "Reelection Brazilian Style: The General Elections of 1998." Unpublished manuscript.

Folha de São Paulo. 1996. "Para Lembrar o que Ele Escreveu." Interview with President Fernando Henrique Cardoso. October 13.

Folha de São Paulo. 1997a. "Desvalorizações Cambiais Competitivas." November 27.

Folha de São Paulo. 1997b. "Real Têm Mais Pobres do que o Cruzado." December 8.

Folha de São Paulo. 1998a. "Latinfúndios Escapam da Reforma Agrária de FHC." January 2.

Folha de São Paulo. 1998b. "Deputados Barganham Voto a Favor da Reeleição de FHC." January 9.

Folha de São Paulo. 1998c. "Ruralistas Negociam Dívida do Setor em Troca de Votos." January 10.

Folha de São Paulo. 1998d. "Uma Tortuosa Divagação." January 15.

Folha de São Paulo. 1998e. "FHC, Estado e Mercado" and "Governo Faz Agenda do Desenvolvimento." February 8.

Folha de São Paulo. 1998f. "Setor Público Gasta Mais no Ano Passado." February 21.

Folha de São Paulo. 1998g. "Boas e Más Notícias," and "Estados Têm Pior Resultado." February 27.

Folha de São Paulo. 1998h. "Dívida Pública Dobra com FHC e Chega a R$306 Bi." February 27.

Folha de São Paulo. 1998i. "Indústria Cortou 38.1% dos Empregos entre 1990 e 1997." February 27.

Folha de São Paulo. 1998j. "Rombo: Malan Responsibiliza Estados por Déficit." February 27.

Folha de São Paulo. 1998k. "FHC Ultrapassa Collor em Número de Medidas Provisórias." March 14.

Folha de São Paulo. 1998l. "Sobre a Nova Safra de Investimentos." March 4.

Folha de São Paulo. 1998m. "FHC Defende Reformas Propostas pelo FMI." March 25.

Franco, Gustavo H. B. 1995. *O Plano Real e Outros Ensaios*. Rio de Janeiro: Livraria Francisco Alves.

Gazeta Mercantil Latinoamericana/El Nuevo Herald. 1999. "La inversión extranjera batió record en 1998." October 4-10: 20.

Goertzel, Ted. 1999. *Fernando Henrique Cardoso: Reinventing Democracy in Brazil*. Boulder, Colo.: Lynne Rienner Publishers.

Hagopian, Frances. 1996. *Traditional Politics and Regime Change in Brazil*. New York: Cambridge University Press.

Hochstetler, Kathryn. 2000. "Democratizing Pressures from Below? Social Movements in the New Brazilian Democracy." In *Democratic Brazil: Actors, Institutions, and Processes*, eds. Peter R. Kingstone and Timothy J. Power, 167-184. Pittsburgh: University of Pittsburgh Press.

Holston, James, and Teresa P. R. Caldeira. 1998. "Democracy, Law, and Violence: Disjunctions of Brazilian Citizenship." In *Fault Lines of Democracy in Post-Transition Latin America*, eds. Felipe Agüero and Jeffrey Stark. Coral Gables, Fla.: North-South Center Press at the University of Miami.

IADB (Inter-American Development Bank). 1997. "Indicators of Structural Reform." *Latin American Economic Policies* 1 (Third Quarter): 8.

INCRA (Instituto Nacional de Colonialização e Reforma Agrária). 1996. *Atlas Fundiário 1996*. Brasília, D.F.: INCRA.

INCRA. 1998. "Reforma Agrária — Metas e Resultados." Brasília, D.F.: INCRA.

Istoé. 1998a. *"Decisão em Casa."* July 22.

Istoé. 1998b. "Quanto Mais Frio, Melhor." August 5.

Istoé. 1998c. "Por Fora do Perfil: Nem FHC Nem Lula Reúnem as Qualidades Desejadas pelo Eleitor." August 19.

Istoé. 1999a. "Itamar Levanta o Topete." January 13.

Istoé. 1999b. "Antes Tarde do que Nunca." January 20.

Istoé. 1999c. "Agora Mais Humilde?" March 10.

Istoé. 1999d. "ACM Põe Tudo de Cabeça Pra Baixo." June 23.

Istoé. 1999e. "Mundo Real: A Crise Visível." June 23.

Istoé. 1999f. "O Quebra Cabeças de FHC." July 21.

Istoé. 1999g. "Os Donos da Pobreza." August 11.

Istoé. 1999h. "A Ira da Professora." Interview with Maria da Conceição Tavares. 18 August.

Istoé. 1999i. "A Hora da Virada." September 1.

Istoé. 1999j. "FHC Está Perdido." Interview with Thomas Skidmore. September 1.

Istoé. 1999k. "A Última Vítima de Malan." September 8.

Istoé. 1999l. "Calhamaço de Promessas." September 8.

Istoé. 1999m. "Ajuste Fiscal: Um Rombo nas Contas." October 6.

Istoé. 1999n. "Embrulho Federal." October 13.

Jornal do Brasil. 1997a. "FH Joga Duro e Enfrenta a Crise com 51 Medidas" and "O Pacote de FH." November 11.

Jornal do Brasil. 1997b. "PSDB Só Vence Com Ajuda do PFL," "Collor e FH Venceram Lula Com Voto do País Arcaico," and "PT É Forte nas Capitais." December 14.

Jornal do Brasil. 1997c. "Atlas Eleitoral Revela Fragilidades do PT." December 16.

Jornal do Brasil. 1998a. "Estados Investem R$13 Bilhões." January 18.

Jornal do Brasil. 1998b. "Pesquisas Apontam Empate." June 6.

Jornal do Brasil. 1998c. "FH Diz que É o Anti Caos" and "PSDB Clasifica Lula como 'Tragédia.'" June 6.

Jornal do Brasil. 1998d. "Índice Mede Bem-Estar." July 2.

Jornal do Brasil. 1998e. "PT Proporá um Pacto de Produção." July 2.

Jornal do Brasil. 1998f. "FH Fará a Campanha Mais Cara de Todos." July 6.

Jornal do Brasil. 1998g. "Governo Quer Retomada de Crescimento." July 12.

Jornal do Brasil. 1998h. "Desempenho Aquém da Previsão Oficial." July 14.

Jornal do Brasil. 1998i. "Programa de FHC Destaca o Combate à Probreza." August 2.

Jornal do Brasil. 1998j. "FH Promete 7 Milhões de Empregos." August 8.

Jornal do Brasil. 1998k. "Desemprego Desafia Lula e FH." August 9.

Jornal do Brasil. 1998l. "Manobra de Emergência." August 13.

Jornal do Brasil. 1998m. "Ajuste É Inevitável." August 13.

Jornal do Brasil. 1999. "Governo Fará Pacote para Servidor." October 3.

Korzeniewicz, Roberto Patricio, and William C. Smith. 2000. "Los dos ejes de la tercera vía en América Latina." Paper presented at the XXII International Congress of the Latin American Studies Association. Miami, Florida. March 16-18.

Kugelmas, Eduardo, and Brasílio Sallum Júnior. 1993. "O Leviatã Acorrentado." In *Estado, Mercado, Democracia: Política e Economía Comparada*, ed. Lourdes Sola, 280-299. São Paulo: Paz e Terra.

Kugelmas, Eduardo, and Lourdes Sola. 1997. "On Statecraft, Economic Restructuring, and Democratization: Theoretical Issues in Light of the Brazilian Experience." Paper presented at the XX International Congress of the Latin American Studies Association, Guadalajara, Mexico, April 17-19.

Lamounier, Bolívar. 1996. "Brazil: The Hyperactive Syndrome." In *Constructing Democratic Governance: South America*, eds. Jorge Domínguez and Abraham Lowenthal, 166-187. Baltimore: The Johns Hopkins University Press.

Latin American Monitor: Brazil. 1997a. "Real Plan Nears Mid-Life Crisis?" July.

Latin American Monitor: Brazil. 1997b. "Crisis Gives a Boost to Reform." December.

Latin American Monitor: Brazil. 1998a. "Rivals Erode Cardoso's Opinion Lead." June.

Latin American Monitor: Brazil. 1998b. "Cash-For-Votes Inquiry Averted." July.

Latin American Monitor: Brazil. 1999. "Brazil After Devaluation." February.

Latin American Monitor: Brazil. 2000a. "Truce in Brasília." January.

Latin American Monitor: Brazil. 2000b. "Brazil: Macroeconomic Data and Forecasts." January.

LARR: Brazil (Latin American Regional Reports: Brazil). 1997a. "Industrial Productivity Soars, Or Does It?" May 27.

LARR: Brazil (Latin American Regional Reports: Brazil). 1997b. "CONTAG Learns from the MST." May 27.

LARR: Brazil (Latin American Regional Reports: Brazil). 1997c. "MST Challenges 'Neo-Liberal' Model." September 9.

LARR: Brazil (Latin American Regional Reports: Brazil). 1997d. "Setback over Ceiling on Salaries." 1 July.

LARR: Brazil (Latin American Regional Reports: Brazil). 1997e. "Portrait of a Massive Shake-Up." November 18.

LARR: Brazil (Latin American Regional Reports: Brazil). 1998a. "MST Warns of More Rural Conflict." January 6.

LARR: Brazil (Latin American Regional Reports: Brazil). 1998b. "Progress on Civil Service, Pensions." March 17.

LARR: Brazil (Latin American Regional Reports: Brazil). 1998c. "MST Links Up With Urban Unions." April 28.

LARR: Brazil (Latin American Regional Reports: Brazil). 1998d. "Investment Turnaround." June 2.

Londoño, J.L., and M. Székely. 1997. *Persistent Poverty and Excess Inequality: Latin America, 1970-1995.* Working Paper Series 357. Washington, D.C.: Inter-American Development Bank.

Lustig, Nora, and Ruthanne Deutsch. 1998. *The Inter-American Development Bank and Poverty Reduction: An Overview.* Revised Version. Sustainable Development Department, Poverty and Inequality Advisory Unit. Washington, D.C.: Inter-American Development Bank. May.

Mahon, James. 1996. *Mobile Capital and Latin American Development.* University Park, Pa.: The Pennsylvania State University Press.

Mainwaring, Scott. 1992-1993. "Brazilian Party Underdevelopment in Comparative Perspective." *Political Science Quarterly* 107: 677-707.

Mainwaring, Scott. 1995a. "Brazil: Weak Parties, Feckless Democracy." In *Building Democratic Institutions: Party Systems in Latin America*, eds. Scott Mainwaring and Timothy R. Scully, 354-398. Stanford, Calif.: Stanford University Press.

Mainwaring, Scott. 1995b. "Parties, Elections, and Society in Democratic Brazil, 1985-1994." Paper presented at the XIX International Congress of the Latin American Studies Association, Washington, D.C. September 28-30.

Mainwaring, Scott. 1997. "Multipartism, Robust Federalism, and Presidentialism in Brazil." In *Presidentialism and Democracy in Latin America*, eds. Scott Mainwaring and Matthew Shugart, 55-109. New York: Cambridge University Press.

Mainwaring, Scott. 1999. *Rethinking Party Systems in the Third Wave of Democratization: The Case of Brazil.* Stanford, Calif.: Stanford University Press.

Martin, Scott B. 1997. "Beyond Corporatism: New Patterns of Representation in the Brazilian Auto Industry." In *The New Politics of Inequality in Latin America: Rethinking Participation and Representation*, eds. Douglas Chalmers, Carlos Vilas, Katherine Hite, et al., 45-71. New York: Oxford University Press.

Melo, Carlos Ranulfo P. 1999. "A Dança das cadeiras." *Conjuntura Política* 11 (September). http://cevep.ufmg.br/bacp/setembro011.

Miami Herald. 1997. "Brazil Will Be Forced to Devalue its Currency, Economist Predicts." November 18.

Montero, Alfred P. 2000. "Devolving Democracy? Political Decentralization and the New Brazilian Federalism." In *Democratic Brazil: Actors, Institutions, and Processes*, eds. Peter R. Kingstone and Timothy J. Power, 58-76. Pittsburgh: University of Pittsburgh Press.

Morely, Samuel. 1997. "Poverty During Recovery and Reform in Latin America: 1985-1995." UNDP/IADB/CEPAL project on "Macroeconomic Policies and Poverty in Latin America and the Caribbean." Washington, D.C.: Inter-American Development Bank. Mimeo.

Morrison, Andrew, Mayra Buvinic, and Michael Shifter. 1999. "The Violent Americas? Causes, Consequences and Policy Implications." Washington, D.C.: Inter-American Development Bank, Sustainable Development Department.

MST (Movimento dos Trabalhadores Rurais Sem-Terra). 1996. *Agenda MST 1997.* São Paulo: MST.

Navarro, Zander. 2000. "Breaking New Ground: Brazil's MST." *NACLA Report on the Americas* 33 (5), March/April.

New York Times. 1998a. "Brazil Pays to Shield Currency, and the Poor See the True Cost." February 5.

New York Times. 1998b. "Brazil's Brighter Future." Editorial. February 19.

New York Times. 1998c. "Brazil's Economic Half-Steps." August 1.

New York Times. 1999. "Candidate's Interest in Debt Renegotiation Worries Brazilian Financiers." October 7.

New York Times. 2000. "After Crisis, Reform Bills Languish in Brazil." January 9.

Nylen, William. 1997. "Reconstructing the Workers' Party (PT): Lessons from North-Eastern Brazil." In *The New Politics of Inequality in Latin America: Rethinking Participation and Representation*, eds. Douglas Chalmers, Carlos Vilas, Katherine Hite, et al., 421-446. New York: Oxford University Press.

Nylen, William. 2000. 'The Making of a Loyal Opposition: The Workers' Party (PT) and the Consolidation of Democracy in Brazil." In *Democratic Brazil: Actors, Institutions, and Processes*, eds. Peter R. Kingstone and Timothy J. Power, 126-143. Pittsburgh: The University of Pittsburgh Press.

O Globo. 1998. "Equipe Econômica Ressalta Ganhos Sociais do Real." July 2.

O'Donnell, Guillermo A. 1978. "Permanent Crisis and the Failure to Create a Democratic Regime in Argentina, 1955-66." In Juan J. Linz and Alfred Stepan, eds. *The Breakdown of Democratic Regimes: Latin America.* Baltimore, MD: The Johns Hopkins University Press.

Pereira, Anthony W. 1997a. *The End of the Peasantry: The Rural Labor Movement in Northeast Brazil, 1961-1988.* Pittsburgh: Pittsburgh University Press.

Pereira, Anthony W. 1997b. "The Crisis of Developmentalism and the Rural Labor Movement of North-East Brazil." In *The New Politics of Inequality in Latin America: Rethinking Participation and Representation*, eds. Douglas Chalmers, Carlos Vilas, Katherine Hite, et al., 95-114. New York: Oxford University Press.

Pereira, Anthony W. 2000. "An Ugly Democracy? State Violence and the Rule of Law in Postauthoritarian Brazil." In *Democratic Brazil: Actors, Institutions, and Processes*, eds. Peter R. Kingstone and Timothy J. Power, 217-235. Pittsburgh: University of Pittsburgh Press.

Pinheiro, Paulo Sérgio. 1997. "Popular Responses to State-Sponsored Violence in Brazil." In *The New Politics of Inequality in Latin America: Rethinking Participation and Representation*, eds. Douglas Chalmers, Carlos Vilas, Katherine Hite, et al., 261-280. New York: Oxford University Press.

Power, Timothy J. 1997. "Quais São os Valores da Social Democracia Hoje? Algumas Reflexões Comparadas sobre a Crise de Identidade do PSDB." Political Science Department, Louisiana State University. Mimeo.

Power, Timothy J. 1998. "The Pen is Mightier than the Congress: Presidential Decree Power in Brazil." In *Executive Decree Authority*, eds. John Carey and Matthew Shugart, 197-230. New York: Cambridge University Press.

Power, Timothy J. 2000a. "Political Institutions in Democratic Brazil: Politics As a Permanent Constitutional Convention." In *Democratic Brazil: Actors, Institutions, and Processes*, eds. Peter R. Kingstone and Timothy J. Power, 17-35. Pittsburgh: University of Pittsburgh Press.

Power, Timothy J. 2000b. *Elites, Institutions, and Democratization: The Political Right in Posauthoritarian Brazil.* University Park, Pa.: Penn State University Press.

Power, Timothy J., David V. Fleischer, and Jales Ramos Marques. 2000. "From Social Democracy to Neoliberalism: The Transformation of the PSDB in Brazil." Paper presented to the XXII International Congress of the Latin American Studies Association, Miami, Florida. March 16-18.

Reich, Gary M. 1998. "The Brazilian Constitution Ten Years Later: Reconsidering an Ugly Constitution." Political Science Department, University of Kansas. Mimeo.

Rosenn, Keith. 1990. "Brazil's New Constitution: An Exercise in Transient Consitutionalism for a Transitional Society." *American Journal of Comparative Law* 38 (Fall): 773-802.

Sáinz, Pedro, and Alfredo Calcagno. 1999. "La economía brasileña ante el Plan Real y su crisis." *Temas de Coyuntura 4*. Santiago, Chile: Comisión Económica de América Latina y el Caribe (ECLAC), División de Estadística y Proyecciones Económicas. July.

Samuels, David. 2000. "Money, Elections, and Democracy in Brazil." Unpublished paper. Morris, Minn.: University of Minnesota, Department of Political Science. January.

Schmidt, Benício Viero. 1999. "A Conjuntura Política e a Agenda Pública no Brasil de FHC." Unpublished manuscript. November.

SECOM (Secretaria de Comunicação Social/Presidência da República). 1998a. *Real: Quatro Anos Que Mudaram o Brasil.* Brasília, D.F.: Secretaria de Comunicação Social. July 1.

SECOM. 1998b. *Brasil em Ação: Resultados do Primeiro Ano*. Brasília, D.F.: Secretaria de Comunicação Social.

SECOM. 1998c. "Agrarian Reform: Brazil's Commitment." Brasília, D.F.: Secretaria de Comunicação Social.

Selcher, Wayne A. 1998. "The Politics of Decentralized Federalism, National Diversification, and Regionalism in Brazil." *Journal of Interamerican Studies and World Affairs* 40(4) Winter.

Simonens da Silva, Luiz Afonso. 1999. "Corrupção e Promiscuidade entre os Setores Público e Privado na Gestão do Sistema Financiero Nacional: A Liberalização Financiera e a Abertura da Conta de Capitais (As Contas 'CC-5')." Comissão Brasileira Justiça e Paz (CBJP) da Conferência Nacional dos Bispos do Brasil (CNBB). November.

Sola, Lourdes. 1994. "The State, Structural Reform, and Democratization in Brazil." In *Democracy, Markets, and Structural Reform in Latin America*, eds. William C. Smith, Carlos A. Acuña, and Eduardo A. Gamarra, 151-182. Coral Gables, Fla.: North-South Center Press at the University of Miami.

Sola, Lourdes. 1995. "Estado, Regime Fiscal e Ordem Monetária: Qual Estado?" *Revista Brasileira de Ciências Sociais* 10 (27): 29-60.

Souza, Celina. 1997. *Constitutional Engineering in Brazil: The Politics of Federalism and Decentralization*. London: Macmillan.

Tardanico, Richard, and Rafael Menjívar Larín, eds. 1997. *Global Restructuring, Employment, and Social Inequality in Urban Latin America.* Coral Gables, Fla.: North-South Center Press at the University of Miami.

U.S. Department of State. 1998. *Brazil Country Report on Human Rights Practices for 1997.* Bureau of Democracy, Human Rights, and Labor. Washington, D.C.: U.S. Department of State. January 30.

Veja. 1998a. Interview with Labor Minister Edward Amadeo. April 15.

Veja. 1998b. "A Contradição de FHC." March 4.

Veja. 1998c. "Procura-se um Candidato." May 20.

Washington Post. 1998. "Study Considers Worst Case of Asian Collapse." August 1.

Weyland, Kurt. 1996a. *Democracy Without Equity: Failures of Reform in Brazil.* Pittsburgh: University of Pittsburgh Press.

Weyland, Kurt. 1996b. "Obstacles to Social Reform in Brazil's New Democracy." *Comparative Politics* 29 (1): 1-22.

Weyland, Kurt. 1997. "'Growth With Equity' in Chile's New Democracy." *Latin American Research Review* 32(1).

Weyland, Kurt. 1998. "The Brazilian State in the New Democracy." *Journal of Interamerican Studies and World Affairs* 39 (4): 63-94.

Zaverucha, Jorge. "The 1988 Brazilian Constitution and Its Authoritarian Legacy: Formalizing Democracy while Gutting Its Essence." Paper presented at the XX International Congress of the Latin American Studies Association, Guadalajara, Mexico, April 17-19.

CHAPTER 3

Global Economics and Local Politics in Trinidad's Divestment Program

ANTHONY P. MAINGOT

This chapter focuses on the complex interaction between local political, social, and economic exigencies and the imperatives of the global economy in Trinidad. Local systems operate according to the perceived needs of their elites and the moral codes and biases of the political culture. In Trinidad, the dominant biases have to do with racial competition. For more than five decades, efforts have been made to use the state to extend economic rights to underprivileged Afro-Trinidadians. Since the mid-1980s, however, a shift in macroeconomic thinking has led to liberalization and a growing gap between the traditional nationalist/statist ideology and the actual decisions of political elites. The chapter explores this unresolved incongruity and discusses Petrotrin, the national petroleum company that oversees the fast-growing oil and gas sector.

PREFACE

This chapter focuses on the complex interaction between local political, social, and economic exigencies and the imperatives of the global economy on the island of Trinidad and Tobago, henceforth referred to as Trinidad. The general context of this study is the global economy and the ideology that explains and justifies it, neoliberalism. While it is true that no nation is an "island," it is even truer that local systems operate according to the perceived needs of their elites and the moral codes and biases of the political culture in general. In Trinidad, the dominant biases have to do with racial competition. The task is to study the consequences of the island's economic insertion into the global economy, as that affects the political, social, and economic competition between the races. This is hardly an academic argument. Data on the level of foreign investments, and the sectors to which they have been directed, make the speed and dimensions of Trinidad's insertion into the global economy quite evident.

Table 1.
U.S. Direct Investments in Trinidad, 1996-1999

	Totals (in US$ millions)	Petrochemicals (%)	Oil/Gas (%)
1996	589	55	34
1997	1,228	51	44
1998 (est.)	1,378	44	42
1999 (est.)	840	32	50

Source: U.S. Embassy, Trinidad and Tobago, July 18, 1998.

Measured on a per capita basis, Trinidad is second only to Canada as a U.S. investment partner in the Western Hemisphere. The investments, and the liberalization program that make them possible, are palpable evidence that the elites are making macroeconomic decisions that conform with the rules of economic conduct recommended by multinational lending agencies such as the International Monetary Fund (IMF) and the World Bank. Together, these rules of economic behavior have come to be known as the "Washington Consensus." However, such economic decisions have not been accompanied by a similar shift in the public rhetoric of the island's elites; the politics of race and the competition for control of the state to further the economic benefits of particular groups is still the ideological standard.

This chapter argues that a major part of the tenacity of the link between control of the state and the economic advancement of specific sectors of the society is that it has had a long existence. In fact, it was in the context of the historical racial antagonism on the island that the British colonial administration began to use the state to extend civil and economic rights to the underprivileged Afro-Trinidadians, a practice that was continued after independence. Despite strong reservations about nationalization and socialism on the part of the major nationalist political elites, they saw the political advantages of expanding the public sector and escalating the rhetoric of the advantages of a "people's sector" even more. The latter was a response to both local and international ideological pressures coming from a resurgent Third World. The elites' rhetoric made an association between capitalism, dependency, the private sector, and racial exclusivity. Although various studies could not establish a direct causal link between racism and job allocation in the private sector, an evident correlation between them established a climate of opinion that drove political actions. The Black Power movement of 1970 intensified this race-private sector association, compelling the Afro-Trinidadian political elites to accelerate the nationalization of major businesses and agricultural enterprises. For more than five decades, all major trends encouraged a significant expansion of the public sector. The nationalization of the petroleum industry, leading to the establishment of Petrotrin, the indisputable crown jewel of the economy, represented the culmination of this nationalization process. It continues in state hands.

In the mid-1980s there began — globally and in Trinidad — a shift in macroeconomic thinking. With little if any public debate, the idea of liberalizing and downsizing the state sector began to gather strength among the island's political elites. This shift, and especially the privatization process and the enormous flow of foreign investments that were an integral part of it, began to increase the evident gap — tg] incongruity — between the traditional nationalist/statist ideology and rhetoric and the actual decisions of the elite. That incongruity has been magnified by the political victory of the Indo-Trinidadians, who have historically been much less dependent on state beneficence than the Afro-Trinidadian sector. Despite all these actual changes in the economy and politics, however, there is no evidence that either the Indo-Trinidadian or Afro-Trinidadian political and intellectual elites are ready to espouse openly an ideology that explains and justifies the type of economic opening they have been pursuing for so long. They are still referring to the state as a "provider" or "server" and not merely a "facilitator" of private initiatives.

Because sociological theory teaches us that at some point publicly espoused ideology and actual behavior will have to become more aligned, it is a matter of speculation as to whether that alignment will be toward a change of ideology (liberalization), a renewal of statist behavior, or some new formula or paradigm engendered by local and international circumstances.

Because it is in the oil and gas sector that the trends toward foreign investment and the development of what Peter Haas calls "epistemic" communities (Haas 1992) are evident, this study gives special attention to that sector through a case study of Petrotrin.

INTRODUCTION: GLOBALISM'S IDEOLOGICAL CONTEXT

The leading principle and ideological influence on American society, wrote Charles A. Beard in 1932, was the idea of progress: a belief in the ever-increasing empowerment of humanity through technological knowledge. This belief in progress, said Beard, "remains, and will remain, a fundamental tenet of American society.... While vigor is left in the race it will operate with all the force of a dynamic idea rooted in purpose, will and opportunity" (Beard 1932, xxxvii).

It is paradoxical that Beard should have been so adamant about the permanency of this idea, for he was much more skeptical about the fixity of ideas in general. During the course of history, Beard noted in the same text, it has been proven that "whole periods are marked by particular types of thought, particular conceptions of life and its values." What is more, these changing constellations of thought affect the whole society. "Neither statesman nor artist, nor writers," Beard concluded, "can escape their pressures" (Beard 1932, xi).

This latter, more general theoretical assertion of Beard is the one that has found the most support in the scholarly literature and is one of the two major theoretical assumptions of this chapter. As early as the 1930s, for instance, Carl L. Becker explored the evolution of the idea of progress, finding its origins in the Middle Ages, even as it changed in content and thrust over the centuries. What determined the interpretation of the idea at any particular stage was the social context. It was this understanding that ideologies change over time that led Becker to formulate the sociological principle that arguments or ideas will command assent not so much "upon the logic that conveys them" but "upon the climate of opinion in which they are sustained" (Becker 1932, 5).

The emphasis on climates of opinion and the societal contexts that engender, sustain, or change them was fully and successfully explored by Karl Mannheim in his 1929 study, *Ideology and Utopia,* which, when published in English in 1936, became the standard text in the field. Suffice it to say that the type of macroeconomic ideas and programs analyzed here — statism and neoliberalism — have not and do not exist in a vacuum; they have both national and international contexts. This analysis emphasizes the local contexts of global ideas, on the assumption that these local conditions — especially those called "maximalist biases," to be introduced later — invariably have the greatest influence on the climate of opinions.

This emphasis on local conditions and actors leads to another major theoretical assumption of this study: that there cannot exist for long an incongruence or divergence between elite ideology and behavior and that of the masses. This assumption holds across schools of sociological theory. Karl Marx's postulate in the *Communist Manifesto* that "the ruling ideas of each age have been the ideas of its ruling class" is not far removed from the position of contemporary structural-functionalists, which asserts that "where the 'ruling ideas' are not those of the ruling class, the latter is correspondingly likely to lose its supremacy" (Lasswell and Kaplan 1950, 208). This explains why elites will always attempt to sustain a condition of compatibility between public predispositions (biases) and the values on which the elites base their programs and, ultimately, their power. When and where there exists an incongruence or incompatibility between ideology (biases) and elite practice, both particular incentives and particular constraints act to reestablish and then perpetuate a condition of compatibility.

This conceptualization goes directly to the concern of this study: that there is in Trinidad an evident gap between existing political elite ideological utterances and public preferences for a particular economic regime, namely, statism, and the quite different macroeconomic policies pursued by these same elites, neoliberalism. Although this is a case study, it certainly is not alone in this concern. There is a widely held belief that in many countries the transition to globalism and neoliberal reforms has taken place without meaningful intellectual debate. And, lack of debate, says Jeremy Adelman, generates memory lapses. To Adelman, the argument that globalization implies a new era does not mean that old themes, debates, and controversies are settled. "What globalization does," says Adelman, "is force us to recast earlier formulations rather than dismiss them" (Adelman 1998, 12).

Part of the debate that has to be reengaged is a clear understanding that neoliberalism and globalism are ideologies, climates of opinion, created and sustained by particular elites. So overlooked is this fact in the new rarefied climate of opinion that Fareed Zakaria sees the need to remind us of a truism: Free markets and free trade "are not naturally occurring and self-sustaining. They rest on an edifice of politics" (Zakaria 1998, 17). To Zakaria this is especially relevant for Asia, where he believes the 1997-1998 economic crisis could undermine support for an open global economy and economic and political liberalization across the world. But why would an economic crisis undermine such a widely held and practiced economic system? In part, it appears, because in some important sectors there has been a gap between political rhetoric and economic practice. In Indonesia and Malaysia, for instance, economic nationalists have been practicing what Zakaria calls "a clever form of duplicity": making fiery anti-Western speeches while adopting Western-style liberal policies. As we shall see, such double-talk, albeit in milder form, also characterizes the case of Trinidad.

It is essential, therefore, that we put the present climate of opinion favoring neoliberalism — in Washington and many other capitals — in the context of contemporary globalization. As the term is used today, globalization refers to the compression of the world, a compression driven by four processes: 1) a world economy with integrated financial productive and trade networks, 2) a communications and information revolution, 3) global consumerism, and 4) a new assortment of political cultures that attempt to coexist with, or resist, processes one through three (Stark 1998; Greider 1997; Sklair 1995). It is not only that the traditional constraints of geography and national politics and economics are receding, it is also that people are keenly aware that this is occurring because they are experiencing the consequences of it. One consequence is a reduced range of economic choices. As Jeffrey Stark puts it, "Delinking from the world economy is no longer discussed as a serious option" (Stark 1998, 71).

There are many places where there is an incongruity between elite ideology and rhetoric and elite practice; and, as the sociological discussion above reminds us, this incongruity cannot be long sustained. This caveat seems especially applicable to official Washington discourse on the hemisphere's "first generation," or "first stage," of reforms, namely, the macroeconomic policies of globalism that were initially put in place in the 1980s and institutionalized on paper in the 1994 Summit of the Americas in Miami. Also known as the Washington Consensus, it represents one of the most comprehensive meetings of minds regarding development between government elites worldwide, Washington, and the major international institutions, such as the World Bank, the IMF, and other regional multilateral lending agencies. To quote Mark L. Schneider, then deputy director of the U.S. Agency for International Development (USAID):

> Those first stage reforms changed the rules guiding macroeconomic behavior. They also got governments to stop doing the things they should not have been doing. They opened markets, privatized state enterprises, provided monetary stability. They brought a consensus on the need for fiscal balance, and unleashed a truly astounding level of private investment and private sector-led trade (Schneider 1998, 6).

In these first years of the new millennium, there is a call to expand this neoliberal consensus into a "second generation" to include wider social and political concerns.

Even though the increasing turmoil in the world's financial markets in the late 1990s gave rise to dissenting voices about the role of global capitalism, generally, and of the IMF, particularly (Rodrik 1997), no one seriously doubts that neoliberal macroeconomic behavior is first institutionalized, and second, that the second generation now has to pick up the pace and correct past missteps of the first generation's program. This second generation had its own debut at the Summit of the Americas II in Santiago, Chile, in March 1998.

Table 2. Selected Economic Indicators

	1986	1987	1988	1989	1990	1991	1992	1993	1994	1995	1996	1997
Nominal GDP (US$billions)	4.8	4.8	4.1	4.3	5.1	5.3	5.2	4.5	5.0	5.2	5.5	5.7
Real GDP Growth (%)	-4.3	-5.3	-3.7	-0.7	-0.1	2.7	-1.7	-1.6	3.8	2.4	3.2	3.7
Inflation Rate (%)	7.7	10.8	7.8	11.4	11.1	3.8	6.6	10.7	8.8	5.3	3.6	3.8
Unemployment Rate %	16.6	22.3	22.0	22.0	20.0	18.5	19.6	19.8	18.4	17.2	16.1	15.5
Gov't Deficit as %-GDP	-8.0	-7.2	-6.5	-4.1	-1.3	-0.2	2.8	-0.2	0.3	-0.2	1.5	0.8
Exchange Rate (TTUS)	3.60	3/60	3.84	4.25	4.25	4.25	4.25	5.35	5.87	5.89	6.00	6.25
Exports (US$millions)	1,358	1,397	1,455	1,535	1,935	1,986	1,870	1,662	1,972	2,477	2,421	2,589
Imports (USSmillions)	1,465	1,175	1,174	1,203	1,109	1,667	1,436	1,499	1,374	1,885	2,041	2,369
Trade Balance	-107	222	281	332	826	319	434	163	598	592	380	220
Current Account Balance	-632	-247	-118	-67	430	-63	35	-107	236	270	92	-105
Gross Official Int'l Reserves	394	224	204	378	466	340	208	236	354	360	482	576
Crude Oil Prices (US$/barrel)	1,487	1,914	1,595	1,958	2,412	2,162	2,057	1,845	1,714	1,781	2,110	2,000

GDP= gross domestic product TT=Trinidad and Tobago

Sources: Central Bank of Trinidad and Tobago; Ministry of Finance; Central Statistical Office, Trinidad and Tobago, 1997.

Sensing that this line of analysis is a clear expression of the U.S. idea of progress, one is hardly disposed to judge it too harshly. It suits the present climate of opinion among U.S. elites. Does it speak for all elites, however? It is precisely because this question raises doubt that one has to deepen and widen geographically the historical analysis of the origins of what is called the first generation. In fact, for much of the world — and certainly for the case analyzed here — we have to understand the immediate post-World War II generation of nationalist decolonizers, reaching beyond the Western Hemisphere to include what used to be referred to as the "South" or "Third World." The purpose of such a task is neither ideological reaffirmation nor the satiation of historical curiosity. By showing the continuities as well as the changes in the various climates of opinion and ideologies in macroeconomic thinking over longer periods of time and greater geographical areas, we avoid the dangers that can result from historical amnesia. A major characteristic of the former condition is to forget that all ideologies have social contexts and that the most important of these is invariably the local, political one. It is precisely this awareness of the intricacies, and, ultimately, unpredictablility, of the interplay between the global and the local that is leading more cautious scholars to make two arguments. The first is a normative one: avoid rushing to judgment with arguments of "betrayal" and "capitulation" by the many former leftists now in power (see Chapter 2.). The other argument is more broadly theoretical and epistemological: a return to the sociology of development as an approach that balances the study of the global with an understanding of individual national socio-historical contexts (Portes 1997). In both approaches there is an awareness that even as national leaders attempt to adjust to the new constraints and opportunities of globalism, they have to contend with their local contexts. This is particularly true regarding politics and the flow of information that governs it.

Noting that the state has proven to be more resilient than the "modernists" anticipated, two of the original formulators of the idea of interdependence now confess that "prophets of a new cyberworld, like modernists before them, often overlook how much the new world overlaps and rests on the traditional world in which power depends on geographically based institutions" (Keohane and Nye 1998, 83). Jeffrey Stark sums up the importance of studying the local even as we accept the realities of a globalized world by cautioning, "it bears repeating . . . that the creation of new intersubjective realms under the force of globalization is ultimately a local and indeterminate process that can just as easily lead to resistance and the construction of intensely parochial identities as to universal values and cosmopolitan solidarities" (Stark 1998, 81).

In this study of changing economic policies in Trinidad, we look at climates of opinion, the national and international forces that engendered them, and the possible incongruence or incompatibilities between the known ideology and rhetoric regarding macroeconomic policies of the elites and their actual decisions. Given our emphasis on the role of local institutions and arrangements, it is important that we review the origins of the island's social structure in the next section.

TRINIDAD: INTRODUCTORY NOTES

The last of the major British conquests in the Caribbean (1797), the twin-island republic of Trinidad and Tobago, is 2,000 square miles in surface with a population of 1,213,000. Because it was conquered by the Spanish and settled by a French group of planters before the British conquest, and because it had a short history of African slavery and a longer history of East Indian indentureship, it has a very diversified population. This ethnic and cultural pluralism is more than just of folkloric interest; it influences everything on the island, including short- and long-range macroeconomic policies. Recent population data available at the Central Statistical Office reveals the following figures as of 1990 (Table 3):

Table 3.
Ethnic Distribution, 1990

Ethnic Group	(%)	Religion	(%)
African descent	39.6	Roman Catholic	29.4
East Indian descent	40.3	Hindu	23.8
White	0.6	Anglican	10.9
Chinese	0.4	Islam	5.8
Mixed	18.4	Presbyterian	3.4
		Other	25.7

Source: Central Statistical Office, Trinidad and Tobago, 1997.

It can be argued that from the time the island was granted self-government in 1956 until the elections of 1995, it was governed by elites representing the island's African descent and mixed populations. Except for the one term governed by the Organization for National Reconstruction (ONR), the period was dominated by the People's Nationalist Movement (PNM). This political party was founded by Eric Williams in 1953 and was, from its inception, identified with a strong commitment to parliamentary democracy and a mild form of statist ideology. It was Williams who took Trinidad to independence in 1962 and governed it until his death in 1980.

Although, as we shall note, the system has not been without its problems, certain key features of the Westminster parliamentary system have proven to be well suited to this particular society. For instance, the split executive position (an appointed, largely ceremonial president and an elected prime minister), the bicameral legislature (appointed Senate and elected House), and the independent judiciary all allow for the optimal use of available talent in this multiracial society. Even members of the small but influential minorities can make their contribution to governance.

Not surprising, political transitions generally have been peaceful events governed by democratic rules of the game. Since universal suffrage was granted in 1946, there have been seven national elections and one during the period of the West Indies Federation (1958-1961). As a result of the most recent elections (1995), the fundamentally Indian-based United National Congress (UNC) and its founding member and political leader, Basdeo Panday, won a similar share of seats as did the

PNM but was put into power after forming a coalition with the smaller, Tobago-based party, the National Alliance for Reconstruction (NAR). Because 1995 represented the first time Indo-Trinidadians have held national power, there were early predictions of racial confrontations and political instability. As far as instability is concerned, there has been little. Part of the explanation is the Westminster-style political system with its single-member constituencies and the tight party discipline (increased in Trinidad by ethnic allegiances). One can expect this coalition to be quite stable. The following additional features of the political system do provide some insight into how the broader society functions:

1. Although the parties are racially based, the wider society as a whole shares a commitment to democratic government and human rights. Note, for instance, the overwhelming rejection of the 1990 attempt to overthrow the government (Table 4). The independent judiciary, with final appeals to the Privy Council, House of Lords, United Kingdom, is widely perceived by the legal profession as a fundamental guarantee of civil rights. In short, the system enjoys legitimacy.

Table 4.
Attitudes Toward Attempted Coup d'État, 1990

Response	African	Indian	Other
Right to attempt overthrow	18	18	12
Wrong to attempt overthrow	75	73	81
No opinion	4	4	5
Refuse to answer	4	4	2

Source: Ryan, 1991b, *The Muslimeen Grab for Power,* 229.

2. Despite the ethnic/racial divisions, there has always been some attempt at ethnic distribution in certain high-profile state institutions. Although as of 1995 the government has been Indian controlled, the chief justice (appointed by the previous administration) belongs to the small white minority, the president is of African descent, and the commissioner of police and commander of the defense forces are of mixed heritage. As our case study of Petrotrin, the crown jewel of the economy, will demonstrate, there is, at least at high technical levels, the beginnings of what are called "epistemic" communities with their emphasis on skills rather than race.

3. There is an active and independent press, radio, and television network that has to be regarded as one of the guardians of the island's democracy. Evidence of the prickly independence of this Fourth Estate was its vociferous reaction to a 1997 government green paper — meant to be a discussion paper, not a policy statement — on the responsibilities of the press. Even though the government suggestions were relatively innocuous individually, the press did not look at the suggestions but rather at the probable intentions behind them. The government's basic approach was perceived as a potentially dangerous encroachment on the autonomy and independence of the press, and, consequently, it was quickly withdrawn.

4. Undergirding all these characteristics is a commendable educational system. Literacy is 98 percent, and school attendance rates at all three levels of education are among the highest in the Third World (World Bank 1998, 80-84). The University of the West Indies, St. Augustine campus, enrolled nearly 5,000 students in 1996, and its scientific and technical departments are highly regarded. Most of the decisionmakers in the oil industry are former members of its faculty. The university is clearly the hatchery for a growing epistemic community on the island.

There is no hiding the most serious problem of the society because it is inherent: the perpetual perception of racial conflict. Perceptions govern behavior, and the perceptions are that there has been an increase in ethnic tensions since 1995. Whatever the perceptions, and aside from rhetorical skirmishes between political leaders that reached a crescendo in mid-1997, there have not been any violent confrontations between Afro- and Indo-Trinidadians. In fact, there never has been such a confrontation in the island's history. Part of the explanation has been demographic: Afro-Trinidadians tend to be urban, Indo-Trinidadians rural.

Up to now, there has been little if any competition for land, housing, or even jobs. Afro-Trinidadians have tended to work in urban crafts and have taken government jobs; Indo-Trinidadians have been agriculturalists, sugar estate workers, and self-employed. As we shall note, all this, in the context of a neoliberal divestment program, might well have resulted in a paradoxical situation: Afro-Trinidadians, who held political power between 1956 and 1995, now find themselves at a greater economic disadvantage than the erstwhile politically disadvantaged Indo-Trinidadians. Will this lead to serious confrontation for the first time in the island's history?

One recalls that the two most serious threats to the established democratic order came in 1970 and 1990 during periods of economic downturn and after significant mobilizations among the urban masses. It is impossible to predict for certain that the present calm will be preserved; let it be recorded, however, that the UNC-led government entered its fifth productive year in power and seemed to have abandoned an early propensity to make alarmist claims about plots and conspiracies. If the present performance of the economy is sustained, chances are that the island will move ahead peacefully. All indications are that the sustained rate of foreign investment, the jobs created in construction for an expanding high-technology industrial park, and the ability to control inflation will compensate somewhat for the dramatic and unexpected drop in world oil prices in 1998, insuring political calm for at least the short term.

RACE, EMPLOYMENT, AND THE ORIGINS OF STATE INVOLVEMENT

Although the growth of the state sector was increased substantially after independence, the activist role of the state did not begin with independence and with the political victory of the Afro-Trinidadian-based PNM.

In the most complete fiscal survey done of the British Caribbean on the eve of federation (1957), English scholar A.R. Prest stated that most of these British

West Indian territories had passed "overnight" from being undergoverned to being almost overgoverned in economic matters. This was due, in large part, to the experiences with a "vast apparatus of direct controls during World War II but also to the shift in political power from the "plantocracy" to newer parties ... "many of them imbued with socialist ideas" (Prest 1957, 8). The results of this government intervention, said Prest, were not encouraging and should, therefore, be considerably reduced. Two specific reasons were given to support a reduced role of the state in the economy: 1) A smaller state sector would minimize the negative effects of the relative lack of personnel with the experience and expertise to direct and administer major economic and social affairs; and 2) it would reduce the negative impact of what the author called the "intensity of special pleading and lobbying of politicians and administrators" for subsidies and handouts. In short, in the Trinidad-Tobago of the 1950s, Prest found a very large state sector expanding because of local lobbying but mostly badly administered and losing money. This was found to be the case with, for instance, the railway, the marketing board, the post office, the electricity and water authorities, and the Agricultural Credit Bank.

What Prest's survey failed to mention, however, was that without government (that is, the Colonial Office) intervention, there would have been little if any infrastructural development or credits for agriculture and small industry. Indeed, without this state intervention, virtually all significant economic activity would have remained concentrated in the hands of a small circle of foreign businessmen. The British-owned sugar industry had long been the darling of the government, and all the private banks at the time were foreign owned and mostly concerned with the financing of external trade. Because of these ties to the large commercial firms, these banks hired the children of that sector. The crucial implications of the virtually perfect correlation between leadership of the economy and race were political. As Williams wrote in one of his early books, "Essentially the difference between capital and labor in the Caribbean is the difference between black and white" (Williams 1942, 68). To early nationalists such as Williams, this racial exclusivity was neither accidental nor the result of "free market forces"; rather, it was the result of the actions of the Imperial state in favor of its elites. The persistence of this pattern a whole decade after independence was apparent in the systematic studies that began to proliferate, a response to the changed climate of opinion (Braithwaite 1953; Camejo 1971; Harewood 1971; Oxaal 1968; Ryan 1972). Because most of these studies could not prove definitely that it was systematic racial discrimination that governed the hiring practices of the major banks and companies (they considered other factors such as the urban-rural divide, levels of education, cultural predispositions, and family ties), the consequences were of little political import; the association had already been made between the colonial state, foreign ownership, and racial discrimination. Harewood's explanation might be perplexing coming from a social scientist, but the political meaning was unequivocal: "In fact, the existence of racial discrimination in employment [in Trinidad-Tobago] is generally accepted as a fact and for the present study could therefore be taken as an assumption rather than as a hypothesis" (Harewood 1971, 300).

As Selwyn Ryan expressed it in his discussion of the appointment of an official commission to investigate racial discrimination, one did not need a commission to report on "what was readily visible to all except the blind" (Ryan

1972, 178). The reasons why it was "generally accepted" are evident in Acton Camejo's findings (see Table 5) showing the dramatic underrepresentation of browns and blacks among the business elite. The move toward political independence could hardly escape the new climate of opinion, which called on the new state to redress the actions of the old state or, at least, to bring about different outcomes from state action.

It is thus not difficult to understand the public's association of private enterprise generally and the private sector's association specifically with racial exclusivity. Be that as it may, the fact is that the literature on this period has missed two essential points of the role of the state, both colonial and after independence, roles that went beyond promoting the white racial sector.

First, it is evident from the pioneering study by Lloyd Braithwaite that in Trinidad the issue of state versus private sectors was not purely an economic debate; it was very much an issue of civil rights, as they enhanced economic opportunities. Because it was not the purview of the private sector to be concerned with civil rights, it certainly was the purview of the colonial state, which had to respond to climates of opinion in the metropolis. The historical fact is that no matter how halfheartedly they did so, the colonial state did work to enhance local civil rights, and, thus, employment opportunities for colored persons. (The word colored is frequently used synonymously for mixed; however, in this paper, the term mixed will be used throughout.)

Given the historical control of the private sector by foreign whites and a few local elites, it was not at all surprising that the black and mixed Trinidadians sought spaces in the public sector. Braithwaite himself had shown that the Colonial Office had been providing increasing opportunities for these sectors. He found that while in 1930 only four of the 42 "principal officers" in the public administration were of mixed heritage, by 1952, 23 out of the 42 were. The number of white Creoles, however, had held steady at 6. This explains why Eric Williams could write in the early 1940s about the rising importance of an educated and politically ambitious middle class. "The colored middle class," Williams wrote, "had arrived" (Williams 1942, 59). Against great odds, to be sure, the members of this class benefited from significant state institutions, like Queens Royal College, and government scholarships to make something of themselves. Ivar Oxaal's 1968 book is thus quite appropriately titled *Black Intellectuals Come to Power.* Any surprise that Braithwaite should conclude with a rare statement of praise for a British empire that, in Trinidad, had worked for a breaking down of the caste pattern? "There may be," he noted, "some benefit in 'Imperialism' after all" (Braithwaite 1953, 173).

The second essential point that the literature on this period has missed is that the standard interpretation of economic nationalism also makes a mistake in not understanding the interest of the local white elites in a more nationalistic state. They, after all, also perceived themselves to be relatively deprived vis-à-vis the expatriate sector. A few examples will suffice to illustrate this point, made by the author elsewhere (Maingot 1962). Although it is true that the top echelons of the "professional and technical" sector were white, it is important to note that only 15 percent of these were native whites; the rest were expatriates. Jack Harewood explains that this "apparent discrimination" in favor of foreign white employees stemmed from the fact that many of the largest and most influential businesses (banks, insurance companies, the oil industry, sugar producers, and so on) were owned and controlled by foreign business organizations, "which prefer to keep their own nationals in the top positions, regardless of the availability of suitable local staff" (Harewood 1971, 280). The local private sector, in a post-World War II expansion, also wished to minimize foreign competition for the import-substitution businesses they were opening. The Alien Land Holding Act, for instance, one of the nationalist moves of the PNM, was much to the liking of the many important, largely Canadian creole-owned businesses. For the same reasons of self-interest, the French and Spanish creole sectors certainly had no reason to oppose the new subsidies for cacao, traditionally one of their economic enterprises much discriminated against by pro-sugar colonial administrations.

Table 5.
Color Distribution of the "Business Elite," 1970

	Color					
Race	**Very Fair**	**Fair**	**Light or High Brown**	**Brown**	**Black**	**Total**
White	111	13	—	—	—	124
Off-white	15	20	1	—	—	36
Chinese	—	20	—	—	—	20
Mixed	—	4	20	—	—	24
Indian	—	—	5	12	3	20
Negro	—	—	2	4	3	9
Total	126	57	28	16	6	233
	55%	23%	12%	7%	3%	100%

Source: Camejo, 1971, "Racial Discrimination in Employment," 300.

The question in the early 1960s, therefore, was hardly ever whether there should be an activist state. The question was who should benefit from such a state, given the climate of opinion, both local and international. It was inconceivable that the nationalist state should be perceived to be doing less than the colonial one. Equally inconceivable was to expect that that newly independent state would not favor those who were its primary constituents, Afro-Trinidadians, at the time perceived as the most economically dispossessed sector on the island. The fact that any study of income distribution even two decades after independence (see Table 6) would show that both Afro- and Indo-Trinidadians could make a claim to such an unfortunate condition was politically immaterial: the state now belonged to the Afro-Trinidadians, and their leaders logically responded accordingly. Additionally, as we shall see, Afro-Trinidadian leaders knew that there were sources of wealth that were not measured in such studies of income distribution. One such source is land, and this is what Indo-Trinidadians were perceived to have in significant amounts. This certainly was the perception of the most influential Afro-Trinidadian politicians.

In January 1956, the nationalist political leader, Eric Williams, gave the new political party, the People's Nationalist Movement, five "responsibilities and obligations": 1) eradicate colonialism, 2) promote democracy, 3) take control of the country's national resources and create a "people's sector," 4) fight for nationhood (independence), and 5) follow the spirit of Bandung.

By the "spirit of Bandung," Williams meant to place Trinidad in the context of the nonaligned nations and their politico-economic orientations. The creation of a people's sector was one key orientation. It was not at all clear, however, just what that meant, a fact evident in the variety of state postures in the Third World. In Trinidad, for one, it was clear that in the early years, neither Williams nor his party were interested in the degree of state ownership, which was already in place in countries such as Ghana, Indonesia, Guinea, and India. In fact, by the mid-1960s, Williams was adamantly opposed to the radical nationalization of the economy being pushed by some intellectuals and labor union leaders. "The inefficiency of [even the] much more modest efforts in the field of public ownership of public utilities," wrote Williams two years after independence, "is, in any case, an inauspicious beginning to public ownership of basic industries" (Williams 1964, 333). He did favor shifting from the British sphere of influence to the North American one, and this was reflected in an attitude that some took to be anticapitalist. It was nothing of the sort, however. As Ivar Oxaal noted when Williams favored Texaco's purchase of British Petroleum's interests on the island, "Greatly expanded production, revenues and wages would develop out of Trinidad's petroleum, not under the red banner of nationalization, as earlier radicals had urged, but under the red star of the Texas Company" (Oxaal 1968, 123).

Williams was certainly not the only nationalist on the island opposed to radically expanding the role of the state. Even the Trotskyite C.L.R. James opposed nationalization. In 1964, he told the special issue on independence of the *Trinidad Guardian* (August 30, 1964) that young West Indians who talk of nationalization, even of revolution, "are either ignorant or crazy. Nationalize what? Oil? That is insanity. . . . We should leave the sugar factories just where they are. . . . Little countries must know their limitations. . . . We clarify the national purpose by discouraging any belief in nationalization as a panacea." And, yet, if the integration of the Afro-Trinidadian sector was to be accomplished, this would have, of necessity, to be through state action, and state action meant central planning, which, as we have noticed, was widely implemented during colonial times. Now, it had to be put to distinct political ends. In the late 1950s, Williams put the planning unit right in the office of the premier. Development planning in the governing process never left Trinidad, a fact that was evident in the changing designations of the office:

1960	Economic Planning Division of the Premier Office
1965	Ministry of Planning and Development
1970s	Ministry of Finance and Planning
1980s	Ministry of Planning and Mobilization

Be these office titles as they may, there is no disputing that much of this planning was oriented toward the creation of a people's sector geared essentially to improving the lot of Afro-Trinidadians. Indian Trinidad hardly figured in this state activity. In a significant study carried out by the Centre for Ethnic Studies of the University of the West Indies in Trinidad, the authors begin by recognizing the ethnic rationale behind much of the statist policies of the past and their simultaneous contribution to further deepening the ethnic divisions on the island:

> It must be mentioned that the first PM of Trinidad-Tobago, Dr. E.E. Williams, strongly believed that disprivileged Trinidadians should be favored by the newly independent government. . . . There was a need to compensate for economic imbalance through the political process. . . . The 'father of the nation' also felt that Indo-Trinidadians were not in need of special treatment because, being a rural-based, and land-owning people, they were more secure than their Afro-Trinidadian counterparts (Centre for Ethnic Studies n.d., xxi).

It is a fact that the early nationalist movement ignored the role of Indians in the creation of the people's sector. As is logical, though, enhanced state resources augment the political competition for their control. The "outs" tend to experience increasing alienation from the state even as they mobilize to control it. This certainly was the case with the Indo-Trinidadians. To be sure, this was not a new situation. By the 1960s, however, Indians had augmented their capacity to articulate their gripes and mobilize for remedial action because they had made very real strides in education, business, and professions. Even though the obstacles they had to overcome had been at least as intractable as those faced by the mixed middle class, the impact on their outlook was different. But it was not because Indo-Trinidadians were as youths any less optimistic than Afro- and mixed-ancestry Trinidadians.

Vera Rubin and Marissa Zavalloni found that, as secondary school boys, they all looked upon the future with extraordinary optimism (Rubin and Zavalloni 1969, 198-199). Yet Indo-Trinidadian elites appeared to be resentful of what they considered their continued subordinate status and were deeply suspicious of Afro-Trinidadian and white Creole elites alike. According to one study, Indians suspect everyone and feel that "no one can be trusted, that everyone would eventually betray them" (Malik 1971, 43). These claims do not appear to have been groundless. The discrimination against Indo-Trinidadians in the state sector was evident and commented on by local and foreign observers (Niehoff and Niehoff 1960; Malik 1971; Bahadoorsingh 1968). To compensate for the slights, Indo-Trinidadians engaged even more fervently in what they were already culturally predisposed to do: create their own opportunities through private initiatives. As Malik put it, "Entry into the civil services being denied to Indians, they seek careers in business and other professions." They also began to open their own schools and build their own housing (Malik 1971, 17).

Precisely because they were not in competition for land, housing, schooling, and social status, the Indo-Trinidadian community hardly figured into the economic planning equation of those who controlled the state. Although the state's efforts were still concentrated fundamentally on the urban Afro-Trinidadian, the Afro-Trinidadian elites were right in being concerned because a situation of incongruity between their ideology and their actions had reached critical proportions by the late 1960s.

THE INCONGRUITY SITUATION IN 1970

The PNM's rhetoric about a people's sector had not been matched by its actions and certainly not in terms of the expectations it had created among the Afro-Trinidadian urban and educated youth. By 1970, both domestic and international forces conspired to resolve the incongruity between the ideology as articulated by the elite for political purposes and the less than equally enthusiastic actions concerning state control of the economy. After months of agitation and mobilization, a mass urban movement proclaiming "power to the people" nearly toppled the Williams regime. The regime's response was to bring its actions closer to the rhetoric of a people's sector.

Right after the rebellion ended, the PNM published the Chaguaramas Declaration, which clearly reflected the new political mood and climate of opinion concerning the role of the state. The publication conveyed this sentiment through two positions in particular: 1) the vow to speed up national control of the commanding heights of the economy with special reference to oil and sugar, and 2) the initiation of an immediate program of ownership and participation in banks and insurance companies (Government of Trinidad and Tobago 1972).

Accompanying this new posture was increased hostility toward the local private sector. Any failure on the part of the private sector to perform, said the government, should be attributed to an inability to seize the numerous investment opportunities in agriculture, industry, fishing, tourism, and housing, and not to the adverse government fiscal and development policies. The indigenous private sector was thought to have little initiative because the firms that existed were believed to be "generally tightly held and do not have the experience, vision and income support needed to take the long view required to introducing fundamental change in the economy." The alternative was clear: "Indeed, the only body in a developing country endowed with characteristics comparable to those of the large corporation in the developed societies is the Government" (Government of Trinidad and Tobago 1972).

Whatever the empirical truth of this comparison, the fact was that the government was leaving nothing up to chance and certainly not to open competition. No new 100 percent foreign-owned enterprises were to be permitted; the existing foreign enterprises were expected to hire nationals and begin to actively transfer "skills, knowledge, and expertise" to them. Alienation of land was prohibited, affecting especially the tourist industry. Finally, this economic nationalism was to be bolstered by two measures:

1. "Certain areas of our economy are reserved exclusively for national effort.

2. Government will take a leading part, including the use of direct participation, to expedite national control and ownership" (Government of Trinidad and Tobago 1972).

Not surprisingly, given the political motivation of the macroeconomic changes, one of the first areas that government focused on was banking. The historical practice of hiring expatriates or local whites made the banks very specific targets of the Black Power movement. And, as Leslie H. Scotland has noted, after the revolt, the government logically "focused on the commercial banking sector"

(Scotland 1988, 66-67). Soon after the end of unrest, the government acquired the Bank of London and Montreal, created the National Commercial Bank, and began construction of the Worker's Bank. Hiring was nearly exclusively from the dominant ethnic groups.

That there were few if any voices opposing this accelerated statism reflected the fact that the climate of opinion created by the intellectuals — especially the politicians cum historians — was hospitable to these actions (Maingot 1992). Among the many examples of such elites, the case of A.N.R Robinson is of particular interest because of who he had been before 1970, deputy leader of the PNM, and what he would be after 1986, the promoter of neoliberal reforms. In his book, written in 1971 at the Massachusetts Institute of Technology while in "exile" from Trinidad, Robinson wrote that the three options open to Caribbean countries were integration of the various islands, the Cuban model of socialism, and "reversion to colonial dependence — this time on the United States." According to Robinson, the third choice was definitely to be rejected, the first preferred, and the second "a real possibility that must be recognized" (Robinson 1971, 167).

To avoid the Cuban path, and outright nationalization in general, Robinson advocated "domestication." Although he provided no hard-and-fast definition of domestication, his arguments tended to indicate that because governments have the responsibility of providing employment for all citizens, there was a fundamental need for state control of resource allocation and mobilization at all levels of the economy. In practical terms, this meant a kind of state-driven affirmative action program. Showing a keen understanding of the existing incongruity, Robinson insisted that there were two things that only the state could do: first, be accountable to the principles of social justice espoused by the nationalist political movement; and second, promote domestic entrepreneurship among Afro-Trinidadians. To do this, governments should begin by managing recruitment into top positions as an effective means of doing away with domination by ethnic minority groups of the private sector.

In 1971, Robinson was proposing a program to deal with some of the major issues that had been identified by Afro-Trinidadian thinkers for years: doing something effective about unemployment among Afro-Trinidadians and also about the white minority control of the economy. Robinson, however, wished to go one step further than the PNM had ever recommended even rhetorically, namely, using the state's coercive power: "Techniques for accomplishing this purpose are not difficult to find. The government must lay down guidelines for recruitment and, in some cases, promotion policies; it should create machinery of its own. . . . It can apply sanctions of one kind or another as a last resort" (Robinson 1971, 154).

If Williams and the PNM were hesitant to go wholeheartedly into state ownership before 1970, by the time Robinson's book appeared on Trinidad shelves, the PNM state had moved dramatically to position itself as the major planner and majority owner of the economy. This was as true in agriculture as it was in the oil industry. Despite this great leap forward, the PNM cannot be said to have embraced nationalization wholeheartedly; it was still attempting to adjust macroeconomic policy to political survival without digging itself into the situation Cuba was perceived to be in, a fact very much on Williams' mind. He called the program of "excessive nationalization" one of the "principal errors" of the Cuban revolution (Williams 1970, 492). As such, Williams calibrated the public sector's participation in terms of three functional needs:

1. Accelerate the transfer of control of foreign-owned firms to local hands. This involved the sugar industry, the telephone company, television, the telegraph company, and the flour mill.

2. Encourage and support new local industry, which explains the Development Finance Company, the Agricultural Development Bank, and the National Fisheries Company.

3. Save jobs, which explains the nationalization of British Petroleum, meat processors, and the Printing and Packaging Company.

The state also expanded its subsidies and incentives in all fields, not the least of which was agriculture, a predominantly Indian sector. The conclusion that the island's agricultural development had been hampered by very strong comparative disadvantages, especially in labor costs but also in other inputs, dated from World War II. The idea was that these disadvantages could be compensated for by two types of state action: 1) direct and indirect subsidies, including minimum guaranteed prices, import restrictions, fiscal incentives, and increased credit; and 2) the expansion of infrastructural and service provisions to include roads, distribution of state lands, land preparation, water (irrigation) schemes, and security of land tenure.

In a subsequent assessment, *Accounting for Our Petrodollars*, it was revealed that between 1973 and mid-1980, the state had invested $2.94 billion in 47 companies, of which $920 million had been spent on energy-based projects. All public utilities — except external communication, which was a joint venture — were government owned. The government was motivated by lingering memories of the 1970 uprising and a sudden windfall of petrodollars. Thanks to the Organization of Petroleum Exporting Countries (OPEC), the island's current revenue, which in 1973 had been $476 million, increased to $2.77 billion in 1978 and to $7.12 billion in 1982. There would be no pulling back from state ownership, especially if this meant restoring foreign interests and the local private sector to their former strengths. As the political leader told the PNM convention in 1980, "The basic aim of the local advocates of free enterprises is to push Trinidad and Tobago into a form of undiluted capitalism, as archaic historically as it is precarious economically, with foreign capital and foreign inspiration, seeking to get more out of the workers whom they will throw on the breadline on the flimsiest of provocations" (Williams 1980, 24).

The key question, of course, is whether this substantial state intervention resulted in increased productivity, better services, or the promised "rationalization" in management, which would make former money losers viable. The answer is clearly no.

As far as food crops were concerned, the acreage under cultivation continued to be small, just as it had been for the past three decades. In 1982, it was still only 98,88 hectares or 12.1 percent of the cropped area. In fact, there was more acreage (12,509 hectares) formerly under cultivation and now listed as "abandoned." It is acknowledged today that much of the money destined for agriculture ended up invested in urban real estate, taxis, and other urban sources of income.

Traditional export crops (sugarcane, cocoa, coffee) together occupied 56,520 hectares, or 69.1 percent of cultivated land. Yet, the results in the state-owned Caroni sugar industry were considerably less than spectacular. With 51 percent equity purchased from the British firm Tate and Lyle, this estate of nearly 14,000 workers occupied 25,000 hectares, or 20 percent of the country's arable land. Far from being rationalized, however, it had become a major money loser: from $21.7 million lost in 1976 to $284 million in 1980. Productivity had dropped by 41 percent during that period. In fact, increases in production costs were making Trinidad completely uncompetitive. In the 10-year period 1972-1983, the costs of producing sugar increased from TT$294 per ton in 1972 to TT$4,429 per ton in 1983, a 1,500 percent increase. By 1986, Trinidad's production costs were 4.5 times that of Belize and three times that of Guyana (Government of Trinidad and Tobago 1988a, 138-141).

Despite this sharp increase, there was no thought of abandoning the subsidies for the production of sugar. Employment was the primary reason for keeping it alive, especially because in 1986, Caroni employed 14,000 mostly Indo-Trinidadians, and there were an additional 5,000 to 10,000 operating as independent cane farmers. These were persuasive numbers, indeed, but also a most unacknowledged and unrecognized indirect subsidy to the Indo-Trinidadian population.

The problems of the cocoa industry differ from those of sugar in that the state has never owned the land and the means of production. Some 5,000 small farmers produce the bulk of the cocoa and coffee, but the state controls the marketing through the Cocoa and Coffee Industry Board, a statutory organization whose agents supervise, regulate, purchase, and market the product. It also sets the prices and determines the level of subsidy through a price support scheme. By the early 1980s, the board was handling 90 percent of the coffee production and 80 percent of that of cocoa. Between 1977 and 1986, cocoa production declined from 3.345 to 1.426 million kilograms. Government involvement has not been able to save the industry.

Fifteen years after the Black Power revolution pushed the PNM to ratchet up its lukewarm statism, the Trinidad public sector was third in relative size in the Caribbean. Only Cuba and Guyana had more of the economy under state control. The old, and quite legitimate, concern over employment opportunities for Afro-Trinidadians was being addressed. Despite the mushrooming of state ownerships, though, it was still not evident just what the government's basic philosophy about state ownership was. The situation is summed up by Selwyn Ryan, who provides the best analysis of these years of state versus private sector strife:

> Even though the PNM had nationalized a great deal more than it had originally envisaged, its approach to nationalization was essentially defensive, pragmatic and non-ideological; at least in the Marxist sense. In many instances, the Government merely "stumbled" into taking over the branch plant of a multinational in order to protect jobs or keep the industry from collapsing (Ryan 1989a, 212).

Be it philosophy, pragmatism, or accident, the widening and deepening of state control are bound to have profound effects on the nature of political power and on the character of those who wield it. By 1980, and after five terms in office, the

PNM's state was, in Williams' own words, "in the driver's seat" as far as the economy was concerned. Government capital expenditure had expanded to 50 percent of gross domestic expenditure, from the 15 percent it had been in 1959. Williams, who also held the portfolio of Finance, must have known the extent of his power. "Williams," says Paul Sutton, "was well aware of this and he used it as the principal foundation upon which he further elaborated the presidential style" (Sutton 1984, 63). As such, Williams was in no mood for political compromise. Those who opposed his schemes — mostly in the private sector — were accused of suffering from "a brown sugar mentality." As he proclaimed in 1975, "We [the state] stand today as the only cohesive force in the society against this [brown sugar] mentality and in vigorous prosecution of our own nationalist economic identity." The Chamber of Commerce retorted by warning about "the spectre of state socialism." They need not have, for neither the PNM nor its leader, Eric Williams, ever thought in those terms. This was made quite apparent in one of his last written pieces, published as an epilogue to his compilation of speeches (Williams 1981). Although he openly ridiculed members of the local business class, calling them "crusaders for the capitalist work ethic" and "capitalist mimic men," he was no less harsh on those who were put in charge of the people's sector, "With the state enterprises, the situation becomes positively impossible: workers demanding higher wages, boards of directors voting bonuses indiscriminately and calling on the treasury for funds . . . dipping hands into the public purse at will and without ministerial approval and parliamentary sanction" (Williams 1981, 441).

Eric Williams died in March 1980. The elections of 1981 pitted the PNM, now led by George Chambers, against the Organization for National Reconstruction, a split from the PNM led by former Attorney General Karl Hudson-Phillips. Hudson-Phillips, who had once described himself as a "Caribbean socialist," presented the first unabashed and undisguised program for a private sector-led development program for the island. The state's functions, he now asserted, should be limited to "facilitating" the role of private initiatives. It was an early version of neoliberalism. Polls, showing widespread public discontent with government corruption and with the inefficiencies and financial losses of the public sector, led many to believe that Hudson-Phillips would beat the lackluster Chambers. It was not to be. Once the PNM accused Hudson-Phillips of wanting to return economic power to the "minorities," race, not economics, became the dominant theme of the campaign. The PNM, having reverted to the theme of the economic empowerment for the black masses, won comfortably. The ONR received 22.1 percent of the vote but not a single parliamentary seat. Quite evidently, Trinidadians in 1981 were not ready for neoliberalism. The ONR was seen, as the presumably objective compiler of the *Historical Dictionary of Trinidad and Tobago* put it, as a "right-wing" party (Anthony 1997, 413).

But even the new Prime Minister, George Chambers, knew that all was not well with the public sector. In fact, he was aware that the fundamental paradox of this statism, with its emphasis on economically empowering the Afro-Trinidadian sector, was that that sector did not feel advantaged. As Table 7 indicates, only 10 percent of blacks believed that they had benefited under the Afro-Trinidadian controlled years of the PNM, but an astonishing 58 percent believed that the Indians had.

Table 7.
Groups Benefiting Most Under PNM Rule (%)

	Group Responses			
Group Benefiting	**Blacks**	**Indians**	**Mixed**	**Total Sample**
Blacks	10	58	26	35
Indians	35	8	21	20
Whites	6	5	9	6
Syrians	5	1	6	3
No group	31	22	24	24
Don't Know	13	6	14	10
	100	100	100	100

Source: Ryan and Barclay, 1992, *Sharks and Sardines,* 190.

With the Black Power movement dissipated, the windfall of OPEC-driven oil prices quickly disappearing, and the examples of Cuba's and Guyana's "socialism" causing increasing disenchantment with the statist model, the times were ripe for changes.

The Shift in Paradigms

It is not at all easy to describe a clear watershed in economic thinking on the part of the island's governing elites. Part of the difficulty is because, with the exception of Hudson-Phillips' 1981 campaign, elections have not been about macroeconomic policy. They have been about race.

There have been no broad studies — certainly none for public discussion — that have analyzed the failure of one phase of government policy as it might relate to the transition to another. There also is no evidence of significant public discussions of alternative economic strategies. As Trinidad economist Dennis Pantin observes, pointing to a dramatic example, the fundamental shift in policy toward a resource-based industries strategy, namely, Point Lisas, took place without any significant debate on broad social issues such as employment creation, income distribution, and national independence (Pantin 1989). But a transition has occurred, and something had to have brought it about.

Interviews on the island point to both internal and external factors, both brought on by the end of the windfall oil profits. Internally, it was evident that what became known as government "giveaways" were at an end. Prime Minister Chambers conveyed the message in typically colorful Trinidadian language in his 1982 budget speech, "The fete is over and the country must go back to work." This domestic vicissitude led to the external factor: the 1983 negotiations between the Trinidad-Tobago government and the IMF for a 1983-1986 "Draft Development Plan." Not insignificantly, the Trinidad-Tobago government team in those negotiations was led by a distinguished Trinidad economist, William Demas, past governor of the island's central bank, and in 1983, president of the Caribbean Development Bank.

Whatever the historical validity of the chronology, none of the governments that have held power since the 1983 negotiations with the IMF have reversed the policy recommendations of the Demas task force.

The PNM, which had initiated the era of economic nationalism, also initiated the shift in paradigms. In the invariably policy-setting budget speeches of 1984, 1985, and 1986, the PNM Prime Minister and Minister of Finance, George Chambers, called for what he had not called for in his campaign, that is, changes in the array of legislation that adversely affected foreign investment.

Although the government did not broadcast its policy changes, and there were no society-wide debates on economic policy, the political opposition did pick up on the new trends and made its thoughts amply known. Led by radical-leaning trade unionist Basdeo Panday and former Deputy Prime Minister Robinson, the opposition began to lambaste the "sell-out" mentality of the PNM. It was in many ways this radical anti-IMF rhetoric, plus the formation of a multiracial alliance, that led to the 1986 defeat of the PNM. The new party, the National Alliance for Reconstruction, had campaigned on the need to administer state services and enterprises more effectively, but to do so "humanely." With Hudson-Phillips a member of the NAR's executive council, the party wished to avoid repeating the mistake of the 1981 elections, namely, maintaining too close an association with the local private sector and the neoliberal ideas with which it was identified.

Despite Robinson's rhetoric during the campaign, immediately upon taking office, he adopted the 1983 IMF-designed restructuring guidelines. He began by changing the nature of central planning, arguing that instead of the top-down approach of the past decades, an attempt would be made to increase consultation and inputs from wider sectors of the society. Institutionally, planning was now to be done by two agencies, the National Planning Commission and the National Economic Advisory Council, both reflecting the changed attitude toward state planning. The National Planning Commission was chaired by the prime minister and the minister of finance. Its membership was drawn from government, business, labor, and academia, and it was to provide broad advice on national policy. The National Economic Advisory Council was a technical body that presented positions for consideration of the NPC and in which the private sector was given a prominent voice.

All was not well with this government, however. The coalition that had campaigned under the theme "One love" soon split. On the surface, the dissension had to do with economic policy; at the core, it reflected the racial divide. Soon, the more radical Indian wing of the government was expelled and returned to a vociferous attack on the NAR's neoliberalism and on Robinson's sell-out to the local capitalists.

In the midst of the attacks, considerable trade union agitation, and clamors to do something about the high rate of unemployment, the government pushed its neoliberal program even more resolutely. In August 1988, it released the most comprehensive restructuring program ever put up for discussion, the *Draft Medium*

Term Programme, 1989-1991. At the core of the program was a call to restructure the local economy in such a way as to make the island attractive to all forms of foreign capital, whether as direct investments, portfolio capital, or monies from multilateral lending institutions. To achieve this, the government proposed doing the following:

1. Reducing government expenditures and, therefore, state deficits by: a) downsizing state bureaucracies, b) privatizing money-losing state enterprises, c) encouraging exports as a means of earning hard currency rather than using hard currency through export-substitution, and d) reducing the scope and depth of the social net.

2. Adopting a new, supportive attitude toward existing elites in the national private sector, regardless of their ethnicity.

3. Accepting the theoretical formulations of international and multilateral agencies such as the World Bank and the IMF regarding competition and the role of foreign investment capital.

4. While not disregarding continued asymmetries, rejecting the paradigm of a basic North-South divide and accepting the idea that even the smallest state is part of an interrelated global economy.

A more complete formulation of what would soon be called the Washington Consensus could hardly be imagined. This newly energized philosophy of liberalization was elaborated on by the Prime Minister and Minister of Finance, A.N.R. Robinson, in his budget speech of December 16, 1988. Robinson noted that the government was open to a range of foreign investment types, from wholly owned joint ventures with foreign majority ownership, "even in medium-sized economic activities." Noting that the whole world, "even Communist Countries," were acknowledging "the realities of today's world," Robinson promised a flexible and receptive approach to foreign investments and initiatives by the native private sector. The latter wasted no time, and under the auspices of the dynamic South Trinidad Chamber of Industry and Commerce, the nation's first Free Zone Area was established at the Point Lisas Industrial Estate.

In 1990, the alien Landholding Act, in many ways the symbol of the economic nationalism of the 1950-1980 period, was abandoned in favor of the Foreign Investment Act.

By 1989, the "structural adjustment" measures began to squeeze. Ryan quotes studies by local academics Ralph Henry and Dennis Pantin showing that between 1982 and 1990, the increase in unemployment was 66,000 while an additional 100,000 had dropped below the poverty level. Between 1986 and 1990, the private sector had retrenched over 8,000, while the public sector laid off 3,529. Additionally, the remaining public sector employees took a 10 percent salary cut and a suspension of their cost of living allowance (COLA). As Ryan noted, "Comparisons were being made with 1970 and 1981 when public servants also took to the streets in protest" (Ryan 1991b, 19). The call was for government to abandon the "IMF-imposed" structural adjustment program.

In the midst of widespread discontent and public protests, the NAR government stood firm on the reforms and was even planning an early election. On July 27,

1990, a militant sect of Black Muslims (Muslimeen) led by Abu Bakr attempted a power grab, taking the prime minister, many of his cabinet, and many in Parliament hostage. The uprising was defeated but not before widespread looting and arson had laid much of the capital city of Port-of-Spain to waste. As in 1970, the 1990 events were led by elements of the urban, Afro-Trinidadian population. Not surprisingly, blacks perceived themselves to be the main losers of the NAR liberalization program (Table 8). The more radical representatives of this black working class were strident in their early opposition to the restructuring program, and after the Muslimeen uprising, they were eager to say, "I told you so!" Some of the representative responses have been recorded by Ryan (1991b, 322-332) and are given below.

National Joint Action Committee (NJAC)

There had been no consultation or public participation in the decisions. "How many times have we warned that policies of privatization and of the IMF would bring unbearable suffering?"

Table 8.
Groups Benefiting under NAR Rule (%)

	Group Responses		
Group Benefiting	**Blacks**	**Indians**	**Mixed**
No group	37	55	47
Blacks	1	16	2
Indians	23	9	18
Whites	9	4	6
Syrians	7	2	5
Don't know	23	14	22
	100	100	100

Source: Ryan and Barclay, 1992, *Sharks and Sardines,* 190.

The Oilfield Workers Trade Union (OWTU)

The NAR government, the union said, "arrogantly" rejected any discussions on the direction of the economy but that "no society which is tied hand and foot to IMF/World Bank Structural Adjustment policies will be a just society." Rejecting the economic program was equivalent to rejecting the government itself.

Council of Progressive Trade Unions (CPTU)

"The NAR Government and the big business elite of Trinidad-Tobago must take the full blame for creating the conditions for the violent uprising of July 27, 1990."

Movement for Social Transformation (MST)

"The so-called 'looting' is . . . better described as an 'IMF Riot.'"

If it were only the radicals in the militant trade unions who had continually attacked the new policies, it would be hard to believe that the reaction would have been so negative and so widespread. The fact is that the liberalization reforms had also been under attack by the local intelligentsia and their students, with no intellectual response from their proponents. Indeed, it is difficult to find a significant written defense of the liberalization approach outside of official statements such as budget speeches. The university student bookstore was stocked with the books of *dependentistas,* world systems theorists, and the five books of Michael Manley, all arguing for a new international economic order. Although there were no books or monographs by Prime Minister Robinson making the case for liberalization, his earlier book, *The Mechanics of Independence,* with its call for "localization," was readily available. His earlier warnings about the disruptive effects of capitalism had come back to haunt him.

Predictably, another election was held and, again, there was hardly a discussion of the policies that every government on the island had been pursuing with different degrees of enthusiasm since 1983. In the elections of 1991, the PNM won a convincing victory as "the party of the people." Whatever the PNM's political rhetoric, there was no backsliding on the policies the PNM itself had introduced after 1983. As the government put it in its major policy paper, *Public Sector Investment Programme,* the purpose of public sector investments is to "secure needed improvements in the country's physical infrastructure, particularly in areas which might be expected to facilitate private sector growth" (Government of Trinidad and Tobago 1995, 1). That the divestment program was proceeding apace is evident in the data in Table 9. It can readily be seen that the years of the PNM, 1991-1995, were years of accelerated privatization, with both the native capitalist and the foreign investor invited to participate in the process. Once in power, the PNM's spokesmen did not dissimulate their neoliberal positions. Terrence Farell, in his former academic life a theoretical statist but in 1992 deputy governor of the central bank, put his administration's position bluntly. Many of the jobs created by government action in the past were jobs that were supported over the years by taxpayers; they were not jobs that would have existed had there not been these structures of protection. Those who cannot survive in the new context "are those who do not have the capacity and what it takes to manage a modern manufacturing operation. And arguably those people don't need to continue in production anyway" (Ryan 1992, 206).

Predictably, the elections of 1995 were about race. Yet, another time, the predominantly Afro-Trinidadian PNM confronted the Indo-Trinidadian United Nations Congress. As it turned out, the ONR of A.N.R. Robinson, based nearly exclusively in Tobago, secured two seats, which ended up breaking the tie between the two larger parties. The coalition, UNC-ONR put Panday in as prime minister and Robinson as president.

Whether as trade union leader, intellectual leader of the Indian community, or leader of the opposition in Parliament, Panday had always been an outspoken opponent of economic liberalization. In fact, he often sounded as if his foremost enemies were the local business sector. During the 1991 elections, his most vehement attacks were directed at the local white business community, whom he invariably referred to as "a French Creole parasitic oligarchy" (Ryan 1992, 203). A review of his speeches up to 1995 does not reveal a single instance of a sympathetic analysis of the neoliberal reforms in place since 1983. Whatever his ideological

Table 9.
Divestments, 1992-1997

Divestment of State Enterprises 1992-1997: Local

	Company	Date Divested	Value (in TT $millions)
1	Farrell House (1975) Limited (100%)	November 1992	4.8
2	Trinidad and Tobago Printing and Packaging (100%)	November 1993	11.6
3	National Fruit Processors (100%)	April 1993	0.2
4	Angostura Bitters (88% preference shares)	December 1993	0.4
5	Angostura Holdings (0.02% ordinary shares)	December 1993	0.1
6	Neal and Massy Holdings (3.12% ordinary shares)	December 1993	5.0
7	National Poultry (18% GOTT)	July 1994	0.1
8	Polymer (Caribbean) Ltd. (25.5% preference shares)	July 1994	0.3
9	Shipping Company of Trinidad and Tobago (100%)	December 1994	5.5
10	Allied Innkeepers (Holiday Inn)	June 1995	2.6
11	National Flour Mills (20%)	May 1995	23.6
12	Reinsurance Company of Trinidad and Tobago Ltd. (TRINRE)	December 1995	10.0
13	Water and Sewage Authority (management contract)	April 1996	
14	National Flour Mills (15%)	November 1996	22.5

Source: Data provided by Divestment Secretariat of Trinidad and Tobago.

Table 9. continued

Divestment of State Enterprises, 1992-1997: Foreign

	Company	Date Divested	Principal Investor	Value (in TT $millions)
1	Fertrin/TTUC (100%)	March 1993	Arcadian	132.1
2	Trinidad and Tobago Methanol (31%)	January 1994	Ferrostaal/Helm	47.0
3	Arawak Cement (49%)	March 1994	Domestic	2.8
4	Trinidad Cement (20%)	August 1994	CEMEX	10.8
5	Petrotrin O_2N_2/UFC plant	August 1994	Domestic	4.4
6	Power Generation Company of TT (49%)	Dec. 1994	SEI/Amoco	107.5
7	Iron and Steel Company of TT (100%)	Dec. 1994	ISPAT	70.1
8	BWIA (51.0%)	January 1995	Acker Group	20.0
9	Trinidad and Tobago Methanol (69%)	April 1997	Ferrostaal/Helm/CMC	150.0

Source: Data provided by Divestment Secretariat of Trinidad and Tobago.

frame of mind has been since 1995, he has taken power just as the program of divestment of government holdings has been accelerating, as the data in Table 9 clearly show.

Also evident in Table 9 is the absence of the oil industry in the divestment program. What the fate will be of what is indisputably the key sector of the island's economy, generally, and the government's, specifically, is a crucial question if one is to understand just how wide and deep the liberalization of the economy will be. Clearly, given the history of the political use (rhetorical and actual) of statism for ethnic mobilization, and in the absence of any public promotion of the advantages of privatization, divesting what is commonly regarded as the nation's main patrimony will not be easy going. According to a study conducted for the Economic Commission for Latin America and the Caribbean (ECLAC), the private sector appears quite solidly behind the new macroeconomic program; it worries, however, that the lack of public discussion and disclosures of the privatization process will harm its chances of total success. According to these business elites, it is the political elites' fear of organized labor that explains this lack of information and proselytizing (Bibo 1994). Be this as it may, the divestment program continues uninterrupted and is knocking on the door of the last bastion of state control, the energy sector.

THE PRIVATIZATION OF THE OIL/GAS SECTOR

THE NATIONALIZATION PROCESS

The nationalization of Trinidad's oil industry took place over a 23-year period. That process can be divided into three stages, each with its own local but especially international dynamics. Although the cumulative effect of the actions over these 23 years was the government's complete ownership of the oil industry, it is hard to identify a single, consistently held motivation or cause behind this nationalization process. Ideological reasons seem to follow, not precede, state acquisition of the foreign oil companies.

First Stage (1969)

This stage is marked by the establishment of the major state-owned company, Trinidad-Tesoro Petroleum Company, Ltd., with an ownership that was 50.1 percent Trinidad-Tobago government and 49.9 percent Tesoro Petroleum Corporation (USA). The particulars of this nationalization (which included purchasing all of the assets of British Petroleum, Trinidad, Ltd., which had already decided to quit the island) have never been fully explained to the Trinidad people. *The Wall Street Journal* (March 12, 1987, 1, 20), in a highly embarrassing (to Trinidadians) front-page story about the "Case of the $3,100 Prostitute" suggested that corruption, rather than benefit to the state, might have been the motivation. It is known that Tesoro received preferential tax treatment and that the Trinidad concession converted it from an obscure Texas company into what *The Wall Street Journal* called "an enterprise whose annual revenue eventually topped $3 billion."

Second Stage (1974)

During this stage, assets of Shell Oil were acquired, including the Point Fortin Refinery, which became Trintoc. Shell had entered the island in 1957, when it bought out United British Oil, and continued to explore for oil and also operate the Point Fortin Refinery until 1974, when it was nationalized. As already noted, the Black Power movement of 1970 had accelerated the pace of nationalizations, but there is no evidence that the government took the leadership in doing so.

Shell's rationalization of its refining operations in the Caribbean included the abandonment of its largest refinery located in Curaçao. Was Trinidad part of this Shell scheme? Even the ever-radical Oil Field Workers Trade Union (OWTU) understood that it was. "B.P. and Shell were shedding crocodile tears about their losses," the OWTU would later write. "The real truth was that, as far as the multinationals were concerned, their Trinidad operations were of no use to them. B.P. had access to North Sea oil, and Shell was analyzing its global refining network" (OWTU 1987, 54). That the same OWTU could then conclude that nationalization, being "the only solution," was at the same time "an extremely viable one at that," reflects the victory of ideology over economic common sense. The fact is that this state acquisition, involving as it did all the refining, producing, and distribution assets of Shell, converted the state into a major employer and thus patronage dispenser, but hardly relieved it of the burdens of operating an industry that was in organizational upheaval everywhere because of the uncertainties of the global oil economy.

Third Stage (1985)

This was the most important stage, and it can be divided into two phases: 1) purchase of Texaco assets, including the Pointe-a-Pierre Refinery to be operated by Trintoc; and 2) acquisition of the outstanding 49.9 percent owned by Trinidad-Tesoro. The Texaco purchase was by far the most important nationalization ever undertaken by the government.

Texaco was established in 1956 when Texaco Oil Company purchased Trinidad Leaseholds. Texaco started secondary recovery pumping from old on-land wells, but, more important, it also began offshore drilling. Its first offshore platform was Soldado Rocks, which began production in 1956. Welcomed by the nationalist movement in the early years, Texaco began a major expansion of the island's refining system in the Pointe-a-Pierre Refinery, whose crude processing capability and complexity it augmented considerably. Texaco survived the Black Power years, and, by 1973, was refining 355,000 barrels per day, including a desulfurization facility to meet new U.S. environmental standards. It had become the mainstay of the island's economy and a major target of opponents of private enterprise, especially those against foreign ownership. And yet, it was not the opposition of these academic, trade union, and radical forces that led to Texaco's decision to leave the island in 1984; nor was it a decision driven by any ideological opposition to the company on the part of the post-Black Power PNM government. The shift in paradigms among government elites had already started. As the cases of Shell and British Petroleum demonstrated, it was the general crisis in world oil and the global move to rationalize refining capabilities that led to the decision. Faced with

Texaco's decision, the government reacted in the way to which it had become accustomed: it bought out Texaco's assets and incorporated them into Trintoc.

On June 1, 1993, the government mandated that the assets of Trintoc and Trintopec be managed jointly, and by an act of Parliament on October 1, 1993, these assets were formally vested into Petrotrin. Petrotrin thus became the largest of the four state-owned oil and gas companies operating in Trinidad-Tobago.

With the nationalization of Texaco, the government was in complete control of the nation's major asset. This happened, however, in a changed international and local environment that had two important characteristics. First, local and ideological governing elites had begun to change their views in 1983; by 1993, the emphasis on state ownership had already dissipated. Second, there was a changed global situation of oil, which no longer appeared to have a brilliant future. The prospects for oil had long been thought to be less than outstanding. By 1978, the island's oil production began to level off and even decline. Since the early 1980s, oil production has been approximately 135,000 barrels a day. By 1997, the country's proven and possible oil reserves had been estimated at more than 1 billion barrels, located in three crude oil "provinces": Land, Marine East, and Marine West. According to British Petroleum's *Statistical Review of World Energy 1997,* at this production rate, Trinidad would have only 11.3 more years of production. It should be added, though, that the recent discoveries by Amoco of offshore oil and the heavy investments that it made in the midst of depressed oil prices engendered new optimism about oil's prospects over the medium term. How this, in turn, will be affected by the purchase of Amoco by British Petroleum, no one on the island seems to know for sure.

As we shall note, those elites knowledgeable about the oil industry are keenly aware that a small country with less than 1 percent of world production — and whose application for membership in OPEC was twice denied — is hardly in a position to act alone. Oil is clearly no longer king in Trinidad.

Where there is unbounded optimism is in the field of natural gas, a resource of much more recent vintage than oil and one that has a different status in the nation's political culture: it carries none of the nationalist burden of being the nation's premier resource and is, thus, not so closely tied to the idea of being a specific national patrimony. Proof of this is that contracts for exploration were being signed even during the late 1960s and early 1970s, when the economic nationalist rhetoric was at its highest. Despite the talk of "empowering the small man" (as in the case of the 1981 elections), exploration by numerous foreign companies (British Gas, Deminiex, Agip, and Occidental) continued undisturbed. It might be argued that "out of sight" is "out of mind," since the significant gas discoveries were well offshore, in the deeper waters off the North Coast.

By 1997, Trinidad was fifth in Latin America in terms of proven reserves of gas, with 8.4 trillion cubic feet and an additional probable and possible 63 trillion cubic feet. That this is where the island's future economy lies is evident in available data that shows that the bulk of the investments coming into the island have been in exploration for natural gas and in downstream, gas-based industrialization.

Interestingly enough, one of the central criticisms of those favoring the nationalization of the energy industry is that the emphasis on that single industry — a "wasting" one — had returned the island to the single-crop, "plantation" mode of yesteryear (Best 1997). That type of analysis misconstrues the nature of this new industry. The data in Table 10 shows that although this energy sector still brings in over three quarters of the island's foreign exchange, its share of both gross domestic product (GDP) and of government revenue has decreased relative to the rest of the economy.

Quite clearly, Trinidad has stopped being a single-industry economy, even as the energy sector still brings in the bulk of the foreign exchange. There is a dynamic and diversified domestic economy operating and paying taxes. Be that as it may, the real and symbolic heart of the economy, to the general society, not just economic nationalists, is still Petrotrin, the most successful of the state-owned enterprises. While not everyone might understand the implications of the company's holdings in gas and oil, they certainly do understand that Petrotrin is the island's largest employer (see Table 11). As such, a review of the government's policies and directives given to Petrotrin and the operating codes of the elites that have its future in their hands will help reveal a great deal about the direction the state has been taking, and intends to take, in its divestment program. Such an inside view will surely be a more accurate gauge of policy than the rhetoric of the politicians that, as we have seen, has proven to be quite different from their actions.

Table 10.
Energy Sector Contribution to Economy

	1975	**1996**
GDP	41%	27%
Government revenues	60%	32%
Foreign exchange earnings	77%	77%

Source: Central Bank of Trinidad and Tobago.

Table 11.
Key Statistics of Petrotrin

Employees	5,313
Crude production (1995 average) with 2,600 active wells, there are also 5,000 "idle" or marginally economic wells.	52,076 bpcd
Gas reserves	308 billion cubic ft.
Primary crude distillation	175,000 barrels of oil per stream day
Conversion capability	100,000 barrels of oil per calendar day

bpcd= barrels per calendar day

Source: Public Relations Office, Petrotrin.

PETROTRIN: A CASE STUDY

From its inception, the team that was to be the future management of Petrotrin spelled out the company's philosophy as market driven. As the then co-Chairman of the Merger Task Force, Trevor Boopsingh, noted in a December 1993 study of the region's energy sector, the region could not keep on doing things the way they had always been done. He revealed the kind of thinking dominant in the creation of the company when he observed that "the development of the proper macro-economic competitive environment is a necessary requirement if private sector capital is to be encouraged to capture any feasible opportunities" (Boopsingh and Beyer 1993, 6).

This philosophy was reiterated five years later by the Minister of Energy and Energy Industries of the UNC government, Finbar K. Gangar, who summarized his energy policy as "driven by concerns for the environment, the Futures Markets and the reality of the global marketplace" (interview, August 21, 1997). To the extent that the thinking within Petrotrin and in the ministry of energy are indicative of broad state macroeconomic orientations, there appears to be little opposition to liberalizing major sectors of the oil industry. This is certainly the impression received from interviews and from the available internal documents. What is significant, of course, is that these sentiments appear to have grown quite independent from the public utterances of the political parties and key leaders. This phenomenon seems to be as much a response to the changing international environment in the energy business as to ideological changes, abroad mostly but also at home. A sort of "law of necessity" in the oil and gas industries compels governmental pragmatism, which, in turn, is facilitated and encouraged by the international climate of opinion.

The fundamental aspect of this law of necessity was that in the mid- to late-1990s the Pointe-a-Pierre Refinery, the island's largest, was losing money (some TT$90 million per year since 1990). The reasoning behind the US$350 million upgrade program at that refinery and the attempts at increasing production from 110,000 to 160,000 barrels a day (and, thus, reducing costs from US$2.90 to US$2.00 per barrel) was the hope that such efficiencies would help find a joint venture equity partner. As Petrotrin's Chief Executive Officer/Managing Director (CEO/MD) Chiang Keith Awong told the press, "An equity partner is probably one of the best ways of enhancing the chances of viability of the Pointe-a-Pierre Refinery, but before you acquire a partner there are some things that have to be done" (*Trinidad Guardian,* August 20, 1997, 4).

There are other reasons pressing the management of Petrotrin to seek fairly dramatic remedies for its situation, to wit: they were using only 50 percent of their total refining capacities; they had only a 30 percent reliability rate in the production of lube oil; and they had a serious debt burden. To quote CEO Awong, "Our biggest single exposure over the next three years is financial, the debt burden. . . . If restructuring is not possible then divestment may be the only solution" (*PetroVision,* February 1997, 7).

None of this should be interpreted to mean that the company was in dire straits. Coopers and Lybrand ranked it as the leading local company in terms of revenues earned (*PetroVision,* November 1995, 1), and *Petroleum Economist* (October 1995) gave it a very favorable review in terms of its cost-cutting efforts. A story in *Oil and Gas Journal, Revista Latinoamericana* (January 1997, 36-40) was glowing about the prospects of gas exploration in Trinidad, noting that Amoco was to spend US$1.2 billion therein over the next 20 years. Gustavo Inciarte of Petróleos de Venezuela, SA (PDVSA) told the South Trinidad Chamber of Industry of Commerce that Petrotrin was doing "a lot better" than his own country in managing the oil sector (*Trinidad Express,* August 19, 1997, 6). This is saying a lot because PDVSA is recognized as a thoroughly professional and honestly run corporation.

To Trinidadians, always interested in the doings of their very proximate neighbor, the case of Venezuela was instructive. There, an ex-Marxist guerrilla leader, Teodoro Petkoff, led the privatization efforts of the Social Christian Party (COPEI) government of Rafael Caldera. A recent in-depth report called Petkoff's efforts "a heroic mission," given the ingrained interests of various groups in continued (unprofitable) state control (Gylden 1998, 32).

Whatever the incongruities between the early rhetoric and the later practices of decisionmakers such as Teodoro Petkoff in Venezuela and Basdeo Panday in Trinidad, there appears to be no such incongruities between the oil sectors of both countries. Relations between Trinidadian and Venezuelan elites in this sector were excellent. The new collaboration seemed to fit Haas' concept of epistemic communities, "networks of knowledge-based communities with an authoritative claim to policy-relevant knowledge within their domain of expertise" (Haas 1994, 55). Such consensual knowledge does not emerge in isolation, but rather is created and spread by transnational networks of specialists (Haas 1992, 1-35). The process by which epistemic communities come into being can be outlined as follows: 1) The technical group experiences increasing professional uncertainty because of a growing awareness of a lack of complete information about technical advancements and also about market, investments, and production opportunities; 2) through contacts with peers, the group is made aware that there are proven benefits from cooperation, as distinct from individual action; and 3) the technical group begins to pursue new forms of cooperation and (after getting the green light from the political authorities) begins the process of institutionalizing the cooperation. At the latter point, the local group becomes part of a global epistemic community.

Clearly, the technical community needs to be in congruity with the political elite in order to institutionalize the technical cooperation. The assumption is that they both make the same opportunity-cost calculations and that this is in itself evidence of paradigmatic flexibility. Given the political commitments (and rhetoric) of the political elites, however, it is the technical elite who have to do the convincing. Under conditions of complex interdependence and generalized uncertainty, says Haas, specialists play a significant role in interpreting the consequences of this uncertainty for the political decisionmakers. Politicians, typically in the dark about such technical issues but always sensitive to high-risk outcomes and state interests, are increasingly disposed to respect the operating space of their epistemic communities. A review of the decisionmakers within the energy sector, generally, and Petrotrin, in particular, shows the outlines of an internationally connected epistemic community in Trinidad that reaches into the political elite.

Table 12.
Board of Directors, Petrotrin, 1997

Name	Race/Color*	Education	Experience/Sector
D. Baldeosingh (chairman)	Indian	BS, electrical engineering MS, electronics	Private sector; founded engineering company
A. Khan	Indian	BS, geology	Public sector; diplomat
C.K. Awong	Chinese	BS, chemical engineering	Private sector; formerly with Shell
G. Bartlett	Mixed	PhD, petroleum engineering	Private sector; founder Bartlett Co.
C.A. Beaubrun	Mixed	BS, chemical engineering	Private sector; formerly with Texaco
D. Hackett	Mixed	BS, economics	Private sector; banking
C. Kumar-Mclean	Mixed	Chartered accountant	Private sector; insurance
E.K. McLeod	Black	—	Trade unionist (OWTU)
A. Niranjan	Indian	MBA	Private sector; insurance
C. Ramkhalawan	Indian	BS, petroleum engineering	Private sector; Texaco
A. Ramlogan	Indian	LLB	Private sector; law practice

*Based on reputation, not self-assessment.
Source: Interviews, Trinidad, August 8-21, 1997.

In the Westminster form of government, general policy is set by the Cabinet, all of whose members have to belong to Parliament, either the elected House or the appointed Senate. Once policy is set, then responsibility for monitoring, regulating, and revenue collecting falls with the particular minister and ministry. After the election of the UNC, the government appointed Finbar K. Gangar to the Senate and then minister of energy and energy industries.

Gangar was 46 years old and held a bachelor of science degree in mechanical engineering (1972) from the University of the West Indies as well as a master of science degree in production engineering management (1986). He joined Trintoc as an engineer in 1974, right after the nationalization, and rose to appraisal manager in the general engineering and technical division. Despite coming of technical age during the period of intense nationalization, the minister of energy believed that the opportunities for private sector investment are particularly strong in the diversification of energy-based industries. This point is emphasized in a 1997 unpublished green paper on energy policy. The thrust of that paper is to highlight and elaborate on the new philosophy in the ENERGY SECTOR, which has two basic visions: 1) "pragmatism vis-à-vis the globalization of markets," that is, moving away from the excessively insular and nationalistic stance in force since the early 1970s; and 2) the need to encourage greater competition in the domestic fuels market. The end result is what the green paper terms the "effective and optimal 'monetisation'" of the nation's natural gas resources. This emphasis on monetization was repeated in interviews. It is taken to mean the development of downstream natural gas-based industries, including petrochemicals, but also the development of the nonhydrocarbon industrial sector that will use natural gas as the prime energy source.

Although the written word is important, Minister Gangar's views on the industry's future are best understood through his actions. On June 20, 1997, he appointed a committee to review and advise on matters pertaining to the domestic energy market. The main terms of reference given the committee appeared also to be the government's main thrusts for the future of the energy sector. The first policy mandate was demonopolization and deregulation. This was in preparation for market liberation of the industry in all its dimensions, from wholesaling to gasoline retailing. The goal was to reduce all subsidies in the domestic market within two years. This plan had three phases:

Phase 1 (1997-1998) involved the introduction of private competition, rationalization aimed at increasing the profitability of operations in the domestic market. The actions already taken in this phase speak to the government's determination to diversify the operations of Petrotrin. The most important of these actions were: 1) lease operations: sublicenses for the operation of certain wells only, without recourse to exploitation of the property; 2) farmouts: sublicenses that permit exploration, drilling, and exploitation of potential hydrocarbon reserves; and 3) more joint ventures, including the following:

- 66 2/3 percent shareholding in Trinmar with Texaco Trinidad, Inc.;
- 80 percent shareholding in Trintomar with the National Gas Company of Trinidad-Tobago;
- 25 percent shareholding in the Northern Basin Consortium, composed of Offshore Trinidad, Ltd., Anderman-Smith, Inc., and Krishna Parsad; and

- 4 percent shareholding of South East Coast Consortium with Enron and the National Gas Company of Trinidad-Tobago.

Phase 2 (1999-2001) called for international marketers to be allowed entry and for partial divestment of the National Petroleum Marketing Company.

Phase 3 (2002- ?) will involve a full deregulation of pump and ex-refinery prices, and the importation of oil products will be allowed.

If the minister of energy were the only technician in the energy domain, we could hardly speak of an epistemic community existing on the island. In fact, the minister was in very immediate and technical communication with the board of directors of Petrotrin. Two weeks of interviews revealed that although race was an issue — judging from the ready attribution by others of each director's race — this factor quickly receded when questions of the industry were discussed. In terms of training, the directors stressed their education and their early years in the private companies, which pioneered the industry. They were, as a group, cosmopolitans.

The company is governed by a board of directors appointed by the shareholder, the government of Trinidad-Tobago. Clearly, the composition of this board will vary over time; the analysis here deals with the board as composed in August 1997. At that point, the office of CEO/MD was in transition. The incumbent CEO/MD was Chiang Keith Awong, who holds a bachelor of science in chemical engineering (Hons.). Awong started with Shell as an engineer and was kept on with the establishment of Trintoc. Awong appears to be typical of the pragmatic and realistic new managerial style in the Trinidad-Tobago industry. In a wide-ranging interview, he analyzed an array of issues that any CEO/MD has to deal with government policies, oil and gas reserves in Trinidad and worldwide, relations with Venezuela (a major supplier of crude for Petrofin's refineries), trade union activists, and stability of government regulatory policies. He was optimistic, citing a "realism" in governing circles and the strong trends in foreign investments as major reasons for that optimism.

The incoming CEO/MD was Lawford Dupres, who holds a bachelor of science degree in applied sciences from the University of British Columbia, Canada. Dupres had years of experience in the private oil world, having worked 11 years with the Imperial Oil Company of Canada in Vancouver, Toronto, and Sarnia. He began his career in Trinidad-Tobago as chief technologist with Trintoc, moved to technical manager and then director. His prior post was chairman of Lake Asphalt Company of Trinidad-Tobago. Dupres' reputation is as a cosmopolitan, active in service clubs such as Lions and Rotary, and an active member of the Southern Chamber of Commerce (the most active member on the island); he is also a musician. The expectation was that the "deprovincialization" of Petrotrin would probably accelerate under his management. What was clear is that the board of directors he would work with (see Table 12) would share his cosmopolitan views, in part, because they shared similar technical educational backgrounds and experiences in both the private and the public worlds of oil.

This new sense of the realities, challenges, and opportunities of the global oil industry was evident also in what appears to be the more moderate stance taken by the historically radical trade union, OWTU. The first Collective Agreement was signed with Petrotrin on September 9, 1996, and new negotiations were undertaken during August 1997. At the signing of the first agreement, the president of OWTU, Errol McLeod, a well-known radical political activist and perennial advocate of nationalization, noted his pleasure of reaching an agreement "without Third Party intervention . . . and certainly without our having had to square off as we did square off over a period of six weeks in 1995." Part of the reason for this change of strategy, he noted, was "the world is not waiting on any one of us. We continue to be impacted upon" (*PetroVision,* September 1996, 6).

Few people interviewed believed that McLeod was converted to neoliberalism, nor did anyone define him and his union peers as members of the island's epistemic community in oil. In fact, the general thrust of a 1990 OWTU mandate to organize a campaign of popular education and mobilization against privatization was still in effect. Given that there was no equivalent public campaign explaining the benefits of privatization, McLeod had a fairly open field. However, interviews in the oil sector indicated that many believed that, in the final analysis, he was a pragmatist. They believed that his stance would vary according to the political winds. On the one hand, it was important that the OWTU's membership was predominantly Afro-Trinidadian and urban and could be expected to have strong sympathies with the general fate of that sector of the society. On the other hand, the union members had long been the aristocracy of labor on the island, with wages to show for it, and could be expected to make opportunity cost analyses of their own. Hence, sentiment, race, and pocketbook were equally important, and it was quite impossible to predict which would carry the most weight in their decisionmaking.

In the final analysis, therefore, one must keep in mind that even as globalization increases the number of epistemic communities, these technical groups still exist and operate within larger national communities. In the broader society, there is most probably much less consensus on the norms and values that characterize an epistemic community. Hence, the latter's wider influence tends to be limited to top governmental elites. Because they do not tend to influence the broader society, they are often at the mercy of dramatic changes in the climates of opinion. They are at their most effective when they present a common front to the political elite and the society. As Haas points out, "Such experts' influence is subject to their ability to avoid widespread internal disagreement" (Haas 1994, 45).

CONCLUSION

It is certainly important to understand the global picture, says John Brown, the CEO of the world's most profitable major oil company, British Petroleum, but it is equally important for leaders to be able to break the big picture down "into bits that are real for individuals." The global economy, he says, has made knowledge about how each specific country and region relates to the whole even more urgent (Prokesch 1997, 17). It is important, for instance, to know that world oil consumption is growing by 2 percent per year, and gas consumption by 3 percent. It is even more important, however, to know about specific growth opportunities in each of the particular countries where British Petroleum operates. Knowing about such opportunities requires one-to-one interactions with the people and the society.

This paper has been concerned with one such specific local political reality: interpreting politics as a composite way of understanding the total social structure and its various groups. We have been particularly concerned with the role of race in the creation of climates of opinion within which elites have to act. We do not take for granted the permanence of any climate of opinion and understand that there is often a wide gap between the ideologies that elites profess to hold or, at least, the rhetoric they use and the actions they take. Sociological theory teaches us that such incongruities between ideology and behavior do not last long. Either ideology adjusts to behavior or vice versa.

This approach differs from the belief in the existence of a hemisphere-wide Washington Consensus: a whole new generation of leaders and societies both adhering to and acting on neoliberal ideas. This latest manifestation of the traditional U.S. idea of progress is certainly a powerful one, and no one is going to dispute its reach. However, as the case study of Trinidad racial politics illustrates, there are local political considerations and biases that indicate that some of the issues neoliberalism takes for granted, namely, the rejection of state involvement in the economy, are far from being settled. Trinidad is not the only example in the Caribbean that can be cited.

A poll by *The Wall Street Journal* and 145 Latin American newspapers in the late 1990s showed a generally favorable hemisphere-wide attitude toward free trade and foreign investments (poll reprinted in *El Nuevo Herald*'s weekly economic review, July 6-12, 1998, 9-14). Opinion was divided, though, on the value and desirability of privatization. In countries such as Argentina, Bolivia, Brazil, Chile, Guatemala, Mexico, Panama, Paraguay, and Peru, those approving of privatization were in the minority. Two explanations for this stance were given: unwillingness to change the tradition, dating to colonial times, of the government providing services in basic utilities; and the pervasive suspicion in these countries that much of the privatization process had been political and riddled with corruption.

Whatever the results of such polls on economic preferences, it would be a mistake to accept them separately from other polls that probed more broadly political conditions in specific countries. For instance, around the same time that *The Wall Street Journal* poll appeared showing Venezuelans favoring privatization by 23 points, local Venezuelan polls indicated that the candidate most opposed to both privatization and foreign investments, Hugo Chávez, was well ahead, leading his closest competitor by 20 points (*El Nuevo Herald,* July 1, 1998, 1, 8). As is to be expected, Trinidadians are now watching their oil-producing neighbor and its state-owned petroleum industry very closely under Chávez's turbulent presidency.

There is the extreme case of Haiti, where a self-denominated, anti-neoliberal bloc opposing privatization completely paralyzed all government functions. A more apropos case that Caribbean elites watched carefully was the popular uprising against the privatization of the Puerto Rico Telephone Company. Fully 65 percent of the islanders opposed the sale. Because the long distance operations had been sold without incident several years before, and in 1990 both major political parties had agreed on the value of such a sale, the uproar in 1998 surprised the elites. There appeared to be much politics and little economic reasoning in the opposition. The opposition to the sale, said the leader of the New Independence Movement, "has become the symbol of the national struggle for sovereignty and for that reason has become a political problem" (*The Miami Herald,* June 29, 1998, 4). Coming from a different political and ideological angle, a leader of the Popular Democratic Party also opposed the sale on political and cultural grounds. The sale, he argued, was an attempt to advance statehood status for Puerto Rico by blurring the differences between the island and the mainland. "One difference [between Puerto Rico and the United States] is ownership of public corporations" (*The New York Times,* June 30, 1998, 14). The sale of the telephone company was in keeping with global trends; politics made it a local issue.

Similarly, the problem in Trinidad is that not only are public expectations of the state's role directly linked with local historical, political, cultural, and even racial considerations, but these considerations are the ones favored and publicly promoted in much of the local intellectual-ideological formulations. If by ideology we mean a systematic set of assumptions concerning the economy as it relates to the wider society and political system, then it is patently evident that in Trinidad, as in much of the Third World, popular ideology favors giving a central role to the state and sustaining a certain degree of economic nationalism. In the language of Michael Walzer, in the Third World, such a nationalist vision of the state and the economy add up to what he calls a "thick," or "maximalist," moral argument or bias. These are locally generated, culturally connected ideas that are relevant in their specific details to the actual experiences and expectations of the society. Neoliberalism, in contrast, as much as its postulates appear eminently rational and beneficial to certain elites, especially epistemic ones, appears to the masses as "thin," or "minimalist," moral arguments: culturally detached, fundamentally abstract, and externally driven. This does not mean that minimalist ideas are any less valid or useful. What it means, as Walzer reminds us, is that precisely because thin moral arguments express no particular culture and attempt to regulate everyone's behavior in a universally defined way, they carry no personal or social signature. "It is everyone's morality," says Walzer, "because it is no one's in particular; subjective interests and cultural expression have been avoided or cut away" (Walzer 1994, 7).

In Trinidad, neoliberal ideas are still fundamentally abstract, culturally detached, and general. Although certainly convincing to the decision-making political and economic elites, to the general society they represent a minimalist moral argument. Keep in mind that the issues of state control — call it "localization," "domestication," "people's sector," or "the aspirations of the Bandung generation"— were creations of very specific historical watersheds and thus rooted in very real biases and expectations as to what a just state should do. And, as we have noted, such expectations predate political independence. Among the intensely believed and culturally connected expectations of the mixed and Afro-Trinidadian populations, in particular, were expectations that the colonial state break the racial caste system to allow them job opportunities. This civil rights issue was translated after independence into the expectation — held by Eric Williams but also by A.N.R. Robinson and Basdeo Panday — of a state-sponsored affirmative action program to compensate for historical disadvantages and, by extension, to protect the mixed and Afro-Trinidadian people from unfair competition, especially if that competition was racial or, worse, racial and foreign.

Such maximalist, or thick, moral reasoning persists in intellectual sectors. The policy of divestment, very specifically, is seen as reversing what has been the painfully slow but, nonetheless, deeply moral commitment to build a people's sector. Even such a moderate political scientist as Selwyn Ryan could not separate his discussion of economics from thick moral issues such as the politics of local race relations. "In 1990," he wrote, "the outlines of the economic counterrevolution were only evident. By 1995, the triumph of the counterrevolution had become unmistakable" (Ryan and Stewart 1995, 16). To Ryan, the counterrevolution meant unemployment, shrinking social programs, the collapse of (especially black) small businesses, a news media again dominated by foreign images, "most of which are white and Eurocentric"; even dress and hairstyles now "imitate America and disdain Africa." The previously nationalized crown jewels of the economy, he continues, are now privatized and again in the hands of the multinationals who have been invited to return with "bargain-basement prices."

To Ryan, the implications for Trinidad, especially since the victory of the Indo-Trinidadian UNC in 1995, were worrisome because they involved a dangerous zero-sum game. "The same factors which led to the growing strength of Indo-Trinidadian culture," he wrote, "have served to weaken Afro-creole social, economic and political power" (Ryan 1997, 21). This decline held especially true for young Afro-creole males who were faring less well in the newer knowledge-based jobs of the rapidly restructuring society.

One does not have to go far to grasp the empirical basis of Ryan's concerns. The racial implications of this dissatisfaction with economic policy are apparent in the data in Table 13. Afro-Trinidadians, by a wide margin, perceived themselves — and were perceived by others — as the big losers in the post-1980s shift from statism liberalization.

Table 13.
Groups Losing Most, 1986-1991

Groups	Response Group			
Losing Most	Blacks	Indian	Mixed	White
Whites	1	3	6	23
Blacks	77	33	66	46
Indians	1	32	4	0
Mixed	1	1	0	0
Chinese	1	3	1	8
Syrians	1	2	1	0
None	5	8	7	0
Don't know	13	18	16	23

Source: Ryan and Barclay, 1992, *Sharks and Sardines*, 191.

An astonishing 77 percent of blacks and 66 percent of the mixed population believed that blacks had lost the most from the opening of the downsizing of the state sector. Although 32 percent of the Indo-Trinidadians believed they had lost the most, not only was this a minority opinion within their own ethnic group, it was an opinion shared by no other group. The reasons for the perception that Indians did not lose from the neoliberal programs and state divestments are not unknown to Ryan and others. Because Indians were never favored by the PNM-dominated state, they got, in Ryan's words, "the best of the bargain in the long run" (Ryan and Barclay 1992, 189). They now enjoyed hegemony in certain sectors of the economy, used their investments in education to secure strong representations in all the professions, and were "now successfully challenging [blacks] for hegemony in the bureaucracy." These gains by Indo-Trinidadians, at least in terms of household income, were corroborated by Ralph Henry in some exacting statistical analyses (Henry 1993, 75-76). A comprehensive study carried out by Selwyn Ryan, John La Guerre, and their colleagues at the Centre for Ethnic Studies gave empirical corroboration to this perception. Graffiti on the island proclaiming "Indian power" and "Indian time" was not empty bravado; it spoke to a real and largely self-generated new identity.

Notwithstanding this admirable advance in social and economic status through private enterprise, Indian politician-intellectuals continued to speak of white oligarchical conspiracies to keep Indians in an alleged subordinate position. Why? What accounts for the fact that these Indian politicians-cum-intellectuals made allegations that, as Ryan notes, "are identical to those made by blacks" (Ryan 1992, 203)?

There are at least two very real reasons why the political elites and intellectuals on the island and elsewhere in the Caribbean hesitated to openly advocate neoliberal ideologies: 1) the demonstrated political strengths of the thick moral arguments that undergird statism and 2) the need for the intellectuals to save face. Let us elaborate.

It is clear that Indo-Trinidadians were as interested as their Afro-Trinidadian compatriots in benefiting from state action; the political possession of the state continued to be a supreme national prize. The direction and beneficiaries might differ, but the maximalist expectations were there. This partly explains why now even the new Indo-Trinidadian leadership has articulated a coherent and public macroeconomic ideology. Given the pluralist and competitive democratic nature of these systems, there are great risks in ignoring public sentiments. No politician ignores a widely held belief that associates the private sector with the local white group. Minimalist arguments, no matter how rational in an international context, are no match for the persuasive moral force of such thick moral biases. This partly explains why the elites who carry out liberalization policies hesitate to campaign forcefully for neoliberal ideas or even to acknowledge that they are being implemented. What is involved is a very rational calculation of costs. The consequence is, of course, that the logic and gains (real or potential) of neoliberalism remain largely unexplained. They remain at the level of a thin, or minimalist, moral argument. From this flows another potential consequence, that is, that public exasperation over the gap between rhetoric and action leads to urban explosions similar to those that occurred in 1970 and 1990.

Intellectual elites face an additional disincentive to publicly champion the neoliberal banner. Even those with a direct or indirect involvement in neoliberal decisionmaking feel that openly accepting it in theory as well as practice means a loss of face. No one acquainted with the literature on Caribbean (and Trinidadian) "respectability" and "reputation" will think "loss of face" a trivial matter (Wilson 1969; Braithwaite 1953; Yelvington 1993). Such a loss often occurs when there is a rejection of theories once strongly held and promoted and still popular among the people. The loss of face is potentially greater when the new ideas are perceived as externally derived and, perhaps, even externally imposed and when the benefits from the switch are not immediately evident. As Lucian W. Pye noted about elites in a different but not unrelated Third World context, changing intellectual paradigms is easier than channeling emotions behind that change because, to the intellectual, "a real effort at change would call for another attempt at changing their personal identities, and it is both too late and too costly for them to commit themselves to such an effort" (Pye 1962, 230).

The findings of this case study should tell us that the longer-term future course of macroeconomic policies in Trinidad, and arguably for the Caribbean, are still not certain at this juncture. As it is not clear that neoliberal practice is being accompanied by the creation of a maximalist moral argument defending, or at least explaining, the urgency and ultimate benefits of liberalization in a global economy, the existing incongruity between thick popular values and expectations and the thin values on which the elites are basing their actions will continue to be as wide, at least for the short to medium term. It cannot continue over the longer haul, however. Sociological theory tells us that pressures toward a compatibility condition will build until the incongruity between ideology and practice is resolved. As such, three possible outcomes are hypothesized over the longer run. First, a situation where the benefits from policies that facilitate an entry into the global economy and market are so evident and widely distributed that politicians and intellectuals see real benefits from embracing and proclaiming the new ideology. Failing such material rewards, a second situation would be the exact opposite: the general social costs from pursuing liberalization are such that mere political survival (that is, the fear of charismatic populists such as President Chávez) would compel politicians to reverse course and return to some form of economic nationalism.

There could, of course, be a third yet-unknown adjustment. The history of changing climates of opinion cautions us that this is possible. This is what makes Allen Hammond's idea that in an age of rapid and profound historical transformations, it is incumbent upon the intellectual and the statesman alike to study not only global but also specifically regional trends and to learn to build alternative scenarios from these as a means of anticipating the future (Hammond 1998). This necessarily means setting aside rigid ideological preconceptions about the way things are going, globally and locally. At present, such flexibility is not evident in Trinidad. There, local politics do have an uncanny way of interfering with grand theories about globalization and universal consensus.

References

Adelman, Jeremy. 1998. "Latin America and Globalization." *LASA Forum* 29:1 (spring).

Anthony, Michael. 1997. *Historical Dictionary of Trinidad-Tobago.* Lanham, Md.: Scarecrow Press.

Bahadoorsingh, Krishna. 1968. *Trinidad: Electoral Politics: The Persistence of the Race Factor.* London: Institute of Race Relations.

Baldeosingh, Donald. 1997. "Activities and Opportunities in the Petroleum Sector." Paper presented to the First Symposium for the Petroleum Sector of the Americas, Caracas, May 17-18.

Beard, Charles A. 1932. "Introduction" to *The Idea of Progress.* London: Macmillan.

Becker, Carl, L. 1932. *The Heavenly City of the Eighteenth-Century Philosophers.* New Haven, Conn.: Yale University Press.

Best, Lloyd. 1997. "Economic Turnaround Is Only an Illusion Says Best." *Trinidad Guardian* March 22, 4.

Bibo, Clemens J. 1994. "The Business Climate in Trinidad and Tobago Through the Eyes of the Private Sector." Unpublished manuscript. Port-of-Spain:-Economic Commission for Latin America and the Caribbean, July 8.

Boopsingh, Trevor M. 1994. "Caribbean Energy Sector: Review and Perspectives." *Caribbean Dialogue* 1:1 (July-August).

Boopsingh, Trevor M., and T.A. Beyer. 1993. "Caribbean Energy Sector Review and Perspectives." Unpublished manuscript. Trinidad, December.

Braithwaite, Lloyd. 1953. "Social Stratification in Trinidad." *Social and Economic Studies* 2:2 (October): 5-175.

Camejo, Acton. 1971. "Racial Discrimination in Employment in the Private Sector in Trinidad and Tobago." *Social and Economic Studies* 20:3 (September): 294-318.

Caribbean Insurance. 1998. July, 10.

Centre for Ethnic Studies. n.d. *Ethnicity and Employment Practices in Trinidad-Tobago.* Vol. 1. St. Augustine, Trinidad: University of the West Indies.

Gangar, Finbar K. 1997a. "An Update on the Energy Sector." Paper presented in China, August 6.

Gangar, Finbar K. 1997b. "Energy Policy Green Paper." Unpublished manuscript. Port-of-Spain:-Ministry of Energy.

Gangar, Finbar K. 1997c. Interview. August 21.

Government of Trinidad and Tobago. 1972. *White Paper on Public Participation in Industrial and Commercial Activities.* Port-of-Spain: Government Printery.

Government of Trinidad and Tobago, Ministry of Food Production, Marine Exploitation, Forestry and the Environment. 1988a. *National Agricultural Development Plan, 1988-1992.* Port-of-Spain: Government Printery.

Government of Trinidad and Tobago. 1988b. *Draft Medium Term Programme, 1989-1991.* Port-of-Spain: Government Printery.

Government of Trinidad and Tobago. 1995. *Public Sector Investment Programme.* Port-of-Spain: Government Printery.

Government of Trinidad and Tobago, Ministry of the Attorney General. 1997. *Reform of Media Law Green Paper.* Port-of-Spain: Government Printery.

Glyden, Axel. 1998. "Venezuela: La grande lessive." *Le Pointe* August 1.

Greider, William. 1997. *One World, Ready or Not: The Manic Logic of Global Capitalism.* New York: Simon and Schuster.

Hammond, Allan. 1998. *Which World? Scenarios for the 21st Century.* Washington, D.C.: Island Press.

Haas, Peter M. 1992. "Introduction: Epistemic Communities and International Policy Coordination." *International Organization* 46 (1): 1-35.

Haas, Peter. 1994. "Regime Patterns for Environmental Management." In *Complex Cooperation: Institutions and Processes in International Resource Management,* eds. Peter M. Haas and Helge Hveem. Oslo: Scandinavian University Press.

Harewood, Jack. 1971. "Racial Discrimination in Employment in Trinidad and Tobago." *Social and Economic Studies* 20 (September): 267-293.

Henry, Ralph. 1993. "Notes on the Evolution of Inequality in Trinidad and Tobago." In *Trinidad Ethnicity,* ed. Kevin Yelvington. Knoxville, Tenn.: University of Tennessee Press.

James, C.L.R. 1962. "Trinidad at Independence." *Trinidad Guardian* (the independence issue) August 30.

Keohane, Robert O., and Joseph S. Nye, Jr. 1998. "Power and Interdependence in the Information Age." *Foreign Affairs* 77:5 (September-October): 81-94.

La Guerre, John. 1991. "Leadership in a Plural Society: The Case of the Indians in Trinidad and Tobago." In *Social and Occupational Stratification in Contemporary Trinidad and Tobago,* ed. Selwyn Ryan. St. Augustine, Trinidad: Institute of Social and Economic Research.

Lasswell, Harold, D., and Abraham Kaplan. 1950. *Power and Society.* New Haven, Conn.: Yale University Press.

Maingot, Anthony P. 1962. "The French Creole of Trinidad." Specialist Thesis, Institute of Caribbean Studies, University of Puerto Rico, Río Piedras.

Maingot, Anthony P. 1992. "Historiography in the Caribbean: Juan Bosch and Eric Williams." In *Intellectuals in the Twentieth-Century Caribbean,* Vol. 2, ed. Alistair Hennessy. London: Macmillan Caribbean.

Malik, Jogendra K. 1971. *East Indians in Trinidad: A Study of Minority Politics.* London: Oxford University Press.

Mannheim, Karl. 1936. *Ideology and Utopia.* New York: International Library.

Miami Herald, The. 1998. June 4, 10.

Miami Herald, The. 1998. June 29, 4.

Mohammed, Kamaluddin. 1995. "Reflections of a Government Minister." In *Power: The Black Power Revolution, 1970: A Retrospective,* eds. Selwyn Ryan and Taimoon Stewart. St. Augustine, Trinidad: Multimedia Production Centre.

New York Times, The. 1998. June 30, 14.

Niehoff, Arthur, and Juanita Niehoff. 1960. *East Indians in the West Indies.* Milwaukee Public Museum Publication.

El Nuevo Herald. 1998. July 1: 1, 8.

El Nuevo Herald. Negocios. 1998. July 6-12, 9-14.

Oil and Gas Journal, Revista Latinoamericana. 1997 (January): 36-40.

OWTU (Oilfield Workers Trade Union). 1987. *50 Years of Progress, 1937-1987.* San Fernando, Trinidad: Vanguard Publications.

Oxaal, Ivar. 1968. *Black Intellectuals Come to Power.* Cambridge, Mass.: Schenkman Publishing.

Pantin, Dennis. 1989. "The Political Economy of Natural Gas-Based Industrialization in Trinidad-Tobago." In *Development in Suspense*, eds. George Beckford and Norman Girvan. Kingston: Friedrich Ebert Stiftung.

Petroleum Economist, 1995, October.

PetroVision, 1995, November, 1.

PetroVision, 1996, September, 6.

PetroVision, 1997, February, 7.

Phillips, D. 1994. "Decentralization and Marginalization in Health Care in Trinidad and Tobago." In *Contemporary Issues in Social Sciences: A Caribbean Perspective,* ed. R. Deosaran. St. Augustine, Trinidad: ANSA McAl Center.

Portes, Alejandro. 1997. "Neoliberalism and the Sociology of Development: Emerging Trends and Unanticipated Facts." *Population and Development Review* 23:2 (June): 229-259.

Prest, A.R. 1957. *A Fiscal Survey of the British Caribbean.* No. 2. London: Colonial Research Studies, no. 23.

Prokesh, Steven, E. 1997. "Unleashing the Power of Learning: An Interview with John Brown." *Harvard Business Review* (September-October): 5-19.

Pye, Lucien. 1962. *Personality and Nationbuilding.* New Haven, Conn.: Yale University Press.

Robinson, A.N.R. 1971. *The Mechanics of Independence.* Cambridge, Mass.: MIT Press.

Rodrik, Dani. 1997. *Has Globalization Gone Too Far?* Washington, D.C.: Institute of International Economics.

Rubin, Vera, and Marissa Zavalloni. 1969. *We Wish to Be Looked Upon.* New York: Teachers College, Columbia University.

Ryan, Selwyn. 1972. *Race and Nationalism in Trinidad and Tobago.* Toronto: University of Toronto Press.

Ryan, Selwyn. 1989a. *Revolution and Reaction.* St. Augustine, Trinidad: Institute of Social and Economic Research.

Ryan, Selwyn. 1989b. *The Disillusioned Electorate.* Port-of-Spain: Imprint Caribbean, Ltd.

Ryan, Selwyn, ed. 1991a. *Social and Occupational Stratification in Contemporary Trinidad-Tobago.* St. Augustine, Trinidad: Institute of Social and Economic Research.

Ryan, Selwyn. 1991b. *The Muslimeen Grab for Power.* Port-of-Spain:-Imprint Caribbean, Ltd.

Ryan, Selwyn. 1997. "The Clash of Cultures in Post Creole Trinidad and Tobago." *Caribbean Dialogue* 3:2 (June): 7-28.

Ryan, Selwyn, and Lou Anne Barclay. 1992. *Sharks and Sardines: Blacks in Business in Trinidad-Tobago.* St. Augustine, Trinidad: Multimedia Productions Centre.

Ryan, Selwyn, and Taimoon Stewart, eds. 1995. *Power: The Black Power Revolution, 1970: A Retrospective.* St. Augustine, Trinidad: Multimedia Production Centre.

Schneider, Mark L. 1998. "Address to the Conference on the Caribbean and Latin America." Washington, D.C., February 2.

Scotland, Leslie, H. 1988. "The Localization of the Banking Industry in Retrospect." In *The Independence Experience,* ed. Selwyn Ryan. St. Augustine, Trinidad: Institute of Social and Economic Research.

Scotland, Leslie, H. 1995. "The Impact of the 1970s Black Power Revolution on Banking." In *Power: The Black Power Revolution, 1970,* eds. Selwyn Ryan and Taimoon Stewart. St. Augustine, Trinidad: Institute of Social and Economic Research.

Sklair, Leslie. 1995. *Sociology of the Global System.* 2d ed. Baltimore: The Johns Hopkins University Press.

Stark, Jeffrey. 1998. "Globalization and Democracy in Latin America." In *Fault Lines of Democracy in Post-Transition Latin America,* eds. Felipe Agüero and Jeffrey Stark. Coral Gables, Fla.: North-South Center Press at the University of Miami.

Sutton, Paul. 1984. "Trinidad and Tobago: Oil Capitalism and the 'Presidential Power' of Erica Williams." In *Dependency Under Challenge,* eds. Anthony Payne and Paul Sutton. Manchester, U.K.: Manchester University Press.

Trinidad Express. 1997, August 19, 6.

Trinidad Express. 1997, August 20, 4.

Trinidad Guardian. 1964, August 30.

Trinidad Guardian. 1997, August 20, 4.

Wall Street Journal, The. 1987, March 12: 1, 20.

Walzer, Michael. 1994. *Thick and Thin: Moral Argument at Home and Abroad.* Notre Dame, Ind.: University of Notre Dame Press.

Williams, Eric. 1942. *The Negro in the Caribbean.* Westport, Conn: Negro University Press.

Williams, Eric. 1964. "Trinidad and Tobago International Perspectives." *Freedom Ways* 4 (Summer).

Williams, Eric. 1969. *Inward Hunger: The Education of a Prime Minister.* London: Andre Deutsch, Ltd.

Williams, Eric. 1970. *From Columbus to Castro.* London: Andre Deutsch, Ltd.

Williams, Eric. 1980. "Political Leader's Account of the Party's Stewardship, 1956-1980." Unpublished manuscript. September 26.

Williams, Eric. 1981. *Forged From the Love of Liberty: Selected Speeches of Dr. Eric Williams.* London: Longman.

Wilson. P.J. 1969. "Reputation and Respectability: A Suggestion for Caribbean Ethnography." *Man* 4 (2): 70-84.

World Bank. 1998. *World Development Indicators.* Washington, D.C.: World Bank.

Worrell, De Lisle. 1989. "Adjustment, Stabilization, and National Experiences in the Caribbean." In *Development in Suspense,* eds. George Beckford and Norman Girvan. Kingston: Friedrich Ebert Shifttung.

Yelvington, Kevin, ed. 1993. *Trinidad Ethnicity.* Knoxville, Tenn.: The University of Tennessee Press.

Zakaria, Fareed. 1998. "Will Asia Turn Against the West?" *The New York Times,* July 10.

PARTIAL LIST OF INTERVIEWS IN TRINIDAD

The Honorable Dr. Trevor Sudama
Minister of Planning

The Honorable Dr. Reeza Mohammed
Minister of Agriculture

The Honorable Mr. John Humphrey
Minister of Housing and Settlements

The Honorable Mr. Finbar K. Gangar
Minister of Energy

Dr. Winston Dookeran
Governor, The Central Bank

C. Keith Awong
CEO/MD, Petrotrin

Mr. Hanza Deave
Editor, *PetroVision*

Ms. Sherifa Hosein
Public Relations Department, Petrotrin

Mr. Emile Elias
President, Trinidad-Tobago Contractors Association

Dr. Selwyn Ryan
Director, Institute of Social and Economic Research, University of the West Indies

Dr. Compton Bourne
Pro-Vice Chancellor and Principal, University of the West Indies

Dr. John LaGuerre
Department of Behavioral Sciences, University of the West Indies

II.
Meeting New Policy Challenges

CHAPTER 4

Toward a Free Trade Area of the Americas: Progress and Prospects

AMBLER MOSS

This chapter discusses the historical antecedents and recent developments of one of the most important initiatives in contemporary inter-American relations — the Free Trade Area of the Americas (FTAA), scheduled for completion in 2005. It begins by reviewing the long history of the idea of economic integration in the Americas, which was given greater seriousness of purpose with the announcement of the Enterprise for the Americas Initiative in 1990 and the launching of the FTAA at the Summit of the Americas in Miami in December 1994. The author then traces the construction of the building blocks of the FTAA in a series of trade ministerials that created working groups, made arrangements for private sector input, and set up a rotating temporary secretariat for the FTAA process. The author also identifies problems encountered along the way, including lack of fast-track authority in the United States, the treatment of smaller economies, and concerns over labor and the environment. The chapter concludes by examining the pro-free trade posture of the new George W. Bush administration, as expressed at the April 2001 Summit of the Americas in Quebec, Canada, and in its pursuit of trade promotion authority (formerly fast track) with the U.S. Congress.

The decade of the 1990s marked the most advanced opening toward economic integration that the Western Hemisphere has ever known. Although progress may seem uneven at times, the construction of a Free Trade Area of the Americas (FTAA) is moving ahead toward an ambitious target date of 2005. While unpredictable economic conditions in the world, as well as in the hemisphere, could upset or retard the time line, there is cause for optimism that the countries of Latin America and the Caribbean will reach their goal. The 2005 finish date has been maintained since it was agreed upon during the Miami Summit of the Americas in 1994.

In examining the FTAA process, it is important to bear in mind that it takes place within the new context of a world trading system, through the completion of the Uruguay Round of the General Agreement on Tariffs and Trade (GATT) and the establishment of the World Trade Organization (WTO) in 1994. What will be the elements of interface between the WTO and regional trading systems? Do the great disparities of economic development and standards of living among Western Hemisphere countries pose serious questions as to the extent of the FTAA's depth and viability? These and other lingering issues, such as the role of civil society and the private sector and the political commitment of the United States (given lack of a presidential "fast track" authorization), continue to cast shadows on the FTAA's process and progress.

A BIT OF HISTORY

Let us begin by putting the FTAA into its historical context. Economic integration in the Americas is not a new idea. None other than Simón Bolívar convoked the Congress of Panamá in 1826 for the purpose of consolidating the newly independent Latin American Republics into a cohesive market. Secretary of State John Quincy Adams appointed two observer delegates from the United States, who, unfortunately, never made it to the conference. The Congress itself never resulted in realizing Bolívar's dream; disunity was to prevail in Latin America.

Later it became the United States' turn to advance the vision. Secretary of State James G. Blaine advocated, in the national interest, an expansion of trade relations between the United States and Latin America. In 1881, he issued an invitation to the independent countries of the Americas (except for Haiti) to meet and discuss trade and measures to prevent war. The invitation was withdrawn, however, after the assassination of President James Garfield. In October 1889 in Washington, D.C., Blaine successfully convened a conference of 17 countries. The result, more symbolic than real, was to set up an entity called the International Bureau of American Republics. In 1910, its name was changed to the Pan American Union (PAU), and its headquarters remained in Washington, with the U.S. secretary of state as its permanent chairman. In 1948, at an inter-American meeting in Bogotá, the PAU was transformed into the present-day Organization of American States (OAS). Security issues, not economic ones, dominated that forum, despite Latin American aspirations for their own "Marshall Plan."

President John F. Kennedy's Alliance for Progress, instituted in 1961, emphasized economic issues. It promised large transfers of capital to Latin America through foreign aid and private investment. As a natural outgrowth of the Alliance, President Lyndon B. Johnson, who had a genuine interest in Latin America, supported a Meeting of American Chiefs of State in Punta del Este, Uruguay, in April 1967. Organized by the OAS, this meeting's philosophy was, "Economic integration is a collective instrument for accelerating Latin American economic development and should constitute one of the policy goals of each of the countries of the region."

The Latin American heads of state at the Punta del Este summit agreed "to create progressively, beginning in 1970, the Latin American Common Market, which shall be substantially in operation in a period of no more then fifteen years." In the summit's final document, "The President of the United States, for his part, declares his firm support for this promising Latin American initiative."[1] Needless to say, the region was not ready for a common market nor even a free trade area — the Latin American Common market was far too ambitious a plan for its time. The prevailing trends were toward increasing state-owned industries and a preference for investment through international lending rather than foreign direct investment (FDI), which, in many countries, would be nationalized or forced out. Protectionism was rampant among the countries, most of which were ruled by military governments, as opposed to democracies. The *Declaration of Presidents and Action Plan*, the Punta del Este summit's final document, was relegated to foreign ministry archives.

In 1969, *The Rockefeller Report on the Americas*, ordered by President Richard Nixon and carried out by Nelson A. Rockefeller, wisely warned of an impending debt crisis. "Heavy borrowings by some Western Hemisphere countries," it said, "...have reached the point where annual repayments of interest and amortization absorb a large part of foreign exchange earnings."[2] The report recommended debt rescheduling on a country-by-country basis. It also urged the United States to grant tariff preferences to stimulate Latin American exports.

The Rockefeller report was ahead of its time. It took over another decade for Latin American debt to reach crisis proportions when, in August 1982, Mexico was unable to meet its debt service obligations. The decade of the 1980s, for most, but not all, Latin American countries, was a period of negative growth and declining standards of living. For a time, nine of the top 10 U.S. banks would have been in jeopardy of failure if the Third World debtor countries had formed a debtors' cartel and renounced their debts. In retrospect, differences among the countries were so great that this could never happen, but it was an ominous economic time for both creditors and debtors. In 1989, the gross domestic product (GDP) per capita in Latin America as a whole stood 9.1 percent below its 1980 level, after adjusting for inflation.

Out of the "lost decade" of the 1980s, however, came the basis for real reform. In the latter part of the decade, Mexico was among the first to set the pace. Reform consisted of lowering trade barriers, courting foreign investment, tightening budgets to eliminate fiscal deficits, privatizing and deregulating industries and services, and adopting policies based on free markets and property rights. Supported by the United States and the international financial institutions, these reforms came to be known as the "Washington Consensus." In the late 1980s, countries of the region began to negotiate free trade agreements (FTAs) with one another. The most significant was the Canada-United States Free Trade Agreement, known as CUFTA, implemented in 1988. Meanwhile, the free trade movement was encouraged by accelerating economic growth rates in most of Latin America and the Caribbean, brought about by fiscal adjustments and market reforms.

THE STAGE IS SET

On June 27, 1990, President George Bush, in a widely publicized White House speech, announced his Enterprise for the Americas Initiative (EAI). Consisting of "three pillars" (trade, investment, and debt initiatives), its boldest goal was the creation of a hemispheric free trade agreement to eliminate both tariff and non-tariff barriers. He called for all countries in the Western Hemisphere to be "equal partners in a free trade zone stretching from the port of Anchorage to the Tierra del Fuego."

What was behind the EAI? It would seem that in 1990, in contrast with 1889, the United States not only wanted the Latin American market for trade but this time actually needed it. The Uruguay Round of GATT was in a precarious state (negotiations would collapse in December of 1990), thwarting the desire of U.S. policymakers for a world trading regime through a world trade organization. The creation of the WTO would not happen until 1994. To Washington in 1990, it appeared the world might divide into regional trading blocs, however defined — certainly Europe, East Asia, and perhaps others. The United States needed a trading bloc to call its own, especially to improve its trade balance. Latin America, where the United States enjoyed a large market share for imports (over 70 percent in Mexico) was the logical place. Its population was over 400 million, with a GDP of US$1 trillion.

An early goal of the EAI was to begin a trade agreement with Mexico similar to the CUFTA. At Canadian insistence, this project soon took on a triangular nature, aimed at bringing the three countries into a North American Free Trade Agreement (NAFTA). The NAFTA negotiations were to be picked up and completed by the incoming administration of President Bill Clinton. As with all contemporary trade agreements, NAFTA was signed as an executive agreement, requiring approval of implementing legislation in both houses of Congress. The House of Representatives was the scene of bitter opposition to NAFTA, even though the accord had been "sweetened" by labor and environmental side agreements in an attempt to mollify some of its opponents. After a heated debate, NAFTA was finally passed in November 1993.

Contemporaneous with NAFTA, Latin America and the Caribbean were going ahead with trade agreements of their own, both bilateral and multilateral. The most significant of these was the Southern Common Market (Mercado Común del Sur —MERCOSUR), a common market among Argentina, Brazil, Paraguay and Uruguay, for which an agreement was signed in 1991 to be implemented in 1995. The growth of other regional alliances proceeded apace — the Caribbean Community and Common Market (CARICOM) in the Caribbean, founded in 1973, now with 14 countries; the Central American Common Market (CACM), originally established in 1961; a renewed Andean Pact, first established in 1969; and a host of bilateral and other agreements. By the time that NAFTA was approved, these other trade agreements added up to more than 30.

THE MIAMI SUMMIT LAUNCHES THE FTAA IN DECEMBER 1994

In late 1993, after the NAFTA victory in the U.S. Congress, Vice President Al Gore traveled to Mexico City. There, on December 1, he announced that President Clinton would invite freely elected heads of state and government to a summit meeting in the United States the following year. The announcement came as a pleasant surprise to Latin American leaders, although its purpose and content were unclear. Aside from approving NAFTA, the Clinton administration's foreign policy had not seemed to consider Latin America a high priority. Moreover, in most respects, NAFTA was primarily domestic policy, in the Latin American leaders' view. In Washington, an interagency task force was set in motion to define the agenda, and in March 1994, President Clinton announced that the Summit of the Americas was to be held in Miami that December.

Although trade was the primary issue of interest to Latin Americans, the fact that trade would be the main issue at the summit was not generally known until just weeks before the meeting. Consultations with hemisphere countries had indicated that Latin American governments wanted from the United States a clear outline of its post-NAFTA trade agenda. When Senior Presidential Adviser Thomas "Mack" McLarty took charge of the agenda-setting processes for the administration, a strong commitment for free trade in the hemisphere finally solidified. Even as presidents and prime ministers prepared to depart for Miami, negotiations were still in progress among all of the participants, eventually resulting in consensus on the FTAA as a goal, with an agreed completion date of 2005. Additional encouragement to the summit participants came with the conclusion of the Uruguay Round of GATT, followed by the creation of the WTO and approval of its implementing legislation by the U.S. Congress.

A noteworthy feature of the Miami Summit was that all 34 of its participants were freely elected, representing the entire hemisphere except for Fidel Castro's Cuba. Although the FTAA was not to be explicitly restricted to democracies, as was the European Common Market, at least the maintenance of democracy was implicit in the language of the *Declaration of Principles*, an official Summit document, signed by all heads of state and government:

> The elected Heads of State and Government of the Americas are committed to advance the prosperity, democratic values and institutions, and security of our Hemisphere. For the first time in history, the Americas are a community of democratic societies.[3]

At the three-day Miami summit, the parties were unable to agree on an overall blueprint or precise plan for achieving the FTAA. However, actually reaching agreement and signing the commitment were landmark events. Intelligently, a timetable was set for annual trade ministers' meetings to launch and oversee items in the *Plan of Action* of the summit and to advance the entire process. The first such meeting was scheduled to take place in Denver in March 1995. At the close of the summit, the leaders of the United States, Canada, and Mexico announced that Chile would be the next country invited to join NAFTA. At that time, Chile and Mexico already had a bilateral FTA in place. Subsequently, Chile has signed an FTA with Canada. The absence of presidential negotiating authority (known as "fast-track" authority), however, never renewed by the U.S. Congress after the passage of NAFTA, has inhibited NAFTA's expansion to this day.

The lack of an overall blueprint at the summit does not imply that there were no visions in the participants' minds. One such vision, in the minds of some Washington officials, involved the rolling southward of NAFTA, beginning with Chile and then picking up countries and groups of countries tied together by regional FTAs. In stark contrast was the Brazilian approach. Brazil favored a slower strategy, calling for distinct stages of negotiation. The most serious stage would not begin until after the year 2000, with liberalization of access for goods and services, investment rule liberalization, and the opening of government procurement to foreign bidders on an equal basis. In fact, Brazil and its MERCOSUR partners wanted to consolidate their own FTA network, then under construction (some have referred to it as a SAFTA, for South American Free Trade Agreement), before negotiating with the powerful United States.

It should be mentioned in passing that the Miami Summit agenda was not confined to trade alone. Important initiatives and specific points in the *Plan of Action* were adopted in the areas of democracy and human rights, civil society participation, corruption, narcotics and money laundering, capital market liberalization, education, health, and sustainable development. All of these items were followed up in some fashion in other forums and eventually in the second Summit of the Americas in Santiago, Chile, in April 1998.

ENTER THE MEXICAN PESO CRISIS

The afterglow of the Miami Summit was dimmed, however, only a few days later. On December 20, 1994, Mexico caused an economic shock felt by the financial markets of the entire Western Hemisphere with the devaluation of its currency, the peso. For some time, many experts had felt the peso was overvalued. Since foreign reserves in the Bank of Mexico were low, the government feared an attack on these reserves by holders of the peso. What Mexico attempted as a correction was a 15-percent increase in the ceiling of the exchange band of the peso with the U.S. dollar. This move, the government felt, would relieve the pressure and keep Mexico in emerging market status.

The Mexican government's optimism was mistaken. Following the devaluation, a massive withdrawal of capital from Mexico and other major emerging markets of Latin America took governments and international financial institutions by surprise. The shock effect was felt right down the hemisphere. In Buenos Aires, it was dubbed the "tequila effect." Most of the capital entering these emerging markets had been portfolio capital (not direct investment), placed there by mutual funds and financial institutions. Some of it was also the return of "flight capital," which Latin Americans had stashed away for safekeeping abroad during the 1980s' debt crisis. Such capital proved to be very portable — and skittish.

The Clinton administration responded on January 12, 1995, by requesting legislation from the Congress, providing $40 billion in loan guarantees to prevent a major default on Mexican government bonds. Congress dithered, and President Clinton unilaterally organized a loan package of $20 billion from the U.S. Treasury's Exchange Stabilization Fund, supplemented by loans from the International Monetary Fund (IMF), the Bank for International Settlements (BIS), and the Government of Canada. The World Bank (WB) and Inter-American Development Bank (IDB) continued their efforts later in separate negotiations with Mexico. Although Clinton's move was subjected to criticism as a "bailout" and its constitutionality has been questioned by legal scholars, the move brought a sigh of relief from congressional leaders and contributed to a rapid recovery by Mexico. By the following year, the country had repaid its debt to the United States with interest.[4]

THE DENVER TRADE MINISTERIAL

If the Miami Summit participants had not shown the foresight to schedule the next trade ministers' meeting, the Mexico peso crisis might have ground the whole FTAA process to a halt or at least seriously impaired its progress. The ministers met in Denver, however, and, on June 30, 1995, issued their first *Joint Declaration*, of which four more would follow annually. In this document, they agreed that, in keeping with the Summit, they would build the FTAA "on existing subregional and bilateral agreements in order to broaden and deepen hemispheric economic integration and to bring the agreements together." Further, they agreed to maximize market openness, to make the FTAA consistent with the provisions of the agreement establishing the WTO, not to raise barriers to other countries, and to ensure that the FTAA would be "a single undertaking comprising mutual rights and obligations."[5]

In this fashion, the meeting set the stage for a process to build the FTAA even in the absence of an agreed blueprint. It also sent a message to Japan and other countries concerned about the FTAA being an exclusive trading bloc. The FTAA would be "open regionalism" — not an attempt to close off markets. Each subsequent ministerial meeting would also repeat the FTAA's adherence to the WTO; this world trading arrangement would clearly take precedence over a regional approach.

The Denver meeting's purpose was not to begin negotiations for the FTAA but to prepare for them. For that reason, the minister established working groups in a number of technical areas, the idea being that these groups would compile information and construct data bases about the subject matter, especially the laws and regulations, tariff and non-tariff barriers, and applicable effects of trade agreements entered into by each member country. The working groups were also charged with making recommendations concerning the negotiations to take place in their areas. The following list describes working groups that were set up and their main areas of work:

- Market Access (identifying market access barriers in the hemisphere, both tariff and non-tariff, covering all industrial and agricultural products);
- Customs Procedures and Rules of Origin (preparing a comprehensive inventory of customs procedures in the hemisphere and the feasibility of developing a general guide to procedures, including a system of rules of origin, measures for the prevention of fraud, and the simplification of customs procedures);
- Investment (drafting an inventory of investment agreements and regimes in the region);
- Standards and Technical Barriers to Trade (TBTs) (compiling information on existing bodies charged with conformity assessment to technical regulations and the organizations that accredit such bodies; making recommendations on ways to enhance transparency and on product testing and certification);
- Sanitary and Phytosanitary Measures (SPS) (preparing an inventory of all hemispheric agreements on SPS, recommendations for enhancing information-sharing, promoting understanding of the WTO Agreement on

SPS, and enhancing mutual understanding of the scientific basis of certification procedures; and the issuance of certificates among countries of the hemisphere);

- Subsidies, Antidumping and Countervailing Duties (identifying agricultural export subsidies and export practices with a similar effect, recommending ways to address all trade-distorting export practices for agricultural products, promoting understanding of WTO obligations with respect to subsidies, and compiling an inventory of subsidies practices in the hemisphere and of dumping and subsidies laws); and
- Smaller Economies (studying the factors that affect the participation of smaller economies in the FTAA process and the ways to facilitate the adjustment of smaller economies, including the promotion and expansion of their trade and requesting certain international organizations to provide pertinent information on their activities to facilitate integration of the smaller economies).

The Denver ministers requested the "Tripartite Committee," consisting of the OAS, the IDB, and the United Nations Economic Commission for Latin American and the Caribbean (ECLAC) to "provide support, technical assistance and relevant studies" to the working groups. Their participation, of course, would be absolutely essential to the success of the working groups, which would have no staffs of their own. Additionally, meetings of vice ministers were prescribed to review the work prior to the next ministers' meeting, scheduled for March 1996.

Finally, the ministers agreed in Denver that at their next meeting four more working groups would be established. The United States had wanted them included immediately, but Latin American political sensitivity precluded their being agreed upon so early. They were listed as follows:

- Government Procurement,
- Intellectual Property Rights,
- Services, and
- Competition Policy.

Following the Denver ministerial, a meeting was held for interested private sector representatives, known as the Americas Business Forum. It was well attended, especially by U.S. members, but it was soon criticized for two reasons. First, private sector members opined that their meeting should be held prior to the ministerial, to give input to the ministers. Second, there should be a better way of designating attendance at the Forum than the one chosen, namely, invitation by ministries of commerce. The next host of a ministerial meeting, Colombia, remedied these two defects.

THE CARTAGENA MINISTERIAL AND AMERICAS BUSINESS FORUM, MARCH 1996

As might be expected, there was some apprehension on the part of trade officials as well as private sector representatives about holding a meeting in Colombia because of security concerns. Nevertheless, these worries were mitigated by two considerations. First, the Colombian coordinator of both events, Jorge Ramírez Ocampo, was obviously an able person who would do an effective job of putting the meetings together, and this inspired confidence. Second, the city of Cartagena, a beautiful colonial-era port on the Caribbean coast, seemed to enjoy immunity from terrorism and kidnapping.

An important step was taken by Ramírez Ocampo in scheduling the private sector meeting, the Americas Business Forum, before the ministerial. In that way, a private sector input could be passed to the ministers. Obvious as this sounds, Ramírez found in his prior consultations that there was still some apprehension in adopting this sequence, even on the part of some U.S. officials. This order of meetings would become the rule for future ministerials, however, as would the practice of Forum participants being self-selecting. The problem of private sector input was not fully solved, nevertheless, as the Forum met immediately before the trade ministerial, not a long enough time in advance to make a great impact on the ministerial. This defect was overcome partially at Cartagena and in future meetings by requesting participants in the Forum to send in written submissions several weeks in advance of the ministerial. Such documents were then furnished to trade ministries.

At Cartagena, the ministers discussed methods of constructing the FTAA that could build on existing subregional and bilateral pacts and arrangements. They also reviewed the work completed to date by the working groups established at Denver. In looking at the timing and means of launching formal negotiations to achieve the FTAA, the ministers agreed that more preparatory work had to be accomplished before making any specific recommendations. They directed their vice ministers to make recommendations to that effect before the next ministerial in 1997. In fact, to gain ground, they directed the vice ministers to meet at least three times, "to ensure significant progress in advance of our next meeting." They also reiterated the pledge that "concrete progress must be achieved by the end of the century."[6]

In compliance with the commitments made at the Denver meeting, new working groups were established on Government Procurement, Intellectual Property Rights, Services, and Competition Policy. Action Plans were issued for each group, as had been the case with the groups previously established, and they added to the Action Plans of the previous working groups. The ministers also agreed to start a working group on dispute settlement procedures by the 1997 ministerial, with the OAS compiling information about actual dispute resolution mechanisms being used in bilateral and subregional trade agreements in the Americas. The Cartagena meeting charged the working groups to go beyond the compiling of information and to develop possible approaches to actual negotiations. It also received from the Special Trade Unit of the OAS a large analytical Compendium of Trade and Integration Accords in the Hemisphere.

THE THIRD MINISTERIAL: BELO HORIZONTE, MAY 1997

As Brazil is often thought to be the most reticent of the participants in the FTAA process, it was interesting to see it host the next business forum and ministerial.

In fact, a sense of progress was maintained. The *Belo Horizonte Ministerial Declaration*, issued May 16, 1997, began by reiterating the commitment to complete the FTAA by 2005 and to make "concrete progress toward the attainment of the objective by the end of this century."[7] The declaration noted substantial progress in trade liberalization throughout the hemisphere since the Miami Summit, not only by the widening and deepening of existing trade agreements and the negotiation of new ones, but also by the implementation of countries' commitments under the WTO. The Brazil ministerial looked forward to a Second Summit of the Americas to be held in Santiago, Chile, in March 1998. That meeting would be preceded by a fourth trade ministerial meeting in February 1998.

The Belo Horizonte ministerial found that, during all the meetings to date, there were many areas of convergence. Consensus among the 34 countries was the fundamental principle of the FTAA, which would be a single undertaking embodying all the rights and obligations of the parties. The FTAA, it reiterated, must be consistent with WTO undertakings. Countries could join the FTAA individually or through bilateral or subregional membership. Special attention must be given to the needs of smaller economies.

The ministers, in their declaration, recognized the need "for a temporary Administrative Secretariat to support the negotiations." They also set the terms of reference for such a body and stipulated a feasibility study concerning alternative sites. These sites would include good flight connections, hotel facilities, meeting facilities, and a multilingual workforce. The Tripartite Committee (the IDB, OAS, and ECLAC) was charged with evaluating nine cities that had expressed their candidacies: Buenos Aires, Kingston, Lima, Mexico City, Miami, Panama City, Rio de Janeiro, Bogotá, and Washington. Although this Secretariat was to be minimal and would have no authority, the idea was expressed that perhaps the city that housed the Secretariat would some day become the "Brussels of the Americas," à la the European Union, and the competition for such a site was on. The lack, until now, of a Secretariat was not just an oversight of the Miami Summit. The fact is that the countries of the Western Hemisphere were not willing to delegate any attributes of sovereignty, or even any appearance of it, to some supranational body. Some may have had in mind the European Commission, which early into the European experience under the Treaty of Rome (1958) had acted to impose its own standards progressively upon the European Common Market.

THE SAN JOSÉ MINISTERIAL PREPARES FOR THE NEXT SUMMIT

In March 1998, the San José Ministerial not only laid the groundwork for the next Summit of the Americas but also outlined the way toward negotiation of the final product in 2005. In effect, although a "blueprint" never emerged from the Miami Summit nor from subsequent ministerials, the San José Ministerial came closest to designing one in practice.

As had become habit, the *Ministerial Declaration*, issued March 19, 1998, led the way with a complete recital of all the agreed-upon principles and areas of convergence, based upon the Miami *Declaration of Principles* and *Plan of Action* as well as those expressed in the Denver, Cartagena, and Belo Horizonte Ministerials. As in these other documents, the San José Ministerial also projected a sense of optimism as to the positive record of trade integration in the hemisphere.

The ministers, having reviewed all of the preparatory work to date, formally recommended that the heads of state and government who were to meet in Santiago, Chile, on April 18 and 19, use that occasion to initiate negotiation of the FTAA, holding to the completion date of 2005. They also reiterated that the FTAA be "balanced, comprehensive and WTO-consistent, and ... will constitute a single undertaking." In addition they stated that the FTAA "can co-exist with bilateral and subregional agreements, to the extent that the rights and obligations under those agreements are not covered or go beyond the rights and obligations of the FTAA."[8]

This statement, then, recognized that there would be three eventual co-existing layers of trade regimes applicable to the Western Hemisphere:

- The WTO,
- The FTAA, and
- The large number of subregional and bilateral agreements that remain in effect and are not superseded by the FTAA to the extent that they are compatible with it. (In fact, throughout the FTAA process, these subregional and other types of agreements have been moving forward, in a parallel process, adding to the overall effect of trade integration.)

The ministers at San José also agreed to an initial structure for the negotiations. For example, they would retain "ultimate oversight and management of the negotiations" and meet at least every 18 months. They established, however, the Trade Negotiations Committee (TNC) at the vice-ministerial level, with a chairman and vice-chairman. The TNC would be responsible for guiding the work of the negotiating groups that were to replace the working groups; to designate the chairman and vice-chairman of each such group (after the first 18-month period, for which the ministers designated the chairs and vice-chairs); and to decide "on the overall architecture of the agreement and institutional issues." The TNC was also mandated, at its first meeting, to develop a work program for each negotiating group.

Nine negotiating groups were established, with chairs and vice-chairs designated to serve for 18 months or until the next ministerial meeting. These groups consisted of the following:

- Market Access,
- Investment,
- Services,
- Government Procurement,
- Dispute Settlement,
- Agriculture,
- Intellectual Property Rights,
- Subsidies,
- Antidumping and Countervailing Duties, and
- Competition Policy.

The ministers, in an annex to their final declaration, stipulated certain specific objectives for each of these issue areas. Moreover, two major differences distinguished between these new negotiating groups from the previous working groups. There had not been a working group on agriculture before; this area, however, was important to a number of countries, especially Argentina, Brazil, and Uruguay. Also, no negotiating group had been established to consider the special problems of smaller economies, a topic of intense interest to the Caribbean and to Central America. Here, the trade-off was a commitment to consider such problems within the mandate of each of the working groups. Additionally, the ministers established a consultative group on smaller economies.

For the sake of efficiency, the ministers also decided that there would be a single venue for meetings of all of the negotiating groups. In this way, a Solomonic decision was applied to the competition for hosting the Administrative Secretariat. During the negotiations, the venue would shift as follows:

- Miami from May 1, 1998, to February 28, 2001;
- Panama City from March 1, 2001, to February 28, 2003; and
- Mexico City from March 1, 2003, to December 31, 2004.

The ministers at San José established the guidelines and procedures for the Administrative Secretariat, tracking the prescriptions of the Belo Horizonte meeting. As was to be expected, this body would be minimal in size and have no authority. The Secretariat was even given a limited life, until 2005, and it would report to the TNC. The body's functions would be to provide logistical and administrative support to the negotiating groups, including translation services; to keep official documents of the negotiations; and to distribute documents as needed.

The ministers also recommended an overall chairmanship of the entire FTAA process, to rotate as follows:

Time Period	Chair	Vice Chair
May 1, 1998 to October 31, 1999	Canada	Argentina
November 1, 1999 to April 30, 2002	Argentina	Ecuador
May 1, 2001 to October 31, 2002	Ecuador	Chile
November 1, 2002 to December 31, 2004	Co-Chair between Brazil and the United States	None

This scheme, of course, was realistic in recognizing that at the end of the process, the hemisphere's two "giants," the United States and Brazil, would be the major players to make the FTAA happen.

In addition to the Consultative Group on Smaller Economies, the ministers also established a Committee of Government Representatives on Civil Society and a Committee on Electronic Commerce. Civil society representatives present at San

José, largely U.S. members of environmental non-governmental organizations (NGOs), were unhappy at this way of responding to the Miami *Declaration of the Presidents of America,* which ruled the FTAA process to be open to civil society participation. In fact, this issue would continue to be a problem as the process went on.

In addition, the final declaration also stressed a commitment to make "concrete progress by the year 2000." What this meant in practice was that the TNC would agree on business facilitation measures, building on the substantive work already achieved by the working groups and negotiating groups.

THE SANTIAGO SUMMIT, APRIL 1998

Western Hemisphere presidents and prime ministers (with the exception of President Fidel Castro) met again on April 18 and 19, 1998. As in the case of Miami, this meeting was characterized by a spirit of conviviality. Unlike Miami, however, trade did not dominate the agenda as a centerpiece, not that trade was considered less important. This agenda, however, focused on other practical issues that needed to be addressed and upon which the success of democracy depended — improving education; strengthening democracy and human rights; alleviating poverty and discrimination; enhancing transparency; and fighting against corruption, crime, and drug trafficking.

With respect to the FTAA, the Summit basically ratified the decisions taken by trade ministers at San José. The *Declaration of Santiago* and its *Plan of Action* instructed trade ministers to initiate negotiations for the FTAA in accordance with the declaration of their last meeting. The presidents also instructed their representatives in the institutions of the Tripartite Committee (the OAS, ECLAC, and especially the IDB) to make available the necessary resources to the Administrative Secretariat and generally to provide technical support to the FTAA process.

REVISITING NAFTA

NAFTA reached its sixth anniversary in January 2000. Are there any object lessons to be derived at this point from the NAFTA experience? As we can recall, the debate over NAFTA in the U.S. House of Representatives in the summer of 1993 was fierce; the trade pact was proclaimed by some as a panacea and denounced by others as a step toward economic catastrophe. Among its critics, there were those doomsayers like Ross Perot, who predicted a "great sucking sound" made by U.S. jobs lost to Mexico's low-wage economy.

In a more technical way and with less passion, debate continues in the United States about the impact of NAFTA. Of course, the results are not easy to assess with precision because NAFTA was born into a worldwide context of market liberalization (the WTO would emerge the following year), economic and financial globalization, and the emergence of the "new economy" of information technology. Change would have occurred with or without NAFTA. However, there is no question that the three large economies of North America are becoming rapidly integrated. At minimum, NAFTA has probably accelerated that process. Mexico has replaced Japan as the second trading partner of the United States, after Canada. There has been serious debate in Mexico about the relative advantages and disadvantages of "dollarization" of the economy, a subject that not long ago would have been so politically incorrect in Mexico as to be absurd. In 2000, a year of presidential elections, that kind of talk did not reach the level of potential action, but the day may not be very far off.

In the United States, there certainly are studies that show job losses due to NAFTA. It is likely, however, that many of the far more numerous jobs that were created can be attributed to NAFTA. One source estimates that NAFTA-related jobs in the United States represent 50 percent of all manufacturing-sector job gains during 1995-2000.[9] The explanation is exports; NAFTA-related exports to Canada were up by 56 percent and up by 90 percent to Mexico. In such an assessment, however, caution is urged. A January 2000 study on employment by the University of California at Los Angeles (UCLA) does not find significant overall changes in employment because of trade with Mexico when all factors are considered.[10]

During the 1993 debate on NAFTA in the U.S. Congress, the effects on labor and the environment were key issues. The Clinton administration felt compelled then to sign side agreements on these issues to make NAFTA more palatable. How well have the agreements succeeded? As Jerry Haar, senior research associate of The Dante B. Fascell North-South Center, points out: "On both the labor and environmental fronts, NAFTA is not delivering all it has promised. Either the Mexican government is not committed, or it has neither the administrative competence nor enforcement authority to do what it should, even with limited resources."[11]

Haar, while being realistic about the present time, is not referring to the long-term prospects for change, however. A recent publication by the Pacific Council on International Policy, entitled *Mexico Transforming,* describes what it calls the "NAFTA effect" in Mexico, a process that is definitively changing a traditional society into a different, modern one. "NAFTA has stimulated powerful forces of changes," the study says, "in trade, investment, the environment, labor practices, finance and corporate governance."[12] The fundamental point to bear in mind here is that the widening of the subregional and bilateral trade pacts all across the hemisphere is unleashing exactly the same sort of forces.

THE FTAA ON TRACK AT TORONTO

Following Santiago, the TNC set into motion an accelerated schedule of meetings in Miami of each of the nine negotiating groups as well as meetings of the three consultative groups — on the topics of smaller economies, civil society, and electronic commerce. Of these, only the electronic commerce group included both private and public sector representation.

The trade ministers met again in Toronto in early November 1999 to review progress and give guidance to the TNC. The meeting's most significant directive was to instruct the negotiating groups to prepare actual draft texts of their respective chapters, which would eventually be included in the FTAA itself. The ministers recognized that these drafts should be considered as "frames of reference" and not "definitive or exclusive outlines of an agreement."[13] In this context, the drafts should include agreed-upon text but also not-agreed-upon text in brackets. All drafts were to be submitted to the TNC no later than 12 weeks prior to the trade ministerial in Buenos Aires in early April 2001. The third Summit of the Americas then followed immediately in Quebec City (April 20-22).

To ensure that the deadline was met, the ministers directed the TNC to meet at least three times before the Buenos Aires ministerial — first in Guatemala (April 2000) and subsequently in Barbados and Peru.

Faithful to the charge of the previous meetings, the Buenos Aires ministerial approved a modest list of agreed business facilitation measures. These consisted of a list of eight specific improved customs procedures and measures aimed to enhance transparency in rules and regulations.

With respect to civil society participation, less progress was made in Toronto, although at least the issue was kept alive. The response to a call for proposals by the committee of government representatives had been very slight, most of the 60-odd papers coming from the United States and Canada. This reflected the great disparity of interest and attention within the hemisphere toward the issue. Civil society groups in North America, particularly the United States and Canada, have been insistent on a greater participation in the process. Governments in Latin America and the Caribbean, when not outright hostile to such a process, are at least indifferent. Nevertheless, the ministerial chaired by Canada included a resolution that directed the committee of government representatives to continue soliciting ideas for civil society input through written submissions.

The ministers at Toronto also reaffirmed their commitment to the world trading system under the WTO and supported the launching of a new round of multilateral negotiations at the Third Ministerial WTO conference that took place in Seattle the following month. Moreover, the ministers stressed the efforts underway in the WTO to eliminate export subsidies on agricultural products.

FAILURE OF THE WTO SEATTLE MEETING

Contrary to the upbeat, businesslike atmosphere of the Toronto FTAA ministerial, the WTO meeting in Seattle of December 1999 ended without the launching of a new multilateral trade round. The reason, however, was not the noisy street riots against the WTO, led largely by members of U.S. unions and NGOs, but the existence of too many differences among WTO members.

These differences had to do with a range of issues that had not been properly resolved in preparatory work for the meeting. In fact, the issues were not all about differences between rich countries and poor countries. The questions were many, including, among others, the contentious issues of including labor and environmental conditions in the trade context. Among rich countries, however, a principal disagreement arose between the United States and the European Union over negotiations to reduce agricultural supports and subsidies. Nevertheless, the failure of a new WTO round spelled good news for the FTAA process in many ways. Why is this so?

In the first place, a WTO round would have absorbed all of the attention of trade negotiators and placed the FTAA on a slower track. Many countries would not have wanted to progress in certain issues on a regional (FTAA) basis if those same issues had been under negotiation at the larger level. These countries would not have been limited to the less developed; certainly, the United States and Brazil place higher priority on worldwide multilateral talks.

Even staffing both the WTO round and the FTAA talks would have been a problem for most countries. The FTAA negotiating rounds taking place in Miami have involved over 700 trade negotiators from the 34 FTAA countries. All of these countries are WTO members. The WTO talks would have drawn off the "first teams" of many countries' negotiators.

Progress in the FTAA negotiations, on the other hand, may actually help the WTO round if and when the WTO becomes more well organized. The flexibility and experience of the FTAA countries in dealing with some of the thorniest issues on a non-polemic basis (labor and environment, private sector and civil society input, transparency, and government subsidies) can provide some beneficial examples to the WTO.

APRIL 2001: THE SIXTH MEETING OF TRADE MINISTERS IN BUENOS AIRES AND THE THIRD SUMMIT OF THE AMERICAS IN QUEBEC CITY

During the first week of April 2001, the Trade Ministers in Buenos Aires were able to review the bracketed draft of an FTAA agreement and make recommendations to the next Summit. That text was a compilation of texts produced by the nine Negotiating Groups in a report of the Trade Negotiating Committee, which included other items on a variety of subjects, such as the overall architecture of an FTAA Agreement. The Ministerial Declaration, dated April 7, stipulated that the TNC hold no fewer than three meetings over the next 18 months, culminating in another ministerial meeting to be held no later than October 31, 2002. It also issued specific instructions to each of the negotiating groups. [14]

The Summit of the Americas was held in Quebec City from April 20 to 22, 2001. It issued a brief *Declaration*,[15] which included a "democracy clause" (see below) and a very lengthy *Plan of Action*[16] with chapters in 18 categories, only one of which was "Trade, Investment and Financial Stability." Reconciling the previously agreed-upon date of 2005 (strongly desired by Brazil and others) with an accelerated date of 2003 (preferred by Chile and, at one point, by the United States), the *Plan of Action* stipulated that the process:

> Ensure negotiations of the FTAA Agreement are concluded no later than January 2005 and seek its entry into force as soon as possible thereafter but, in any case, no later than December 2005, in conformity with the principles and objectives established in the San Jos(Ministerial Declaration, in particular the achievement of a balanced, comprehensive agreement, consistent with WTO rules and disciplines, the results of which will constitute a single undertaking embodying the rights and obligations, as mutually agreed: . . . .

It also stated that the FTAA countries should:

> Foster, through their respective national dialogue mechanisms and through appropriate FTAA mechanisms, a process of increasing and sustained communication with civil society to ensure that it has a clear perception of the development of the FTAA negotiating process; invite civil society to continue to contribute to the FTAA process; and, to this end, develop a list of options that could include dissemination programs in smaller economies, which could be supported by the Tripartite Committee or other sources . . . .

The George W. Bush Administration and the FTAA

The Quebec Summit was, of course, the debut of the new U.S. president in the FTAA process and his first meeting at a gathering of heads of state.

On April 28, 2001, President George W. Bush gave a radio address to the nation about his first 100 days in office. His reference to foreign policy in the talk highlighted his participation in the Third Summit of the Americas, attended by 34 heads of state and government in Quebec City, Canada, a few days earlier. He said:

> But it's just as important for us to listen as it is to speak. A week ago, I attended the Summit of the Americas in Quebec City, where I met with the democratically elected leaders of Canada, Mexico, Central and South America and the Caribbean. We talked about how we can handle common challenges — everything from education and the environment to drugs, energy and trade. I said my piece, and I listened, as well. That's how good neighbors behave.

President Bush said at the concluding press conference after the Summit, "There should be no doubt in anyone's mind that I would come to Quebec City to promote trade."

At the same time, the presidents stipulated that the Summit process would be limited to democracies. The "democracy clause" states that any interruption of the democratic order in any state would constitute "an insurmountable obstacle to the participation of that state's government in the Summit of the Americas process." The United States worked hard for the inclusion of the clause. It remains to be seen, however, whether the "democracy clause" will be written into the FTAA itself.

President Bush had already signaled, on April 17, in a speech at the OAS in Washington, D.C., that the FTAA and free trade in general were at the top of his agenda. He also stated that he would push for fast-track negotiating authority, now renamed "trade promotion authority"(TPA), from the Congress, to be in place in 2001.

The president also stated his intention to go ahead with bilateral trade agreements, such as those being negotiated with Chile and proposed for Singapore. He acknowledged that there were opponents of free trade in the United States and elsewhere. However, he said, citing the success of NAFTA, "It's not going to change my opinion about the benefits of free trade, not only for my country and the people who work in my country . . . but the benefits of free trade for all the countries of this hemisphere are strong."

President Bush reiterated his strong commitment to the FTAA and free trade in a speech to the Council of the Americas in Washington, D.C., on May 7, 2001. Promising an active stance toward the Congress, he said, "We must make those [trade] benefits a reality for all the people of our hemisphere. And that's the task ahead. I accept it with enthusiasm. And I'm counting on the Council's help to bring sanity to the United States Congress."

President Bush followed up this promise quickly by presenting his "2001 International Trade Legislative Agenda" to the Congress on May 10. The eight-page document made a strong case for a trade promotion authority (TPA) with three objectives in mind: 1) opening a new round of the World Trade Organization (WTO), 2) completing the FTAA, and 3) concluding "other regional and bilateral trade negotiations," citing Chile and Singapore as examples. (The presidents of Argentina and Uruguay both indicated interest in pursuing bilateral free trade agreements with the United States.) In the International Trade Legislative Agenda, President Bush acknowledged the need to make progress on labor and environmental issues, but he avoided including those issues in the TPA itself. The phrase, "trade promotion authority," has been coined by the Bush administration to replace previous administrations' terminology, "fast track authority," often shortened to "fast track." Both terms mean that the U.S. Congress would grant the executive branch the authority to present trade agreements that could come before the Congress for a yes-or-no vote, with the stipulation that congressional committees may not propose alternative wording for or amendments to the agreements.

As of the Trade Act of 1974, trade agreements were always handled as executive agreements that were subject to approval by a majority of both houses of Congress. The fast track procedure was adopted so that such agreements could be handled quickly. However, fast track authority expired after the approval of the World Trade Organization in 1994. This partially explains why the United States is a party to only two free trade agreements in comparison with the European Community (28) and nearly all Latin American countries today.

Only a few days later, on May 17, 2001, President Bush unveiled an $880 million proposal to the Congress, called the "Andean Regional Initiative"(ARI). Designed to strengthen democratic institutions, promote respect for human rights, reduce poverty, and engage regional cooperation in fighting drug trafficking, it would be administered largely by the U.S. Agency for International Development (USAID). In many ways, the ARI seemed aimed at meeting the criticism from Latin America and Europe against the highly militarized aid package for Plan Colombia. It also added key components to the overall goals of hemispheric integration.

WHY IS LATIN AMERICA OF SPECIAL IMPORTANCE TO PRESIDENT BUSH?

From the beginning of his administration in January 2001, it has been obvious that President Bush has a special interest, among the regions of the world, in Latin America. During the presidential campaign, in fact, he gave a major speech at

Florida International University in Miami devoted entirely to the Western Hemisphere, something that his opponent Al Gore never did.

George W. Bush's first visit as president outside the United States was to Mexico's President Vicente Fox's ranch, and all reports of the visit indicated that the two presidents have a special rapport. In fact, it seems fairly safe to predict that the United States' relationship with Mexico will be a foreign policy cornerstone of the Bush administration. President Fox has not so jokingly referred to himself as President Bush's adviser for Latin America. But he is not alone. Before the Quebec Summit took place, President Bush held private meetings with a number of other Latin American presidents.

Moreover, this interest seems to be his personal inclination. None of his closest advisers, including Vice President Richard Cheney, Secretary of State Colin Powell, Secretary of Defense Donald Rumsfeld, and National Security Adviser Condoleezza Rice, have ever emphasized the importance of Western Hemisphere affairs in their public statements or publications.

On May 5, 2001, President Bush gave a radio address from the White House in Spanish, believed to be the first time that a president of the United States has done so. The occasion was the commemoration of a Mexican holiday, the "Cinco de mayo," also celebrated by Mexican-Americans. (It marks the Battle of Puebla, in 1862, when Mexican patriots defeated the French occupying forces.) The holiday's domestic political symbolism is obvious; Spanish is no longer a "foreign" language in the United States.

Of course, there is the element of family legacy that certainly informs President Bush's interest in the Western Hemisphere. His interest in the FTAA stems, in part, from an initiative begun by his father, former President George Herbert Walker Bush, the Enterprise for the Americas (EAI), described earlier. With the Cold War over, the Bush presidency in 1990 was the first time in recent memory that the United States could look at Latin America and the Caribbean in other than geopolitical terms.

BUSH ORDERS A MOVE AHEAD ON TRADE TO COMPLETE THE FTAA

President George W. Bush wasted no time in moving toward his father's dream. Following the president's instructions, United States Trade Representative Robert Zoellick spent most of his time on Capitol Hill developing congressional support for TPA, twice denied (as fast track authority) by the Congress to President Clinton. The sticking points were still labor standards and environmental protection: whether they should be included in a trade agreement and, if so, to what degree. Controversy over these points caused the congressional vote over NAFTA to be extremely close, after a heated debate, in late 1993. Yet, at the Summit in Quebec, President Bush acknowledged the importance of these issues and the fact that they must be dealt with in a meaningful way.

This is not to say that all of the obstacles to the FTAA are domestic. In Quebec, Brazil's President Fernando Henrique Cardoso referred to the need for agreed-upon rules for antidumping, reduction of nontariff barriers, avoidance of protectionism in sanitary regulations, and overcoming the "asymmetries" in the agricultural sector. These were clear references to Brazilian unhappiness with U.S. rules and practices regarding such Brazilian products as steel, orange juice, sugar, and shoes, among others. Brazil has been against speeding up the FTAA process, because of these unresolved controversies. Brazilian officials have repeatedly said that it is unfair for North Americans to characterize them as anti-FTAA, that trade issues important to Brazil simply must be dealt with.

WHAT IS THE OUTLOOK FOR THE FTAA'S SUCCESS?

There are reasons for optimism. To date, despite problems along the way, including the significant U.S.-Brazil differences noted above, the FTAA process has kept to its timetable and to its businesslike methods, aimed at producing draft texts for a final agreement. There is, of course, a long way to go to complete the FTAA by 2005. At this juncture, the unresolved issues are the following:

- Will President Bush have trade promotion authority (fast track authority), which is needed to continue his leadership posture supporting the FTAA negotiations? The conventional wisdom says that if he does not get TPA this year, he will have to wait until after the next congressional elections, that is, until after November 2003.
- How will the FTAA process deal with the contentious issues of labor and environmental considerations, the role of civil society, and the role of the private sector?
- Will treatment of smaller economies be handled in a way that allows them to adopt the consensus position required by the FTAA guidelines?

Apart from these known potential difficulties, will there be unforeseen economic conditions or political crises between now and the conclusion of the negotiations? The security crisis in Colombia, the political uncertainties of Venezuela's direction, and the economic straits of Argentina and Ecuador are a few such wild cards.

On the positive side, economic integration along the lines of the subregional and bilateral arrangements continues to produce benefits for the FTAA's member countries. As the FTAA is to build upon and add to these agreements, not replace them, its chances for success are enhanced. All along, the FTAA has been designed as a structure of open regionalism. Its member countries are free to negotiate with Europe (as Mexico has done and MERCOSUR is doing); to join the Asia-Pacific Economic Cooperation (APEC) group (as Mexico and Chile have done); and to engage in other similar agreements. The FTAA's lack of exclusivity is one of its inherent strengths.

Finally, there are no strict guidelines as to the exact content of the FTAA. While the FTAA definitely will not be a common market or a customs union, it will be — on a consensus basis — whatever its members want it to be. That is why the FTAA will probably succeed.

Notes

1. *Declaration of the Presidents of America*, 1967, Meeting of American Chiefs of State, Punta del Este, Uruguay, April 12-14.

2. Nelson A. Rockefeller, 1969, *The Rockefeller Report on the Americas* (Chicago, Quadrangle Books).

3. *Declaration of Principles*, 1994, First Summit of the Americas, Miami, Florida, December 9-11.

4. On this topic, see the trenchant analysis given in Sidney Weintraub, 1997, *As Mexico Imploded: Action and Inaction in the United States*, North-South Agenda Paper No. 28, July.

5. *Ministerial Declaration*, 1995, First Western Hemisphere Trade Ministerial, Denver, June.

6. *Ministerial Declaration*, 1996, Second Western Hemisphere Trade Ministerial, Cartagena, Colombia, March.

7. *Ministerial Declaration*, 1997, Third Western Hemisphere Trade Ministerial, Belo Horizonte, Brazil, May.

8. *Ministerial Declaration*, 1998, Fourth Western Hemisphere Trade Ministerial, San José, Costa Rica, March.

9. Mary Jane Bolle, 2000, *NAFTA: Estimated U.S. Job "Gains" and "Losses" by State Over 5 1/2 Years*, Congressional Research Service Report for Congress, Washington, D.C., February 2, 8.

10. Raúl Hinojosa-Ojeda, et al., 2000, *The U.S. Employment Impacts of North American Integration After NAFTA* (Los Angeles: University of California, School of Public Policy and Social Research) <http://www.sppsr.ucla.edu>.

11. Jerry Haar, 2000, Presentation on Capitol Hill by The Dante B. Fascell North-South Center, March 24.

12. Pacific Council on International Policy, 2000, *Mexico Transforming*, Report by Binational Study Group of PCIP, March. <http://www.pcip.org/html/pub/pub_studyreports.html>.

13. *Ministerial Declaration*, 1999, Fifth Western Hemisphere Trade Ministerial, Toronto, Canada, November.

14. *Ministerial Declaration*, 2001, Sixth Meeting of Ministers of Trade of the Hemisphere, Buenos Aires, Argentina, April 7.

15. *Declaration of Quebec City*, 2001, Third Summit of the Americas, April 22.

16. *Plan of Action*, 2001, Third Summit of the Americas, April 22.

References

Bolle, Mary Jane. 2000. *NAFTA: Estimated U.S. Job "Gains" and "Losses" by State Over 5 1/2 Years*. Congressional Research Service Report for Congress. Washington, D.C., February 2.

Declaration of Quebec City. 2001. Third Summit of the Americas, April 22.

Declaration of Principles. 1994. First Summit of the Americas. Miami, Florida, December 9-11.

Declaration of the Presidents of America. 1967. Meeting of American Chiefs of State, Punta del Este, Uruguay, April 12-14.

Haar, Jerry. 2000. Presentation on Capitol Hill by The Dante B. Fascell North-South Center. Washington, D.C., March 24.

Hinojosa-Ojeda, Raúl, et al. 2000. *The U.S. Employment Impacts of North American Integration After NAFTA*. Los Angeles: University of California, School of Public Policy and Social Research. <http://www.sppsr.ucla.edu>.

Ministerial Declaration. 1995. First Western Hemisphere Trade Ministerial. Denver, Colorado, June.

Ministerial Declaration. 1996. Second Western Hemisphere Trade Ministerial. Cartagena, Colombia, March.

Ministerial Declaration. 1997. Third Western Hemisphere Trade Ministerial. Belo Horizonte, Brazil, May.

Ministerial Declaration. 1998. Fourth Western Hemisphere Trade Ministerial. San José, Costa Rica, March.

Ministerial Declaration. 1999. Fifth Western Hemisphere Trade Ministerial. Toronto, Canada, November.

Ministerial Declaration. 2001. Sixth Meeting of Ministers of Trade of the Hemisphere. Buenos Aires, Argentina, April 7.

Pacific Council on International Policy. 2000. *Mexico Transforming*. Report by Binational Study Group of PCIP, March. <http://www.pcip.org/html/pub/pub_studyreports.html>.

Plan of Action. 2001. Third Summit of the Americas, April 22.

Rockefeller, Nelson A. 1969. *The Rockefeller Report on the Americas*. Chicago: Quadrangle Books.

Weintraub, Sidney. 1997. *As Mexico Imploded: Action and Inaction in the United States*. North-South Agenda Paper No. 28 (July). Coral Gables, Fla.: The Dante B. Fascell North-South Center at the University of Miami.

CHAPTER 5

Democratization, Health Care Reform, and NGO-Government Collaboration in the 1990s: Catalyst or Constraint?

ALBERTO CARDELLE

The diminished role of the state in Latin America has been accompanied by decentralization of health care delivery and an enhanced role for the private sector in delivery of services. Simultaneously, in the process of regional democratization, the number of organized civil society groups has expanded, increasing the alliances formed between non-governmental organizations (NGOs) and governments in the process of state reform. This chapter examines the experiences of NGO-government collaborative health care reform projects undertaken in Guatemala, Chile, and Ecuador. Assessments are made as to how factors such as civil society-state relations, democratization, state reform, and international pressure have catalyzed or constrained policies promoting the collaborations. The projects' implementation processes are analyzed with an emphasis on determining their sustainability, and various aspects of the collaborations are evaluated. The chapter includes a set of policy recommendations for future implementation of such collaborative projects.

INTRODUCTION

During the 1980s, the traditional, state-centric health care delivery systems that had dominated Latin America collapsed as a result of the regional economic crisis. By 1995, concerned with the economic performance and sustainability of health care delivery systems and following the advice of international financial institutions, 34 of the 38 countries in Latin America and the Caribbean had begun implementing health care reform projects. The economic crisis had exposed the imbalance and mismanagement plaguing the regional health systems and further constrained the states' ability to remedy the systems' inequality and inefficiency (Musgrove 1992). Reflecting the major trends in the political economy of the hemisphere and responding to the new consensus regarding the diminished role of

The research for this paper was supported by the Pan American Health Organization with funding from the government of the Netherlands.

the state in Latin America, health care reform in the region has decentralized the delivery of health care. In addition, it has enhanced the role of the private sector in the delivery of services. Simultaneously, a regional democratization process has expanded the number of organized civil society groups, compounded the complexity of civil societies, enlarged the number of political interests, and promoted the demand for greater respect for social rights and citizenship.

The need for states to respond to stronger civil societies within a context of fiscal constraint has led to development schemes characterized by new alliances. Collaborative projects between non-governmental organizations (NGOs) and governments have emerged as important strategies in the process of state reform. Although the opportunities for NGO-government partnerships in health care have increased, the success of these new arrangements is affected by myriad national and local factors that determine the degree and sustainability of the collaboration.

This chapter examines the experiences of a variety of different projects promoting NGO-government collaboration in Guatemala, Chile, and Ecuador. It is divided into three parts. The first part reviews the global trends within which the policies are being implemented and assesses the degree to which different factors, such as civil society-state relations, democratization, state reform, and international pressure have served to catalyze or constrain policies promoting NGO-government collaboration. Interspersed within this part of the chapter are several brief, country-specific case studies. The second part analyzes how the goals, objectives, resources, and planning processes associated with the implementation of collaborative projects influenced project sustainability. The third section identifies the different ways in which NGOs and governments collaborate (for example, funding, coordinated planning, and training) and examines how each affects the project's outcome. The paper concludes with a set of policy recommendations for the implementation of future collaborative projects.

GLOBAL TRENDS

The Evolution of NGOs and Their Relations with the State

The NGO sector associated with the delivery of social services such as health evolved in three stages or generations (Korten 1987). The first generation of NGOs lasted from colonial days to the 1960s. It was characterized by organizations charged with providing relief and welfare services designed to address the short-term needs of the population. The first NGOs were closely associated with the Catholic Church, which was the strongest institution in Latin American civil society. These organizations were charitable in nature and employed an "assistantialist" approach — providing housing for the homeless, soup kitchens for the indigent, and free hospitalization for the poor. (Hospitals were the venue of care for the poor, while the wealthy received care at home.)

A second generation of NGOs emerged during the 1960s and was dominated by groups that emphasized a technical, modernization approach to development. The shift in logic, from charity to technical assistance, helped NGOs become significant recipients of international aid. Their growing professionalization made aid agencies more responsive to using them as vehicles of development.

The third phase of NGO development came during a period of growing political repression and collapsing state-centered industrialization in the 1970s and early 1980s. It accelerated the formation of NGOs desirous of influencing national policies in favor of the poor, providing services that weakened states could not, and helping to open new political spaces in the face of growing repression. It was during this phase that the NGO sector and popular sector movements began to work more closely together. This spurred NGO involvement in popular education, community organizing, and consciousness raising. The coupling of the popular movements and NGOs was a significant factor in the sector's orientation toward the state. With these new objectives, NGOs developed a strong sense of autonomy. During the third phase, NGOs championed themselves as the antithesis of the state, which relies on the legitimate use of force and coercion, and of the private for-profit sector, which responds to profit-maximizing incentives (Macdonald 1997a).

Observers have noted that had NGOs aligned themselves more closely with the labor movements that emerged in the region during the period of populist governments, they would have necessarily developed more collaborative tendencies. The social movements, on the other hand, refused this kind of neo-corporatist framework and eschewed the conventional politics of interest mediation, political parties, and elections. By identifying themselves closely with the popular movements, NGOs rejected political negotiation in favor of collective claims and personal liberation (Foweraker 1995). This was clearly evident in the countries of Central America, where many NGOs became important political instruments for insurgent social movements. At the same time, it is important to note that many NGOs did not follow this evolutionary path, but instead remained within the developmentalist approach and continued to provide high-quality technical assistance to international development organizations and even the state.

The personnel who came to staff the NGOs at this time were a significant factor in determining the NGO sector's positions vis-à-vis the state. NGOs became a refuge for professionals from the public sector and academic centers. This migration not only assisted the rapid professionalization that allowed NGOs to become powerful groups within civil society, but also reinforced the sector's anti-state posture. Many NGO personnel had been forced to abandon previous positions by an increasingly coercive state and, therefore, fiercely defended the NGO sector's autonomy (Cox 1992).

While the NGO sector was gaining strength, the public sector was losing both capacity and institutional strength. For some in the public sector, NGOs were responsible for diverting international aid away from state programs and challenging the authority of the state by strengthening the collective action of a multitude of groups within civil society. NGOs were also seen as fueling a growing international scrutiny of the state in Latin America.

In many instances, NGOs felt that collaboration with the state could compromise funding from independent sources. From the state point of view, NGOS were judged according to their former and current political program. Today, in countries like Guatemala and El Salvador, NGOs are closely identified with the opposition groups they supported during the period of civil war. The state's reluctance to collaborate is directly related to this association. In order to alter the existing competitive relationship, significant incentives and guarantees must be assured.

Democratization

In countries in which nondemocratic regimes limited the political space available for civil society to express its collective ideas and demands, NGOs served as a crucial forum for the expression and articulation of those political and social interests (Jelin 1997). NGOs performed a critical role in the processes of democratization because the traditional forms of political organization had very little room for political action under nondemocratic governments. They mobilized civil society into new organizational structures that increased both subnational and international pressures on nondemocratic governments. It was in this spirit that the first attempts at NGO-government collaboration emerged. The onset of democratic regimes and the presence of powerful NGOs were viewed as an opportunity for governments to integrate civil society, increase participation, and improve social services. Indeed, in many countries, NGOs became integral partners in the reconstitution of democracy. NGOs that were part of the opposition became active participants in the electoral processes in the countries, in the writing of constitutions, in the creation of new governments, and in designing new social service systems.

Yet, as countries in the hemisphere continued to exhibit rising economic and social inequality and the breakdown of democratic institutions (legislatures, the judiciary, political parties), advocates of democratic institutions began to demand a broader definition of democracy. No longer were electoral processes enough. Rights of citizenship had to be guaranteed. Proponents argued that alliances among the dominant political, economic, and social groups were limiting democratization (Amini 1996). Advocates of more institutionalized democracy claim that greater levels of participation of institutions of civil society such as NGOs are required in order to hold the state accountable.

Despite the success of early NGO-government collaboration during the reemergence of democratic governance, it has been during the recent process of expanding the rights of citizenship when collaboration has been most difficult. Collaboration during these processes requires new structures of governance and public administration, including collaborative decision-making bodies and arenas that allow for consultation between NGOs and the public sector. There has been a recurring assumption that the decline of authoritarianism and the rise of electoral processes would precipitate a shift in the anti-statist position of social movements and NGOs to one more open to collaboration with governments. Yet, the evidence points to the possibility of a different outcome (Díaz 1997). It seems that as the process of democratization advances, there is a parallel decline in civil society participation and in the number of NGOs. As part of a somewhat counterintuitive process, this occurs in part because authoritarian regimes provide environments conducive to the creation of NGOs as a matter of necessity. In times of authoritarian regimes, NGOs are havens of democracy and, therefore, find a broad base of support. In contrast, as the new democratic regimes pursue electoral legitimacy and battle to institutionalize themselves, the rationale behind NGOs becomes less compelling, and NGOs find it more difficult to articulate their goals and objectives.

CASE STUDY 1: NGOS IN A PACTED DEMOCRACY

During the authoritarian regime of General Augusto Pinochet in Chile, among the most active organizations in the opposition were the NGOs working for women's rights. Organizations such as the Colectivo Mujer Salud y Medicina Social and the Centro de Estudios de la Mujer were active in the struggle for democracy. Following the victory of President Patricio Aylwin in 1990, these NGOs were viewed as integral groups that could continue to motivate the social participation of civil society. The new government was hopeful that "the work of the NGOs in the previous phase (struggle for democracy) [would] continue in this next phase and that NGOs [would] continue serving as a conduit of international solidarity and support" (Jiménez 1996). The democratic government of President Aylwin issued a document entitled "Policies for Private Development Corporations and NGOs" in which it was stated that "...the new government recognizes the value that these organizations [NGOs] have in the promotion of development and it therefore promises to respect their autonomy, support their institutional development and in those areas where it is possible, establish working agreements so they may cooperate with the implementation of public policy." This period of opportunity resulted in very concrete manifestations of collaboration, including the creation of a department specifically dedicated to NGO-government collaboration within the Ministry of Development and Planning (MIDEPLAN) and a new agency of the executive branch, the National Service for Women (SERNAM), a coordinating body aimed at promoting programs for women. The Ministry of Health (MINSAL) along with SERNAM and the Pan American Health Organization (PAHO) funded a project aimed at improving the quality of health services for women. The project combined the resources and services of the state via MINSAL and SERNAM and the expertise of NGOs working on women's issues. The project provided these NGOs with project funding in order to design and implement new service delivery models targeting women, analyze the existing needs of women in the country, design and evaluate health policies and their impact on women, and examine the existing legal framework regarding women's rights. Between 1991 and 1993, the program funded 10 different projects throughout the country, which resulted in the development of important health policies and a strong relationship between the state and NGOs. Yet three years later, many of the NGOs were disillusioned with the process. Most felt that the democratization process had weakened them. While during the period of authoritarian government NGOs were the primary beneficiaries of international aid, now more aid went directly to the state, leaving the state as the primary contractor of NGOs. This forced NGOs to respond to the state's programmatic agenda instead of having the opportunity of developing their own programs. In addition to losing direct contact with international financing, the international perception that Chile had undergone an economic recovery had led to an overall decline in international aid.

NGOs have also suffered from a diminution of staff. Many of the people, who came to NGOs from the public sector or academia, eluding political repression, have moved back to the public sector. Another important factor, according to the NGOs, is the increasing role played by technocrats within the government. As the state moves to strengthen its institutional structures, it has emphasized greater technical efficiency in policymaking, leading to a technocratic style of policymaking. According to the director of a consortium of NGOs working on women's health issues, this new technocratic bureaucracy is not conducive to collaboration because NGO-government collaboration requires a process of social and political dialogue, which, in turn, requires a significant investment in time and resources. Since the short-term rate of return for collaboration is minimal, given the level of negotiation and compromise required, collaboration is an unattractive strategy to technocrats. NGOs in Chile also feel that the pact between the authoritarian regime and the Chilean democratic forces generated a self-imposed censorship among groups within civil society against criticizing and making demands upon the state. The confluence of these factors constrained the type of environment required for NGOs and the state to collaborate.

State Reform

With guidance from international financial institutions (IFI) and the Paris Club of donor countries, Latin American countries responded to the economic crisis of the 1980s with austere economic stabilization programs. Structural adjustment programs aimed at curbing inflation, decreasing fiscal deficits, shrinking the state, liberalizing the economy, and privatizing state enterprises followed stabilization programs. The traditional state-centric health care delivery system in the region, despite some successes, collapsed during the economic crisis. As a result, state revenues dedicated to public health programs and capital investment fell from a regional average of 9 percent in 1980 to 5 percent in 1985. The crisis exposed the health system's imbalance and mismanagement, while the rapid debt accumulation that triggered the crisis further constrained the state's ability to address the system's inequality and inefficiency. Proponents of the need for fiscal austerity saw the health sector as an integral component for the overall reform and economic development of the state, since the health sector's lack of financial viability presented a threat to the broader economic structural programs. Investments in health began to be seen as essential in order to ensure a productive workforce. Communicable diseases such as HIV/AIDS and tuberculosis cumulatively account for millions of years of lost life annually, and health sector expenditures in the hemisphere account for an average of 11 percent of gross national products (GNPs), representing a considerable economic component of productivity and employment (PAHO and ECLAC 1994). In response, a regional health care reform "fashion trend" emerged. Reform programs were undertaken or planned in 34 of the 38 countries in Latin America and the Caribbean.

Health care reform in Latin America and the Caribbean has resulted in decentralizing health care delivery and has increased the role of the private sector in the delivery of social services by altering the way the system is financed. The delivery of health services is being decentralized to regional health entities, municipal governments, and local health systems. Proponents of decentralization claim that local entities will increase responsiveness to local needs, improve access of the poor to health services, and increase management adaptability and flexibility. This has meant that these local structures are charged with the delivery of services, purchase and allocation of resources, contracting and management of personnel, selection of technologies, design of programmatic interventions, and coordination of both governmental and non-governmental entities providing health care.

The new health care financing schemes are designed to provide the decentralized health entities with a more efficient, streamlined funding mechanism. Under the existing financing scheme, service has been segmented according to where patients access their services. The social security system is responsible for workers in the formal sector, whose employers pay into the system (about 15 percent of the population), while the central Ministry of Health provides care for the remainder of the population (with a small percentage of the population using the private health care market). Within each of these structures, the respective institutions finance and administer the funds, and they provide health services to their target populations in a vertically integrated system in which each institution is the sole participant.

In the health systems envisioned in various reform proposals, the entire system (especially ministries of health services) would be open to more institutions in the hope of diversifying the providers and increasing competition. Under these new systems, the Ministry of Health and Social Security would regulate and finance services, while the administering of the system and the provision of the services would be provided by decentralized institutions of the national government, by local government entities, or by private entities.

Both the decentralization of the health care system and the new financing schemes being established are designed to open the system to a greater number of private providers. It is expected that by aggregating private decisions, the market represents "public interests" better than the political realm, which is affected by personalism, clientelism, and populism (Mahon 1995). In advancing the role of the overall private sector, the health care reform processes promote a greater role of the private non-profit (NGO) sector in the region. The expectation is that the limited technical and organizational capacity of the new decentralized health entities, as well as the pressure to contain costs, will persuade the entities to contract with private sector groups such as NGOs that have experience in delivering services locally.

In general, health care reform has increased the opportunities for NGO-government collaboration. Most importantly, reforms have lifted the financial and administrative barriers that prevented NGOs from serving as contractors. Under these systems of open competition, the opportunities for collaboration are strengthened by the market advantage NGOs enjoy over other private sector entities. NGOs have experience in providing health care services in the regions that are being decentralized. They have a good reputation with international donors and communities, and they usually provide a wide array of social services, such as community organizing and participatory health education and training, which go beyond the services found in a "basic package of services" financed by governments.

Paradoxically, reform programs also limit collaboration because they emphasize a contractual type of NGO-government collaboration for the provision of more efficient and cost-effective social services. This is in contrast to the perspective and interest of NGOs, which seek a broader-based relationship — one in which NGOs can continue their work as strong advocates for the basic needs of the population and in which they may truly collaborate. The reform context favors considerations of efficiency, emphasizing NGO program management and administration. Less attention is paid to the qualitative dimensions of collaboration and the possibility of a greater role of the NGOs in project planning and design. The importance placed on "collective goods" by NGOs makes them more likely to provide such needed services as free care to the poor, public health services, and popular education, but these are services that the new reformed health systems will not finance. Under health care reform, collaboration is not only defined but also implemented and governed through economic and market strategies (contracts, bids, capitation reimbursement, basic package of services, and so on). Additionally, the contract regime usually reimburses the entities after the provision of services, in many instances months after the NGOs have provided the services. This requires NGOs to continue to underwrite a considerable amount of their activities. The emphasis on pecuniary considerations also includes greater emphasis on complex financial and administrative procedures and reporting mechanisms. This, coupled with the limited institutional capacity and weaker financial foundations that characterize NGOs, makes it difficult for NGOs to collaborate with the state through a "contractual regime." The fragile economic foundations of NGOs limits their capacity to participate as equal partners in traditional bidding processes, reimbursement procedures, procurement practices, and contractual restraints.

CASE STUDY 2: DIFFICULTIES OF NGOS IN THE CONTEXT OF HEALTH CARE REFORM

In cases where economic reform measures have been vigorously implemented, as in Chile, policies promoting collaboration have failed to produce collaborative relationships that satisfy the needs of both sectors. NGOs such as Fundación Cristo Vive (FCV) and La Caleta are what can be considered the "new proto-typical NGO," in the sense that they are subcontractors of the ministries of health. These NGOs are among the few service-providing NGOs that have made the transition from international aid recipient to government contractor. The shift has required that these two NGOs strengthen their financial and administrative capacity.

In the case of FCV, the organization was forced to secure funding beyond the government contract so that they could have the financial flexibility required to cover their operating expenses, since the government required 12 to 18 months to reimburse the NGOs for the services rendered. The organization has also found itself subsidizing many services because it provides services beyond those covered by the government contract. This also means that they begin to attract patients outside their target population (the population for which they are paid) because of their growing reputation. FCV has had to integrate its reporting system and preventive health care program with that of the state, forcing it to modify its administrative system and increase its personnel. According to organization officials, the new contracting system has also increased competition among providers. While previously the organization was more likely to coordinate and collaborate with other clinics and NGOs, now each clinic is in competition for patients and funding and is less likely to coordinate and cooperate with others in the provision of services.

In a similar vein, organizations like La Caleta, a small NGO specializing in substance-abuse treatment and intervention programs, have found it difficult to sustain their activities because government contracts in specialized health care areas have tended to be short-term and renewable through competitive bidding processes. This has meant that the organization has found it difficult to carry out long-term planning because it never knows what resources it will have at its disposal. For three months at the end of every contract, the organization is also required to re-compete for funds, increasing the need for an administrative capacity able to produce sophisticated proposals and financial reports.

The International Health Regime

A common underlying factor running throughout these national and global trends has been the role played by international organizations. International financial institutions, intergovernmental cooperation organizations, and bilateral aid agencies form part of a powerful international health regime capable of affecting the policy agendas of sovereign nations. The capacity of international organizations to impact national development policies with regard to the role of NGOs in national development has been evident for some years. After the collapse of the state-centric systems and the rise of authoritarianism, donors worked on the assumption that NGOs were more effective than the public sector in delivering social services to the poor. NGOs therefore acquired the reputation of being reliable alternatives for the disbursement of international cooperation aid in places where donors had lost confidence in the public sector. In Chile, for example, the number of NGOs grew by 87 percent after the 1973 coup, due to the international community's growing skepticism regarding the public sector. The influence of the international community in the rise of the NGO sector is reflected in the dramatic increase in the international aid being channeled through NGOs. NGOs channeled US$0.9 billion in 1970, US$1.4 billion in 1975, US$4 billion in 1985, and in 1990, NGOs channeled US$5.2 billion in the area of health alone and about 20 percent of all "official development assistance" (World Bank 1993; Bebbington and Thiele 1993). More recently, causal evidence of the role played by the international regime in the implementation of state reform is detectable in the synchronized fashion in which health care reform policies have been implemented across the majority of the countries of the region. Policies promoting the greater involvement of NGOs in the delivery of health care portray similar patterns, given that nearly 20 countries in the region have implemented similar policies within the last decade without any apparent groundswell of support in favor of greater NGO collaboration from within the countries.

A great part of the interest in NGOs in health emerges from the recent interest by the World Bank, the Inter-American Development Bank (IDB), and the Pan American Health Organization (PAHO) in promoting greater civil society collaboration. This interest is evident in the growing role the World Bank, previously somewhat uninterested in non-state actors, is granting NGOs. In 1988, for instance, only 6 percent of the organization's projects included NGO-government collaboration, while in 1994, the projects in the hemisphere that involved NGO-government collaboration accounted for 50 percent of the organization's project portfolio (Malena 1995). Over the last few years, these organizations have begun to recommend liberal democratic governance as an important condition for the sustainability of economic reform and growth. Since the early 1990s, the multilateral organizations are no longer prescribing or making loans solely contingent upon economic reform, but rather are emphasizing the implementation of strategies promoting democracy, decentralization, community participation, and respect for civil liberties (Vacs 1994).

As a result, most, if not all, of the major international multi- and bilateral organizations have instituted an initiative encouraging NGO-government collaboration. These organizations have been promoting such collaboration using different strategies, which include the strengthening of NGOs, the creation of NGO networks, and the inclusion of NGOs in aid programs. These organizations have also employed NGOs as a mechanism to improve their ability to deliver technical cooperation and assistance. NGOs have been used to help the organizations better identify the needs of communities, give representation to underserved populations, and channel resources to isolated groups. These organizations have emphasized the inclusion of NGOs in the process of policy formulation and social development by facilitating the creation of suitable mechanisms that foster the collaboration between NGOs and the state. The idea is to establish channels of representation so that the society as a whole may be ensured participation in the health policy process. PAHO has actively supported the inclusion of NGOs in the health reform debate and in the reform process in countries such as Belize, Guatemala, Ecuador, and Chile. The basic strategies for these objectives include the promotion of systematic work alliances for program planning and execution, taking into account the institutional comparative advantages of NGOs and governments.

The influence of the international community is also illustrated in the declarations and documents presented at international intergovernmental summits. Initiative 17 of the Plan of Action of the 1994 Miami Summit of the Americas, states "... health care reforms will include decentralizing services, reorienting budgetary allocations to favor the poor, developing new financial mechanisms and encouraging greater use of NGOs" (Summit of the Americas 1994). In the program of action of the International Conference on Population and Development, Chapter 15 is dedicated to partnerships with the NGO sector and states that "governments and intergovernmental organizations should integrate NGOs and local community groups into their decision-making..." (UNFPA 1994).

Until now, the projects funded by international organizations seeking to create an enabling environment for NGO-government collaboration have produced intense but unsustainable projects. International organizations influence national policymaking and therefore transmit their policy preferences using two major mechanisms. First, organizations use their financial leverage via loan and aid conditionality in order to compel states to implement specific policy packages. Many of the health care reform loans arranged by both the World Bank and the IDB will have specific requirements for NGO involvement. A second mechanism, a dense network of policymakers who permeate both national institutions and transnational organizations, allows policies to become part of the technocratic consensus within the network. In many cases, policymakers move with ease from positions within international organizations to positions within the national governments and vice-versa. That allows these policies to become important components of reform packages. Yet while these policy-influencing strategies can precipitate the rapid implementation of policy packages (because they are usually linked with aid and financial resources), they are difficult to sustain because once the financial incentive ends, policymakers are less committed to the policy objectives. This is in contrast to approaches in which the incentives and the proponents of collaboration are internal and, therefore, can count on long-term political commitment.

CASE STUDY 3: THE WORLD BANK, NGOs, AND FAILED COLLABORATION IN GUATEMALA

PACT, an international consortium of NGOs, worked closely with the Association of Service and Development Institutions (Asociación de Instituciones de Desarrollo y Servicios — ASINDES), a Guatemalan consortium developed in the late 1980s, at a time when the NGOs decided on a strategy of closer collaboration with the state. In the early part of the 1990s, the World Bank approached the government of Guatemala with the idea of creating a Social Investment Fund (SIF), an autonomous public entity designed to promote local development initiatives through financial support of projects carried out by community groups, local governments, NGOs, and other private groups. At that time, ASINDES was the largest NGO consortium group with a stated strategy of greater cooperation with the state, and it agreed to participate with the World Bank and the government in negotiating the SIF. ASINDES viewed such participation as a way of influencing national development strategies, diversifying and increasing the NGOs' financial base, increasing coordination among NGOs, and proving the strength and effectiveness of the NGO sector. For the Christian Democratic government, the negotiations would work toward the fulfillment of government promises of decentralization, create effective mechanisms to address poverty, increase the faith of foreign donors in the state, gain the World Bank's stamp of approval so as to attract more foreign funds, and respond to pressure from the Bank to work with NGOs.

From January 1989 to March 1990, six different World Bank missions came to Guatemala to help the government and NGOs develop mechanisms that would allow for NGO participation in the SIF. Throughout this 18-month period, there was close collaboration among the parties and even an agreement by which ASINDES would provide 1.5 million quetzales (from other funding) to support SIF non-NGO projects. After the last World Bank mission, negotiations fell apart, the government accused the NGOs of reneging on agreements of NGO support for the SIF, and the NGOs accused the government of politicizing the SIF. In the absence of an outside source like the World Bank to mediate and provide incentives, the collaboration fell apart even before it entered the programmatic stage. According to evaluations, the process failed to create a sustainable environment where the three actors were able to work together within a cooperative decision-making model. The incentives for the government to depoliticize and for the SIF to allow nonpolitical control of the fund and greater NGO involvement were not strong enough. There was little internal support within the government for collaboration. As stated earlier, a primary motivation for the government to participate was to satisfy international pressure, but that did not translate into a real desire to increase the collaboration with civil society.

Case Study 4: Efficiency, Expanded Coverage, and NGO Participation in Guatemala

A few months before the final Guatemala peace accords were signed in December 1996, the country began to implement a health care reform project that called for the reorganization, integration, and modernization of the health sector (Pan American Health Organization 1998). The process was catalyzed by the peace accords, in which the government agreed to lower infant mortality by 50 percent and assure health coverage for 100 percent of the population. The principle goals of the health care reform project were to: a) extend the coverage of basic health services, targeting those who are poorest; b) increase public spending and expand the sources of financing for the health sector; c) redirect the allocation of resources; d) increase the efficiency of the public sector in performing its functions and producing health services; and e) generate an organized social response, with a base of broad social and community participation.

Within the overall reform plan, the core reform project is the Comprehensive Health Care System (Sistema Integral en Atención de Salud — SIAS). It is the principal mechanism by which the Ministry of Health (MOH) expects to increase coverage and improve access in areas already partially covered. The SIAS seeks to decentralize health care delivery to the lowest possible political-administrative level capable of responding to the health needs and demands of the population. In Guatemala, the SIAS provides basic health services to the population through the creation of a basic health team for every 10,000 people, or about every 3,200 homes. Each SIAS unit consists of a health team that includes a mobile physician, a service coordinator, a community organizer, and 50 volunteer community health workers. The SIAS is also linked with a secondary hospital to which patients can be referred. The set of basic services covered by the local SIAS unit consists of maternal childcare, nutrition, communicable disease control, health education, and improved basic sanitation in coordination with other agencies. At the local level, the administration of each individual SIAS unit is subcontracted to NGOs, private for-profit companies, or even local governmental entities such as municipalities. Once contracted, these organizations contract the appropriate personnel and establish the local level delivery system. These organizations are financed on a per capita basis depending upon the number of people to whom they offer services. Most importantly, the SIAS reforms lifted the financial and administrative barriers that prevented NGOs from serving as contractors. Under this system of open competition, the opportunities for partnerships are strengthened by the market advantage NGOs enjoy over other private sector entities. Government entities promoting greater efficiency do understand, albeit reluctantly, that NGOs have greater experience in providing health care services in the more isolated and underserved regions than does either the traditional private sector or the state. In addition, NGOs usually provide a wide array of social services, such as community organizing and participatory health education and training, which go beyond the services found in a "basic package of services" financed by governments.

Most of the national NGOs in the country that had been working in health were fearful of working with the SIAS because, despite some attempts at devolution of power to the local level, its implementation (and more specifically the contracting of NGOs) was being administered by central MOH officials. NGO leaders felt that the government was eager to approach NGOs because it was a conditionality of the Inter-American Development Bank, which was funding the reform program. NGOs viewed the SIAS as a channel through which to influence the national health system. By signing service contracts with the MOH, the NGOs were able not only to formalize their relations with the ministry but also to expand the relationship, something they had not previously been able to accomplish. The strategy of centralizing implementation and of placing the SIAS under the direct administration of a vice-minister allowed the program to bypass the political and bureaucratic obstacles that had previously restricted the expansion of the local level NGO-state partnerships.

By early 1998, the government of Guatemala had integrated about 50 NGOs throughout the country in the SIAS program. Although the experiences with the central government had been mixed, there was a growing consensus among NGOs that they needed to engage the MOH in this process. In fact, NGOs that did not sign a service agreement to provide services in their areas could be shut out. The SIAS would look for another contractor (a local NGO or an outside organization) if it determined that it had to expand coverage in the area. The SIAS program implemented this practice in various parts of the country when no local NGO was willing to sign a service agreement. In two departments (Quetzaltenango and Huehuetenango), SIAS contracted the provision of local health services to NGOs that were newly formed or NGOs from outside the community. NGO officials reported that part of their urgency in signing SIAS agreements had been the fear created by this policy.

The experience in Guatemala highlights the tensions between the goals of structural reforms that undertake a fundamental modification of political, economic and social structures and the ideal of local development. Centralization has driven the SIAS to focus more on the technical goal of expanding coverage and less on the social goal of expanding coverage with an emphasis on community participation. As in Chile, the reform strategy favors considerations of efficiency, emphasizing NGO program management and administration. The limited institutional capacity and weaker financial foundations of the "social change" NGOs makes it difficult for them to collaborate with the state through a "contractual regime."

As a result, these reforms are spurring a new generation of NGOs in Guatemala. First, there is a set of traditional, community-based NGOs with a history of working for social change that are becoming more entrepreneurial, reorganizing their structures and missions in order to allow them to compete for government contracts. A large number of these NGOs have over time slipped somewhat reluctantly into a range of close partnerships with state development agencies, which, in turn, have changed their profile in terms of size and administration.

There is also the emergence of a second type of NGO — "astro turf NGOs"* — that emerge without any grassroots identification in order to take advantage of the contracting regimes being established by state reform processes. These "astro turf NGOs" are almost exclusively technical in nature and very entrepreneurial. Such "astro turf NGOs" are usually organizations formed by former public sector employees, created solely to compete for and acquire government service contracts.

As the NGO sector at large becomes increasingly more interested in the business side of their work, individual NGOs tend to lose their "oppositional" legitimacy (Bebbington and Lehmann 1998). Increasingly, NGOs are reluctant to bite the hands that feed them (Loveman 1996; Browning et al. 1998). NGOs are adapting to the new political agenda of aid, which emphasizes business cooperation, investment climates, and efficiency over concepts of solidarity and distribution (Grugel 1997). The new economic and political realities, have led to a migration of NGOs from organizing civil society for articulation of social rights to organizing civil society for the purpose of improving the efficiency of the state.

It remains unclear how the new generation of NGOs will impact the access of citizens to health care. What is certain is that the traditional relationship between NGOs and central governments is being altered. A likely scenario is one in which central governments (because of political considerations and international pressure) expand efforts at social participation by increasing partnering with NGOs, but without broad-based internal support within government bureaucracies. Under these conditions, partnerships are implemented in a circumscribed fashion and are aimed at incorporating only a small segment of the NGO sector, recruiting NGOs less involved in political and social activism, thereby closing opportunities for diverse representation. Partnerships with NGOs are established both because of the need to expand services to isolated underpopulated areas that would not be profitable for the private sector and because such areas have historically been served by the NGOs. NGOs are seen as a mechanism to implement a kind of low-intensity privatization of health services. In this model, however, the government relinquishes only the provision of services to the private sector, limiting the influence of NGOs as representatives of civil society.

---

*Astro turf is adapted from the term "astro turf lobbying," which describes lobbying efforts that are manufactured and passed on as grassroots movements (Patel and Rushefsky 1995, 201).

If reform programs are to alter existing inequitable health systems, they need to be implemented with a process of consultation that allows for controlled and constructive debate and compromise. This consultation is a reciprocal process that requires give and take, recognizing the obligations both of civil society and of government. Governments should not institute reform programs for political reasons but for the attainment of very concrete programmatic outputs, whose progress can be measured in both the short and long term.

Some Preliminary Conclusions on Global Trends

Efforts to promote greater NGO-government collaboration in Latin America and the Caribbean have been working under the assumption that, within an environment dominated by health care reform and democratization, heightened levels of NGO-government collaboration would automatically emerge. Although the opportunities for NGO-government collaboration in health care have increased as a result of political and economic reforms, competing influences have actually hampered their implementation. Therefore, it is overly simplistic to talk about a direct causal effect between state reform, democratization, and greater NGO-government collaboration. There is a considerable delay in the appearance of collaboration after the implementation of democratization and economic reform policies, in part because these catalyzing factors are double-edged — creating opportunities but failing to construct an enabling environment for the collaboration of NGOs and the government.

The specific historical relations between the government and NGOs in a particular country is a significant factor that can be a barrier to collaboration, despite the easing of tensions as a result of democratization. One of the primary roles the NGO sector views itself as playing is as an arena for discussing issues regarding civil society vis-à-vis the state. That the NGO sector grew rapidly when political space was curtailed and that it still seeks to play an important role in demanding transparency and accountability from the state leads to a situation in which NGOs find it necessary to defend their autonomy and independence.

Democratization has produced significant social and institutional changes, which have permitted once illegal and marginalized groups and social movements to enter the national political and social arena and obtain legal incorporation. Yet the process has not automatically led to the integration of these marginalized sectors or groups into the political process. Democratization has broken down many of the existing relationships that sustained these marginalized groups. Democratization in some ways has weakened the social base from which NGOs emerged without truly creating a secure and coherent means of participating in the new political system.

The space available for integration into the national political, economic, and social space is usually crowded out by more mainstream social movements and groups, thereby leading to similar or even greater levels of marginalization and exclusion for other NGOs and social movements.

Economic reform has replaced the existing unsustainable welfare functions of the health sector with neoliberal reforms that have allowed for contractually based systems of collaboration between civil society groups and the state, leading in some instances to more efficient systems and better quality of services. Nonetheless, the problems that plagued the previous state-centered system — an inability to provide equitable access to health care services, which in turn increased costs and inefficiency — have not been addressed by the market forces introduced by neoliberal reforms. The health care reform processes being introduced are market-based systems without the incentive for contractors to implement programs that address issues of inequality. The contractual bases of collaboration promoted by reform actually constrain the NGO sector's expertise in providing collective and social goods.

The influence of international organizations is also double-edged. They rapidly create incentives for governments to view NGO-government collaboration as favorable policy and a strategic alternative. Unfortunately, they fail to create long-term and sustainable motivations that allow for the formulation of permanent state policies.

THE IMPLEMENTATION PROCESS

The implementation of NGO-government collaboration redefines the state-centric social contract between the public sphere and civil society. The process, in addition to the influences created by global trends, is affected by the political conflict that arises as institutions that are threatened by the new relationship resist changes to the existing social contract. The successful implementation of collaborative projects in this context requires skillful statecraft. The implementation process becomes as important as program content, in which poorly designed, executed, and funded implementation plans negatively impact the quality of the collaborative project. The following analysis looks at four basic implementing conditions that serve as a checklist against which to score the quality of the implementation process. These include the level of time and resources available for implementation; the degree of consensus on the validity of the policy; the level of interdependence, communication, and coordination of the implementing actors; and the presence of a coherent implementation process (Hogwood and Gunn 1984).

Level of Time and Resources Available for Implementation

Funds are often readily available during the initial phases of NGO-government collaborative projects. Problems tend to arise when complementary counterpart funding, especially from the ministries, is required. In Chile, between 1991 and 1993, international and bilateral organizations financed a program designed to generate NGO-government collaboration in the extension of primary care services. The program funded 90 NGOs in 86 communities throughout the country. The services offered by the funded NGOs ranged from general community health to specialized services in mental and occupational health. Dr. Roberto Belmar, the director of primary care services for the Ministry of Health at that time, believes that the project was successful because the NGOs' flexibility allowed them to pool resources from other projects, while their social embeddedness permitted them to mobilize additional resources, resulting in programs that would have otherwise cost the ministry many times more. However, as the international funding for the program diminished and the health care reform emphasized privatization and contractually based relations with NGOs, the shift in priorities made collaboration less intense. By 1996, only 10 percent of the 90 NGOs that the Ministry of Health funded in the early 1990s maintained a relationship with the public health care system. In Ecuador, Dr. Patricio Abad Herrera, the second of three ministers of health during the administration of former President Sixto Durán (1991-1996), supported efforts to increase NGO-government collaboration. Dr. Abad developed a strategy for increasing collaboration and established a unit directly under his administration to coordinate the efforts. Because of a decrease in state expenditures on health (from 8 percent of the national budget in 1994 to 4 percent in 1996), the efforts and the unit were reduced upon his departure.

The experiences in Chile and Ecuador demonstrated intense periods of collaboration because of a significant initial injection of funds. In Guatemala, collaborative projects were slow in developing, but they still exist today and show a greater chance of sustainability than the projects in Ecuador and Chile. The Ministry of Health in Guatemala has been involving NGOs in the implementation of Integrated Systems of Health Delivery (Sistemas Integrales de Atención en Salud — SIAS). SIAS are the new administrative local-level entities of the Ministry of Health promoted by the health care reform process. These are allowed to contract NGOs to deliver health care and, in the first 10 months of implementation, five major NGOs were already contracted. The Guatemala experience is an example of collaboration being implemented with funds controlled by the Ministry of Health (mainly from loans from the international financial institutions destined for health care reform).

The limited evidence from these experiences shows an inverse relationship between initial external funding and long-term project sustainability. The problem is not that efforts are poorly funded from their initiation. On the contrary, the influx of initial funds, usually from international sources, while producing initial intensive collaboration, fails to secure sustainability in the absence of complementary domestic funds.

Agreement Upon the Validity of the Policy

If the implementing agents of a policy or a program of activities do not agree with the validity of the theory upon which the policy is based, its implementation is difficult. All of the cases observed in this analysis show an initial lack of consensus among the diverse set of implementing actors on the validity and the goals of collaboration. Importantly, the reservations concerning the policy were not based on political considerations per se, but many of the technical personnel within the ministries of health had serious reservations regarding the capacity of the NGO sector.

Personnel from the Chilean Ministry of Health's maternal and child health program feel that the very same attributes that make NGOs attractive to international donors make them problematic for the public sector. Dr. René Castro of the Chilean Ministry of Health explained that while NGOs' effectiveness emerges from their small scale, this same characteristic makes them unable to expand their scope of work to a wider scale or to "scale up" their projects. Therefore, despite even the greatest efforts by NGOs, their inability to broaden their scope makes them ineffective partners for the Ministry of Health, which is responsible for the delivery of care to an entire nation. According to Castro, NGOs are more of a drain on the ministry than an asset because of the need to subsidize their work continuously.

Personnel from the Ministry of Health in Guatemala highlighted their frustration with a lack of NGO compliance with national health plans. According to ministry officials, the NGO sector's reliance on external sources of funding makes it difficult for NGOs to follow guidelines established by the national institutions (in many instances, private international donors encourage the NGOs to remain autonomous of the Ministry of Health) since they are more accountable to international donors than to national entities. Officials in Guatemala are very sensitive to this issue, given the country's more than 300 NGOs. Officials complain that this has led to isolation, duplication of services, and a squandering of a good part of the international assistance since the activities are uncoupled from other national-level interventions. This perception is not without some merit. There is significant evidence that NGOs do not have a monopoly on flexibility and client-centered behavior. The presence of undesirable traits cannot be assigned to either the public or private sector; instead, the divide runs across both sectors (Tendler 1997).

Even within the international organizations that promote greater collaboration between sectors, there is no consensus on the comparative advantages of the NGO sector. In a collaborative paper by staff from the International Monetary Fund (IMF) and World Bank, the authors analyzed strategies promoting popular participation using social choice and public choice theory (Gerson 1993). Among the paper's conclusions are assertions that organizations like NGOs are unlikely to represent broad public opinion and that close NGO-government collaboration may actually diminish social participation. In addition, the paper states that social participation is a commodity that might not always yield sufficient benefits to justify the costs. Officials from other international organizations, including PAHO, find NGOs to be difficult counterparts because of the nebulous distinction between their social and political roles and argue that collaboration with NGOs can limit democratic representation and social participation.

Levels of Interdependence, Communication, and Coordination of the Implementing Actors

The process of implementing any policy is long and involves an intricate progression of events and linkages, any of which may derail the process. The more complex the dependency and the relationship among the different implementing actors, the greater the difficulty in implementing the policy. With regard to NGO-government collaborative projects, the programmatic area that the collaboration is intended to address will be a strong determinant of the ease of implementation. The public sector's functions in health include 1) development of health policy, 2) research, 3) regulation, 4) education and training, 5) provision of clinical services, and 6) implementation of public health initiatives. Each of these functions occurs at different levels of the state administrative structure and results in varying degrees of dependency.

If schematically depicted as a multilayered box, with the outer layers corresponding to the provision of public health interventions and the inner layers representing the health policy environment, the interdependency and overlap of areas of authority among the actors, as well as the difficulty related to program implementation, increase as the program being implemented addresses activities in the inner layers.

The more enterprising the collaborative project (the more policy-oriented the work), the greater the interdependency among the decision-making actors, and the greater the overlap of the areas of authority, the more negotiation required and the greater the difficulty in implementing the project. In the policy-making realm, there is less space for complementarity of tasks, so any collaboration in this area is dependent upon formal institutionalized coordination with a greater number of public sector entities. The more periodic and short-term the area of collaboration (vaccination campaigns, for example), the less interdependency among relevant actors, less impact on the different jurisdictions of the institutions, and a greater likelihood that the NGO-government collaboration will succeed.

An example of this escalating interdependence was evident in Ecuador in the collaborative project between Fundación Sol Mayor and Health Area Nine (a health area on the outskirts of Quito). The director of the local health area, Dr. Jorge Albán,

Health System Activity and Actors Involved

Public Health Programs — governed by the Ministry of Health

◊

Clinical Services — governed by the Ministry of Health, hospitals, and professional associations

◊

Health Education and Research — governed by the Ministry of Health, hospitals, professional associations, the Ministry of Education, and universities

◊

Health Policy and Regulation — governed by the Ministry of Health, hospitals, professional associations, Ministry of Education, universities, legislature, executive, the Ministry of Finance, and judiciary realizing that many of the patients were accessing their health care from the local *curanderos* (traditional healers), decided to coordinate the efforts of the formal health system with the Fundación Sol Mayor, which had a project with the local *curanderos*. The resulting project integrated the services of the *curanderos* and the physicians so that physicians working in the local health area and *curanderos* referred patients to each other. Although Dr. Albán and the Fundación Sol Mayor characterized the collaboration within the local health area as a success, their efforts to develop policy promoting this coordination at the national level were fiercely opposed. According to Dr. Albán, the collaboration was easy at the local level because it was negotiated between two local entities. However, as soon as the project tried to influence policy, it made contact with the sphere of influence of a multitude of actors, which made the development of the policy a highly political process. For example, the Ministry of Justice opposed any policy recognizing the *curanderos* because collaboration with "non-western" medical practices is prohibited by statutes still on the books. The same held true with the national medical association, which felt that a legitimization of the *curanderos* devalued their role as physicians.

The Presence of a Coherent Policy

The lack of a rational and coherent policy represents a major barrier not only to the implementation of collaborative projects but to the enactment of health care reform. Health care reform advocates claim that the traditional health system needs increased efficiency, cost effectiveness, and quality and that these may be attained by rationing state resources, while increasing the power of the private sector. In contrast to the interventionist approaches advocated by the state-centric model, the neoliberal foundations upon which much health care reform is based encourage countries to reduce the role and size of the public sector and increase that of the private sector. The concrete manifestation of the strategy is a process of unchecked decentralization and privatization with little coherence and rationality. This is an understandable consequence given the inherent contradiction in a strategy that asks public sector entities to support, fund, and press for measures that are going to reduce their own power and sphere of influence. What emerges is a declared process of decentralization and rationalization, without a guiding coherent state policy. Since NGO-government collaboration is embedded in these health care reform policies, collaborative projects also often lack a coherent process and system capable of instituting an effective implementation process.

The experience of the Fundación Eugenio Espejo (FES) in Ecuador highlights the effect of this contradiction. As part of the health care reform process, FES worked with the Ministry of Health to set up a collaboration that allowed the NGO to administer a local health area (Tabacundo, Ecuador). FES, the Ministry of Health, and PAHO implemented a project by which FES would coordinate the health services of the area's multi-institutional delivery system (ministry services, UNICEF projects, UNFAP projects, church programs). Although officials in the higher echelons of the ministry agreed to the program, the project was never supported by the local health director, the other institutions, and the area's health personnel. The director resented the loss of control, the health personnel viewed the project as "low-intensity privatization," and the other NGOs saw it as a threat to their autonomy.

Although certain sectors of the ministry had supported the project and even provided funding, the ministry as an institution could not compel the local entities to collaborate, and after the first year the project collapsed. Ministry of Health personnel explained that without any explicit state policy, there was no leverage for them to support the NGO over other public sector employees who, through strikes and protests, could not only exact significant political costs but who also represented the interests of the public sector more than did the NGO.

Some Preliminary Conclusions on the Implementation Process

Although the model from which these preconditions were derived is a linear, top-down approach to policymaking, the application of the four factors selected to the process of implementing NGO-government collaboration actually highlights the nonlinearity of the process. In reality, the implementation of collaborative projects is an interactive and reciprocal process in which policymakers and proponents of collaborative projects may adapt and modify strategies as well as the policy-making process itself. As the cases analyzed demonstrate, the process is not exclusively top-down and allows for a variety of implementation mechanisms, including informal and extra-institutional processes. Regardless of the direction of the process, these four factors were a source of friction in all the attempts at implementation. Attempts to increase the role of NGOs represent a significant alteration of the status quo. The conspicuous conflicts between the public sector and NGOs have been embedded in the institutional behaviors of each sector, and for the NGO sector it has even served as the raison d'être behind their existence. This level of institutional discord requires that collaboration advocates take the political and institutional reality that governs the state and civil society relations into account when implementing cross-sectoral collaborative projects. These are conditions that proponents of greater collaboration need to integrate into project implementation plans and are examples of why implementation plans are as critical as the programmatic contents of the projects.

OUTCOMES AND MECHANISMS OF COLLABORATION

Another key linkage is the correlation between the mechanism employed to operationalize the collaboration and the success of the project. The existing literature indicates that the linkage mechanism is a significant determinant of the sustainability and impact of the collaboration program. In experiences in other fields (education and agriculture), linkages that employ mechanisms such as contracting tend to be short-term and result in low levels of satisfaction. This is in contrast to programs that employ a more structural mechanism, such as planning bodies with public-private sector representation, which lend themselves to higher levels of success because of their institutional nature (Bebbington and Thiele 1993).

Based on the examples of NGO-government collaboration observed in this analysis, the modes of operationalizing the collaboration can be classified as either operational linkages or structural linkages. Operational linkages refer to modes of collaboration based on activities in which personnel from both sectors are actively involved. These include professional activities, such as training, research, conferences, and collaborative project planning committees. Structural linkages are modes of collaboration more administrative in nature, such as resource allocation systems (in which NGOs are contracted or are government grantees), units within state agencies with the goal of coordinating NGO activities, and policy-making committees with both NGO and government representation.

Table 1 is a roster of the NGOs involved in the collaboration analyzed in this research, along with the collaborative mechanism used in each case. The table also describes two outcome indicators — one measured by the ability to sustain the project at least 18 months beyond the life of the original project funding and a second by the satisfaction of both the public and private sector personnel involved in the project. This was measured using a battery of questions to measure individual satisfaction with the extent of the collaboration and its accomplishments. In the last column, the expressions describing the modes of collaboration for those projects that showed positive outcomes in both categories are highlighted.

The most revealing information in Table 1 is the positive correlation demonstrated between the eight cases of NGO-government collaboration that demonstrated positive outcomes and the presence of collaboration mechanisms that included professional activities, collaborative project planning committees, and policy-making units with corepresentation (factors A, C, and E).

Interpreting the Results

In interviews, government officials argue that in order to collaborate with NGOs, governmental entities must be able to verify the professional and technical capacity of the NGOs and be able to hold NGOs accountable. NGO officials, by contrast, look for mechanisms that allow them to retain autonomy and recognize their long experience. It appears that modes of collaboration that in some way increase the contact among the personnel of both sectors give those involved a greater sense of control. Professional activities, collaborative project planning, and policy-making units with corepresentation are conducive to alleviating the apprehensions of both sectors. Arenas of dialogue, debate, and exchange allow the government to supervise and hold the NGOs accountable and provide the NGOs with a minimum level of exchange that allows them to feel that they are retaining their autonomy and that their contribution and experience is respected.

The negative correlation between "resource allocation" mechanisms and satisfaction is significant. The presence of resource allocation was not a sufficient or even necessary factor in making collaboration outcomes positive. This finding is critical, since many of the international initiatives promoting collaboration concentrate their efforts in providing the state with funds to finance NGOs. The experience of NGOs like Fundación Cristo Vive (FCV) and La Caleta in Chile shows that the financial difficulties involved with receiving funding from the state, either because of reimbursement problems or the short-term nature of the contracts, negatively impacts the NGO sector's satisfaction with collaboration.

A second interesting correlation is the minimal role that formal NGO coordinating units played — another mode of collaboration prompted by international organizations. In Ecuador, for example, the NGO tied closely to the NGO

Table 1.

Countries	NGOs	(A) Professional Activities	(B) Resource Allocation	(C) Planning	(D) NGO Units	(E) Decision-making Bodies	Outcome measured satisfaction/ sustainability	Isolation of the determining factors
Chile	La Caleta		+		+	+	negative/positive	
	CEMS	+	+	+	+	+	POSITIVE/POSITIVE	A B C D E
	CORSAPS	+	+	+	+	+	POSITIVE/POSITIVE	A B C D E
	Fundación Cristo Vive		+		+	+	negative/positive	
	COMUSAMS	+	+	+	+	+	POSITIVE/POSITIVE	A B C D E
	Hogar de Cristo	+	+	+		+	POSITIVE/POSITIVE	A B C E
	Fundación Sol Mayor			+	+		negative/positive	
Ecuador	Fundación Eugenio Espejo			+	+	+	negative/negative	
	CEPAR	+		+		+	POSITIVE/POSITIVE	A C E
	CIUDAD	+		+		+	POSITIVE/POSITIVE	A C E
	CARE/Ecuador	+		+		+	POSITIVE/POSITIVE	A C E
	CEPAM	+					negative/negative	
Guatemala	Médicos Descalzos	+		+		+	POSITIVE/POSITIVE	A C E
	ATI	+				+	negative/positive	
	ASINDES	+		+		+	negative/negative	

unit, the Fundación Eugenio Espejo, collapsed entirely because of the disappointment that resulted after the NGO unit was given little support and status. The presence of NGO units, in and of themselves, is not enough. Instead, positive outcomes require contact among differing levels of the bureaucracy in various institutions and not just contact between the NGOs and the governmental NGO unit.

This seems to indicate that the NGOs interested in collaboration perceive the state's openness to using the NGOs' professional experience in training, sharing planning responsibilities, and decisionmaking as even more valuable than the allocation of state resources. An example of the importance played by units of corepresentation is the experience of Hogar de Cristo (HDC) in Chile. HDC is one of the oldest NGOs in the country and counts on a broad-based presence throughout Chile. The organization has centers throughout the country and is a very successful philanthropic organization, receiving much of its operating budget from private contributions. Although the organization is not the typical post-1973 Chilean NGO and was not a major organization in the pro-democratic movement, it has maintained very close contact with the state through an advisory board that includes people from the organization, politicians, and government bureaucrats. Médicos Descalzos, a Guatemalan NGO established in 1990 to research and promote the use of medicinal plants, has also been able to establish and sustain a successful relationship with regional health officials in the department of Quiché without initially receiving funding from the state. Local ministry officials initiated the relationship so that the NGO would not only provide services to the patients, but train ministry personnel in the use of medicinal plants. The collaboration has been highly successful, with the NGO now included in the strategic planning sessions of the local health services. Among the most successful public-private collaborations in Ecuador is that between CIUDAD, an NGO concerned with urban issues, and the health secretariat of the municipality of Quito. Without the need for a formal agreement or any transfer of funds between the two institutions, the NGO and mid-level civil servants at the municipality designed, developed, and implemented a computerized epidemiological surveillance system for the capital city. After the program had been developed and tested, it was presented to municipal and ministry officials. CIUDAD officials attributed the success of the project to the confidence that had been built up between the state civil servants and CIUDAD personnel in everyday programs as well as in planning sessions.

POLICY RECOMMENDATIONS

Despite the perception that Latin American health care systems were state-centric, the reality is that by the 1980s the state was a weak and disinterested actor in health policy. Governments and NGOs in the region often have an adversarial relationship embedded in the political, religious, and ethnic polarization that has dominated the region's sociopolitical structure. Although the opportunity for comprehensive NGO-government collaboration could have been an instrumental mechanism through which the state-centered system could have been made more flexible, responsive, and efficient, the polarized political landscape that governed the region in the 1970s and 1980s made the collaboration impossible. Yet, with the end of the Cold War and its accompanying ideological currents, the emergence of the proponents of democratic market economies were able to seize health care reform processes and champion the benefits of decentralized, market-governed health care systems.

Under the current model of health care reform, NGOs reemerge as private sector entities that can improve the system's efficiency and effectiveness, and collaboration is defined, implemented, and governed through market strategies (contracts, bids, per capita reimbursement, and so on). The cases explored in this analysis show that democratization processes and decentralized health care systems in and of themselves were not enough to create an enabling environment for NGO-government collaboration. The merits of democracy and market capitalism have been agreed upon, and specific policies sometimes followed, but the mechanisms and institutions by which to generate and maintain greater NGO-government collaboration have been given very little priority. The attempts at NGO-government collaboration have lacked appropriate resources as well as established administrative practices characteristic of good governance. It is through good governance that states put mechanisms and procedures in place that facilitate NGO competitiveness, including contractual and reimbursement procedures that are sensitive to the NGO sector's financial, technical, and administrative constraints and bidding and contracting systems that allow the NGO sector to use its expertise not only in the implementation of projects but also in the planning and designing of programs.

The cases also demonstrate the need for bureaucratic commitment and institutional learning. The potential benefit of decentralization is visible in the successful collaborative efforts that have emerged at the local level, but at the same time its limitations are evident in the difficulty encountered in sustaining efforts and replicating them in a context devoid of institutional state support. The lack of a bureaucratic commitment and the loss of accumulated knowledge as a result of frequent bureaucratic reshuffling does not engender cohesive governmental structures and policies, which are the precursor of effective government-NGO collaboration. Greater collaboration between the sectors depends upon the will demonstrated by the state to promote actively and create an enabling political and economic space for the NGO sector to interact with government. An active, participatory, and collaborative non-governmental sector requires a determined, active, and guiding state, willing to modernize through a participatory and inclusionist process.

The evidence in this analysis points to three pillars upon which successful NGO-government collaboration may be developed and implemented. The first is the need for a broad-based commitment to the policy, that is, a belief in the validity of the theory underlying NGO-government collaboration and in the cause-and-effect relationship of the policy. The second is an adequate system of procedures and processes able to guide the financial and programmatic relationship between NGOs and the state. The third is the critical role played by the structural mechanism of dialogue and debate that allows both sectors to air contested matters and to compromise. These three pillars are attainable through various mechanisms of good governance.

Broad-based commitment to policy is a component that emerges from an inclusion of various levels of bureaucracy in the development and implementation of the policies. Both top-down and bottom-up approaches of policymaking are inadequate in and of themselves. The policy in either approach encounters significant barriers from the mid-level bureaucracies. Some advocates promote a process of "cluster implementation," in which the process does not focus either on top-down or bottom-up approaches (Walt 1994). Instead, policy is implemented by choosing strategic clusters at the three levels of bureaucracy: the macro or political will level; the local level bureaucrats or the micro-level; and the mid-level bureaucrats, which include local area health directors, regional health directors, and ministerial division heads. The approach is enhanced by instituting policies through a system of open dialogue and debate among different levels of bureaucracy and by focusing the policy implementation on the attainment of specific programmatic outputs. The governmental sector should institute and implement policies not for the sake of political cover but for the attainment of very concrete programmatic outputs whose progress can be measured in the short and long terms. The process of consultation allows for all levels of government to agree to the availability of political, financial, and technical resources for the implementation of the policies. This strategy requires more effort at the early stages of policy implementation, but the political gains in terms of reduced intergovernmental conflict outweigh the initial investment. Hence, the state needs to accompany the rhetoric of stated policy with the required effort at the initial stages of policy implementation.

Collaboration mechanisms that respect the uniqueness of NGO characteristics are critical. Among the most destabilizing factors in the contracting and granting system between NGOs and the state is the myth that contracting operates according to market principles. This results in under-investment in the NGO sector, short funding cycles undermining fiscal stability, and a predominant concern with efficiency and cost-cutting that puts pressure on service quality (Smith and Lipsky 1993). Instead of retaining this belief, the practice of collaborating with NGOs through contracting and grantmaking needs to be recognized as a social service delivery system and viewed as a public investment. Among the strategies governments may use to help alleviate the poor performance of contracting regimes (Magnusson 1993) are the following:

1. Extend funding cycles to three-to-five-year grants and contracts. This would allow NGOs to improve their financial stability and long-term strategic planning, which in turn would allow them to secure and hold personnel and staff.

2. Build contingency funds into the contracts; in other words, allow NGOs to make a minimal "profit" as a buffer against temporary setbacks and for times in between contract periods in which the organization has few sources of income.

3. Provide NGOs with tax incentives that facilitate their importation of necessary technology and equipment and the purchase of infrastructure resources such as land, buildings, and other capital investment components. This is important because NGOs cannot use their contracts as assets in seeking mortgages and loans.

4. Develop accountability measures that satisfy public sector regulations (such as strict financial reporting and annual audits), respect the autonomy and independence of the NGOs, and respond to the administrative limitations faced by

NGOs — yet that are based on programmatic outcomes. This would not only reduce regulatory interference and allow NGOs to exploit their advantage of efficiency, but it would also protect the interest of the NGOs to respond quickly and thoroughly to community needs.

5. Provide NGOs with small one-time grants that recognize their contributions as laboratories for the invention of social services. These grants would allow NGOs to pursue independent research and practice, which not only help the organizations retain their programmatic autonomy but also contribute to the production of knowledge in the social service sector.

Arenas of dialogue allow for controlled and constructive debate and compromise. The social service sector is an integral component of the relation between the state and civil society. This exchange is a reciprocal process that requires give and take, which recognizes the obligations both of civil society and of government. This requires participation, protections, and privileges. The establishment of arenas of dialogue makes decisionmaking transparent, allowing the goals and objectives of policies to be made clear to all the actors involved. Policy decisions should be undertaken after consultation with sectors of civil society, providing accessible and reliable information. The arenas of dialogue allow the NGO sector to provide input into the policy-making process. Even if these bodies are only consultative in nature, they allow NGOs to voice their experience, present empirical data, and put forth philosophical arguments to policymakers. These arenas of dialogue also provide a vehicle through which the strong historical antecedents that have governed the two sectors' adversarial relationship can be taken into account and discussed. The implementation of policies or of funding regimes that do not recognize these historical antecedents will be unable to establish a well-founded collaborative relationship.

Some of the countries of the hemisphere are rediscovering democracy, while others are discovering it for the first time. This is occurring simultaneously with a retrenchment of the state and a championing of the private sector. The challenge facing the countries of the hemisphere is to find a formula that allows them to balance the social responsibilities of the state with the efficiencies of the private sector. NGO-government collaboration has emerged as a mechanism to attain this equilibrium, but this relationship requires a third factor, namely, engaging the inventiveness of the NGO sector. It is with this goal in mind — the pursuit of a balance among the state, the market, and civil society — that these recommendations are made. The state is responsible for its citizens; the private sector provides efficiency; and the NGO sector is more caring and inventive. Conversely, the state needs to become more efficient; the private sector, more caring; and the NGO sector, more accountable. Future paths to development lie in the balance of these three arenas, and international organizations must work to exploit the advantages and minimize the disadvantages inherent in this new framework.

References

Abel, Christopher. 1996. *Health, Hygiene and Sanitation in Latin America: 1870-1950.* London: University of London.

Alleyne, George. 1995. "Introductory Statements." Paper at the PAHO Seminar on Health Care Reform, Washington, D.C.

Álvarez, Sonia, and Arturo Escobar,eds. 1992. *The Making of Social Movements in Latin America: Identity, Strategy, and Democracy.*Boulder, Colo.: Westview Press.

Amini, Ash. 1996. "Beyond Associative Democracy." *New Political Economy* 1: 9-34.

Badelt, Christopher. 1990. "Institutional Choice and the Nonprofit Sector." In *The Comparative Studies of The Third Sector,* eds. Helmut Anheier and Wolfgang Seibel. New York: Walter de Gruyter.

Bebbington, Anthony, and David Lehmann. 1998. "NGOS, the State, and the Development Process." In *The Changing Role of the State in Latin America*, ed. Menno Vellinga. Boulder, Colo.: Westview Press.

Bebbington, Anthony, and Graham Thiele. 1993. *NGOs and the State: Rethinking Roles in Sustainable Agricultural Development.* New York: Routledge.

Brown, David. 1989a. *Voluntary Development Organizations: Expanding Their Development Role.* Washington, D.C.: Institute for Development Research.

Brown, David. 1989b. *Voluntary Development Organizations: Guidelines for Donors.* Washington, D.C.: Institute for Development Research.

Browning, Félix Alvarado, Maribel Guerra, and Abel Girón. 1998. *Perfil de las Organizaciones No Gubermentales en Guatemala.* Guatemala City: Foro de Coordinaciones de ONGs en Guatemala.

Carroll, Thomas F. 1992. *Intermediary NGOs. The Supporting Link in Grassroots Development.* West Hartford, Conn.: Kumarian Press.

Chalmers, Douglas, Scott Martin, and Kerianne Piester. 1997. "Associative Networks: New Structures of Representation for the Popular Sectors?" In *The New Politics of Inequality in Latin America: Participation and Representation,* eds. Douglas Chalmers et al. New York: Oxford University Press.

Clark, John. 1993. "The Relationship Between the State and the Voluntary Sector." Unpublished. Washington, D.C.: World Bank.

Cox, Stephen. 1992. "El Papel de las ONGs en los Procesos de Desarrollo en América Latina." Paper presented at ODN conference on NGOs in Latin America, Washington, D.C.

Díaz, Álvaro. 1997. "New Developments in Economic and Political Restructuring in Latin America." In *Politics, Social Change and Economic Restructuring in Latin America,* eds. William C. Smith and Roberto P. Korzeniewicz. Coral Gables, Fla.: North-South Center Press at the University of Miami.

Escobar, Arturo. 1992. "Reflections on Development: Grassroots Approaches and Alternative Politics in the Third World." *Futures* 24(5) June:411-436.

Evans, Peter. 1994. *Embedded Autonomy.* Princeton, N.J.: Princeton University Press.

Fishlow, Albert. 1990. "The Latin American State." *Journal of Economic Perspectives* 4: 61-74.

Foley, Michael, and Brian Edwards. 1996. "The Paradox of Civil Society." *Journal of Democracy* 7: 38-52.

Foweraker, Joe. 1995. *Theorizing Social Movements.* London: Pluto Press.

Foweraker, Joe. 1998. "Social Movements and Citizenship Rights in Latin America." In *The Changing Role of the State in Latin America,* ed. Menno Vellinga. Boulder, Colo.: Westview Press.

Garoz, Bartolomé. 1995. "La ONG y el Desarrollo Sostenible." Paper presented at El Primer Congreso Nacional de Organizaciones No Gubernamentales, Guatemala City.

Gerson, Peter. 1993. "Popular Participation in Economic Theory and Practice." Manuscript. Washington, D.C.: Inter-American Development Bank.

Gobierno de Guatemala. 1996. *Acuerdos de Paz.* Guatemala City: Asamblea de la Sociedad Civil.

Gobierno de Guatemala. 1997. *Program for Peace: an Opportunity for Guatemala, Investing in National Reconciliation, Democracy and Sustainable Development.* Guatemala City: Fondos Para La Paz.

Grossi, Francisco V. 1989. *Primero la gente: ONG, estado y cooperación internacional en el Tercer Mundo.* Santiago: CEAAL.

Grugel, Jean. 1997. "NGOS Coopted, Independent or Networking? British Overseas Development NGOS and Democratization in Latin America." Paper presented at the Latin American Studies Association Meeting, Guadalajara, Mexico.

Hall, Peter. 1986. *Governing the Economy: The Politics of State Intervention in Britain and France.* Cambridge: Polity Press.

Hirschman, Albert. 1981. *Exit, Voice and Loyalty: Responses to Decline in Firms, Organizations and States.* Cambridge, Mass.: Harvard University Press.

Hogwood, Brian, and Lewis Gunn. 1984. *Policy Analysis for the Real World.* Oxford: Oxford University Press.

Hunt, Raymond, and John Magenau. 1984. "A Task Analysis for Research on Decision Making in Organizations." In *Decision Making in the Public Sector,* ed. Lloyd Nigro. New York: Marcel Dekker.

Jelin, Elizabeth. 1996. "Citizenship Revisited: Solidarity, Responsibility and Rights." *In Constructing Democracy : Human Rights, Citizenship, and Society in Latin America,* eds. Elizabeth Jelin and Eric Hershberg. Boulder, Colo.: Westview Press.

Jelin, Elizabeth. 1997. "Emergent Citizenship or Exclusion? Social Movements and Non-Governmental Organizations in the 1990s." In *Politics, Social Change, and Economic Restructuring in Latin America,* eds. William C. Smith and Roberto P. Korzeniewicz. Coral Gables, Fla.: North-South Center Press.

Jiménez, Marcela. 1996. "Gobierno y Tercer Sector en Chile: Hacia una relación sinérgica." Paper presented at the "Seminario Sobre Iniciativas Privadas para el Desarrollo Local," Santiago, Chile.

Japanese Organization for International Cooperation in Family Planning (JOICFP). 1995. "An Invisible Sector. The Need for Private, Nonprofit or Non-governmental Organizations." *Integration* 44: 78-89.

Kingdon, John. 1984. *Agendas, Alternatives and Public Policy.* Boston: Little Brown and Company.

Korten, David. 1987. "Third Generation NGO Strategies: A Key to People-Centered Development." *World Development* 15 (supplement): 145-159.

Krasner, Steven, ed. 1983. *International Regimes.* Ithaca, N.Y.: Cornell University Press.

Loveman, Brian. 1995. "Chilean NGOS: Forging a Role in the Transition to Democracy." In *New Paths to Development in Latin America,* ed. Charles Reilly. Boulder, Colo.: Lynne Rienner.

Macdonald, Laura. 1997a. "A Mixed Blessing: The NGO Boom in Latin America." *NACLA Report* 28 (3): 35-36.

Macdonald, Laura. 1997b. *Supporting Civil Society: The Political Role of Non-Governmental Organizations in Central America.* New York: St. Martin's Press.

Magnusson, Warren. 1993. "Social Movements and the State: Presentation and Representation." In *A Different Kind of State? Popular Power and Democratic Administration,* ed. Gregory Albo. Toronto: Oxford University Press.

Mahon, James. 1995. *Mobile Capital and Latin American Development.* University Park, Pa.: Pennsylvania State University Press.

Malena, Carmen. 1995. *Working with NGOs. A Practical Guide to Operational Collaboration Between The World Bank and Non-governmental Organizations.* Washington, D.C.: World Bank.

Mettessich, Paul, and Barbara Monsey. 1992. *Collaboration: What Makes It Work. A Review of Research Literature on Factors Influencing Successful Collaboration.* St. Paul, Minn.: Amherst H. Wilder Foundation.

Musgrove, Philip. 1992. "The Economic Crisis and Its Impact on Health and Health Care in Latin America and the Caribbean." In *Health Services Research Anthology,* ed. Kerr White. Washington, D.C.: Pan American Health Organization.

Myrdal, Alva. 1945. *Nation and Family: The Swedish Experiment in Democratic Family and Population Policy.* London: Paul, Trench, Trubner & Co.

O'Donnell, Guillermo. 1994. "The State, Democratization, and Some Conceptual Problems." In *Latin American Political Economy in the Age of Neoliberal Reform,* eds. William C. Smith, Carlos Acuña, and Eduardo Gamarra. Coral Gables, Fla.: North-South Center Press.

O'Donnell, Guillermo. 1996. "Otra institucionalizaci6n." *Política y Gobierno* 3: 3-18.

PACT. 1990. *Steps Toward a Social Investment Fund.* Washington, D.C.: PACT.

Pan American Health Organization (PAHO) and Economic Commission for Latin America and the Caribbean (ECLAC). 1994. *Report on Health, Social Equity and the Changing Production Patterns in Latin America.* Report to the XLVI PAHO Regional Committee Meeting, Washington, D.C.

Pan-American Health Organization (PAHO). 1998. *Health Conditions in the Americas.* Washington, D.C.: Pan-American Health Organization.

Patel, Kant, and Mark Rushefsky. 1995. *Health Care Politics and Policy in America.* London: M.E. Sharpe.

Pereira, L.C., José María Maravall, and Adam Pzeworski. 1994. "Economic Reforms in New Democracies: A Social-Democratic Approach." In *Latin American Political Economy in the Age of Neoliberal Reform,* eds. William C. Smith, Carlos Acuña, and Eduardo Gamarra. Coral Gables, Fla.: North-South Center Press.

Reilly, Charles. 1996. "Topocrats, Technocrats and NGOs." In *New Paths to Development in Latin America,* ed. Charles Reilly. Boulder, Colo.: Lynne Rienner Publishers.

Ritchey-Vance, Marion. 1993. *The Art of Association: NGOs and Civil Society in Colombia.* Washington, D.C.: Inter-American Foundation.

Ritchie, Margaret A. 1995. "NGOs for Health. Roles and Approaches of Nongovernmental Organizations in Health Development." *World Health Forum* 16: 34-38.

Rodríguez-García, Rosalía. 1994. "The Role of NGOs in Community Health and Development." *Promotion and Education* 1: 4-10.

Schmitter, Philip. 1984. *Community, Market, State and Associations?* Florence: European University Institute.

Smith, Steven R., and Michael Lipsky. 1993. *Non-Profits for Hire.* Cambridge, Mass.: Harvard University Press.

Solimano, Giorgio, and Judith Salinas. 1992. *Salud con la gente.* Santiago: CORSAPS.

Stallings, Barbara. 1992. "International Influence on Economic Policy: Debt, Stabilization and Structural Reform." In *The Politics of Economic Adjustment,* eds. Stephan Haggard and Robert Kaufman. Princeton, N.J.: Princeton University Press.

Summit of the Americas. 1994. *Summit of the Americas Plan of Action.* Miami, Florida.

Tendler, Judith. 1997. *Good Government in the Tropics.* Baltimore: Johns Hopkins University Press.

Unidad de Participación Social. 1994a. *Cooperación Servicios de Salud-ONG 1990-1993.* Santiago: Ministerio de Salud de Chile.

Unidad de Participación Social. 1994b. *Políticas de Salud y Organismos No Gubernementales en Chile, Balance de Gestión 1990-1993.* Santiago: Ministerio de Salud de Chile.

United Nations Fund for Population Acitivites (UNFPA). 1994. *Program of Action.* International Conference on Population and Development. New York: UNFPA.

Vacs, Aldo. 1994. "Democracy, Markets, and Structural Reform in World Perspective." In *Latin American Political Economy in the Age of Neoliberal Reform,* eds. William C. Smith, Carlos Acuña, and Eduardo Gamarra. Coral Gables, Fla.: North-South Center Press.

Vargas, Carlos H. A. 1992. *Acerca de la Naturaleza y Evolución de los Organismos No Gubernamentales (ONGs) en Colombia.* Bogotá: Fundación Social.

Walt, Gill. 1994. *Health Policy: An Introduction to Process and Power.* London: Zed Books.

World Bank. 1987. *Financing Health Services in Developing Countries: An Agenda for Reform.* Washington, D.C.: World Bank.

World Bank. 1993. *The World Development Report: Investing in Health.* Washington, D.C.: World Bank.

Chapter 6

Lessons on Sustainable Development from Costa Rica's Forests

Eduardo Silva

Costa Rica's innovative efforts to implement a policy of sustainable development raise a number of questions. What trade-offs have the forest and biodiversity conservation policies of the 1990s generated with respect to the different components of sustainable development? Are the measures adopted likely to be successful? How were those policy choices made? By what means can the components of sustainable development that have been neglected be incorporated, especially those related to livelihood? This chapter addresses these questions by analyzing Costa Rican forest policy, one of that nation's most sharply contested environmental issue areas.

Costa Rica enjoys a reputation as a peaceful, democratic, and equitable Central American country with a strong commitment to nature protection. Government environmentalism began with a focus on nature preservation during the administration of Daniel Odúber (1974-1978), the presidential father of the national parks system. Under President Oscar Árias (1986-1990), Costa Rica's leaders became aware that responses to the problems of environmental protection versus development required more than the creation of national parks. Since then, they have worked tirelessly to weave the norms and principles of the concept of sustainable development into their nation's policies and institutional framework. Costa Rica's institutional and programmatic innovations have turned it into a laboratory for sustainable development, especially with respect to the forest. It is seen as a leader and pioneer in community forestry, bioprospecting, green taxes, carbon emissions trading, and administrative decentralization in the management of protected areas. As occurs with all trailblazers, Costa Rica's efforts to implement a policy of sustainable development raise a number of questions. What trade-offs have the forest and biodiversity conservation policies of the 1990s generated with respect to

The author acknowledges with thanks Amb. Frank McNeil's helpful commentary and Greg Basco's able research assistance. This chapter was originally published as North-South Agenda Paper 45 in May 2001 under the same title.

the different components of sustainable development? Are the measures adopted likely to be successful? How were those policy choices made? By what means can the components of sustainable development that have been neglected be incorporated, especially those related to livelihood? This paper will address these questions.

SUSTAINABLE DEVELOPMENT

Since the 1980s, sustainable development has evolved into a complex, multifaceted concept that seeks to balance economic growth, environmental protection, social equity, and citizen participation in decisionmaking (WCED 1987; World Bank 1992). Economic growth is necessary for political stability and for raising standards of living, which, in developing countries, means poverty reduction. Poverty alleviation is thought to have positive effects on the environment because poor people put great strains on natural resources, pasture, water, and forests. Yet economic growth alone will not suffice to restore environmental quality or to cover the livelihood concerns of impoverished people.

With respect to environmental quality, the consequences of economic growth (health hazards of pollution, climate change, biodiversity loss, and resource scarcity) can no longer be ignored by treating them as externalities. The costs of those consequences must be incorporated into economic decisionmaking. Where natural renewable resources are concerned, environmental economists have cultivated the concept of sustained-yield use (Pearce and Turner 1990). This means that a resource's rate of extraction (fisheries, timber, or game, for example) should not exceed its rate of replacement. The minimum goal is to keep stocks of resources constant; ideally, they would also increase over time, adding to a country's capital stock.

Neither economic growth nor sustained-yield use[1] of natural resources adequately addresses the issues of combating poverty and bringing about social equity. These tasks require the empowerment of local, usually poor communities (Redclift 1992; Friedmann and Rangan 1993). This is one of the reasons why citizen participation has become a crucial component of sustainable development. Citizen participation in decisionmaking (democracy, in a word) is a key element in the process. However, participation in the policy process is not a sufficient condition for the improvement of livelihood. Other factors include institutions, organizations, and funds in the state and in civil society that support social organization, community control over economic resources, and the generation of community enterprises. Without such support it is unlikely that the efforts of local communities will succeed in improving the supply of employment, education, health, and other social services to the community. The asymmetries of knowledge and of economic and political power between poor communities and other sectors of society are simply too great to expect otherwise. Of course, in the context of sustainable development, the economic activities of local communities must incorporate mechanisms to conserve local environmental resources. Some analysts believe that, if properly planned, smaller-scale use and less capital-intensive technology allow economic development to be more sensitive to the nuances of local ecosystems. In the forest sector, this approach is called community or social forestry (Browder 1989).

Nature protection and ecosystem management have become increasingly important components of sustainable development, especially after the signing of the biodiversity convention at the Rio Earth Summit in 1992. Environmentalists stress that ecosystems perform numerous environmental services. Forests, for example, help to control greenhouse gases by capturing and storing CO_2; they are crucial for watershed stability, constrain soil erosion, and provide habitat for flora and fauna. These environmental functions also have value, though they may be difficult to quantify. Thoughtlessly destroying them may adversely affect human health and welfare, for natural systems protect us, and the maintenance of biodiversity is crucial to ensure the well-being of future generations.

Moreover, growing awareness exists — especially in developing countries — that parks isolated from people do not provide a workable solution for biodiversity conservation. The livelihood needs of rural populations put pressure on parks. Thus, conservationists are beginning to emphasize land-use planning around protected areas in which mixed-use zones surrounding parks buffer core areas from further encroachment. The incorporation of local people into park management dovetails with the goals of meeting basic needs and community participation in sustainable development.

Any country would be hard-pressed to address all of the elements of sustainable development simultaneously, all the more so for developing countries. Giving priority to some elements over others implies trade-offs. For example, an emphasis on urban areas usually means neglect of rural regions. A focus on market-led economic growth at the global and domestic levels, combined with an emphasis on sustained-yield resource use, frequently signify postponement of community development and participation in favor of large-scale industry; these priorities also tend to call for technocratic instead of participatory approaches to policymaking. A preference for biodiversity protection often means abandonment of sustained-yield harvesting of natural renewable resources, either industrially or, especially, by local populations. To complicate matters, cutting across the policy debates over these trade-offs are two deeper, "classical" policy issues: 1) the role of the state in the economy and society and 2) (re)distributional concerns or the "who benefits" question.

Yet, these trade-offs are not inevitable. It is possible to craft policy that is more inclusive of seemingly competing goals. However, a focus on traditional policy analysis — description of the problem and prescriptions for corrections — may not suffice. Clarifying policy options and the technical rationales for them are important steps. But the environment and sustainable development in particular are new issue areas. Therefore, they are the subject of contentious politics, the politics of reform and change (Tarrow 1994, 1996). Conflict and cooperation among major stakeholders deeply influence policy outcomes; therefore, reformers interested in a more inclusive approach to sustainable development would benefit from knowing the major stakeholders, their interests, and their sources of influence. This information would place reformers in a better position to cast policy prescriptions for incremental change in ways that bring diverse interests together. Understanding the political opportunity structure that affects environmental policymaking in Costa Rica reveals that prescriptions for improvement — implementing a more integrated version of sustainable development — do not require political sea changes. They can be acted upon within the existing structure.

To answer the questions raised at the beginning of this paper, the first section examines government environmentalism prior to the 1990s, introducing the main stakeholders. The next two sections focus on the contributions and limitations of current policy for the sustainable development of Costa Rica's forests. The concluding sections analyze the policy process that generated those policies and explore the potential for a more inclusive approach to sustainable development.

COSTA RICAN FOREST POLICY: SETTING THE STAGE

Three major tendencies have shaped Costa Rica's forest policy. One champions conservation either as strict preservation or as a search for economic uses of the forest that support preservation, mainly in the form of protected areas. The second and third tendencies focus on the economic uses for the forest's timber and non-timber products as tools to promote incentives for the sustainable development of the forest inside and outside of protected areas. The differences between the second and third approaches depend on the characteristics of the producer and the producer's relationship to the market. Tendency two mainly draws its inspiration from economic liberalism, focusing on landowners (mostly large-scale) and other actors, each connected to the market individually. Tendency three has more communitarian roots, focusing on cooperative behavior — building social capital — among peasants and small-scale farmers as a prerequisite for more successful participation in the market. The following sections show how, over time, Costa Rican and international stakeholders with philosophies and interests anchored in these three tendencies have shaped Costa Rican forest policy. At present, the differences among them remain unreconciled. How to achieve reconciliation in the context of a still fairly poor country remains a question.

Conservation

Historically, Costa Rica has suffered from high rates of deforestation, a testament to the unsustainable nature of the forest sector's development. In 1900, 85 percent of the nation's territory was covered by tropical forests; that decreased to 56 percent in 1950 and to 29 percent in 1987 (Lutz et al. 1993). Of an estimated 1.5 million hectares of remaining primary forest, approximately 400,000 are not in protected areas, thus are available for production (Kishor and Constantino 1993). The Forest Service (Dirección General de Forestal —DGF) estimated that deforestation rates decreased from an average of 50,000 hectares per year in the 1980s to 17,000 in the early 1990s. In a hotly debated study released in 1998, the Ministry of Environment and Energy (Ministerio de Ambiente y Energía — MINAE) proudly announced that deforestation had been halted. The calculation was based on a controversial definition of secondary forest as forests that regenerate naturally.

Costa Rica's forests have succumbed to many sources (Carriere 1991; Peuker 1992; Hopkins 1995). Conversion to agriculture and ranching by large-scale commercial farmers, agribusiness, and ranchers have been significant sources of deforestation. Government subsidies to expand cotton, sugar, and meat production for export spurred them on. Shifted cultivators[2] also contributed to deforestation by settling on heavily forested parcels of land made available through the agrarian reform agency. Legal and illegal logging destined primarily for domestic markets, of course, have been a perennial source deforestation. Moreover, legal logging practices condoned high-grading,[3] which degrades the market value of the forest.

Since the 1950s, concern in Costa Rica has steadily mounted over the effects of these high rates of deforestation on the country's efforts to preserve its diverse flora and fauna, and abundant watersheds and to prevent soil erosion. Early responses focused on the control of timber production and habitat preservation (Hopkins 1995). A forest service had existed in Costa Rica since 1948. However, the 1969 forest law, which created the DGF, greatly strengthened the institutional framework for Costa Rica's forest sector (Asamblea Nacional 1969). Originally housed in the Ministry of Agriculture, the DGF had two departments: National Parks and Forest Protection. The DGF's functions were to control timber extraction and land-use change on public property. It also regulated timber extraction on private property but only when landowners wanted to avail themselves of concessions to public lands or use public subsidies for agricultural development. Otherwise, private property owners could dispose of their forests as they saw fit, which they did, and deforestation continued at a rapid pace.

As the forests dwindled, government environmentalism began to focus on nature preservation during the administration of President Daniel Odúber (Hopkins 1995). Odúber turned the National Park Service into a General Directorate, thereby establishing it as an independent agency on equal footing with the DGF. He also sponsored the creation of a national parks system. His efforts earned him international recognition and put Costa Rica on the environmental map. The emphasis on nature preservation continued during the presidency of Rodrigo Carazo (1978-1982), who took an active interest in the parks system and had a personal role in the establishment of Parque Amistad, an innovative bi-national park overlapping the borders of Costa Rica and Panama.

The contributions of these political leaders notwithstanding, at bottom, the parks system was the creation of Costa Rica's pioneering environmentalists. These individuals formed a community of knowledge rooted in a scientific background, a common vision, and shared experiences, often dating from university student days. They persuaded successive presidents that parks were the best way to protect the environment. Their influence, in no small measure, stemmed from the fact that they formed a cross-party coalition on behalf of environmental protection (Boza 1997). This tightly knit community of knowledge and its followers steadfastly championed conservation over use in policy debates. They have placed Costa Rica in the forefront of the biodiversity movement in the developing world and, among other achievements, have played a leading role in getting environmental education into the curricula. This community of knowledge continues to exercise a powerful force for conservation in Costa Rica today.

Introducing Sustainable Development

Of course, parks and reserves were just the beginning. The harder challenge had to do not only with how to manage the parks but also the wise use of the environment, especially throughout the country. Continuing high rates of deforestation and the emergence of the concept of sustainable development in the 1980s underscored the shortcomings of Costa Rica's initial policy and institutional responses to unrestrained land-use change. The Forest Service's domain and focus were too narrow. Advocates of sustainable development stressed that environmental problems cut across economic sectors. Yet, the DGF had little control over privately held forests, colonization policy, or the expansion of the agricultural frontier. Moreover, its focus on timber production meant that the DGF had little concept of forests as ecosystems and the value of their environmental services and non-timber products. The Park Service's exclusive focus on preservation necessarily entailed a lack of attention to the relationship between human pressure over natural resources (especially by rural poor) and habitat protection. Awareness of these deficiencies sparked over a decade's worth of legislative and administrative efforts to reform these institutions and their policies to try to implement sustainable development in Costa Rica.

The administration of Oscar Árias opened political opportunities for policymakers captivated by the concept of sustainable development (many of them had been closely connected to the United Nations or other development aid institutions, usually as consultants). Backed by the president, whose party, National Liberation (Liberación Nacional), enjoyed a majority in the legislature, these policymakers and their supporters generated a number of institutional, administrative, and legislative reforms. First, they conceived a program, Conservation Strategy for Sustainable Development (Estrategia de Conservación para el Desarrollo Sostenible — ECODES), that squarely placed Costa Rica's environmental policy in the context of sustainable development (MIRENEM 1990). With legislative approval, they created the Ministry of Natural Resources, Energy, and Mines (Ministerio de Recursos Naturales, Energía y Minas — MIRENEM) in 1987 (Segura, Gottfried, Miranda, and Gómez 1997). It housed the Forest Service, the Park Service, and the Wildlife Service. The ministry's cabinet-level rank revealed the Árias administration's will to imbue natural resource-related environmental issues with a modicum of political authority. Separating the various services from the Ministry of Agriculture and adding the energy and mining sectors also signaled an aspiration to confront the intersectoral and development-related dimensions of environmental problems.

This arrangement entailed two omissions that caused serious difficulties. First, there was no coordination of environmental problems at the ministerial level. This inhibited more serious attention to the crosscutting and intersectoral nature of the issue area. Second, the MIRENEM minister had limited control over the various services. Each had its own law that had not been abrogated, giving them independent powers. Thus, to varying degrees, the minister's role was reduced to that of a coordinating agent among rival services. This adversely affected administrative efficiency, policy formulation, and policy implementation. Both omissions reflected political concerns: an attempt to create a coordinating institution or to abolish the independence of the services would have been too politically costly or unattainable. Moreover, policymakers lacked a vision of how to integrate the functions of the various independent services.

Despite these shortcomings, Costa Rica was a cauldron of experimentation in the 1980s. Because the nation was in the grip of economic stabilization programs, much of that experimentation relied on international funding. Those sources championed pilot projects in sustainable, participatory community forestry and reforestation for timber and fuel wood; and they also provided resources for wildlife and protected area management.

Reliance on foreign funding had other benefits as well. Many projects trained Costa Ricans in the concepts, techniques, and administration of community forestry and reforestation. Another benefit was that the environmental and socioeconomic problems of regions that had suffered after the collapse of cotton, sugar, beef, and banana markets were finally being addressed, most notably in the peninsulas of Guanacaste and Osa (E. Rodríguez 1997). Buffer zone projects for the people surrounding parks, especially in central Costa Rica, sensitized Parks Service personnel to the connection between preservation and development. Finally, the participatory nature of the projects nurtured a grassroots leadership for the community-based non-governmental organizations (NGOs) created by them (Solís 1993).

Dependency on foreign financing had its disadvantages too. Policy coordination was problematic. The country was more or less carved up into areas of influence for each of the major donors (often the development aid agencies of European governments and the United States) and their Costa Rican allies. Of course, the fate of the projects when the foreign funding ended was the most serious problem. Although Costa Ricans participated in the design of international projects, the funding priorities of international donors affected the Costa Ricans' proposal submittals. As trends changed among international donors, internationally funded, established projects faced grave difficulties. Since many experiments found it difficult to become selfsustaining, extinction threatened as soon as the official, internationally backed project ended.

Institutional and legislative reforms followed apace with the new focus on sustainable development. The DGF expanded its regulatory mandate to private as well as public forests and over the transport of timber. Economic incentives for reforestation were adopted on the assumption that people care for resources they value. Because they were initially on a reimbursement basis, tax credits and subsidies mainly benefited a few relatively large companies and landowners (Segura, Gottfried, Miranda, and Gómez 1997).

All of these measures were legally enshrined in the forestry law of 1986, with more reforms added over the next two years (Asamblea Nacional 1986). By disbursing funds in advance, a reforestation incentive program for smallholders was established with the help of the Dutch and Swedish governments (Solís 1993). The Dutch made funding conditional on the establishment of a Department of Peasant Forestry (Departamento Campesino Forestal — DECAFOR), thus ensuring that smallholders received an institutional toehold in the DGF. In effect, DECAFOR became the nexus between grassroots NGOs and the DGF/MIRENEM (Canet 1995). These measures enhanced the socioeconomic development, that is, the satisfaction of basic needs, and the participatory dimensions of the concept of sustainable development in Costa Rican forest policy.

Meanwhile, the Park Service designed its first plan for a National System of Protected Areas (Sistema Nacional de Áreas Protegidas — SINAC), which melded ideas from the United Nations' Man-In-Biosphere program with those of sustainable development. The project advocated strict preservation of an ecosystem's core area, allowing for small-scale land use in buffer zones around it to prevent encroachment by local communities. Proponents assumed that, perceiving a benefit, local populations would protect the core area and buffer zones from encroachment by more distant communities.

These policy choices evinced trade-offs that contained the seeds of sharp political conflict. First, they emphasized government regulation of the private sector by the DGF over market incentives. Second, the participatory component focused more on smallholders and their organizational development than on large-scale landowners; however, the government (via the DGF) dominated over the organizations of civil society on policy-making and funding boards. Third, the policies emphasized reforestation over the management of old-growth or native forests. Fourth, the focus remained on timber production and preservation instead of incorporating ideals of nontimber use and valuation of the environmental services performed by the forest. Fifth, the measures privileged a participatory approach to sustainable development, centered on direct and indirect subsidies rather than a more technocratic and market-oriented style.

REORIENTING INSTITUTIONS AND PROGRAMS, 1990-2000

Attempts to consolidate this approach to the sustainable development of Costa Rica's forests through a reform of the 1986 Forest Law met with stiff resistance in the 1990s. When the dust settled in 1996, Costa Rica's Ministry of the Environment had been thoroughly reorganized, and policy for the sustainable development of the forest bore little resemblance to the 1980s. By the year 2000, conservationists had regained the upper hand; timber interests struggled to retain state incentives, and community forestry all but lost its tenuous foothold in the state and in forest legislation.

The Politics of Containment

Toward the end of the Árias administration, the DGF presented the Congress with a new forest law. It was essentially the same as the 1986 law with the addition of clauses meant to give more permanence to the regulatory, participatory, and incentive-oriented direction of policy as it had evolved between 1986 and 1988. A constitutional challenge to the 1986 law at the beginning of the conservative Rafael Calderón administration (1990-1994) halted the DGF's reform efforts (Mendoza 1990). The Constitutional Tribunal mandated a revision of the law to conform to constitutional law. This opened a prolonged policy debate over forest policy and the

MIRENEM's institutional structure. A new forest law was not signed until April 1996.

During Calderón's government, a broad coalition of social and state actors sought to reverse the trade-offs over sustainable development established by the Árias government. That coalition included the new minister and vice minister of MIRENEM; prominent environmental NGOs such as the Tropical Science Center (Centro Científico Tropical — CCT) and the San Carlos Forest Development Cooperative (Cooperativa para el Desarrollo Forestal de San Carlos — CODEFORSA); the regional headquarters of the U.S. Agency for International Development; and landowners (Barrau 1993; Peralta 1993; Salazar 1994). These forces advocated market incentives for sustained-yield forestry, state support for large-scale plantations, and a sharp reduction in the regulatory powers of the DGF.

This, however, was mainly a rear-guard action. The minister and vice-minister of the MIRENEM were actually more interested in preservation than sustainable development (Boza 1997). Their priority was passage of legislation that would reorganize the DGF, the Park Service, and the Wildlife Service into a SINAC — a schema in which the Park Service would take center stage. Nevertheless, the DGF, due to its significant administrative autonomy, together with its supporters in the Agricultural Committee of the legislature (in charge of the bill), managed to block the minister of the MIRENEM (Salas 1993, 1994; Vargas 1993). Consequently, both the forestry law and the SINAC bill languished in Congress for the rest of the Calderón administration.

Biodiversity Conservation Ascendant

Matters came to a head in the administration of José Figueres Olsen (1994-1998). A leader of the Liberation Party, Figueres Olsen's was one of the first governments in the world to make sustainable development a central theme of its administration. MIRENEM's new Minister, René Castro, and his team injected fresh ideas into the policy debates and brought new perspectives to existing conflicts. By 1997, Costa Rica's institutional and legal landscape had changed radically in matters related to conservation in general and the forest in particular.

Minister Castro and his team were decidedly more technocratic than past heads of MIRENEM had been. They relied on cutting-edge technical and administrative skills and ideas learned abroad to formulate policies, which emphasized administrative decentralization, underscored the biodiversity conservation component of sustainable development, and relied on market-oriented policy instruments for both regulation and financing. With respect to the forest, they focused on its contributions to the global environment, especially its role in regulating greenhouse gas emissions. This was a sharp shift from the state activist and social forestry approaches of the Árias administration and from the more traditional conservationist and laissez-faire tacks of the Calderón administration.

Castro and his team had three main, politically conflictual goals (Segura 1997; Martínez 1997; J. Rodríguez 1997). Administrative restructuring of MIRENEM was their top priority. The thorough overhaul of financing for MIRENEM projects ran a close second and entailed developing new projects more appealing to international donors whose interests had shifted away from social forestry, community reforestation, and sustained-yield production in general. Reformulating the forest bill in light of these ends was the third item on the agenda.

Minister Castro was keen on a permanent administrative restructuring of MIRENEM in the mold of a refurbished version of the SINAC. This meant getting a SINAC bill passed into law through the Congress. The Legislative Assembly, however, stifled him at every turn. In frustration, Castro implemented the SINAC as an act of administrative reorganization created by decree toward the middle of 1995 (Segura 1997). A few years later, the Biodiversity Act gave the SINAC permanent standing (Asamblea Nacional Legislativa 1998). The SINAC fused the DGF, the National Parks Service, and the Wildlife Service into a single administrative unit. (Lobbying by these three agencies to remain independent had been a major source of gridlock in the Congress.) The operative mechanism for the fusion was to be the appointment of the same person to head all three directorates. It was theorized that the fusion would break down bureaucratic rigidities among the three services, rigidities that hindered effective natural resource management, especially in the forest sector. For example, as separate departments active in the same physical areas, they often denied each other necessary cooperation for effective management and oversight. As a result, the overall quality of service and resource conservation efforts declined accordingly.

The SINAC had four general objectives (MINAE 1997). First, to consolidate Costa Rica's protected areas to guarantee the conservation of the nation's biodiversity. Second, to strengthen the management of those areas and their environs. Third, to establish conditions that facilitate the responsible use of natural resources for the economic and social development of the country. Fourth, to ensure — with the participation of civil society — compliance with technical and legal norms established to achieve sustainable management of natural resources.

The guiding principles to achieve these objectives were administrative decentralization, functional deconcentration, client service, and democratization (MINAE 1997). Decentralization meant that most decisions that had been taken in San José's central office would devolve to 11 regional administration centers called conservation areas (*áreas de conservación* — AC). Each AC was further divided into subregions. Decentralization also ensured that most personnel would be stationed outside the capital city. Functional deconcentration meant that the separate departments, DGF, National Parks (Parques Nacionales — PN), and Vida Silvestre (VS), would no longer exist as such. Instead, at the regional and subregional levels, the personnel who used to belong to those agencies would be "polyfunctional," attending to all problems involving resource use, preservation, and protection. In theory, decentralization and functional deconcentration would create the conditions necessary for the provision of better services to the clients (both human and nonhuman) of MIRENEM. Regional and local offices would issue use permits for forests to landowners, process applications for incentives, take care of forest fires, attend to accusations of abuse of protected areas, and manage parks. A streamlined SINAC central office (SINAC Central) would be in charge of defining overall policy and strategy and would standardize rules and regulations for the ACs. Democratization called for greater citizen participation in the regions through local organizations (MINAE 1997).

The ACs were territorial units modeled on the principles of the United Nations' Man in the Biosphere program. Each AC contained core zones focused on protected areas such as national parks or wildlife refuges; economic exploitation in core areas — called nuclei — was prohibited, as preservation was the main goal. Around the core areas were buffer zones, where humans were allowed to exploit nature only in carefully controlled ways. Beyond the buffer zones were areas of unrestricted production.

The establishment of the SINAC was an advance over former administrative structures for several reasons. First, it facilitated the implementation of a key tenet of sustainable development — that environmental problems cross sectoral lines. Second, the SINAC rationalized and streamlined policymaking by strengthening the minister's office, placing it over the heads of departments. Thus, third, the SINAC fundamentally changed the institutional setting for the formulation of forest policy and its financing. This allowed the executive to press forward with an agenda that previously had been blocked by the DGF. The minister's office was aided in November 1995, a few months after the SINAC decree, by the passage of an environmental law that transformed the MIRENEM into the Ministry of Environment and Energy (MINAE). The statutes of the MINAE further strengthened the minister's power over the heads of departments, which, in turn, facilitated implementation of the SINAC.

The DGF had been one of the main stumbling blocks for the reorientation of forest policy along more market-oriented principles. It had steadfastly resisted reduction of its myriad regulatory, financial, and control functions. Yet, there was a general consensus in the MIRENEM/MINAE, civil society, and international agencies that the DGF had too many responsibilities. As a result, it was unable to accomplish any of them well. By law, the DGF controlled permitting, managed finances, exercised control and oversight over extraction, carried out research, engaged in long-range planning, conducted extension services, designed forest management plans, and formulated industrial policy for the sector (Asamblea Legislativa 1986). In short, the DGF had nominal authority over all aspects of forest policy. Yet, the DGF lacked the personnel and equipment to carry out all of these functions. As a result, the DGF concentrated on issuing permits and managing its financial funds to the detriment of control and oversight of extraction (Árias 1997). Worse, costly and time-consuming red tape in the permitting process, handled by personnel who were overly centralized in the capital city of San José, invited corruption. These characteristics contributed to policy failure in the form of continued deforestation and the lack of sustainable development for the forest sector. Given this diagnosis of the situation, the problem was how to reduce the DGF's responsibilities so that it might concentrate on control and oversight. The SINAC offered one solution to the problem by effectively dismantling the DGF.

A restructuring of financial service delivery was high on the list of necessary reforms. Previously, the DGF had administered four separate trust funds set up to finance the various incentive programs, each with its own board of directors and procedures. Now, the MIRENEM entrusted the management of the four funds to a single independent board, the National Forest Fund (Fondo Nacional de Financiamiento Forestal — FONAFIFO). In addition to administrative efficiency, it was assumed that this move would improve services to users. Individuals, companies, and organizations would only need to fill out one set of forms and deal with fewer offices once a petition was in the bureaucratic pipeline.

In a separate but related move, Minister Castro and his team aggressively pursued new international sources of financing for conservation based on market-oriented instruments. One was the establishment of an office to manage joint implementation projects (Segura 1997). In such ventures, foreign companies (frequently energy utilities) that emitted greenhouse gases could buy "pollution rights" by paying Costa Rica for the conservation of forest areas. This involved agreements between specific polluting companies and the Costa Rican government. For much the same purpose, the MIRENEM also participated in the creation of a market for tradable pollution instruments in U.S. financial markets. On the domestic front, one-third of a "green" gasoline tax was earmarked for conservation.

These innovative financing arrangements were grounded in a recognition that biodiversity conservation, interpreted as nature protection, had become the highest priority of international donors. This shift toward a preservationist emphasis in the meaning of sustainable development occurred during the United Nations Conference on Environment and Development in 1992. However, Castro and his team were not just pragmatists responding to a shift in circumstances. They shared with the international community a conviction that incentives should support the non-timber environmental services performed by the forest.

Accordingly, the MIRENEM followed a two-track policy. One track established an economic incentive for conservation in 1994: the Certificate for Forest Protection.[4] To be eligible, owners of forest tracts ranging from one to 300 hectares had to refrain from all exploitation with the exception of ecotourism (Segura 1997). The other track contemplated the elimination of existing incentives for sustained-yield timber production and reforestation and their replacement by credit (Barrantes 1997; J. Rodríguez 1997). In addition to philosophical changes regarding the role of markets in sustainable development, this move also responded to fiscal austerity measures adopted by the government of Costa Rica. Like the rest of Latin America, Costa Rica was also undergoing a process of structural economic adjustment along more free-market lines. Eliminating traditional incentives, however, proved to be a highly charged political issue, and Castro had to settle for their gradual phase-out.

Taken together, these measures were part of a conscious effort to emphasize biodiversity conservation and to establish a more technocratic, market-oriented approach to forest policy. The FONAFIFO and the changes in the incentive programs became enshrined in the 1996 forest law. By not authorizing its existence, the new legislation also officially killed the DGF (Asamblea Legislativa 1996). Joint implementation and tradable pollution certificates were pursued separately.

Forest policy also took a decidedly more market-friendly turn concerning private-sector timber production. Command and control were out. Liberalizing and privatizing permitting, extraction, and transportation were in. Castro and his team believed that the myriad rules and regulations related to extraction were cumbersome and invited corruption. They also argued that strict rules regarding extraction hindered the economic development of the timber industry. The focus had been on control over trees, rather than on forest management. Moreover, the requirements were the same for native forests, plantations, and secondary forests. Consequently, it was felt that a reduction in direct government involvement and a liberalization of forest management would be beneficial, adding economic value to the forest, thus, at least in theory, providing incentives not to change land use (Árias 1997; Alfaro 1997).

Given this diagnosis, the new forest law simplified and streamlined permitting for timber extraction to reduce the costs of bureaucratic transactions. Permits were also made valid for longer than one year; less paperwork was required for plantation timber; and conditions were eased to remove trees from fields, small forest remnants, secondary forests, and for the using timber for improvements on farms as opposed to commercialization. Policymakers assumed that landowners would not take advantage of increased private responsibility over compliance with the law to enhance their own gains.

The deregulation of log transportation was also undertaken to reduce private-sector costs and to remove incentives for official corruption. Before 1996, each tree was stamped to certify legal extraction, and each load had to have a manifest stipulating the origin and destination of the timber, the amount approved for extraction, and the proportion of that amount on the truck. The new forest law replaced individual tree stamping with a single symbol for the entire load and a reusable manifest.

In keeping with goal of administrative decentralization and devolution of responsibility to the private sector (meaning less burden and expense for the public sector) as of 1996, private-sector organizations replaced many of the DGF's functions (Asamblea Legislativa 1996; Árias 1997; Barrantes 1997). The institution of the regencies (*regencias*) as a mechanism to improve control and oversight of timber extraction was the most important innovation. Private agents, the regents (*regentes*), were granted the right to take over most oversight and control functions that were once the purview of the DGF. Regents must be members of the College of Agronomists; they are bonded; and they have been granted *fe pública*, meaning the legal presumption of operating in good faith. Regents can design management plans and have the duty to police their clients' compliance with rules and regulations. Regents can be held liable if forest management is found to be out of compliance by MINAE spot checks. Of course, forest owners who could not afford a regent have the right, in due course, to be attended to by a MINAE forester.

Castro and his policy-making team believed that the institution of the *regencia* would increase the efficiency of the MINAE in the forest sector (Árias 1997). The regency freed public-sector personnel to concentrate on inspection and oversight rather than on spending so much time on the permitting process. Although MINAE personnel still had to approve regents' management plans, it was now a one-stop process. A regent presented MINAE with the whole management package; if it was procedurally correct, it was approved. In the past, petitioners had to go to multiple departments for the permitting process and submit to field inspections. All of this had cost time and money and opened opportunities for corruption.

In keeping with the participatory principle of sustainable development, new forest policy offered a space for private-sector and NGO participation in policy formulation and policy implementation through the National Forest Office (Oficina Nacional Forestal — ONF) and the Certifying Commission (Asamblea Legislativa 1996). The ONF, a private-sector institution, is essentially an advisory board to the MINAE, and it is also responsible for research and information campaigns. The Certifying Commission is a voluntary program in which forest owners open tracts under exploitation to inspection to certify that the extractive process is in compliance with norms of sustained-yield management, as defined by law and further private-sector criteria. Once certified, forest owners are free from government oversight for a number of years.

Conservation vs. Sustainable Timber Production

During the current Christian Social Union Party (Partido Unión Social Cristiano) government of Miguel Ángel Rodríguez (1998-2002), MINAE Minister Elizabeth Odio, who is also the second vice president of Costa Rica, has concentrated on the consolidation and expansion of the market-oriented approach to sustainable development. Most policy debates with respect to the forest centered on the Environmental Services Act, which was sent to the National Assembly in February 1999, where it still awaits final deliberation on the floor of the National Assembly. This act seeks to codify and institutionalize the new system of government funding for the sustainable development of forests, based on payment for environmental services (Pago por Servicios Ambientales — PSAs), established during the Figueres administration. The debate has been couched mainly in the language of market-style development, with social forestry concerns only rarely discussed in legislative commission hearings. At its core, this bill, as did the Biodiversity Law of 1998, addresses the incorporation of biodiversity and environmental services into overall economic growth plans.

The debate over the PSAs and the Environmental Services Act, which replicates many of the controversies aroused by the earlier Biodiversity Law, has been contentious. It reveals a fundamental divide in the market-based environmental discourse between the advocates of biodiversity conservation and forest industrialists, including the logging complex. In other words, the main cleavage is between those who promote absolute forest protection to maintain biodiversity and those who urge state support for sustainable timber production from forests and reforested lands and. Consequently, the central question has become whether forests should be used for wood at all. Environmentalists argue for strict protection of the primary forest, on the assumption that sustainable management is a code term for deforestation. The forest sector counters that absolute protection stifles economic growth and takes large areas of land out of the hands of potentially productive sectors (Basco and Silva 2000).

Meanwhile, advocates of community forestry as a means to address the livelihood component of sustainable development have lost the foothold they had achieved in the past. The debates over the 1995 forestry law at least saw substantial discussion of peasant livelihood issues. Current debates largely avoid discussion of concrete measures to support poor small landowners as a means to address the social equity component of sustainable development.

Worse, peasant organizations have lost state support due to the phasing-out of government agencies and funds that formerly supported agroforestry and small-scale native species reforestation. First, the demotion of the Department of Peasant Development (Departamento de Desarrollo Campesino) from a full-fledged agency to a small program within the MINAE has robbed organizations built on the ideals of community forestry of effective support within the state (Canet 1997). Second, funds specifically earmarked for community forestry have been terminated. The Fund for Forestry Development's (Fondo de Desarrollo Forestal — FDF) replacement by the system of payment for environmental services has tended to favor larger landholders. This shift has led to a general state of disillusionment in the peasant sector with regard to sustainable development and forest conservation. It has also contributed to substantial disarray among peasant organizations interested in those ideals.

The struggle among conservationists, timber interests, and advocates of community forestry has taken place in a complicated policy-making setting that involves the MINAE, the National Assembly, and policy-making boards created by the Rodríguez administration. Environmentalists mainly interested in biodiversity conservation have gained the upper hand in the MINAE, where Minister Odio has centralized decisionmaking, and used their ascendancy to define policy agendas. This, for example, was the purpose of initial drafts of the Environmental Services Act sent to the legislature. However, two additional institutions ensured wider participation in the policy-making process. One of those venues was the Concertation Commission (Mesas de Concertación), a consensus-building mechanism for setting policy agendas during the Rodríguez administration. The other was the Agriculture and Natural Resources Committee of the National Assembly. As a result, the final bill was a more well-balanced document, one that included the demands of a broader spectrum of stakeholders.

How did these actors and institutions shape the Environmental Services Bill? Upon taking office in mid-1998, the Rodríguez government issued a decree that established a national consensus-seeking commission — the Mesa Nacional de Concertación — covering a number of conflictive topics, including environmental policy. This proved to be a valuable exercise that brought together actors whose interests were often in conflict with one another, such as supporters of biodiversity conservation, market-oriented sustainable timber production, and peasant interests. For peasant organizations in particular, the Concertation Commission provided an option other than protests by which to influence policy. The resulting documents, which required the signatures of all participating organizations, would serve as the basis for bills the administration intended to submit to Congress.

Yet, this attempt to incorporate diverse viewpoints into lawmaking was only partially successful. The documents emerging from Concertación commissions often changed substantially when presiding ministries edited them for presentation to the relevant legislative commission in the National Assembly. This occurred with the Environmental Services Commission and the translation of its work into the Environmental Services Act, an attempt to codify the system of payment for environmental services into law (Basco and Silva 2000). The Environmental Services Commission focused on three areas: the definition of environmental services, financing, and participation in administrative institutions. Recommendations included provisions for biodiversity conservation, timber extraction, and, although fainter, community forestry and mixed-use. Thus, the commission took into account the interests of conservationists, timber producers, and poor peasants.

The MINAE, however, revised the document strongly in favor of conservationists when it crafted the Environmental Services Act (MINAE 1998b). The definition of environmental services in the bill was skewed toward non-timber functions, such as carbon storage and watershed and habitat protection that reinforce opportunities to pursue bioprospecting, and scenic beauty. The fiscal incentives for environmental services were biased in favor of conservation, emphasizing the protection of primary forest over reforestation and logging. The proposed administrative structure strongly favored conservationists, weakly included market-oriented timber producers, and shut out environmental and peasant organizations that supported more community forestry-oriented approaches. Yet, the MINAE did not have the last word in the policy-making process; it had to undergo legislative review.

The MINAE presented its draft bill to the Legislative Assembly's Agricultural and Natural Resources Committee in late November 1998. A timber producer alliance of the Costa Rican Forestry Council (Cámara Costarricence Forestal — CCF) and the National Peasant Forestry Coalition (Junta Nacional Forestal Campesina — JUNAFORCA) lobbied strenuously against the MINAE bill in committee hearings (Barrantes 1999; Vega 1999; Alfaro 1999). The CCF, which represented timber industrialists and large-scale reforesters, dominated the coalition. JUNAFORCA, which by then mainly represented medium-sized holdings instead of a poor peasant base, joined the CCF because that it believed the principle of forest use for wood production took precedence over other interests that might divide the two organizations. The CCF gladly accepted aid from an organization that gave its arguments greater legitimacy by including more disadvantaged social groups. Moreover, the CCF/JUNAFORCA alliance had an institutional base of power in the ONF. The ONF gave them official advisory rights in the policy-making process.

Testimony from the ONF/CCF/JUNAFORCA alliance convinced key deputies on the committee of two of their major concerns: first, that the proposed bill shut producers of biodiversity and environmental services (the owners of forests and plantations) out of the decisionmaking process and, second, that the bill, as written, was redundant. It added unnecessary bureaucracy to the system established by the 1995 forestry law, principally to the FONAFIFO and the regents.

The Agriculture and Natural Resources Committee remanded the text to an ad hoc subcommittee composed of the major members of original Concertación working group to formulate a new bill. There, the private sector (including JUNAFORCA), allied with the Costa Rican Network for Private Nature Reserves (Red Costarricence de Reservas Naturales Privadas — RCRP) to write a draft. This version gave preference to their economic interests and granted them a strong presence in the executive committee (Junta Directiva) of the new National Fund for Environmental Services (Fondo Nacional de Servicios Ambientales — FONASA), which would replace FONAFIFO (MINAE 1999b). Significantly, organizations representing poor peasants or indigenous groups were largely absent from committee hearings and meetings of the subcommittee that recast the bill. Based on the subcommittee's recommendations, the MINAE sent a new draft back to the legislative committee in February 1999. After additional debate, the Agriculture and Natural Resources Committee approved a bill on April 28, 1999, and forwarded it for full floor debate (Basco and Silva 2000; *Tico Times* 1999). As of early 2001, the bill remains on the plenary agenda of the Legislative Assembly.

In the end, a more well-balanced bill that addressed nearly every objection raised by the major organizations that participated in the policy process was presented to the Legislative Assembly (MINAE 1999a). Duplication of bureaucracy, a major critique of the ONF/CCF/JUNAFORCA alliance, was eliminated by replacing FONAFIFO with FONASA. Fiscal incentives — including a substantial proportion of funds generated by hydroelectric projects — favored the protection of primary forests over their sustainable use by limiting their disbursement mainly to forest conservation and plantations. This was a key demand of environmentalists as represented by the CCT and the Conservation Federation (Federación Costarricence para la Conservación del Ambiente — FECON) in opposition to timber interests. By the same token, funds generated by hydroelectric projects on private land would not be used to pay state debts to landowners whose property had been expropriated to form national parks. A separate account was established for that purpose. Medium- and small-scale producers received a nod, in that FONASA was specifically charged with benefiting them via credits and other mechanisms for forest management, reforestation, establishment of tree nurseries, recovery of degraded areas, and financing technology for the extraction, industrialization, and commercialization of timber. These measures, however, fell short of establishing a specific account for poor smallholder peasants. This was a critical omission. Individual peasants and their generally weaker organizations would have to compete for scarce resources on nearly equal footing with economically and organizationally stronger social groups: the timber interests.

Representation on the executive board of the FONASA proved to be another contentious issue that was partially resolved in the final bill. The board includes two representatives from the public sector; one from MINAE and one from the Ministry of Agriculture (Ministerio de Agricultura y Ganadería — MAG); two representatives from the private sector to be nominated by the ONF; one from the timber industry; and one from the organizations of medium and small timber producers. In practice, this meant that the CCF would represent medium producers and JUNAFORCA would represent the smaller producers. One spot was also reserved for a national NGO representing private nature preserves, the RCRNP. These were the organizations that would, in the first instance, wrestle with decisions over how to distribute FONASA's benefits. Although they clearly leaned toward market and timber producer interests, a legal definition of environmental services that privileged conservation and plantations over forest management constrained them.

To overcome objections to such narrow representation by environmentalists, organizations of poor peasants, and other government agencies, the Environmental Services Bill mandates the creation of a second policy-making arena, the Environmental Services Advisory Council (Consejo Asesor de Servicios Ambientales — COASA), which is supposed to be an advisory, consensus-building arena for FONASA's decisionmaking process. The COASA is, indeed, a well-balanced organ of representation. It includes one representative each from the following government agencies: the MINAE, the MAG, the Institute for Agrarian Development (Instituto de Desarrollo Agrario, the land reform agency whose inclusion was a key demand of the Mesa Nacional Campesina), the Tourism Institute, the Costa Rican Electricity Institute, and the Costa Rican Institute of Sewers and Aqueducts. Two places each are reserved for the following sectors of civil society: the forest sector, the tourist sector, organizations of agricultural producers, environmentalists, and universities. The interaction of COASA and the executive board of FONASA will determine the distribution of credit, the environmental services to receive incentives, and the form of distribution.

These arrangements notwithstanding, the Rodríguez administration has seen the rift among market-oriented stakeholders widen. Conservationists and timber producers disagree on the definition of environmental services, which services should receive priority, and the selection of sources of financing. For now, conservationists seem to have the upper hand, based on their ascendancy in the MINAE and that ministry's financial distress. As will be seen in the next section, forest policy debates beyond the Environmental Services Act also support this conclusion.

SUCCESSES, PROBLEMS, AND TRADE-OFFS

Costa Rica's forest policy reforms are too recent for rigorous evaluation; however, some impressionistic data exist. On the positive side, the red tape involved in receiving and administering the incentive funds has diminished dramatically. This frees both landowners and public officials to carry out other work. By the same token, the *regente* system has increased the supply of people and offices allowed to draw up forest management plans. Again, this has positive benefits for landowners and public officials. The same applies to liberalization of transportation.

What are public officials freer to accomplish? The SINAC has a central office in San José and regional offices, one for each conservation area. Deregulation frees central office personnel to devote more time to agenda-setting, planning, and policy formulation. For the moment, this has meant pursuing cutting-edge, market-oriented strategies to fund biodiversity conservation: joint-implementation, internationally tradable pollution permits, and biodiversity prospecting. Meanwhile, the regional and subregional offices of SINAC carry out policy implementation, mainly interpretations of regulation and oversight. This division of labor allows for more rapid responses to regional and subregional problems.

The creation of the National Forest Office and the Certification Commission have expanded and intensified intra-private-sector communication, enabling these groups to focus on defining goals and elaborating strategies for action. Since the second half of the 1990s, this strategy has concentrated on ensuring that payments for environmental services also include production in the form of sustained-yield timber extraction, reforestation, establishing tree plantations, and industrialization. These private-sector institutions strengthen the participatory component of sustainable development, at least in terms of formal civil society participation in the policy process. The proposed National Fund for Environmental Services and Environmental Services Advisory Council would expand such participation to conservation groups and organizations of poor peasants as well.

A number of difficulties temper these positive assessments. The bureaucratic process may have been streamlined, but the decline of public-sector commitment to adding value to the forest and plantations in order to manage them sustainably leaves substantial tracts of privately owned forests open to destruction by unsustainable extraction. From the very beginning of José Figueres' administration in 1994, Minister Castro and his team wanted to dismantle the incentive system, with the exception of the conservation certificates (Certificados de Conservación del Bosque — CCBs). During the Rodríguez administration, Minister Odio has continued the trend. The two ministers' views were in keeping with their governments' commitments to fiscal austerity, economic stabilization, and free-market economic restructuring programs.

Declining budgetary allocations for the various forestry incentive programs (managed forestry, reforestation, plantations, and conservation) were part of the problem. The 1996 Forestry Law stipulated that one-third of a new gasoline "green" tax should be apportioned to FONAFIFO. But the Treasury Department refused to release those funds to MINAE and instead sent the "green" revenues to a general fund (Caja Única) and disbursed them for different purposes. During the Figueres administration, the private sector (primarily timber industrialists and JUNAFORCA) put intense political pressure on President Figueres himself to keep incentives for production and reforestation (CCF 1997; Rivera 1997). His administration negotiated with the Treasury Department for a much smaller share of the gasoline tax, less than 20 percent. In 1998 (the date of the latest available complete annual figures), the Rodríguez administration had received about the same share of the tax (Barrantes 2000b).

These funds were barely enough to cover existing commitments and were insufficient for program expansion. Not only that, but the disbursement of incentives for reforestation and forest management has been slow and erratic (Barrantes 1997). Meanwhile, although FONAFIFO is accepting new contracts, most are for conservation (Barrantes 2000a). Further proof of declining state commitment for sustainable forestry came in May of 2000, when Minister Odio abolished the managed forestry category of the payment for environmental services system. MINAE's rationale — in part echoing conservationist critiques — was that under tight budgets, it made no sense to pay the forestry industry for the production of products they planned to profit from in the marketplace (Sánchez 2000). Timber interests suspect that Minister Odio welcomed environmentalists' complaints because she wants to reassert state control over the forests. They warn that landowners now have an incentive to cut trees without any type of sustained-yield management plans, increasing deforestation (Barrantes 2000a). And it is not as if most of the budget for fiscal incentives goes to forest management. Only one-tenth was allocated for that purpose. The forest protection category accounted for seven-tenths of total expenditures for environmental services, although the payment per hectare was less than for forest management (Barrantes 2000a).

The sources of additional funding sought by FONAFIFO underscore the trend away from managed forestry. FONAFIFO has pinned many of its hopes on a World Bank loan (Asamblea Legislativa 2000). As the World Bank no longer supports timber production, one assumes the funds will be allocated to conservation. FONAFIFO is also relying on money from power companies for watershed protection, which centers on conservation and reforestation, not timber use. Furthermore, FONAFIFO is searching for new private-sector funds, such as payments from tourism-related companies that use forests as business capital as well as new joint implementation contracts — all biased toward conservation (Basco and Silva 2000).

The implementation of administrative decentralization has introduced uncertainties that make it difficult for the public sector to carry out its roles of planning, regulation, and oversight or to provide prompt attention to those eligible for government services. For example, substantial confusion over rule interpretation reigns at the regional and subregional levels. The variation in interpretation across administrative boundaries hampers program implementation, which now hinges on the actions of private-sector, small farmer, and peasant organizations and producers. There are no clear signals for them to follow. Moreover, companies and NGOs have to deal with each regional and subregional headquarters separately, more work than these organizations are equipped to handle. As a result, their efficiency declines, and members become discouraged. Extraction and conservation programs begin to suffer because individuals have fewer incentives to comply with rules and regulations (Barrantes 1997).

MINAE personnel cutbacks aggravate the problem. Fewer public-sector officials are available to handle the claims at the regional and subregional levels. They are swamped with petitions for rule interpretations. Uncertainty over their regulatory function hinders them from carrying out their oversight roles, which require time to go out into the field and inspect. The lack of adequate transportation for those officials further hampers their oversight capabilities, as does the absence of coordination between departments when conservation area boundaries do not coincide with those of local ecosystems (Araya 1997; González 1997; Martínez 1997; E. Rodríguez 1997).

Questionable MINAE commitment to the decentralization process under Minister Odio compounds these difficulties. Her tendency to centralize management led to antagonism between MINAE and the regional councils of the conservation areas. Moreover, despite some success stories, many environmentalists consider decentralization a failure because they are underrepresented on the regional councils (Mora 1999). In part, SINAC local councils have failed to achieve the promised level of civil society participation because of MINAE's difficulties in motivating local groups to participate in discussions. However, there is some evidence that this may be largely due to a lack of effort and commitment by MINAE itself (Gutiérrez 2000).

What lies at the root of MINAE's flagging interest in decentralization? Perhaps Minister Odio is more interested in restructuring the MINAE to provide for more effective and cohesive policymaking in concert with the Ministries of Health and Agriculture to avoid duplication, complexity, and turf battles (Odio 2000). After all, air, soil, and water pollution had been overlooked by existing legislation. Such a goal would be compatible with her recent attempts to have the Constitutional Tribunal (Sala IV) of the Supreme Court abolish the National Commission for the Management of Biodiversity (Comisión Nacional para la Gestión de la Biodiversidad), which was established under articles 14-22 of the Biodiversity Law. That commission placed MINAE in competition with other line ministries.

Declining budgets and problems with decentralization have a negative impact on the public sector's oversight capacity (González 1997; Martínez 1997). This invites corruption of public officials and cheating by the private sector, making it next to impossible to control extraction rates. Moreover, less ethical regents are tempted to draw up extraction plans based solely on data provided by the client (who has an incentive to extract as much as possible), without field visits in either the planning or extractive stages. Forest industry representatives seem unconcerned, arguing that state control of tree-cutting under the DGF system was no better than the current system (Barrantes 2000a). Others in the sector, such as the RCRP, argue for reforms of the *regente* system (Marín 2000). They believe that abuses can be reduced by using biologists and ecologists as forest inspectors or at least including them on inspection teams. Environmentalists currently hope to address these issues in the MINAE commission assigned to evaluate and change the 1998 Biodiversity Law.

However, insufficient oversight has other sources as well. Under current guidelines, the deregulation of transportation contributes to overextraction (González 1997). With the current manifest forms, it is impossible to control for sustained-yield logging. Moreover, liberalization of extraction from small landholdings lends itself to abuse because farmers have begun to subdivide their land among relatives and associates in order to reap the economic benefits of timber on their property (J. Rodríguez 1997). Their extraction patterns are clearly not oriented toward sustained-yield extraction.

As currently implemented, the *regente* system allows larger landowners to have advantages over smallholders and poor peasants (Cárdenas 2000). Between 1999 and 2000, environmentalists — who oppose any logging of primary forests — criticized the system for promoting deforestation, as it helped larger landowners (the only ones who can afford *regente* services) to extract timber from forests more freely. Evidence from frontier regions such as Osa Peninsula and Tortuguero/Barra Colorado supports such conclusions (Evans 1999, 180-181). Meanwhile, organizations that offer *regente* services, such as CODEFORSA, prefer larger projects because they make more money per unit of staff time than with a number of smaller projects. The fact that small-scale landowners who could not afford *regente* services had a right to service by MINAE foresters was of little help. Most had difficulty understanding bureaucratic procedures or lacked time to comply with them. Moreover, MINAE lacked sufficient personnel to supply timely service.

Forest policy reform from 1994 to 2000 has implied the acceptance of two common trade-offs regarding the major components of sustainable development. The first one has been a preference for conservation over sustained-yield management or multiple use of the forest.[5] As currently designed, the turn to global market-oriented instruments for the funding of forest policy has tied revenues to conservation of core areas over buffer-zone management and sustainable-ecosystem management beyond that. The money raised is to be spent on the preservation of forests and reforestation. Meanwhile, deregulation, liberalization, privatization of oversight, and slashing incentives for the economic use of the forest are clear signals that the public sector is giving up on sustained-yield and multiple-use management of native forests. For all intents and purposes, native forests in the hands of private individuals who are not interested in conservation have been abandoned to their fate.

The second trade-off in Costa Rica's forest policy is a clear choice in favor of market-oriented conservation and reforestation instead of support for community development or cooperative behavior. It is up to individuals to respond or to adjust to the incentives offered. Cooperative behavior for the development of peasant or smallholder communities is discouraged. Existing cooperatives and peasant and smallholder organizations are threatened by diminished revenues; their operating budgets partly depend on a percentage of the funds generated by government incentives. As a result, cooperatives that offer *regente* services have a strong incentive to ignore small, poor peasants. They get more revenue per staff member by accepting large projects. Other cooperatives collapse as a result of poor business decisions when they decide to establish private enterprises (Canet 2000). The most common problem is size. Organizations attempt ventures on too large a scale. They overreach their human resources as well as technical, managerial, and financial (debt) capacities. Bankruptcy and the end of the cooperative is often the result. Stronger peasant-specific state agencies could help prevent this problem by offering timely advice.

The SINAC and decentralization have also negatively affected the provision of advocacy services. The social services organizations have to maintain a presence in many regional offices (instead of just one central office) and keep up with sui generis interpretations of rules to do the paperwork for their members, one of their primary functions. Social services organizations have also lost institutional presence and support in the executive branch of government with the dismantling of the DGF, which effectively gutted the DECAFOR (Canet 1997; Bauer 1997). Price competition from regents saps organizational strength by luring away members (Barrantes 1997).

The bias toward the market extends to ecotourism, an integral element of SINAC's strategy. Established Costa Rican and foreign firms and conservationist, urban-based NGOs dominate. The SINAC does publicize grassroots ecotourism as an attractive land use option for peasants. But the lack of concrete support has led to the failure of many attempted ventures. This has generated a climate of frustration and resentment among peasants. Moreover, the Certificate for Sustainable Tourism (Certificación para la Sostenibilidad Turística — CST)[6] provides little room for participation by local communities (Baez 2000). Problems with the CSTs are caused, in part, by budgetary constraints that restrict the Costa Rican Institute for Tourism's (Instituto Costarricence de Turismo — ICT) extension programs. Meanwhile, a national consortium of grassroots tourism projects is in discussion with the ICT to modify the CST program (Monge 2000).

What are the implications of these developments for the implementation of sustainable development in Costa Rica's forests? Costa Rica's new forest policy emphasizes a market-oriented view of sustainable development that favors conservation (understood as habitat preservation) over sustainable use, and it stimulates reforestation by large-scale corporations or landowners. It is hoped that those same agents will engage in sustained-yield management of natural forests, but there is resignation over the fate of privately owned forests if they do not. The moral imperative is not to subsidize timber extraction, especially from primary forests. Under these circumstances, priority must be given to the conservation of primary forests protected in expanding national park systems and by concentrating incentives on the restoration of pasture, secondary forests, and tree plantations. The global, regional, and local environmental functions of forests are stressed (greenhouse gas emission control, soil erosion control, watershed maintenance). Focusing on these environmental services allows policymakers to emphasize conservation while sidestepping thorny questions of social order; in this way, they can avoid the difficulties of formulating and implementing redistributive policies.

Costa Rica's new forest policy neglects the basic needs component of sustainable development. It reveals little interest in integrating the satisfaction of basic needs with biodiversity conservation and the sustainable use of resources. This is a paradox, given the dominant discourse of including local communities in conservation policy. The irony is compounded by the struggle between timber interests and conservationists for the support of peasant organizations. Each side claims it has the interests of the peasantry at heart.

The problem is that since the middle of the 1990s, Costa Rican forest policy has dismantled or ignored the sociological and institutional requirements for effective programs to meet the basic needs component of sustainable development. Gone is the support for collective action to build cooperatives to pool resources, generate autonomous peasant organizations, train personnel (thus raising skill levels), add value to timber, and encourage nontimber use. Thrust into the market, established cooperatives find it difficult to resist the temptation to overreach themselves and be destroyed, as occurred with the Guanacaste Forest Development Association (Asociación Guanacasteca de Desarrollo Forestal — AGUADEFOR). Crucial state support in the form of specialized, independent agencies, budgets, credit, and trust funds specifically allocated for peasant development have been dismantled, gutted, or terminated. The majority of unorganized, poor, smallholders and peasants are left to their fate in the market. The entrepreneurial among them may individually attempt microenterprises only to find they cannot succeed, as has been the case with ecotourism. The eligibility requirements, paperwork, and bureaucratic rules for meager per hectare conservation benefits discourage individual participation in the conservation certificate or reforestation program. From the small, poor peasant's point of view, the market encourages them to sell or abandon their holdings, migrate to cities, or become day laborers on banana plantations. At best, smallholders might be able to sell timber to established companies.

The discourse of participation has displaced the vital sociological and institutional conditions to meet the basic needs criteria of sustainable development. Including organizations that represent smallholders in the policy-making process becomes the primary criterion. Concerns over the organizations' effectiveness or representativeness are not at issue. Little thought is given to whether an organization can actually make its voice heard, much less heeded, when it is but one of many on a policy-making board — a role that is potentially even more marginal if the institution is only an advisory board, as so often is the case. Moreover, there is the question of the organization's representativeness. Does it really represent poor, smallholding peasants, or does it articulate the interests of its more prosperous segments?

In conclusion, a crude pluralist image of policymaking informs the discourse: the mere inclusion of an interest group in the policy process implies that policy output will address their substantive demands. Such an image ignores the economic, institutional, and political asymmetries of power among peasant organizations, the private sector, and mainstream well-established NGOs. This conception of participation accompanied by programs that offer jobs and training to only a few individuals (park rangers and parataxonomists) or that emphasize environmental education will not suffice to meet the basic needs criteria of sustainable development. Participation in the policy process is a necessary but not sufficient condition. The problem of power asymmetries for peasant organizations and their representativeness must also be addressed. Under current conditions, mainstream state institutions, private-sector groups, and environmental NGOs benefit the most. However, the tug of war between centralizing and decentralizing trends has left even these relatively privileged sectors of civil society uncertain over the effectiveness of their participation.

THE POLITICS OF INCLUSION

The trade-offs discussed above are more the result of politics and ideology than inherent incompatibilities between biodiversity conservation and the satisfaction of basic needs through the sustainable use of resources. The forest policies of the 1980s and the 1990s were shaped by shifts in the political fortunes of opposing political camps. One camp encompassed a network of professionals who believed in community development and cooperative behavior as an approach to satisfy the basic needs component of sustainable development (Silva 1997). These professionals gained ascendency in the Árias government from 1986 to 1990. Their positions in the state and consultancies to the MIRENEM gave them a base of political power. Because Costa Rica is a country rich in associational life, it was an easy step for these officials to ally with peasant and smallholder cooperatives seeking a solution to the depressed economic conditions of their regions in the wake of the collapse of cattle, sugar, and cotton markets. Those cooperatives grew, multiplied, formed networks, and federated as the National Peasant Forestry Coalition (JUNAFORCA) (Solís 1993).

The external sector, mainly social democratic Scandinavian governments (the Netherlands in particular), provided much-needed, in fact, pivotal support. Programs, funding, and their insistence on a special office for peasant affairs in the DGF — the DECAFOR — were key to the flourishing of a community development approach to sustainable development in the forest sector (Segura 1997). A myriad of other international programs, sponsored by developed countries, emphasized community participation in buffer zone management around national parks (Umaña and Brandon 1992).

Costa Rica's industrial timber interests — from both the natural forest and plantation subsectors — compose the other camp, along with influential, well-established environmental think tanks, such as the CCT. These groups have opposed the emphasis on community development and growing government regulation on the exploitation of the forest. However, to all intents and purposes, they had no political organization or allies. The Calderón administration changed that. New appointments to the MIRENEM provided the private sector with more sympathetic ministerial leadership (Silva 1997).

Nevertheless, once again, external actors proved pivotal. The United States Agency for International Development's (USAID) regional office for Central America helped to organize the private sector and gave it programmatic orientation. The director of USAID's rural development office worked hard to model Costa Rican timber interests along the lines of those of Chile. To that end, together with key private-sector figures, he ultimately helped to establish the Costa Rican Forestry Council (CCF) (Barrau 1993; Peralta 1993; Barrantes 1994). Private-sector timber interests in it lobbied for liberalization and deregulation of the timber sector — both for plantations and for native forests under private ownership (Peralta 1993; Sage 1994; Alfaro 1997).

During the Figueres administration, USAID dropped into the background, and the CCF took center stage. The CCF was dominated by producer organizations representing larger-scale timber interests. However, organizations that included small-scale producers also participated, including the JUNAFORCA, although the latter had an ambivalent position. JUNAFORCA's members wanted less government regulation and believed the CCF provided a vehicle to protect peasant interests effectively in the struggle to reform forest policy (Solís 1995). For its part, the CCF advocated deregulation, liberalization, and the maintenance of the incentive structure. It also wanted institutionalized, effective participation of the private sector in future policymaking (J. Rodríguez 1997). JUNAFORCA tirelessly added modifications to CCF proposals in keeping with peasant-sector interests (JUNAFORCA representation in production and policy-making boards, control over revenue earmarked for the peasant sector, and so on) (Solís 1995).

The Figueres administration shifted the balance of forces in the CCF in favor of large-scale timber interests and away from the organizations built around the incentive system, which helped landowners navigate bureaucratic regulations, carry out silvicultural tasks, and facilitate access to the funds (J. Rodríguez 1997). The directors of the SINAC and the framers of the law's regulatory body had long been part of the forces that favored liberating private-sector timber interests from government oversight and regulation. These officials were more interested in effective promotion of ecosystem management, with a specific focus on forest conservation. Some of their critics imply that these officials are not very concerned about what happens to the forest under private ownership and simply want well-run parks.

Moreover, key SINAC officials vigorously supported the private sector's interest in developing Chilean-style plantations to export timber (Alfaro 1997; Árias 1997). Key private-sector organizations, such as the National Forest Office, the Certification Commission, and the CCF championed the project. As in the Chilean model, large-scale private timber interests and reforesters control those institutions. In a system where markets dominate, the private sector uses the peasant sector's lack of resources and the absence of government institutional support (after dismantlement of the DECAFOR) to corral peasant interests and to force their acquiescence to large-scale timber interests. Brandishing efficiency arguments, they maintain that peasants have no place in production, development of multiple use of forests, or in reforestation with commercial intent.

Although the situation has remained essentially unchanged under the Rodríguez administration, there have been changes in emphasis. For example, the policy debate hardened between timber interests who wanted state support for wood production and conservationists who advocated absolute forest protection to maintain biodiversity. This narrowing of the policy debate influenced a second change. It generated differences among peasant organizations over the definition of their own best interests and who their allies might be. JUNAFORCA, the principal umbrella association for forest-based peasants during the policy debates of the 1980s and 1990s, experienced the biggest transformation.

In the late 1990s, JUNAFORCA's leaders concluded that the peasant sector was at heart a productive sector and that its best chances for development lay with the forest industry rather than with environmentalists (Vega 2000). JUNAFORCA felt environmentalists had abandoned peasants by transferring their support to private nature reserves in an attempt to promote strict protection of forests above all else. Moreover, JUNAFORCA resented the fact that environmental organizations, such as the National Institution for Biodiversity (Instituto Nacional de Biodiversidad — INBio), have monopoly access to public land in protected areas, while peasants may not even utilize isolated pasture trees for their wood needs (Espinoza 2000). Further, environmentalists had made wood production more expensive by pushing for regulations at every step in the production process that undermined the peasants' ability to contribute to the development of the national forest industry (Barrantes 2000a).

Based on these redefinitions, during the Rodríguez administration, JUNAFORCA has reestablished its 1995 alliance with the forest industry, as represented by the Costa Rican Forestry Council within the National Forest Office. Once again, the perception of a greater danger emanating from the conservationist camp spurred JUNAFORCA to sublimate its ambivalence over timber industrialists. This was a significant step because later in 1995, JUNAFORCA had concluded that the CCF had merely used their organization to claim broad societal support for the retention of state subsidies for managed forestry and plantation forestry (Solís 1995). Once the timber industry had achieved its goal, it ignored the programmatic demands of JUNAFORCA.

In addition to its perception that environmentalists posed a greater threat than timber industrialists, two other factors contributed to the change in JUNAFORCA's posture. One was a redefinition of the social group it represented. The organization's revised focus is on "peasants" whose holdings permit them to participate individually in a market-driven timber industry. JUNAFORCA now speaks mainly for relatively well-to-do peasants who are, in fact, in the Costa Rican context, medium-sized landowners. In JUNAFORCA's view, a landowner with a 100- hectare farm is still considered a peasant; broader yet, a peasant is anyone who makes his/her livelihood from use of the land in rural areas. By the same token, JUNAFORCA now pays little attention to poor, small landholders because they cannot contribute much to the development of the forest industry — they have inherent limitations in producing uniform high-quality timber in a timely fashion (Espinoza 2000).

A change in JUNAFORCA's organizational center of gravity — from AGUADEFOR to CODEFORSA — accompanied this redefinition of the social sector it served. AGUADEFOR had had a strong commitment to small, poor peasants as well as to those who were better off. AGUADEFOR promoted grassroots development, independence from the timber industrialists, and had strong links to the municipal peasant organizations of Guanacaste. But AGUADEFOR collapsed as a result of an ill-considered expansion into the marketplace, as it tried to create a timber company capable of competing with established private-sector firms.

CODEFORSA, from the more central region of San Carlos, had been in competition with AGUADEFOR for leadership of the peasant forestry movement throughout the entire period. Its principal organizers had always been strong supporters of market approaches to sustainable forestry. They had been in the forefront of medium-sized landowners' efforts to break the more cooperative-centered approach to grassroots development. CODEFORSA was more interested in finding a niche within the established forest industry than in creating an independent peasant sector.

Because of these changes within JUNAFORCA, many grassroots forestry organizations do not consider it as representative of their interests. Moreover, they are rarely, if ever, consulted or contacted by it (Cárdenas 2000). Consequently, peasant-friendly forestry groups, such as the Indian Peasants for Community Agroforestry Coordinating Committee (Coodinadora Indígena Campesina de Agroforestría Comunitaria — CICAFOC), conclude that JUNAFORCA's policy stance is unrepresentative of peasant needs. Yet, if the wood sector seems to have little to offer, more grassroots-oriented peasant forestry organizations see equal or less potential support from environmentalists at the national level (Acosta 1999). By and large, these organizations have been left on their own in their search for projects and funding sources that emphasize multiple use of the forest. The redefinition of JUNAFORCA's interests and representativeness suggests that peasants — defined as poor, small landholders — have largely been shut out of participation in policy formulation at the national level. JUNAFORCA, after all, is the only organization within the CCF and the National Forest Office that claims to represent peasant interests.

This conclusion may seem at odds with claims by the timber sector and environmentalists alike that peasants are a desirable strategic ally in Costa Rica's forest policy debate. Both sides have argued forcefully that their proposals more effectively fulfill the participatory criteria of sustainable development. The problem is that, for the most part, the timber industry's and the environmentalists' overtures to peasants are in word only. For example, the National Plan of Forest Development, prepared by the ONF/MINAE, focuses on strengthening the capacity of Costa Rica's industrial forestry sector (MINAE 1998a). Conversely, the National Biodiversity Strategy, prepared by INBio/MINAE, focuses on the protection of primary forests through economic valuing of the environmental and biodiversity services these ecosystems provide (MINAE 2000). Both claim that their plan attacks rural poverty and ensures the active participation of local communities in the management of natural resources. Yet, both plans have little, if any, concrete measures that include the social criteria necessary to implement those claims. Mere promises of a few jobs and training programs are certainly insufficient. This strategy allows the ONF to include JUNAFORCA as an integral member in its lobbying efforts while ignoring the interests of poor peasants. By the same token, peasant organizations are reluctant to ally with environmentalists because they perceive that social criteria are only of secondary concern to conservationists, if they understand them at all (Basco and Silva 2000).

Framed this way, the political and ideological divisions among three opposing forces seem unsurmountable. Resurgent conservationists and large-scale timber interests are the strongest. Conservationists seek to blend traditional concerns about primary forest protection with new ideas drawn from conservation biology and environmental economics, mainly through the concept of payment for environmental services. They seek to limit payment of public funds to forest protection (parks and reserves), restoration, and reforestation. Timber interests want to retain access to primary forests (preferably with public incentives for managed extraction), receive subsidies for plantation forestry and technological improvements of their enterprises, and benefit from reduced regulation. Timber interests have also sought to break down independent peasant-sector organizations in the state and civil society to eliminate competition for markets and scarce public and international resources. Meanwhile, peasant organizations favor community development (organizational aid) with small-scale multiple use of resources for the satisfaction of the basic needs component of sustainable development.

Costa Rica's democratic political system and pluralist style of policymaking offer an arena for reconciliation of these divergent interests. However, its institutions are not neutral. After a brief interlude in the 1980s, conservation and timber interests have fared better than peasant organizations. Current international attention on market instruments for biodiversity conservation in addition to domestic political factors (control over institutions) favor conservationists over others. International organizations and multilateral lending institutions frequently target conservation over use, and conservationists dominate the MINAE. However, this does not mean that timber interests are helpless — they are adept at using Costa

Rica's democratic and pluralist policy-making process to advance their cause. Conservationists may have gained the upper hand in the MINAE, but timber industrialists have strong, effective representation on MINAE policy-making boards, and the legislature also protects their interests, as was seen in the case of the Environmental Services Bill.

In this context, peasant organizations have become the third and least powerful interest group by far. The discourse of sustainable development demands their inclusion. But their involvement is limited to participation in policy-making boards in a highly subordinated manner. No thought is given to the provision of the organizational and material aid necessary for peasants' success. Moreover, their principal officially recognized interlocutor — JUNAFORCA — has changed in ways that call its representation of peasants into question. It has recast its demands in terms of narrow timber interests and has given up representing poor, small-scale peasants and cooperative efforts for multiple use of the forest.

This situation suggests that Costa Rican policymakers and many international organizations have made their choice with respect to trade-offs among the components of sustainable development. Policy mainly supports conservation and market-oriented forestry. Meanwhile, rhetoric and discourse aside, commitment for community development and small-scale multiple use by poor peasants has declined precipitously.

However, this trade-off is not necessarily permanent. Bringing together domestic and international actors to include peasant concerns over livelihood via community development and multiple use of the forest is possible within existing conditions. Because Costa Rica depends strongly on international agencies to support its environmental policy, the international arena offers peasant organizations a promising entry point. Most important, although most international agencies currently focus on market instruments for biodiversity conservation and sustainable development, their posture does not axiomatically exclude peasant development. To the contrary, these agencies officially recognize the need for it.

Unfortunately, most international agencies' efforts toward peasant development have been misguided. Project proposals consistently downplay the elements necessary to implement community development: organization and long-term technical assistance for small-scale projects (that may be scaled-up later). Programmatic lapses are probably a function of the professional training of those drafting the projects, who are frequently steeped in conservation biology and environmental economics. Yet, these disciplines also stress that satisfaction of basic needs and community involvement in projects is necessary for project success.

What conditions, then, might lend substance to the discourse on community development as the means to fulfill the livelihood component of sustainable development in Costa Rica? At minimum, three factors are necessary. First, peasant organizations themselves and the national and international NGOs that support them must continue their unflagging efforts to influence the policy agenda. The social afforestation projects of the 1980s had an important organizational consequence. They spawned several strong peasant organizations that are likely to persist, given Costa Rica's rich tradition of a strong civil society. That organizational base provides a platform from which to act, from which to participate in project formulation and policymaking. Crucial, however, is that such participation must include the creation of stronger, independent, peasant-specific departments within the MINAE (such as DECAFOR had been); special accounts for community forestry; and organizational assistance for peasant associations. These are key elements of the sociological context necessary for the success of social forestry.

Recent events suggest that movement in this direction is possible. For example, when JUNAFORCA still represented groups that supported social forestry, it helped to force the Figueres administration to keep the incentives for reforestation and managed forests for smallholders as well as large-scale producers. During the Rodríguez administration, the peasant organizations involved in the Mesa Campesina, with help from legislators, managed to attain representation on a significant policy-making board, the Environmental Services Advisory Council (Consejo Asesor de Servicios Ambientales — COASA). This was a small but important step. It included peasant organizations other than JUNAFORCA — which had ceased to represent them adequately — in the policy-making process on a permanent basis.

The divisions and dissensions among in the organizations that represent peasants, smallholders, and owners of medium-sized landholdings are debilitating but could be transitory. The JUNAFORCA's alliance with the timber industry may be only a marriage of convenience in light of the perceived danger conservationists pose, and JUNAFORCA may well walk away from it again.

For now, however, the main task of peasant organizations is to continue to prove the viability of their models. Currently, Central American regional organizations are their main source of support (Brenes 1999; Madrigal et al. 1997). In 1994, Costa Rica ratified the Treaty for the Conservation of Biodiversity and Protection of Protection of Priority Forestry Areas in Central America (Convenio para la Conservación de la Biodiversidad y Protección de Áreas Silvestres Prioritarias en América Central). As part of that treaty, the Central American Countries agreed to make the Central American Commission for Environment and Development (Comisión Centroamericana de Ambiente y Desarrollo — CCAD) the main organ for coordinating region-wide forest policy (Asamblea Legislativa 1994). Peasant interests are relatively strongly represented in the CCAD, with CICAFOC from Costa Rica receiving funding from the International Union for the Conservation of Nature (IUCN) to influence policy and implement projects (IUCN 2000). By the same token, the Forest, Trees, and Peoples Programme (FTPP) of the United Nations Food and Agriculture Organization also represents and aids peasant interests (Chinchilla 2000; *La República* 1997). In terms of policymaking, these organizations have made some headway at the regional level; however, at the national level they have concentrated on influencing project design and have little influence on high-level policymaking.

These sources of support and small successes offer peasant and smallholder organizations breathing room for survival, a space for reorganization in a relatively hostile policy environment. Part of that process of organizational reconstruction should involve intellectual growth to take advantage of new opportunities in the international arena. Peasant and smallholder organizations might be well advised to study the core concepts of conservation biology and understand how peasant interests fit into them. From there, they can formulate innovative arguments about how peasant life contributes to maintaining the ecological balance that allows forests to provide their myriad environmental services. The question these organizations need to answer is: how do peasants enhance, facilitate, or preserve the forest's ability to provide its environmental services? How would the absence of those activities be detrimental? In short, peasant organizations must become intellectually and technically more sophisticated. This they can do with the patient, diplomatic, and sensitive help of international organizations, NGOs, and universities. Then peasant organizations will be in a position to influence the programmatic content of biodiversity conservation projects in ways that include peasant concerns over livelihood.

External conditions are more favorable to such activism than in the recent past. International institutions such as the World Bank, under pressure from NGOs and developing country governments, are increasingly concerned about livelihood needs and biodiversity conservation and are more committed to forming interdisciplinary teams for project design and implementation than they once were (IUCN 1980; Hopkins 1995,84). This is partly a direct result of the fact that social equity questions are once again taking center stage in policy debates, now that the basic issues of economic restructuring and transition to democracy in Latin America seem to have been settled. Grassroots organizations and their supporters stand to gain much from constructively showing how livelihood fits in with the new discourse of biodiversity conservation along with sustainable development. Conservation groups cannot be expected to make livelihood issues their first priority, but they may be persuaded to deal with them more effectively. If conservation groups perceive that peasant organizations understand their issues, can contribute to winning funding, and can help with project implementation, livelihood issues may again become higher priorities on Costa Rica's policy agenda.

Notes

1. Sustained-yield use occurs when natural renewable resource extraction equals or is slightly lower than the rate of replacement.

2. "Shifted cultivators" refers to poor peasants who depend on slash-and-burn agriculture for their subsistence, meaning that they clear a plot of land from the forest, cultivate it for a few years, and when the soil gives out, they move on to clear new sections of the forest.

3. "High-grading" is the practice by which loggers quickly extract all of the commercially valuable trees, leaving behind a degraded and economically devalued forest stand.

4. The fiscal incentive system René Castro wanted to dismantle had been established between 1988 and 1995, and it included the following principal elements: Certificados de Abono Forestal (CAFs); the Certificados de Abono Forestal por Adelantado (CAFAs), and the Certificado de Abono Forestal para Manejo del Bosque (CAFMA). Castro wanted to keep the Certificados de Conservación del Bosque (CCBs), which compensated forest owners who did not cut down their forests for their non-timber environmental services.

5. Multiple use of the forest is a concept that assumes that forests have many economic uses besides timber extraction. Therefore, plans for the sustainable development of forest areas should not focus exclusively on the commercial value of the trees in a timber stand. One can also practice small-scale agriculture and husbandry, cultivate honeybees and ornamental plants, grow cash crops that require shade (cacao, for example), and so on.

6. The Certificate for Sustainable Tourism (CST) program was established by executive decree in 1998 as a response to extensive allegations that the hotel industry was hyping environmentalism without real commitment to ecological sensitivity, a practice known as "green wash." Under the CST program, hotel owners and lodges are certified if the environmental and socioeconomic impacts of their business practices meet specified standards. Certification gives them an official "green" ranking (like a five-star system) that appears in tourist guides. Nonetheless, there are indications that participation in the CST program is biased toward larger hotels and elite-owned ecolodges, and although the Costa Rican Tourist Institute is working with the grassroots tourism groups, progress will be difficult, given the strength of the larger-scale tourism interests.

Acronyms

AC	Area de Conservación (Conservation Area)
AGUADEFOR	Asociación Guanacasteca de Desarrollo Forestal (Guanacaste Forest Development Association)
CCAD	Comisión Centroamericana de Ambiente y Desarrollo (Central American Commission for Environment and Development)
CCF	Cámara Costarricence Forestal (Costa Rican Forestry Council)
CCT	Centro Científico Tropical (Tropical Science Center)
CICAFOC	Coodinadora Indígena Campesina de Agroforestría Comunitaria (Indian Peasants for Community Agroforestry Coordinating Committee)
CST	Certificación para la Sostenibilidad Turística (Certificate for Sustainable Tourism)
COASA	Consejo Asesor de Servicios Ambientales (Environmental Services Advisory Council)
CODEFORSA	Cooperativa para el Desarrollo Forestal de San Carlos (San Carlos Forest Development Cooperative)
DECAFOR	Departamento Campesino Forestal (Department of Peasant Forestry)
DGF	Dirección General de Forestal (Forest Service)
ECODES	Estrategia de Conservación para el Desarrollo Sostenible (Conservation for Sustainable Development)
FDF	Fondo de Desarrollo Forestal (Forestry Development Fund)
FECON	Federación Costarricence para la Conservación del Ambiente (Conservation Federation)
FONAFIFO	Fondo Nacional de Financiamiento Forestal (National Forest Fund)
FONASA	Fondo Nacional de Servicios Ambientales (National Fund for Environmental Services)
FTTP	Forest, Trees, and Peoples Programme (under UN's FAO)
ICT	Instituto Costarricence de Turismo (Costa Rican Institute for Tourism)
IUCN	International Union for the Conservation of Nature
JUNAFORCA	Junta Nacional Forestal Campesina (National Peasant Forestry Coalition)
MAG	Ministerio de Agricultura y Ganadería (Ministry of Agriculture and Animal Husbandry)
MINAE	Ministerio de Ambiente y Energía (Ministry of Environment and Energy)
MIRENEM	Ministerio de Recursos Naturales, Energía y Minas (Ministry of Natural Resources, Energy, and Mines)
NGO	Non-governmental Organization
ONF	Oficina Nacional Forestal (National Forestry Office)
PSA	Pago por Servicio Ambiental (payment for environmental services)
RCRP	Red Costarricence de Reservas Naturales Privadas (Costa Rican Network for Private Nature Reserves)
SINAC	Sistema Nacional de Áreas Protegidas (National System of Protected Areas)
USAID	United States Agency for International Development
VS	Vida Silvestre (Wildlife)

References

Acosta, Ilse. 1999. Testimony of the president of the Mesa Campesina at the Hearings of the Comisión Permanente de Asuntos Agropecuarios y de Recursos Naturales, Asamblea Nacional Legislativa, Acta de la Sesión Ordinaria No. 105, March 3.

Alfaro, Marielos. 1997. Author interview with then CCF vice president, San José, July.

Alfaro, Marielos. 1999. Testimony of the president of the Cámara Costaricence Forestal at the Hearings of the Comisión Permanente de Asuntos Agropecuarios y de Recursos Naturales, Asamblea Nacional Legislativa, Acta de la Sesión Ordinaria No. 94-95, January 20.

Araya, Marco Vinicio. 1997. Araya was one of the directors of the new Fondo Nacional de Financiamiento Forestal (FONAFIFO). Author interview. San José, July.

Árias, Guillermo. 1997. Árias is a highly placed consultant to government, on the staff of COSEFORMA, wrote regulations for 1996 forest law, and works with SINAC. Author interview. San José, July.

Asamblea Legislativa. 1969. "Ley Forestal No. 4465." *La Gaceta*, November 25.

Asamblea Legislativa. 1986. "Ley Forestal." *La Gaceta*, No. 85, 7 May. (Also known as Ley Forestal No. 7174 of June 28, 1990).

Asamblea Legislativa. 1994. "Ley 7433: Convenio para la Conservación de la Biodiversidad y Protección de Áreas Silvestres Prioritarias en América Central." *La Gaceta*, No. 193, October 11.

Asamblea Legislativa. 1996. "Ley Forestal, No. 7575." *La Gaceta*, No. 72, April 16.

Asamblea Legislativa. 1998. "Ley de Biodiversidad No. 7788." *La Gaceta,* No. 101, May 27.

Asamblea Legislativa. 2000. "Proyectos: Aprobación del contrato de préstamo entre el Gobierno de la República de Costa Rica y el Banco Internacional de Reconstrucción y Fomento para Financiar el Programa de Pago por Servicios Ambietales." *La Gaceta*, No. 178, September 18.

Báez, Ana. 2000. Greg Basco interview of Báez, president of Turismo y Conservación Consultores. San José, February.

Barrantes, Alfonso. 1994. Barrantes was a functionary of the Comisión de Desarrollo Forestal de San Carlos (CODEFORSA). Author interview. Ciudad Quesada, November.

Barrantes, Alfonso. 1997. Barrantes was general secretary of CODEFORSA. Author interview. Ciudad Quesada, June.

Barrantes, Alfonso. 1999. Testimony at the hearings of the Comisión Permanente de Asuntos Agropecuarios y de Recursos Naturales, Asamblea Nacional Legislativa, Acta No. 92-93, January 19.

Barrantes, Alfonso. 2000a. Interview by Greg Basco of Barrantes, executive director of the Oficina Nacional Forestal and of the CODEFORSA. Ciudad Quesada, September.

Barrantes, Alfonso. 2000b. "Servicios ambientales: Necesidades mínimas a partir del 2001." San José: Oficina Nacional Forestal.

Barrau, Enrique. 1993. Author interview with Barrau, an agricultural development officer, USAID. San José, May.

Barrau, Enrique. 1994. Author interview. San José, November.

Basco, Greg, and Eduardo Silva. 2000. "Campesinos, Timber Interests, and Environmentalists: The Making of Forest Policy in Costa Rica." Mimeo (October).

Bauer, Jan. 1997. Author interview with Bauer, the first secretary of the Dutch Embassy in Costa Rica. San José, June.

Boza, Mario. 1997. Author interview with Boza, the former vice minister of MIRENEM during the Calderón administration. San José, June.

Brenes, Carlos. 1999. "Del paradigma de ordenamiento forestal y de rendimiento sostenido al paradigma de ordenamiento sostenible de los ecosistemas forestales." *Agroforestería Comunitaria y Gestión Local del Desarrollo*, special edition: 7-18.

Browder, John O. 1989. *Fragile Lands of Latin America: Strategies for Sustainable Development.* Boulder: Westview Press.

Cámara Costarricence Forestal (CCF). 1997. "Aspectos más relevantes de la negociación con las autoridades del MINAE." *Desde El Bosque* 5, No. 23, May-June: 1.

Canet, Gilbert. 1995. Author interview with Canet, at that time director of the Departamento Forestal Campesino. San José, February.

Canet, Gilbert. 1997. Author interview with Canet, the director of the Programa Forestal Campesino. San José, June.

Canet, Gilbert. 2000. Greg Basco interview with Canet, the director of the Programa Forestal Campesino. San José, October.

Cárdenas, Pablo. 2000. Greg Basco interview with Cárdenas, an environmental law specialist, FECON. October.

Carriere, Jean. 1991. "The Crisis in Costa Rica: An Ecological Perspective," In *Environment and Development in Latin America*, eds. Michael Redclift and David Goodman. Manchester, UK: University of Manchester Press. 184-203.

Chinchilla, Alberto. 2000. Greg Basco interview with Chinchilla, a functionary of CICAFOC. San José, March.

Espinoza, Héctor. 2000. Greg Basco interview with Espinoza, a JUNAFORCA functionary. San José, September.

Evans, Sterling. 1999. *The Green Republic: A Conservation History of Costa Rica.* Austin: University of Texas Press.

Friedmann, John, and Haripriya Rangan, eds. 1993. In *Defense of Livelihood: Comparative Studies on Environmental Action.* West Hartford, Conn.: Kumarian Press.

González, Orlando. 1997. Author interview, July. González was a PUSC deputy on the Agrarian Committee of the National Assembly and heavily involved in the formulation of the forest law.

Gutiérrez, Rafael. 2000. Greg Basco interview with Gutiérrez, a SINAC functionary. San José, March.

Hopkins, Jack W. 1995. *Policymaking for Conservation in Latin America.* Westport, Conn.: Praeger.

International Union for the Conservation of Nature (IUCN). 1980. *World Conservation Strategy.* Washington, D.C.: IUCN.

IUCN. 2000. *Comunidades y gestión de bosques en Mesoamérica.* San José: Impresión Comercial La Nación.

Kishor, Nalin, and Luis Constantino. 1993. "Forest Management and Competing Land Uses: An Economic Analysis for Costa Rica." The World Bank Latin America Technical Department Environmental Division, Note No. 7 (October).

La República. 1997. "Un repunte de la agroforestería en Centroamérica." October 30: 38

Lutz, Ernst, Mario Vedova, Héctor Martínez, Lorena San Román, Ricardo Vázquez, Alfredo Aravena, Lucía Marino, Rafael Celis, and Jeroen Huising. 1993. *Interdisciplinary Fact-finding on Current Deforestation in Costa Rica.* World Bank Environment Working Paper No. 61 (September).

Madrigal, Patricia, Vivienne Solís Rivera, Ivannia Ayales Cruz, and Marino Marozzi Rojas. 1997. *Uso sostenible de la biodiversidad en Mesoamérica: Hacia la profundización de la democracia.* San José: Programa de Vida Silvestre para Centroamérica, UICN.

Marín, Martha. 2000. Greg Basco interview with Marín, leader of the Red Costarricence de Reservas Privadas. September.

Martínez, Leonidas. 1997. Martínez was the Partido Liberación deputy who sponsored the Forest Law Bill in the Figueres administration. Author interview. San José, July.

Mendoza, Dixie. 1990. "Sala IV anula Ley Forestal." *La Nación*, 25 May, 5A.

Ministerio del Ambiente y Energía (MINAE). 1997. "El sistema nacional de áreas de conservación de Costa Rica: Concepto, funciones y avances en su implementación." Mimeo, May.

MINAE. 1998a. *Plan Nacional de Desarrollo Forestal: Integración y Participación Activa del Sector Forestal en El Desarrollo Humano Sostenible.* San José: MINAE.

MINAE. 1998b. Proyecto Ley de Valoración y Retribución por Servicios Ambientales. Asamblea Legislativa, Comisión Permanente de Asuntos Agropecuarios y Recursos Naturales, Expediente 13, 472, 2-13.

MINAE. 1999a. Ley de Valoración y Retribución por Servicios Ambientales: Dictamen, Afirmativo de Mayoría. Asamblea Legislativa, Comisión Permanente de Asuntos Agropecuarios y de Recursos Naturales, Expediente 13, 472, April 28: 742-754.

MINAE. 1999b. Propuesta: Texto Sustitutivo de Ley de Valoración y Retribución por Servicios Ambientales. Asamblea Legislativa, Comisión Permanente de Asuntos Agropecuarios y de Recursos Naturales, Expediente 13, 472, February 17: 193-219.

MINAE. 2000. *Estrategia Nacional de Conservación y Uso Sostenible de la Biodiversidad.* San José: MINAE.

Ministerio de Recursos Naturales, Energía y Minas (MIRENEM). 1990. *Estrategia de Conservación para el Desarrollo Sostenible de Costa Rica.* San José: MIRENEM.

Monge, Rosaura. 2000. Greg Basco interview with Monge, the coordinator of the Natural Resources Department of the Instituto Costarricence de Turismo, August.

Mora, Jorge. 1999. "El doble discurso ambiental." *Semanario Universidad*, February 17-23: 16.

National Assembly. 1994. *Comisión Permanente de Asuntos Agropecuarios y de Recursos Naturales.* File nos. 11,003, pp. 13-30, 549-69, 727-75; and ledgers nos. 54, August 23; and 56-57, August 24.

Odio, Elizabeth. 2000. "Política ambiental nacional," *La República*, editorial, March 12.

Pearce, David W., and R. Kerry Turner. 1990. *Economics of Natural Resources and the Environment.* Baltimore: The Johns Hopkins University Press.

Peralta, Alfredo. 1993. Author interview, with Peralta, a leader of timber industrialists who became vice president of the Cámara Costarricence Forestal. San José, May.

Peuker, Axel. 1992. *Public Policies and Deforestation: A Case Study of Costa Rica.* World Bank Latin America and the Caribbean Technical Department Environment Division Report No. 14 (February).

Redclift, Michael. 1992. "Sustainable Development and Popular Participation: A Framework for Analysis." In *Grassroots Environmental Action: People's Participation in Sustainable Development*, eds. D. Ghai and J. Vivian, 23-49. London: Routledge.

Rivera, Sileny. 1997. "Cambian destino a gravamen de combustibles." *Al Día* May 4: 3.

Rodríguez, Emel. 1997. Author interview. E. Rodríguez was director of the Área de Conservación Tempisque. San José, July.

Rodríguez, Jorge. 1997. Author interview. J. Rodríguez is a senior consultant to Central American governments on forestry and was the chair of the Reconciliation Committee. San José, July.

Salas, José Luis. 1993. Author interview. Salas is the former director of the Tropical Forestry Action Program (TFAP-Costa Rica) San José, May.

Salazar, Edgar. 1994. Author interview. Salazar was executive director of the Comisión de Desarrollo Forestal de San Carlos (CODEFORSA). Ciudad Quesada, February.

Sánchez, Oscar. 2000. Greg Basco interview with O. Sánchez, a FONAFIFO functionary. San José, September.

Segura, Olman, Robin Gottfried, Miriam Miranda, and Luis Gómez. 1997. "Políticas Forestales en Costa Rica." In *Políticas forestales en Centroamérica: Análisis de las restricciones para el desarrollo del sector forestal,* eds. Olman Segura, David Kaimowitz, and Jorge Rodríguez. San Salvador: IICA-Holanda.

Silva, Eduardo. 1997. "The Politics of Sustainable Development: Native Forest Policy in Chile, Venezuela, Costa Rica and Mexico." *Journal of Latin American Studies* 29, 2: 457-493.

Solís, Magda. 1993. *Junta Nacional Forestal Campesina: Una experiencia de organización campesina.* San José: Junta Nacional Forestal Campesina (Junaforca).

Solís, Magda. 1995. Author interview. San José, February.

Tarrow, Sidney. 1994. *Power in Movement.* Cambridge: Cambridge University Press.

Tarrow, Sidney. 1996. "Social Movements in Contentious Politics: A Review Essay." *American Political Science Review* 90, 4: 874-883.

Tico Times. 1999. "Worry Over the Environment Growing." February 5.

Umaña, Álvaro, and Katrina Brandon. 1992. "Inventing Institutions for Conservation: Lessons from Costa Rica." In *Poverty, Natural Resources and Public Policy in Central America,* ed. Sheldon Annis. Washington, D.C.: Overseas Development Council.

Vargas, Ronald. 1993. Author interview with the director of the Dirección General Forestal, San José.

Vega, Luis Felipe. 1999. Hearings of the Comisión Permanente de Asuntos Agropecuarios y de Recursos Naturales, Asamblea Nacional Legislativa, Acta de la Sesión Ordinaria No. 92, January 19.

Vega, Luis Felipe. 2000. Greg Basco interview with Vega, the chair of the Executive Committee of the Oficina Nacional Forestal and executive director of JUNAFORCA. San José, September.

World Bank. 1992. *World Development Report 1992: Development and the Environment.* New York: Oxford University Press.

World Commission on Environment and Development (WCED). 1987. *Our Common Future.* New York: Oxford University Press.

Contributors

Alberto J. Cardelle is assistant professor of public health at East Stroudsburg University in Pennsylvania. A specialist in international health policy, his current research and writing focus primarily on health care reform and the increasing collaboration between non-governmental organizations and the state for delivery of health care in Latin America. He received his Ph.D. in comparative development and international health policy from the University of Miami and a master's degree in public health from Boston University. Cardelle has served as a program officer for Oxfam America, and he was a resident fellow in international health at the Pan American Health Organization in Washington, D.C., and a research associate at The Dante B. Fascell North-South Center.

Anthony P. Maingot is professor of sociology at Florida International University (FIU). An adjunct senior research associate of The Dante B. Fascell North-South Center, he has been adjunct professor of Mexican and Caribbean studies of the U.S. Air Force School of Special Operations since 1985. Born in Trinidad, he received his doctorate from the University of Florida, Gainesville, and was director of the Antilles Research Program in both Yale University and FIU. A member of the Constitutional Reform Commission of Trinidad from 1971-1974, Maingot has also held one-year visiting appointments in Tokyo, Aix-en-Provence, and at The Rand Corporation in California. Awarded FIU's Professional Excellence Award in 1997, he is the author of numerous monographs, journal articles, and other major publications such as a *Short History of the West Indies; Small Country Development and International Labor Flows: Experiences in the Caribbean;* and *The United States and the Caribbean: Challenges of an Asymmetrical Relationship.* Maingot is the founding editor of the magazine of Latin American and Caribbean studies, *Hemisphere*, and serves on the editorial boards of several other important publications in Geneva, Costa Rica, and Trinidad.

Nizar Messari is assistant professor of international relations at Akhawayn University in Ifrane, Morocco. He holds a master's degree from the Instituto de Relaçãoes Internacionais of the Pontifical Catholic University of Rio de Janeiro, Brazil. In 1998, he completed his Ph.D. in international studies at the School of International Studies at the University of Miami. He has published articles in several scholarly journals, including *Contexto Internacional* and *Shuun Maghribia*. His current research interests focus on constructivist approaches to international relations theory as applied to questions of identity and foreign policy analysis. He has applied this framework to U.S. foreign policy toward Islam and to the analysis of Moroccan foreign policy since independence.

Ambler H. Moss, Jr., is the director of The Dante B. Fascell North-South Center, professor of international studies at the University of Miami, and of counsel to the law firm of Greenberg Traurig in Miami. He holds a bachelor's degree from Yale University and a law degree from George Washington University. As deputy assistant secretary of state for congressional relations, Moss was involved with the negotiation of the U.S.-Panama Canal Treaties and their ratification. He served as ambassador to Panama and as a member of the U.S.-Panama Consultative Committee from 1978 until 1982. President Bill Clinton re-appointed him to the same committee in 1995. Moss has practiced law in Washington, D.C., Brussels, and Miami. He is a member of the Council on Foreign Relations, the Inter-American Dialogue, the Royal Institute of International Affairs, and the International Institute of Strategic Studies. He also serves on the board of the Espirito Santo Bank of South Florida, the Florida International Banking Advisory Council, and the Association of American Chambers of Commerce in Latin America. Moss teaches graduate courses at the School of International Studies of the University of Miami on U.S.-Latin American relations, U.S. foreign policy, and diplomatic negotiation.

Manuel Pastor, Jr., is professor of Latin American and Latino studies and director of the Center for Justice, Tolerance, and Community at the University of California, Santa Cruz. He holds a Ph. D. in economics from the University of Massachusetts, Amherst, and has received fellowships from the Danforth, Guggenheim, and Kellogg foundations as well as grants from the Irvine Foundation, the Ford Foundation, the National Science Foundation, The Dante B. Fascell North-South Center, among others. His most recent books include a co-edited volume, *Modern Political Economy and Latin America: Theory and Policy,* and a co-authored work on urban development, *Regions that Work: How Cities and Suburbs Can Grow Together.* Pastor's research on Latin American and urban problems has also been published in journals such as *International Organization, World Development,* the *Journal of Latin American Studies, Latin American Research Review, Economic Development Quarterly, Social Science Quarterly,* and numerous others. Pastor is currently studying several environmental justice issues, with support from both the California Endowment and the California Policy Research Center. He serves on the Advisory Council of the Public Policy Institute of California.

Eduardo Silva is associate professor of political science and fellow at the Center for International Studies at the University of Missouri, St. Louis; he is also an adjunct senior research associate of The Dante B. Fascell North-South Center at the University of Miami. He received his Ph.D. in political science from the University of California, San Diego, in 1991. Dr. Silva is author of *The State and Capital in Chile* (Westview 1996); co-editor of *Elections and Democratization in Latin America* (University of California Press, San Diego 1986); and co-editor of *Organized Business, Economic Change, and Democracy in Latin America* (North-South Center Press, 1998). His articles have appeared in *World Politics, Comparative Politics, Development and Change*, the *Journal of Latin American Studies*, the *Journal of Interamerican Studies and World Affairs* (now *Latin American Politics and Society*), the *Latin American Research Review*, and the *European Review of Latin American and Caribbean Studies*.

William C. Smith is professor of political science at the University of Miami's School of International Studies and a former senior research associate of The Dante B. Fascell North-South Center. He is the author of *Authoritarianism and the Crisis of the Argentine Political Economy* (1989) and a contributor to and co-editor of several volumes, including *Latin American Political Economy in the Age* *of Neoliberal Reform* (1994); *Security, Democracy, and Development in Latin America* (1994); *Democracy, Markets, and Structural Reform in Latin America* (1994); *Latin America in the World-Economy* (1996); and *Politics, Social Change, and Economic Restructuring in Latin America* (1997). With Roberto Patricio Korzeniewicz, he co-authored "Poverty, Inequality, and Growth in Latin America: Searching for the High Road to Globalization" in the *Latin American Research Review*. Smith is the editor of *Latin American Politics and Society*.

Jeffrey Stark is director of research and studies at The Dante B. Fascell North-South Center. His work focuses on issues of democratic governance, globalization, and environmental security. He co-edited, with Felipe Agüero, *Fault Lines of Democracy in Post-Transition Latin America* (North-South Center Press, 1999), which won a Choice Award for Outstanding Academic Books. He is also the editor of *The Challenge of Change in Latin America and the Caribbean* (North-South Center Press, 2001). Stark is currently working on a project studying common policy challenges in Latin America and Southeast Asia. He was a program officer for exchange programs at the U.S. Information Agency and the U.S. Department of State. He has taught political science at St. Thomas University in Miami. In addition to his research activities, Stark is editor of the *North-South Agenda Papers*.

Carol Wise is assistant professor at the School of Advanced International Studies at Johns Hopkins University, where she teaches graduate courses on Latin American politics, economy, and transition. After obtaining her Ph.D. from Columbia University, she was Fulbright Scholar in Argentina, Chile, and Colombia; Rockefeller Foundation Faculty Fellow at the University of Cape Town, South Africa; and she has also taught at Georgetown University. Dr. Wise has also worked as research consultant for the emerging markets division of Salomon Brothers, Inc., and headed one Ford Foundation project in Lima, Peru. Her publications include *The Post-NAFTA Political Economy: Mexico and the Western Hemisphere,* which she edited, and two forthcoming works entitled *Reinventing the State: Economic Strategy and Institutional Change in Peru* and *Twenty Years After: The Politics of Economic Transformation in Mexico,* co-authored with Manuel Pastor, Jr. Since the early 1990s, she has contributed articles to the *Latin American Research Review,* the *Journal of Interamerican Studies and World Affairs, Business and Politics,* and the *Journal of Democracy.*

Index

D

E

I

J

L

M

N

U